D1275719

FAMILY: THE FIRST IMPERATIVE

A Symposium in Search of
Root Causes of Family Strength
and Family Disintegration

Edited by William J. O'Neill, Jr.

Published by The William J. and Dorothy K. O'Neill Foundation, Cleveland, Ohio

Copyright © 1995 by William J. O'Neill, Jr.

All rights reserved. No part of this book may be reproduced or transmitted in any form or by any means, electronic or mechanical, including photo-copying, recording, or by any information storage and retrieval system, without permission from the publisher.

Published by The William J. and Dorothy K. O'Neill Foundation, 30195 Chagrin Blvd., Cleveland, Ohio 44124.

Printed in the United States of America

Library of Congress Catalog Card Number 95-071661

ISBN 0-9649220-0-2

TABLE OF CONTENTS

When the William J. and Dorothy K. O'Neill Foundation elected to direct a substantial portion of its grant-making to the area of "family," its Disbursements Committee concluded it had much yet to learn about the area before it could select an "actionable" activity. To assist it in this learning, the Committee decided to hold a Symposium and to invite leading practitioners, academicians, thinkers, writers and researchers in the field of family to come together and dialogue with members of the O'Neill family on the subject.

The Symposium, held in October of 1994 and entitled "Family: The First Imperative," was structured to lead discussions from symptom to cause and was formatted in small working groups to encourage candid and intimate discussion of each aspect of the topic. A rural retreat site was chosen, and the Symposium approach emphasized an open and collegial atmosphere.

Because of this structure, which was necessary to achieve the purposes of the Symposium, it was not possible to invite the public at large to attend and participate. The O'Neill Foundation, however, wished to share the Symposium proceedings with anyone and everyone who might have an interest in what transpired.

Consequently, a commitment was made to publish the Symposium proceedings in book form and to make the book available to anyone who might be interested in it. This book then is the result of that commitment.

ACKNOWLEDGEMENTS

No book can be written without the time and talent commitments of a number of people.

This book, which reports the proceedings of a Symposium entitled "Family: The First Imperative," owes its existence to the twenty-two distinguished Symposium participants whose papers are published in Part II. The knowledge and experience they brought to the Symposium, and the papers they prepared for it, provided the platform from which Symposium discussions began. Beyond any doubt these participants are, collectively, the real authors of this book.

Members of the William J. O'Neill family also played key supporting roles. William J. O'Neill, Jr. (hereinafter referred to as Mr. O'Neill) founded the William J. and Dorothy K. O'Neill Foundation, designed its strategy and planned and managed the Symposium project. Other family members serving on the Foundation's Disbursements Committee selected the subject of "family" as a focus theme and decided to hold a Symposium to learn more about the subject. In particular, Molly O'Neill Sweeney was actively involved throughout as Chairperson of the Disbursements Committee.

Still other O'Neill family members participated by attending the Symposium and actively engaging in dialogue and debate with the professionally-expert participants. Their contributions often brought a practical and plain-spoken reality to the discussions.

Another key contributor was the keynote speaker, Leodis Harris, then Judge of the Juvenile Division of the Cuyahoga County Court of Common Pleas. The scope and depth of his real-world experience, and his energetic style, invigorated the discussions that followed.

A special thanks goes to Jack G. Wiggins, Ph.D. (hereinafter referred to as Dr. Wiggins) who advised in the planning stages of the Symposium and also acted as Symposium moderator.

Behind the scenes, helping with the Symposium planning and also with the subsequent publication of this book, were a number of people. In particular, Martha A. Barry, Patrick F. X. Gallagher and Debra A. Stoner made significant contributions.

And finally, acknowledgements are due: to William J. O'Neill and Dorothy K. O'Neill, who raised their children to truly believe that "family is the first imperative"; to Katherine T. O'Neill, who patiently accepted the Symposium project's imposition on the time of her husband; and to the many friends and associates who encouraged and counseled throughout.

PART ONE:

The Symposium

BACKGROUND

The traceable lineage of the O'Neill family name goes back to the year 360 A.D., making it the oldest lineage in Europe. Perhaps this is one of the reasons that members of the O'Neill family have an abiding conviction about the importance of strong, healthy families.

The William J. and Dorothy K. O'Neill Foundation was founded in Cleveland, Ohio, in 1987 as a private family foundation. Like many family foundations, it is not particularly large. It has, however, become increasingly active and engaged in the philanthropic areas of greatest interest to O'Neill family members.

In 1992 Mr. O'Neill, the founder and President of the Foundation, developed a comprehensive strategy for it. This strategy was designed to improve and focus the Foundation's philanthropic activities and to provide for governance, administration, resource allocation and disbursements decision-making well into the next century. It directs that one-third of the Foundation's disbursements be channelled to a specific focus area which is to be chosen from time to time by the Foundation's Disbursements Committee. It is the hope of O'Neill family members that they can make a substantial impact in the focus area they choose by virtue of their contributions of money, time and talent.

Through a series of meetings held in 1993, the Foundation's Disbursements Committee, chaired by Molly O'Neill Sweeney, worked to select its first focus area. The Committee, consisting of ten O'Neill family members spanning three generations, took an evolutionary approach and ultimately selected the theme of "family."

In its deliberations, the Committee first set forth some of its basic beliefs. It recognized that people over time have held different family values; but it also recognized that the value of family itself has been almost unanimously upheld by all people throughout recorded history. Families bring us joy and happiness, support, comfort and understanding. As an institution, family both enables us and restrains us. It provides the arena in which we develop and form character. It can develop and promote strong values and support its members when they are in need. It is the natural environment for individual growth and well-being. And throughout the world family is the oldest, most fundamental, most enduring and most important of all human institutions. Consequently, family has an enormous impact on the quality of life for all people.

Because the institution of family is affected by the social mores and value systems which are prevalent from time to time and from place to place, and because these mores and value systems are affected by the structure and quality of families, the institution of family and the problems of society are intimately intertwined. They are each both causes and effects and enormously impact one another.

With these beliefs as background, the O'Neill Foundation's Disbursements Committee concluded that family disintegration is a root cause (and indeed perhaps *the* root cause) of most of the major social problems that beset our nation, and indeed much of the world. These problems include the erosion of economic well-being for large segments of our society; the increase in crime, particularly in the underclass; the vastly increased use of illegal drugs; the epidemic of young, unwed mothers; the erosion of our schools; the debasement of much of our art, film, literature and music; and the mean-spiritedness often experienced in daily life. Notwithstanding the billions of public and private dollars directed at alleviating the symptoms of these problems, both the problems and their symptoms seem to continually worsen.

Because of the enormous importance of family to the entire human race, and because the disintegration of family may well be the root cause of the pervasive social problems our nation faces today, the O'Neill Foundation concluded that "family" was indeed a worthy theme. The question remained, however, of how to turn this theme into an "actionable" focus area.

INTRODUCTION

As members of the O'Neill Foundation's Disbursements Committee worked to select and refine their focus theme of "family," it became increasingly clear that they lacked the knowledge and experience to develop this theme into an "actionable" focus area. The need to do so however was apparent, as they believed that the widespread social problems plaguing our nation today are largely caused by, or at least permitted by, the weakening of family structures and the epidemic of individual family disintegrations. If the institution of family could be restored to its rightful role as the basic unit of our society, and if the vast majority of individual families could again become strong and functional, then, they believed, these major social problems would eventually evaporate.

As discussions progressed, a conceptual approach to the problem gradually evolved. If family disintegration is a root cause of major social problems, then are there root causes of family disintegration, and, if so, what is the ultimate root cause? Diagrammatically, this conceptual approach looked like this:

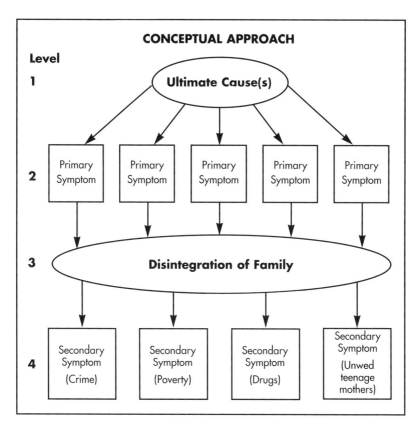

The Committee recognized that real world answers to these questions would not be as simple and clean as might be implied by this "medical model" approach; and indeed it recognized that its linear approach might be somewhat oversimplified and that a more circular concept of causes and effects might ultimately evolve. Mr. O'Neill, however, as the principal Symposium planner, felt that a concentrated effort should be made to climb the ladder of symptoms and causes in an attempt to get all the way back to ultimate causes of family disintegration. He felt that, both publicly and privately, our society directs enormous amounts of time and money to treat level 4 secondary symptoms (as shown on the Conceptual Approach diagram above). We also bemoan the disintegration of family at level 3. And many professionals have attempted to intervene at the primary symptom level, level 2. But all this seems to be of little avail as the problems seem to worsen. Perhaps, he reasoned, prevention at level 1 was the answer. Perhaps this is where the focus should be. If indeed ultimate causes could be discovered and exposed, then concentrated work at this level would create a highly leveraged effort to again make strong and functional families the norm of our society, and thereby solve the insidious social problems that plague us.

The O'Neill Foundation acknowledged that its resources are small (in fact, minute compared to the problems it is seeking to solve). But it felt that, if it could define the real essence of what makes for strong and self-reliant families and what ultimately causes families to disintegrate, and then make this its actionable focus area, it could indeed make a difference. If it could isolate the ultimate causes of family success and family failure, then, notwithstanding the fact that it is a small and relatively unknown foundation, it could become of real service to mankind.

With this background, and recognizing the very real limits of its knowledge and experience, the O'Neill Foundation decided in March of 1994 to sponsor and host a Symposium entitled "Family: The First Imperative." With the knowledge gained from this Symposium, the Disbursements Committee could then identify and define the Foundation's actionable focus area.

The Symposium took place on October 21, 22 and 23 of 1994, and was sited in a pastoral setting on the outskirts of Cleveland, Ohio. The Symposium planners (principally Mr. O'Neill and Dr. Wiggins) first identified about one hundred leading program administrators, researchers and practitioners, each professionally expert in the field of family. These candidates were sorted by professional background and geographic location, and thirty-six nationally-recognized members of the group were then selected with an eye to diversity in both background discipline and location. These thirty-six outstanding professionals, two-thirds of whom were from outside the Cleveland, Ohio area, were then invited to participate in the Symposium in the hope that twenty-four would in fact be able to attend.

Concurrently, thirty-four adult members of the O'Neill family were also invited to participate. The group included members by marriage and it spanned three generations. Its members reside in various parts of the country.

The professional invitees were each asked to prepare a paper explaining one or more of the primary (level 2) symptoms which cause families to disintegrate, and to opine on what (in the invitee's opinion) were the ultimate causes of these symptoms. The papers (which are broadly overviewed in a subsequent section of Part I of this book, and published in their entirety in Part II) were submitted a month in advance of the Symposium and distributed to all participants to be read before the Symposium began. The papers were limited to twenty pages in length and the authors granted the O'Neill Foundation a non-exclusive right to publish them.

The Symposium was built upon four separate working groups, each of which was balanced with professional participants and O'Neill family members so that each working group would be comparable to the others. Heading these groups as facilitators were James F. Alexander, Ph.D., James H. Bray, Ph.D., Florence W. Kaslow, Ph.D. and Sherrod D. Morehead, Ph.D. The four working groups (named "Oak," "Maple," "Buckeye" and "Hickory") stayed intact throughout the Symposium.

The Symposium was structured in four discrete sessions. The first session started with a luncheon for the assembled group and was followed by an overview of participant papers. This session then broke up into separate working groups which were to discuss the primary (level 2) symptoms leading to family disintegration. The working groups then reassembled, and each reported its conclusions back to the assembled group. A group dinner and keynote address followed to wrap up the first day of the Symposium.

The Symposium's second session started in breakout fashion and each working group was to discuss the ultimate (level 1) causes which produce the primary (level 2) symptoms. The working groups then reassembled and each reported its findings to the assembled group. After a group luncheon, the third session started, again in breakout fashion, and each working group was to discuss strategies to prevent further disintegration of families and strategies to strengthen families at the ultimate cause level. Then the working groups again reassembled to report their conclusions. A group dinner followed to end the second day.

The third day of the Symposium was spent in assembled group, and at this session participants offered proposals for what they felt should be the actionable focus area of the O'Neill Foundation. The Symposium then concluded with a group lunch.

The Symposium's structure generated considerable camaraderie among the professional participants and family members, and ultimately led to a willingness to speak openly and candidly. The atmosphere throughout was casual and relaxed. But the intensity with which the participants cared about the subject, and their very diverse backgrounds and points of view, often led to spirited debate. Indeed, the Symposium planners expected this and did not seek unanimity of opinion. They asked only that participants try to think in a linear way and reason back behind obvious symptoms to ultimate causes, at least to the extent that this might be possible given the interrelationship between cause and effect inherent in the subject. In the end, they hoped to achieve the wisdom of consensus that comes when competent people dialogue together to make progress.

In planning this Symposium, Mr. O'Neill sought to achieve five basic objectives:

• First, to uncover ultimate causes of family disintegration and to thereby help identify the best possible actionable focus area for the O'Neill Foundation (one which would help restore healthy, functional families to again becoming the norm of our society).

• Second, to build a network of resource people who could be called upon from time to time in the future to advise and assist the Foundation in its focus area activities.

• Third, to broadly educate members of the O'Neill family on the subject of family.

• Fourth, to eventually share the content and results of the Symposium with the public at large.

• And finally, to have everyone involved thoroughly enjoy the process.

With these objectives in mind, the Symposium planners launched their efforts to undertake this noble but awesome task.

PARTICIPANTS

Twenty-one professional participants attended the O'Neill Foundation's Symposium on "Family: The First Imperative." Alphabetically listed, they were:

James F. Alexander, Ph.D.
(Salt Lake City, Utah): Professor and Past Director of Clinical Training, Department of Psychology, University of Utah.

James H. Bray, Ph.D.
(Houston, Texas): Director, Family Psychology Programs and Associate Professor in the Department of Family Medicine, Baylor College of Medicine.

Helen Cleminshaw, Ph.D.
(Akron, Ohio): Professor of Child and Family Development, University of Akron.

William J. Doherty, Ph.D.
(St. Paul, Minnesota): Professor in the Department of Family Social Science and Director of the Marriage and Family Therapy Program, University of Minnesota.

Stephen J. Dohner
(Cleveland, Ohio): Director of training in areas related to marriage and family life for the staffs of 250 churches and agencies served by Catholic Charities Services Corporation of Cleveland.

John M. Gottman, Ph.D.
(Seattle, Washington): Professor in the Department of Psychology, University of Washington.

Bernard C. Guerney, Ph.D.
(State College, Pennsylvania): Professor Emeritus of Counseling Psychology and founder of the Individual and Family Consultation Center, Penn State University.

Dorothy V. Harris, ACSW, LCSW-C
(Silver Spring, Maryland): Conference Director, National Conference on Child Abuse and Neglect and past President of the National Association of Social Workers.

Richard L. Jones, Ph.D.
(Cleveland, Ohio): President and Chief Executive Officer of the Center for Families and Children.

Florence W. Kaslow, Ph.D.
(West Palm Beach, Florida): Director of the Florida Couples and Family Institute, Adjunct Professor of Medical Psychology, Department of Psychiatry, Duke University Medical School, and Visiting Professor of Psychology, Florida Institute of Technology.

Nadine J. Kaslow, Ph.D.
(Atlanta, Georgia): Associate Professor in the Department of Psychiatry and Behavioral Sciences, Emory University School of Medicine.

Nina McLellan, M.A.
(Cleveland, Ohio): Senior Planning Associate, Federation for Community Planning.

Sherrod D. Morehead, Ph.D.
(Cleveland, Ohio): Clinical psychologist in full-time private practice at University Suburban Health Center, and Assistant Clinical Professor of Psychology, Case Western Reserve University Medical School.

Arthur J. Naparstek, Ph.D.
(Cleveland, Ohio): Professor of Social Work and former Dean of Case Western Reserve University's Mandel School of Applied Social Sciences.

David R. Reines
(Cleveland, Ohio): Deputy County Administrator of Health and Human Services for Cuyahoga County.

Lynne Bravo Rosewater, Ph.D.
(Cleveland, Ohio): Licensed psychologist in private practice.

Jetse Sprey, Ph.D.
(Cleveland, Ohio): Professor Emeritus of Sociology, Case Western Reserve University and past editor of the "Journal of Marriage and the Family."

Jose Szapocznik, Ph.D.
(Miami, Florida): Professor of Psychiatry and Psychology, and Director of Center for Family Studies/Center for Minority Families/Spanish Family Guidance Center, University of Miami.

Peter A. White, J.D.
(Washington, D.C.): Founder and President of International Skye Associates, Inc.

Barbara Dafoe Whitehead, Ph.D.
(New York, New York): Vice President of the Institute for American Values.

Jack G. Wiggins, Ph.D.
(Cleveland, Ohio): Past President of the American Psychological Association and now President of the Psychological Development Center in Cleveland. Though not a formal participant, Dr. Wiggins moderated the Symposium proceedings and submitted a paper for it.

Joan Levy Zlotnik, ACSW
(Bethesda, Maryland): Formerly Government Relations Associate of the National Association of Social Workers.

More complete biographical data on each of these professional participants is contained at the end of each of their respective papers, which are published in Part II of this book.

O'Neill family participants attending the Symposium were:

Dorothy O'Neill Donahey and her husband John D. Donahey
(Cleveland, Ohio): Parents of four children and grandparents of four; he is a retired insurance executive.

J. David Donahey, Jr.
(Chicago, Illinois): Single and an officer of a national investment bank.

Kathleen A. Donahey
(Cleveland, Ohio): Single and a recent graduate of the University of Virginia.

Robert W. Donahey and his wife Colleen M. Donahey
(Cleveland, Ohio): Parents of two children; he runs his own business and she is a registered nurse.

William M. France, Jr.
(Cincinnati, Ohio): Married, father of four children and a co-owner and executive in a start-up business.

Kelly Sweeney McShane
(Washington, D.C.): Married, mother of one child and Executive Director of Hannah House, a social service agency.

John H. O'Neill
(New York, New York): Married and a rehabilitation counselor teaching at the graduate level at Hunter College.

Sara O'Neill Sullivan
(Cleveland, Ohio): Single then (now married) and teaching kindergarten.

Timothy M. O'Neill
(Annapolis, Maryland): Married, father of one, and an executive with International Paper.

Dorothy K. O'Neill
(Delray Beach, Florida): Widowed, mother of five children, grandmother of seventeen, and great-grandmother of thirteen.

William J. O'Neill, Jr. and his wife Katherine T. O'Neill
(Cleveland, Ohio): Parents of five children; he is the past President of Leaseway Transportation, and the founder and manager of the O'Neill family office and the Foundation; she is a fashion editor.

Molly O'Neill Sweeney and her husband George B. Sweeney, Jr.
(Houston, Texas): Parents of five children and grandparents of one; she is chairperson of the Foundation's Disbursements Committee; he is a retired Exxon Chemical executive.

Kevin F. Sweeney
(New Orleans, Louisiana): Single, and a senior at Tulane University.

The Symposium's keynote address was delivered by **Leodis Harris**, then Judge of the Juvenile Division of the Cuyahoga County Court of Common Pleas.

Each of the Symposium's twenty-one professional participants and the Symposium's moderator submitted a paper prior to the start of the proceedings and these papers were distributed to all participants in advance. The papers are published in their entirety in Part II of this book, but they are briefly overviewed here because they were the platform from which Symposium discussions began.

Dr. Alexander's paper suggests that it will be difficult to find "ultimate causes" of family disintegration, which in turn causes behavior disorders in youth. To reverse the process he states that we must understand what these youths feel they need for positive change.

Dr. Bray focuses on step-families, offering statistical evidence that children from divorced, single-parent and remarried homes are at greater risk. He argues, however, that a sense of commitment and supportive relationships can make these families work.

Dr. Cleminshaw points out that there is a strong and interdependent relationship between families and the communities in which they exist. She concludes that unless families and their communities work in unison with each other, with respect, equality and commitment, there can be neither healthy families nor healthy communities.

Dr. Doherty argues that the breakdown of the father-child relationship is a central problem in contemporary American society. He concludes that this breakdown is rooted in the disintegration of male-female relationships.

Father Dohner focuses on the symbiotic but complex relationship between families and the societies in which they exist. What happens to one inevitably affects the other. He concludes that the health of a family is definitely related to its support network.

Dr. Gottman concentrates on "meta-emotion" (which deals with parents' feelings about feelings). He states that it affects almost every important aspect of family patterns and communication, and that responding negatively to the negative emotions of a spouse is the most consistent indicator of an unhappy marriage. He concludes that we must change the way that boys, in particular, are socialized with respect to emotion.

Dr. Guerney reminds us that causes and effects in family disintegration are intertwined, with each contributing to the other; they also tend to be multiple in nature. He warns that working at the highest level of causality entails a greater risk of unintended and harmful side effects.

Ms. Harris articulates the importance of full-time jobs which offer liveable wages and benefits. She says that these jobs are a key ingredient to family success, particularly in the black community.

Dr. Jones argues that the high incidence of poverty, particularly among blacks, must be resolved. He also argues that "community" offers a tremendous potential to act as a protective factor and help restore hope.

Dr. F. Kaslow deplores the fact that our contemporary society has developed hordes of "throwaway children" who are neither loved, nurtured, protected nor guided. This of course, leads these children to have very low self-esteem and causes them to grow up angry.

Dr. N. Kaslow urges that we develop culturally-sensitive preventive interventions that address the familial and socio-cultural issues which particularly concern children. These interventions should be built upon strengths and resiliencies, and should take into account the perspective of children.

Ms. McLellan suggests that we take an asset-oriented approach, rather than a deficit-oriented approach and re-design services around interlinked neighborhood resources, safety-net services and public systems. She argues that the deficit approach we have been using has created a daunting array of public and private agencies which compete for funds, and a system which, collectively, doesn't work.

Dr. Morehead devotes his paper to describing the role which genetic factors play in family functioning. He also highlights the importance of leadership in families.

Dr. Naparstek argues that community and the family are inextricably intertwined, and that our challenge is to develop strategies that build strong communities. The work must be comprehensive and integrated, must focus on assets not deficits, and must build self-esteem, obligation and faith.

Mr. Reines points out that existing public assistance programs are not conducive to maintaining family structure, and often contribute to the demise of families in the welfare system.

Dr. Rosewater focuses on violence in the home (marital rape, wife-battering, child abuse and incest). She argues that this is the root cause of family disintegration, and that it stems from an unequal distribution of power among males and females.

Dr. Sprey opines that the institution of family and the institution of marriage are separate issues. Family, which exists in both the animal kingdom and human society, can be viewed as the institution which is socially responsible for the care and raising of children. Marriage however, which exists only in human society, exists to legitimatize offspring, but does not in and of itself provide the care and companionship which children require.

Dr. Szapocznik concludes that the ultimate cause of family disintegration is the breakdown of a social ecology characterized by active participation and a sense of collective identity.

Mr. White states that family is the vessel of responsibility in our society, and that the principal task of the modern family is to raise children who can take charge of their lives as adults. As families increasingly fail to raise children to responsible adulthood, society as a whole moves increasingly towards chaos. The source of power to reverse this situation, he says, is community (which is the coming together of people with a common mission, interest and commitment).

Dr. Whitehead points out that marriage and parenthood are rapidly coming apart, and that this is severely damaging our children. She points to the shift of Western parents from a concern for their children's futures to a self-orientation that gives priority to the individual. The challenge, she believes, will come in reconciling the adult's desire to pursue individual happiness with the child's needs for a secure and stable family environment.

Dr. Wiggins discusses the priorities of family, work and leisure. He points out that external forces change these priorities and can thereby create stress. Active dialogue and a willingness to understand and adjust can help families weather this stress, however.

Ms. Zlotnik argues that how family is defined, and what set of social and economic supports are created for families, will be crucial issues, particularly as our government struggles with welfare reform. She acknowledges that there is no single solution for all families, and urges that we focus on strengths and build an array of prevention and early intervention services.

The keynote address, delivered by Judge Leodis Harris, enumerated many of the pervasive and enormously negative influences which shape the environment under which children grow up today. These include: the "future shock" effect of rapid changes in technology; the stupefying effect of television; the repetitive acts of violence assimilated through television addiction; the overwhelming influence of a pop culture that seems to eliminate absolutes in terms of right and wrong and to make all moral principles appear debatable; the widespread pornography that has invaded our songs, magazines and television; a national welfare system that has decimated the family, created a matriarchal society and, among blacks, has essentially replicated slavery; a culture that teaches young girls the value of motherhood, but not the value of marriage; a culture that distances young men from the responsibility of fatherhood and impairs their ability to bond with their children; a culture in which children are taught that there is something wrong with getting old and in which they see adults in general, and their parents in particular, as largely irrelevant; a culture in which religion, too, seems to have become irrelevant; and a culture in which everyone insists on their rights, but few recognize their responsibilities.

Overall, the papers submitted in advance of the Symposium painted a frightening picture of the state of family in our society today; it is a picture in which marriage and parenthood are coming apart and in which children are often born unwanted and unwelcome. There was widespread recognition, however, that we all share responsibility for the conditions which affect families. Many of the papers also exhibited a commonality around concepts such as responsibility, commitment, bonding, support, communication, conflict resolution, and building on strengths.

Acknowledging this responsibility we all have, and recognizing that there are common themes which may lead us to solutions that work, the Symposium participants gathered in the hope that they could learn more about that which they did not yet know. The undertaking was indeed a noble one, but the task was awesome.

IMPLEMENTATION

The Symposium planners adopted a linear approach when they structured the Symposium. The plan was to identify the primary causes of family disintegration, and then attempt to find the ultimate cause of these primary causes. If an ultimate cause could be identified, then it was hoped, the professional participants and the family participants working together could identify meaningful actionable focus areas for the Foundation which would attack the problem of family disintegration at the ultimate cause level. The plan called for the Symposium to conclude with all participants debating the pros and cons of each actionable focus area proposed, and then collectively selecting the one best suited for the O'Neill Foundation given the limitations of its time, talent and money.

In the actual implementation, however, this plan was modified. The working groups generally thought that linear reasoning was not very effective in the context of the Symposium's subject matter because causes and effects are so intertwined, interdependent and interrelated. Consequently, much of the discussion in these groups was free-ranging and often strayed quite far from the particular topic assigned for each session. Reports back to the assembled group reflected these wide-ranging and creative discussions.

As a result, the Symposium took a somewhat different approach from that which was originally planned. The planned approach would have resulted in a report which covered: primary causes of family disintegration; the ultimate cause of these primary causes; various actionable focus areas which could effectively address this primary cause; and, finally, the selection of an actionable focus area best suited to the O'Neill Foundation. The approach adopted changed all this; it recognized multiple causes and concluded that families can be threatened by a wide variety of stressors that are complicated in and of themselves and difficult to prioritize in the abstract.

The discussions that in fact took place at the Symposium on "Family: The First Imperative" can best be reported in five parts:

• the generic types of *activity* suggested for consideration;

• the specific *issues* that were considered most important;

• the general advice that was offered and the *themes* emerging from this advice;

• the *constraints* that limit what the O'Neill Foundation will in fact be able to do;

• and the actionable *focus areas* which were suggested for consideration.

The report which follows is consequently organized along these lines.

ACTIVITIES

In the course of the Symposium proceedings, participants suggested various generic types of activity for consideration by the Foundation in order to meaningfully impact the institution of family in a favorable way. While some of these activities were not specifically discussed as such, they can be implicitly deduced from the discussions and conversations that took place. The types of activity suggested were:

1) Multi-disciplinary team building

2) Convening and establishing networks, both professional and philanthropic

3) Leadership in establishing collaborative efforts

4) Collection, organization and dissemination of important information

5) Scholarly and scientific research

6) Training and teaching

7) Advocacy, particularly in areas of public social policy

8) Mentoring

Issues

Participant papers started to suggest specific issues that must be successfully dealt with in order to restore family to its most important and rightful position in our society. Symposium discussion expanded this list of issues and amplified upon them. They tend to be hardcore problems that reflect basic values which are missing from our society; their absence leads to family disintegration and all the social problems that follow. The most widely mentioned specific issues were:

1) Widespread feelings of disconnectedness

2) Insufficient living-wage jobs

3) Lack of marriageable black males

4) Absent, disconnected and unsupportive fathers

5) Social policy programs that undermine the family

6) Lack of hope, despair and isolation

7) Unwanted and unloved children

8) Disintegrating male-female relationships

9) Inept communication abilities

10) Low self-esteem and anger, particularly in children with irresponsible parents

11) Separation of marriage and parenthood

12) Negative influence of the media (TV in particular) on our children

13) Absence of a dominant and shared moral value system

14) Lack of individual responsibility and commitment

15) Narcissism, sense of entitlement, and demand for instant gratification

16) Stress created by the rapidity of change and dual working parents

17) Violence in the home

18) Children in crisis

19) Illegal drugs

Sprinkled throughout the Symposium was a great deal of wisdom and advice from Symposium participants, wisdom and advice that reflects their years of experience working in the field of family. Some of this advice was conflicting (i.e., "employ the scientific method and rely upon it" vs "beware of the scientific method because it can lead to false conclusions"). Most of it, however, reflected a very strong consensus of opinion.

From this advice, ten principal themes can be deduced. These themes, and the advice which supports each, are as follows:

1) **Theme:** The focus area project should be appealing and emotionally satisfying to family members and to members of the community at large. The project should generate excitement, but the family must remember that it may not have as great an impact as hoped for.

   Supporting Advice: Embrace something that excites the O'Neill family... Don't become frustrated if initial efforts fail... Enjoy the work... Be content with a satisfying solution even if it is not an optimizing one... And look for an enormously compelling intervention that appeals to the very hearts of people.

2) **Theme:** The focus area project should be primarily child-centered, while recognizing the fact that a child's development is highly dependent upon the well-being of the adults in his or her life.

   Supporting Advice: Focus on the children; they need love, nurturing, protection and guidance... Consider children's needs for security as well as adult needs for individual happiness... And today's society has shifted from child-centered to adult-centered.

3) **Theme:** To be successful, the O'Neill Foundation needs to network and collaborate with Symposium participants, other foundations, and existing programs and groups that are already working on family issues. It should strive to foster a sense of belonging both within its funded projects, among family members, and among other groups with which the Foundation collaborates.

   Supporting Advice: Use Symposium participants as ongoing resources... Employ a collaborative team approach... Try to work with individuals or groups that are already bonded... Take advantage of existing programs... Be interactive... Identify and utilize resource people... All people need to be needed (even, and perhaps especially, men)... Modernization has impersonalized relationships and thereby helped to break down the bonds between people... All people breathe the same social air (problems anywhere affect everyone)... Widespread support creates a sense of belonging... And network with others (both professional and philanthropic).

4) **Theme:** There are a number of developmental and cultural stressors that families experience, and these stressors should be considered when selecting a focus area project.

    Supporting Advice: It is increasingly difficult for families to balance work, family and leisure activities... Two-career families put stress on marriages... The complexity in today's society contributes to its stress... Extended families and regular families are getting smaller with the passage of time (world society has gone from extended families to single mothers, and in Brazil, to orphans in the streets)... Longer life spans and rapid advances in technology are having fundamental effects on today's families... The way parents feel about emotions is important to the way children turn out... Peer influence on children often increases as parental influence decreases... And the different socialization of young boys and girls creates difficulties in communications when they grow up.

5) **Theme:** The Foundation's focus area activities should provide strong moral leadership by using the media and other outlets for popular culture to transmit positive values that are supportive of families.

    Supporting Advice: Look for institutions that transmit values and virtues... The media has an incredible impact on the impressionable and fragile minds of children... Strong and outspoken moral leadership is needed... "Work" must be made better than "welfare"... The O'Neill Foundation brings prestige to a community not only because of its money, but also because of its influence, perceived power and experience... Control of the contemporary pop culture is control of the society... And the average child has seen 7,000 simulated homicides on TV by the time he or she finishes the first grade.

6) **Theme:** Focus area projects should emphasize the disadvantaged or those at the fringes of society where the need is greatest.

    Supporting Advice: Welfare, as it is structured today, enslaves its recipients... The fringes of society are where the problems are the greatest, and the fringes are getting larger... Focus on those who are disadvantaged... Many inner-city black males don't expect to be alive beyond age 25 because of violent crime... And even with abortion, out-of-wedlock births today are: 68% of black children; 37% of hispanic children; and 23% of white children.

7) **Theme:** Focus area projects should be grounded and empowering in the sense that recipients of "help" should be directly involved at every level of the project, including its planning, implementation and evaluation.

   Supporting Advice: Use a bottom-up approach... Empower individuals... Get feedback from program beneficiaries... "Help" should be defined by the recipient... Setting up self-help efforts is better than doing it all for the disadvantaged... And build on strengths; use an asset approach (rather than a deficit approach).

8) **Theme:** When selecting and monitoring a focus area project, the Foundation needs to be strategic and it must purposefully plan and manage the project. It should have a systematic process for selecting, monitoring and evaluating projects using the advice given at the Symposium as its criteria.

   Supporting Advice: Build continuity into the program selected... Be creative... Be mindful of possible negative side-effects of well-intentioned programs, particularly those that work at the highest level of causality... Adopt a holistic approach... Symptoms and causes may be related in a circular, rather than in a linear, way... Try to develop programs which can be replicated... Take care not to duplicate what others are already doing well... Measure results of the efforts... Take advantage of existing programs... Employ a systemic approach... Use a "Request For Proposal" as an initial tactic if necessary... Be systematic... Process is important... While long-term fixes are the ultimate aim, short-term fixes are also needed... Find bridges between empirical approaches and bottom-up approaches... Looking at same data, people often come to different conclusions... And ideas lead to inventions which lead to innovations which produce effective and efficient results.

9) **Theme:** How "family" is defined will have a profound effect on the selection and impact of the project selected for funding.

   Supporting Advice: How family is defined will affect the design and structure of programs established to help families... Family is more than a set of feeling relationships; it should be an institution built on a set of commitments, and as such a source of "social capital" as well as a source of emotional well-being... Extended families and regular families are getting smaller with the passage of time... Successful marriages and successful families are not necessarily the same... And the structure of family is important; but the functioning is more important.

10) **Theme:** The selection and replication/dissemination of a focus area project should actively reflect the great cultural and class diversities within our country.

   Supporting Advice: Be sensitive to cultural diversity... All regions of the country may not have the same influences and values... And family problems are not only in poor urban settings; they cross financial lines and exist in suburban and rural settings as well.

CONSTRAINTS

In selecting an actionable focus area for the O'Neill Foundation, family members were aware of the real constraints that must be considered. While they might overcome any, or even all, of these constraints over time, these constraints are real at this time and they limit the options from which the Foundation can select. These constraints are:

1) **In terms of *time*:** Who in the family will be able and willing to commit the very significant amounts of time some of the suggested focus area projects will require? Without doubt, some of the proposed activities could require from 1,000 to 2,000 hours per year by one or more family members in order to be successful; other proposed activities may not require as much time but would probably require 300 to 500 hours per year at a minimum. And, if the activity is centered in the Cleveland, Ohio, area, will only Cleveland area family members be candidates? While the Foundation's small staff can help, a significant commitment of time from other family members will undoubtedly be required. The ability and willingness of family members to make a significant time commitment may be the most critical constraint.

2) **In terms of *talent*:** It must be recognized that O'Neill family members are all "lay people" in the field of family. They learned a lot at the Symposium and are much better educated than they used to be; but they are still far from experts. Help is available, but they are going to have to identify it, solicit (and perhaps pay for) it, and work with it. They are also going to have to lead the effort.

3) **In terms of *money*:** For the time being, the Foundation can probably deploy $150,0000 to $200,000 per year to its focus area. Over time, this amount may increase. While this is a significant amount of money to the family, it is a very small amount in relation to the size of the problems it is about to tackle. The Foundation must therefore deploy its resources very carefully and wisely if it hopes to make a real difference.

FOCUS AREAS

All of the thoughts expressed in the prior sections of this book, and particularly those reflected in the sections entitled Activities, Issues, Themes and Constraints, were considered as Symposium participants discussed possible focus area activities in the field of family for consideration by the O'Neill Foundation. Some of the suggested activities were carefully crafted by very strategic-thinking groups; some were almost spur-of-the-moment suggestions. Some enjoyed widespread consensus among Symposium participants and some had only a single advocate. Some were rather fully developed and some had to be pieced together from widely separated comments.

The focus areas recommended for consideration were as follows. The order of listing does not imply any sort of prioritization, and indeed, no particular attempt was made to prioritize them:

1) **The Active Team Working In a Local Community:** Form a multi-disciplinary team (O'Neill family members, Symposium members, knowledgeable local community resources, and other resource people as needed) and partner with leaders who are bonded to their local community in a joint effort to establish connectedness among the community members and between them and their community. Build this program on existing strengths that are already there. Determine what is needed for success in the community, then work to see that it is provided and follow up until it works.

2) **A Central Source For Sound Data On The Status of Families In America:** Determine what data accurately reflects the condition of families in America and whether this condition is getting better or worse, then periodically collect this data and widely disseminate it to the media, becoming the acknowledged central source of expert opinion on family status. Use this position to favorably influence all those things that benefit families in general.

3) **Discovery And Promotion Of Existing Programs That Work:** Create a wide area network that can identify existing programs which try to strengthen families, identify which of these programs really work as evidenced by measurable results, then widely disseminate information about such programs, encouraging other communities with like situations to adopt them. Invite media to meetings at which these programs are described and explained by their sponsors.

4) **Cost-Benefit Accounting For Government Policies Affecting Families:** Develop a sound accounting methodology to determine the cost of government social policies which affect families and the benefit (or detriment) of these policies to families. Then apply it to existing government programs, and also to proposed programs, in an effort to discourage and terminate programs which are bad for families and encourage and sustain the ones that are good.

5) **Focus On Fatherhood:** Recognizing that fathers who are absent and disconnected from their families are one of the root causes of family disintegration, develop a communication program which highlights the importance of fathers to their children and establishes role models for good fatherhood. Promote the program in a way that encourages young males to be responsible fathers.

6) **Catalyst For Professionals In The Field Of Family:** Become a catalyst to bring together diverse professionals in a community who all work in some aspect of the field of family, and encourage them to regularly dialogue together in order to improve the results they each achieve by sharing knowledge of what works and what doesn't, and by working to eliminate overlap and duplication.

7) **Promotion Of Relationship And/Or Parental Skills Training:** Recognizing that people with relationship skills and parental skills make for better families, search out the existing skills training programs which work the best, and widely disseminate and promote them to other groups that might use or employ them for the benefit of people in their communities.

8) **Grantmaker Catalyst In The Family Program Area:** Establish the O'Neill Foundation as a grantmaking thought leader in the program area of family, then use this position to regularly convene grantmakers interested in this program area. At these sessions, exchange helpful information on the focus area, introduce grantmakers to the best programs, and encourage more grantmaking in support of families.

9) **Annual Symposiums:** Periodically arrange and convene symposiums modeled after the Symposium on "Family: The First Imperative," programming timely topics on the subject of family and inviting appropriate participants. Then publish and disseminate the results for the benefit of all interested parties.

10) **Identification Of Community Strengths:** Develop a method to identify and assess existing strengths (assets) in a community, and using this knowledge, advise the community leaders on how they can best build upon these strengths. Once the model is built and successfully tested, deploy and widely use it throughout the country.

11) **Job Creation:** Try to develop a model for the creation of jobs in communities with high joblessness, jobs which offer a living wage, reasonable security and some hope for advancement. If such a model can be developed, test it, and if it works publicize and widely disseminate it.

12) **Decrease Illegitimate Births:** Recognizing that a disproportionately large percent of societal problems stem from the birth of children to young, unwed, often poorly educated and impoverished women, particularly black women, strive to find an effective way to decrease the unwed birth rate, particularly in this segment of our society. If such a way can be found, widely publicize and promote it.

13) **Stressors And Supports:** Conduct a study of the major stressors that afflict families then determine which types of support most effectively and cost efficiently counteract these stressors. When the work is complete, publish and widely disseminate it.

14) **Mentoring Programs:** Develop a model mentoring program, test it in the Cleveland area and measure its outcomes. If it works satisfactorily, disseminate and promote it widely throughout the country.

In addition, two other possible focus area projects emerged as a result of the Symposium and subsequent efforts to prepare this book; they are:

15) **The Statue Of Responsibility:** Recognizing that the Statue of Liberty on the East Coast represents freedom of the individual, but also recognizing that a sound nation with strong families requires an equal amount of responsibility, become the catalyst in forming a group to design, fund and erect a "Statue of Responsibility" on the West Coast. The Statue of Responsibility would be comparable in size, scope and importance to the Statue of Liberty, and would symbolize that true peace, joy and prosperity for the nation which lies between these Statues requires not only liberty but also responsibility. The Statue of Responsibility might feature a male father image.

16) Uniting People In A Simple Common Cause: Recognizing the importance of community and connectedness, and that it requires a common mission, interest and commitment, establish a model program to bring people in a community together in a very simple but appealing common endeavor. The endeavor should be fun, multi-generational, social and replicable. An example might start with the acquisition of a derelict neighborhood home which would then be torn down and replaced by a small neighborhood park. A role-model family in the neighborhood could be appointed to give lay supervision to the park's development with trees, shrubs, plants, flowers, playground equipment, etc. The funds to pay for this would come from the Foundation and the labor to do it would come from people in the neighborhood; professional nursery people could lend the expert advice needed. When the neighborhood park is complete, it could be named after the family that provided the local supervision and then perhaps turned over to an appropriate agency to hold in perpetuity.

Evaluation

The William J. and Dorothy K. O'Neill Foundation tries to approach its philanthropic activities not so much in terms of "giving away money," but more in terms of "making an investment." As an investor, the Foundation seeks a return on its investment, not a monetary return to itself, but a return to society in terms of improving the human condition. And to maximize this return, it is first necessary to evaluate it. Consequently, the Foundation tries to evaluate whatever it does, including the performance of its Disbursements Committee, the achievements of its larger grants, and even the results obtained from this Symposium on "Family: The First Imperative."

While evaluations of this sort are often difficult and quantification is rarely precise, it is still necessary to make the effort; without it, "investment returns" will not improve.

Going into the Symposium, Mr. O'Neill started with the belief that the O'Neill Foundation could make a difference, and that it wanted to help people help themselves in fundamental ways that would restore strong and healthy families. The O'Neill family committed to bring values, passion, focus, time and money to the undertaking, but they knew they needed guidance to expose the ultimate causes of family disintegration. Mr. O'Neill wanted to know what was *really* important that needs to be done, that is not being done now, that is within the Foundation's capabilities, and that turns family members on with excitement.

With this in mind, Mr. O'Neill established the five objectives which are outlined in the Introduction section of this book. Whether and how well these objectives were achieved is, of course, very much a matter of individual opinion. O'Neill family members, and perhaps the professional participants as well, might well differ with one another in their assessments of how well the Symposium went. Mr. O'Neill, however, evaluates it as follows:

• With reference to uncovering the ultimate causes of family disintegration, a great deal of progress was made. While no single ultimate cause was discovered (indeed, it may not exist), a number of root causes were exposed. It remains to be seen, however, if the family can develop a meaningful and actionable focus area which effectively addresses one of these root causes in a manner which not only works, but can also be replicated if successful. This was the principal objective of the Symposium. Only time will tell for sure if it was accomplished and to what degree. While the achievement here may not have been as great as Mr. O'Neill had hoped, all participants, including O'Neill family members, clearly recognized that a great deal was in fact achieved.

• With reference to building a network of resource people who would be available to the Foundation to call upon in the future, the Symposium clearly achieved this objective. The twenty-one professional participants constitute an enormously talented pool of expertise in the field of family and represent a wide diversity of viewpoints and multiple backgrounds. Most of them have volunteered to help out in the future in any way they can, and the Foundation has already done some further work with some of them.

• With reference to educating members of the O'Neill family on the subject of family, the Symposium was a great success. The collegial atmosphere that prevailed quickly built bonds of trust between all participants, and this led to candid discussions which probed the depths of the subject. While family members did not leave the Symposium as knowledgeable as the professional participants, they did receive what one member described as the equivalent of an undergraduate degree in the field of family. With this greater knowledge, the Foundation is much better positioned to do meaningful work in the field.

• With reference to sharing the content and results of the Symposium with the public at large, it is hoped that this book will adequately meet that objective. It attempts to not only report on what transpired, but also to present the background leading up to the Symposium and a candid assessment of how well it achieved its objectives. Should any readers of this book desire additional information, they may call Mr. O'Neill at the Foundation's office (216-831-9667).

• With reference to having all participants thoroughly enjoy the process, it appears that they did in fact have fun. There was much camaraderie from the very beginning and each of the four break-out groups quickly became strong "family" units within the context of the Symposium community. Professional participants appreciated working with other high caliber professionals, and also enjoyed the new experience of working with non-professional members of the O'Neill family; collectively, they rated the experience a 4.6 on a 5.0 scale. The O'Neill family members thoroughly enjoyed meeting and working with this diverse group of highly capable professionals; they were treated with respect and urged to participate. Collectively, they rated the Symposium at 4.4.

In terms of evaluating the Symposium as a *process* for learning, most of the participants would say it worked out quite well. It got quickly into the major issues and stimulated in-depth discussion. The diverse backgrounds of the participants, and the wide range of views they held, resulted in lively debate. The fact that they each cared deeply about the subject matter caused thoughtful ideas to be advanced and created an atmosphere of mutual respect.

But it should be recognized that a Symposium like this is a considerable undertaking for a small family foundation. It was seven months in the planning, and from initial concept through the publication of this book it probably consumed over 2,000 hours of Foundation staff time. The out-of-pocket cost was approximately $76,000 (mostly for honorariums and travel and lodging expenses), and the cost of publishing this book will be in addition to that amount.

It should also be recognized that the plan of attack adopted by Symposium planners may in fact be modified in implementation by the participants. While Mr. O'Neill had planned a linear approach, the participants adopted a more circular, interactive approach, perhaps in recognition of the dynamic interplay of causal forces on the multiple roles that family plays. Because family serves so many purposes, a breakdown in its ability in any one of these areas can be viewed as a root cause of its disintegration. This approach to the problem makes linear reasoning back to an ultimate cause all but impossible.

Finally, the free-ranging discussions which took place during the Symposium's working group sessions made it more difficult to extract and organize the Symposium's major messages. This delayed the publication of this book and slowed the Foundation's ability to select its actionable focus area.

Notwithstanding these difficulties however, the Symposium process proved itself a worthy way of accomplishing the Foundation's objectives.

As this book was going to press, the O'Neill Foundation's Disbursements Committee selected its first actionable focus area in the field of family. Working through the Center For Families & Children in Cleveland, Ohio (CFC), the Foundation will fund and participate in a two-year project entitled "Fathers & Families Together." This replicable demonstration project will take place in Cleveland's Glenville community, a community of 25,000 residents which is racially homogeneous but socio-economically diverse. Glenville has 12,000 households and a significant number of its adult male population is unemployed, or underemployed due to limited education and unpreparedness. The project will target a group of 60 fathers per year, and will be conducted as part of CFC's family services initiative.

The aim of "Fathers & Families Together" will be to strengthen the father-child bond, to help fathers assume greater parenting responsibility, and to enhance the self-sufficiency of fathers. The program will integrate a number of services, and will build on family strengths. It will seek to give men a space and place for psychologically safe bonding and articulation of their concerns about the role of father and husband; it will also address career development, job training and educational enrichment.

The core conceptual frameworks which form the basis for the program are Village Based Development and the Competence Model. The program's goals are: to strengthen father-child bonding; to strengthen families; to help fathers assume greater parenting responsibilities; to enhance the self-sufficiency of families and fathers; and to strengthen values that encourage family success, achievement and community.

The program will be administered by CFC's Project Safe Harbor Director, and will employ three full-time people: a professional social worker, an outreach worker, and a job developer. Members of the O'Neill family will be involved on a committee which advises the program, and periodic evaluations of the program will be made.

The O'Neill Foundation believes that this program meets all of the major requirements it established for its actionable focus area in the field of family, and is responsive to most of the major concepts and ideas which emerged from its Symposium. Family members indicate that they are prepared to contribute whatever time and talent they might have to help this program succeed, and they are energized by the prospect of getting started and committed to bringing values and passion to the undertaking.

PART TWO:

The Papers

Family Disintegration and Behavior Disorders of Youth: An Inevitable Cycle?

JAMES F. ALEXANDER
CHRISTIE PUGH
DONNA GUNDERSON
CRYSTAL DELOACH
University of Utah

FAMILY: THE FIRST IMPERATIVE —

IN SEARCH OF THE ULTIMATE CAUSE(S) OF FAMILY DISINTEGRATION

In selecting this theme, the William J. and Dorothy K. O'Neill Foundation has undertaken a noble but awesome task: Organizing an effort to identify "the ultimate cause(s) of family disintegration." To meet this challenge, the Foundation has gathered an impressive array of professionals to participate in this conference, and I am honored and most appreciative to have the opportunity to attend.

However, even with this concentration of experts the task can be daunting. In myriad domains — cancer, heart disease, birth defects, low socioeconomic status, and (in the case of this conference) family disintegration to name just a few — the search for "ultimate causes" has been frustrating; this in large part because none of these topics represents a unitary "end product." Instead, these convenient phrases organize several, sometimes quite distinct, processes that have multi-variate and diverse etiological and developmental pathways.

As a result, it is most likely that few, if any, absolute ultimate causes can be found. Instead, we must reframe our approach as one of identifying "risk factors" that, singly or more likely in combination, increase the likelihood of undesirable consequences in certain contexts. In recognizing this contextual caveat we give up some comforting delusions such as the "single issue platform" proposed by some politicians and the "one size fits all" solutions we often encounter in the media and popular literature.

At the same time, what can look like a potentially overwhelming array of potential contributors to family disintegration can be organized into more manageable conceptual "chunks," and that is one goal of this paper. Rather than simply reviewing many factors[1] and selecting "front runners," we will instead propose a framework for ordering and interrelating the effects of many variables, suggesting a "dynamic systems" (Fogel and Thelan, 1987), as opposed to a "linear cause-effect," conceptual strategy for understanding their effects. Further, in order to avoid platitudes and overgeneralizations, we will use a particular set of secondary symptoms to organize the framework. *Disruptive Behavior Disorders (DBD's)* (Costello & Angold, 1993) of youth will represent our focus, largely because family disintegration is so often invoked as an important cause. We also choose this problem because without effective intervention these behaviors are very expensive: Expensive in economic terms, in physical (property and people) damage, in legal and medical costs, in lost productivity, and even in lives. Finally, we choose this problem because we have extensive research and clinical experience with demonstrated and frequently cited positive impact on DBD's of youth with a family-based intervention model (Alexander & Barton 1976; Alexander, Barton, Schiavo & Parsons, 1976; Alexander & Parsons, 1973, 1982; Barton, Alexander, Waldron, Turner & Warburton, 1985; Gendreau & Ross, 1980; Gurman, Kniskern & Pinsof, 1986).

DISRUPTIVE BEHAVIOR DISORDERS (DBD'S) OF YOUTH

DBD's often emerge with the following labels and diagnostic categories: Oppositional Defiant Disorder (ODD), Conduct Disorder (CD), Juvenile Delinquency (JD), Adolescent Substance Abuse, and Disorders of Impulsivity and Attention (ADHD: Attention Deficit Hyperactivity Disorder). These various labels, and numerous specific behaviors such as truancy and sexual aggression that are subsumed under them, represent a heterogenous group of overt behaviors and possible etiologic patterns (Farrington, 1987; Kazdin, 1987; Loeber, 1988; Rutter & Giller, 1983). For some of the most troublesome youth, the development of DBD's generally begins with Oppositional Defiant Disorder (ODD), or at least disruptive behavior patterns that satisfy some of the criteria for that diagnosis (Loeber, 1990). For a subset of these youth, perhaps with preexisting intraorganismic (genetic, physiological, anatomical, neurocognitive: Costello & Angold, 1993) vulnerabilities, the problematic behaviors evolve into more dramatic, and at times violent, forms of Conduct Disorder. Without effective intervention, such children are at extremely high risk for developing antisocial personality disorder and being arrested for multiple crimes (Loney, 1988; Mannuzza, Guittleman-Klein, Horowitz Korning, & Giampino, 1989). These youth also become progenitors of a new generation of problems by virtue of being at higher risk for marital and occupational adjustment problems (Kazdin, Siegel, & Bass, 1992) and by having children who in turn demonstrate a much higher rate of the same type of problems (Costello & Angold, 1993).

Other youth do not show early oppositional signs, but nonetheless during mid-adolescence develop serious forms of Conduct Disorder. These youth, which include a much larger percentage of females, are more likely to desist their troublesome behavior as they enter late adolescence, and are characterized by more covert (e.g., stealing) than violent forms of conduct disorder (Hinshaw, Lahey & Hart, 1993; Loeber, 1990; Roff & Wirt, 1984).

DOMAINS OF INFLUENCE IN DBD'S

Four interdependent major domains of influence have been implicated in the development of the various expressions of DBD's. These domains (Extrafamilial, Larger family system, Parent(s) subsystem, Child/youth Intraorganismic factors) include myriad specific variables, many of which will be identified briefly below. However, extensive lists of potential contributing variables, even with documentation of their independent correlations with DBD's, do little to advance our quest for "ultimate causes;" as such they also do not translate readily into widely applicable and coherent prevention and treatment programs, or to coherent social policy. Unfortunately, most formal investigations have focused on only a subset of these variables, and only in relation to specific populations of youth. As a result, the relationship between these variables is often left to supposition. In addition, many of these variables can act as toxic influences or as sources of hardiness that can buffer the negative effects of other variables. Thus, as a first step, it is necessary to develop an omnibus model of effects that focuses on the larger systemic relationships between variables. Such a model, represented in its molar (and as a result only heuristic) form in Figure 1, identifies the reciprocity and embeddedness that characterizes the sources of influence in the environment of youth in the process of developing DBD's.

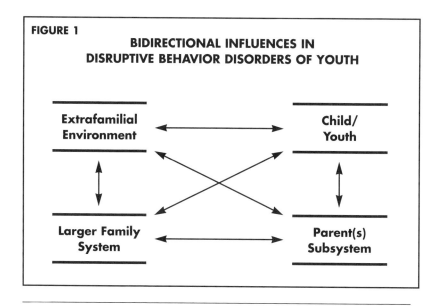

FIGURE 1

BIDIRECTIONAL INFLUENCES IN DISRUPTIVE BEHAVIOR DISORDERS OF YOUTH

Extrafamilial Environment

Child/ Youth

Larger Family System

Parent(s) Subsystem

Specific definitions and variables that constitute these four domains will be presented in later sections. However, it is first important to emphasize "non-content" aspects of the model, including:

1) Reciprocity, not linear cause-effect relationships, characterize the influence processes. For example, while a number of investigations have examined the effects of parent variables on DBD's, other researchers have noted the powerful reciprocal effect child behavior can have on the marital relationship and parenting practices (Bell, 1968; Emery, Fincham & Cummings, 1992; Lytton, 1990). Further, oppositional and aggressive behavior on the part of the child can increase the likelihood of abuse by the parent(s) (Reid, Taplan, & Loeber, 1981). In other words, the variables that are thought to produce DBD's are at the same time elicited by them. Thus, while most of our subsequent discussion will focus on influences that operate on the child/youth, the bidirectionality of effects, including those of the child/youth, should not be forgotten.

2) Each domain can have a direct effect on several others. For example, a crime-ridden neighborhood can directly influence the parent(s) subsystem by creating fear, it can directly influence the child through peer pressure and the modeling and reinforcement of violence, and it can directly influence the larger family system by recruiting siblings into a violent peer group. A highly pathological and conflicted parental relationship can likewise directly alienate a potentially beneficial Extrafamilial environment (e.g., neighbors, school, church), it can directly influence the child via abusive and negligent parenting, and it can alienate a potentially supportive extended family.

3) At least as important as direct influences, are the three-way, indirect effects domains can have on one another. A culture (Extrafamilial domain) that supports and values the extended family (Larger Family System domain) can indirectly affect the child by facilitating positive ("buffering") extended family involvement with a youth in circumstances when the parent(s) do not provide sufficient positive influence. Conversely, in a culture which places much more emphasis on the independence of the nuclear family, the larger family system and the extrafamilial environment may not be able to provide as effective a buffering role for inadequate parents. Further, Lambert, Weisz and Knight (1989) provided evidence that conduct problems are more common in American children than in youth from areas where undercontrolled behavior is viewed as less normative and acceptable.

Dual membership in minority and majority cultures represents a particularly troublesome situation for families. The "acculturative stress" is sometimes dealt with in maladaptive ways, and family members' responses to this stressor can create or exacerbate interpersonal and intergenerational conflict (Yates, 1987) since oftentimes youths are quicker to adopt the beliefs, attitudes, and values of the majority culture than are adults (Szapocznik, et al., 1984; 1994).

Finally, institutions such as school and juvenile justice systems can facilitate good parenting process (thereby indirectly influencing the child) through support, therapeutic involvement, and education for the parents and family. In contrast, they can actually worsen parenting process by adding stress, by creating reactance through insensitivity, and by failing to recognize and accommodate to the fact that parents' needs and agendas may differ from theirs.

The implications of the relationships between and within domains of influence are profound, adding complications as much as they provide hopeful alternatives to our current level of understanding. For example, the effects of a negative extrafamilial environment can be obviated, but it requires a different type of parent and/or larger family situation than would be necessary in a less toxic environment. Similarly, the potentially damaging effects of predisposing child "temperament" variables such as impulsivity, learning disability, and even some intrauterine toxins can be minimized with particularly adept parental, larger family system, and extrafamilial environment responses. Unfortunately, many of these specific "positive paths" for particular configurations are wiped out in typical research designs that independently correlate each variable at a molar level with the rate of DBD's. So-called "qualitative" and "transactional" approaches to developing explanatory models are better designed to evaluate the complexity and uniqueness of particular configurations, but such models have yet to evolve to a point where they are useful in the developmental epidemiology (Costello & Angold, 1993) of DBD's.

As a result, we are still faced with a large number of variables that are modestly related to DBD's in youth. From the data, we can safely infer that the presence of many of the negative influences work additively to predict a poor prognosis. Conversely, the complete absence of any of these with respect to a particular youth can lead to a highly confident conclusion that DBD's will not emerge. But for the majority of youth, for whom various patterns and combinations of some of the variables are present, our predictive validity becomes quite low. Thus while we must identify the variables, we must also develop a more refined model that can guide researchers, clinicians, and policy makers as they struggle with particular patterns of these variables. To that end, the next section briefly identifies a number of variables and combination of variables, and a subset of the references to them, that have been found to relate to some form of DBD's. These variables are organized within the domains of influence introduced above, and are found in Table 1.

TABLE 1 - IMPLICATED VARIABLES IN DISRUPTIVE BEHAVIOR DISORDERS OF YOUTH:

1 A: Child Intraorganismic (Genetic, Anatomical, Physiological, Neurocognitive) Variables.

• Comorbid impulsivity/ADHD (Krinshaw et al., 1993; Ferrington et al., 1990)

• Academic underachievement (Krinshaw et al., 1993)

• "Predisposing factors such as difficult child temperament" (Patterson, 1986)

• Genetics and possible neurotoxins (Loeber, 1990; Needleman & Bellinger, 1981)

• Aggressive subtypes, most likely with some sort of biological predisposition (Quay, 1993)

• Early maturation for females, with effects being mostly through association with older males (Cairns, Gariepy & Hood, 1990; Stattin & Magnusson, 1990)

• Child emotional disregulation which represents a learned pattern as a function of parent negativity (Cole & Zahn-Waxler, 1992)

• History of disruption in caretaker continuity (Loeber, 1990)

1 B: Extrafamilial Environment Variables.

• Culture/acculturative stress (Yates, 1987)

• Variations in acculturation rates among family members (Szapocznik et al., 1994)

• Cultural attitudes about undercontrolled behavior in youth (Lambert, Weisz & Knight, 1989)

• Cultural attitudes relative to child abuse and neglect, including value of children, involvement of extended family, attitudes regarding child rearing (Korbin, 1981)

• "Counter culture environments" (Richters & Cicchitti, 1993).

• Low socioeconomic level (Frick, 1981; Rey et al., 1988; Schachar & Wachsmuth, 1990—see also Lakey et al., 1991)

• Peer influences, which emerge after family influences have their early effects, but become equally important and remain roughly comparable to family influences for quite some time (Loeber, 1990).

• Peer rejection (Frick et al., 1991; Cole, Lochman, Terry & Hyman, 1992) and other peer problems (Schachar & Wachsmuth, 1990)

• Peer drug use (Swadi, 1992)

• Minority status (Guerra, Huesmann, Tolan, VanAcker & Eron, in press)

• Low SES (Guerra et al., in press)

• Community context of high crime rate (Guerra et al., in press)

• School suspensions (Frick et al., 1991)

• Police contacts (Frick et al., 1991)

TABLE 1 - CONTINUED

1 C: Larger Family System.

- Sibling problems (Schachar & Wachsmuth, 1990)

- Family of origin

- Extended family/kin (Dilworth-Anderson, 1992; Friedman & Andrews, 1990)

- "Family variables are a consistently strong predictor of antisocial behaviors" (Henggeler, et al., 1989; McCord, 1991; Loeber & Stouthhamer-Loeber, 1987; Tolan & Loeber, 1993)

- Lack of emotional warmth, family disorganization and lack of support, family beliefs & values (Tolan, Gorman-Smith, Zalli & Huesmann, 1994)

- Unemployment (Patterson, DeBaryshe, & Ramsey, 1989)

1 D: The Parent(s) Subsystem.

- Parental antisocial personality disorder (Faraone et al., 1991; Frick et al., 1991)

- Substance abuse (Faraone et al., 1991; Frick et al., 1991)

- Parent aggressiveness (McCord, 1980)

- Parental conflict (McCord, 1980)

- Lack of maternal affection and paternal criminal behavior (McCord, 1980)

- Low parental warmth, low acceptance and affection, high conflict and hostility (Henggeler, 1989; Tolan & Lorion, 1988; West & Ferrington, 1973)

- Inadequate discipline and supervision, low involvement in daily activities with child (Darling & Steinberg, 1993)

- Poor monitoring, coercive discipline, inconsistent discipline, absence of positive parenting (Patterson, 1982, 1986; Frick et al., 1992; Patterson & Stouthhamer-Loeber, 1984)

- Parent Rejection (Hetherington & Martin, 1986-Review)

- Marital conflict predicts externalizing behaviors (Porter & O'Leary, 1980; Snyder, Klein, Gdowski, Faulstich & LaCombe, 1988; Van Wickle-Palma & DiGuisecpe, 1992)

- "Perturbations in parenting" predict child behavior disorders (Patterson, DeBaryshe & Ramsey, 1989, p.33)

ENHANCING POSITIVE PARENTING: A UNIFYING SOLUTION

Based on the wealth of information exemplified by the numerous sources cited above, we propose an "Influence Process" model of DBD development, prevention, and change. This organizing framework helps us understand and hopefully redirect what currently appears to be an increasingly negative reciprocal cycle of youthful DBD's and a variety of environmental factors. Certainly the popular media and official statistics point to an ever increasing magnitude (rate and severity) of these problems. Further, for purposes of clarity and simplicity, this model (see Figure 2) artificially punctuates the influence process as a more linear effect sequence than actually exists. However, it also organizes the effects in such a manner that they are amenable to positive change. A colleague (C. Turner, personal communication, September, 1994) has likened the problem to one of entering a turbulent river to rescue a child in danger of drowning. A number of complex and interdependent variables undoubtedly have led to this situation, possibly including contributions by the child. In addition, a number of complex physical forces (e.g., uneven terrain beneath the water which creates eddies and small whirlpools), as well as current maladaptive "coping" behaviors of the child, complicate the situation. In such a context, the intervenor must understand the interdependent and reciprocal systemic effects of the variables involved (in a manner consistent with the model presented in Figure 1), but at the same time must in a more linear fashion introduce a new and very powerful intervention in order to dramatically change the potential trajectory that characterizes the situation.

Conceptually, we see the current context of Disruptive Behavior Disorders in youth as representing a similar situation; in particular a number of variables exist that we cannot control retroactively or directly in the present. However, if our intervention strategy can understand and negate or buffer some of the powerful effects of neg-atively influencing variables, we can have dramatic positive impact.

Most of the domains and specific exemplars contained in Figure 2 already have been introduced. The important new conceptual element is the separation of influence processes on the child (see the middle section of the Figure) from the sources of those processes (i.e., extrafamilial environment, larger family environment, parental sub-system). This model suggests that the various sources of influence converge to represent one final common pathway in which the pro-portional magnitude of any given source of influence is dependent upon the relative magnitude of the other sources. For example, as extrafamilial factors (e.g., peers) increase in influence potential, other sources of influence decrease by a like amount, unless they also act to increase their relative impact. Because of this, we can conceptually assign "weights" to the various paths of influence that converge on the child, with the possibility of automatically reducing the impact of some paths by increasing the potency of others. Based on numerous legal, cultural, social, economic, technical, pragmatic, and (for some) spiritual considerations, we propose that in the current Zeitgeist par-enting process should represent our primary focus. Our goal is to enhance the positive influence potential for this avenue of influence, both absolutely and relative to others.

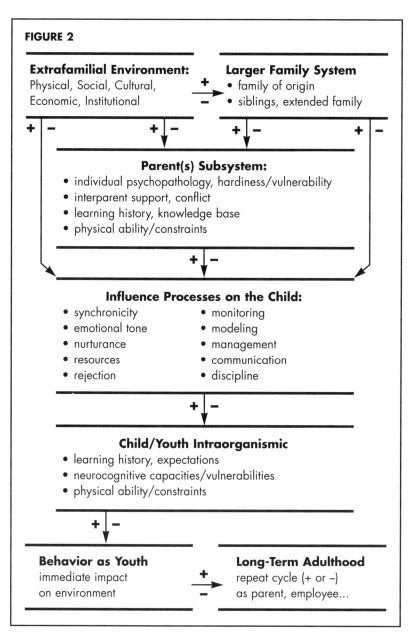

FIGURE 2

Extrafamilial Environment:
Physical, Social, Cultural, Economic, Institutional

Larger Family System
• family of origin
• siblings, extended family

Parent(s) Subsystem:
• individual psychopathology, hardiness/vulnerability
• interparent support, conflict
• learning history, knowledge base
• physical ability/constraints

Influence Processes on the Child:
• synchronicity
• emotional tone
• nurturance
• resources
• rejection
• monitoring
• modeling
• management
• communication
• discipline

Child/Youth Intraorganismic
• learning history, expectations
• neurocognitive capacities/vulnerabilities
• physical ability/constraints

Behavior as Youth
immediate impact on environment

Long-Term Adulthood
repeat cycle (+ or –)
as parent, employee...

Please note, however, that "traditional" parent configurations are not the only configurations required to meet our goal. Arguably in many contexts, a traditional parental configuration may be the most efficient, but for many children an alternative avenue to parenting may be the only one(s) available, or even desirable. Thus, we must develop alternative pathways that can still provide Positive Parenting Process, especially in light of the multigenetic, multicultural, multiclass, and multiple, as well as diverse physical environments, within which a large proportion of youth live. To insist on a single form of solution to the problems of parenting would be comparable to insisting on a single genetic or dietary or lifestyle or medical solution to cardiovascular disease or cancer. One can stop smoking to decrease the risk for such disorders, but for people who don't smoke very different paths must often be taken to facilitate longevity.

At the same time, regardless of their form, certain basic positive processes must be available to all children and youth. We must do all that we can to facilitate the provision of these processes, listed in Figure 2. For example, synchronicity (Gelfand & Teti, 1989) in parenting nurturance, monitoring, and the use of "proximal zones of development" (Vygotsky, 1987) will exist to a greater or lesser extent somewhere in the environment of any given child. If such factors as parental psychopathology, relational conflict, and economic deprivation decrease the likelihood that such synchronicity will occur within the immediate home environment, it is more likely that such a process will be located (and even sought out) by the child in the Extrafamilial environment. If a parent models and reinforces effective prosocial behaviors for the child (Bandura, 1965; 1973), the modeling influences of less desirable alternatives outside the home will be lessened. Conversely, if parent(s) provide less nurturance, the appearance of fewer resources, and a more negative emotional tone which includes hostility and coercion, the child will be more likely to seek out and respond to alternative sources of influence potential outside the home.

The specific process variables that influence the childrens' behaviors both positively and negatively, have been referenced in Table 1 and are well developed in related literature (See also Bandura 1965, 1973; Patterson, 1986; Steinberg, 1985, 1989; Dornbush et al, 1985). At this juncture our goal is to provide a context in which to understand how Positive Parenting Process can be enhanced through direct intervention (e.g., education, therapy), through the indirect effects of decreasing psychopathology and other intraorganismic factors in future parents, and through more diffuse extrafamilial support (media, cultural, economic) for positive parenting. An example might be providing monetary resources to parent(s) based more on positive parenting process rather than parent status per se. Psychopharmacological and other medical interventions which reduce child/youth vulnerability, as well as the negative impact of certain youth behaviors on parents, may also enhance positive parenting process, but such interventions must not be used merely to suppress troublesome behavior.

Finally, we wish to emphasize the multiplicative effect of enhancing positive parenting process. This will directly benefit the child in many ways, but will also decrease the relative influence of other sources (e.g., peers and media in the extrafamilial domain) should they be less positive. It also allows us to bring one of our main social goals (to facilitate the role of the family) in line with other legal, economic, and social goals such as achieving lower crime rates and less dangerous neighborhoods. Finally, a focus on enhancing Positive Parenting Process does not preclude or negate the need for intervention in other domains. In fact, improvement in the functioning of many other variables (educational, economic, physical) is generally highly consistent with enhancing positive parenting. But without the latter, other levels and domains of intervention are generally doomed to (expensive) failure.

IMPLICATIONS

Promising avenues of change. The drowning child, a metaphor introduced earlier, can likely be rescued given sufficient knowledge of the variables maintaining the crisis and sufficient resources to obviate their influence. As a caring culture, we would also like to prevent such crises as much as possible through various possible mechanisms; we could, for example, install electrified fences around all rivers and streams, outlaw children within 300 feet of these waters, outfit all children with permanently attached life jackets, educate children and parents in ways to avoid such circumstances, etc., etc.

Such solutions, mostly "tongue-in-cheek," are offered to make a point: Prevention and intervention programs, for most if not all social (and for that matter physical) ills, involve issues of motivation and implementation, as much as they involve the challenge of developing "technology." Some solutions are difficult or impossible to implement for economic reasons, and some violate other principles or create side effects that are unacceptable even if they might serve to impact the problem. In the case of juvenile DBD's, for example, it is both technically and ethically difficult, if not impossible, to eliminate many of the child/youth Intraorganismic variables identified in Table 1 (e.g., genetics, some intrauterine processes, neurotoxins, ADHD). Intrusive genetic manipulation and severe constraints on who may or may not give birth are not options society is ready to adopt, even if we were technically able to do so. In addition, many Extrafamilial System variables (e.g., unemployment and poverty, physically dangerous neighborhoods, polluted air and water, deteriorating schools with too few resources to meet students' needs, violent and otherwise exploitative images on television, and so on), while representing desirable foci for change, are part of larger system processes (social and economic, to name two of the more obvious) that would appear to be difficult to change immediately without major, perhaps revolutionary, forms of intervention.

Finally, we must admit to resembling the old phrase: "When all you have is a hammer, the whole world looks like a nail." As mentioned earlier, we are interventionists who have developed an effective family-based (Functional Family Therapy) model to deal with juvenile DBD's. We and others who emphasize some form of family or parenting focus in the treatment of child/youth behavior problems (Borduin, Henggeler, Blaske, & Stein, 1990; Brunk, Henggeler, & Whelan, 1987; Dishion, Patterson, & Reid, 1985; Dumas, Blechman, & Prinz, in press; Henggeler & Borduin, 1990; Henggeler, Melton, & Smith, 1992; Henggeler, Rodick, Bourduin, Hanson, Watson, & Urey, 1986; Larzelere & Patterson, 1990; Liddle, 1991, 1992; Liddle & Dakof, 1993, in press; Mash, 1989; Nye, 1958; Patterson, 1982, 1986; Reid, Taplin, & Loeber, 1981; Szapocznik, Perez-Vidal, Brickman, Foote, Santiseban, Hervis, & Kurtines, 1988; Tolan & Mitchell, 1989) represent one of the few consistently efficacious treatment philosophies in the mental health and juvenile justice literature (Alexander & Barton, 1994; Alexander, Holtzworth-Munroe, & Jameson, 1993; Bednar, Burlingame, & Masters, 1988; Cedar & Levant, 1990; Forehand, 1993; Gendreau & Ross, 1980; Gurman, Kniskern, & Pinsof, 1986; Hazelrigg, Cooper, & Borduin, 1987; Henggeler, Borduin, & Mann, in press; Kazdin, 1987, 1993; Markus, Lange, & Pettigrew, 1990; NIDA Notes, 1991; Patterson, Dishion, & Chamberlain, 1992; Selekman & Todd, 1991; Tolan & Guerra, 1993). As a result, it is no surprise that we see a focus on "the family," in the various forms it may take, as a (if not the) most promising avenue to prevention and treatment of juvenile DBD's. The extensive literature cited above, from which the domain of "Positive Parenting Process" was distilled, also points to this avenue.

Prioritizing the foci of change. Since each of the major domains of influence discussed above (Intraorganismic, Extrafamilial, Larger Family System, Parent(s) Subsystem) contribute to the problem of DBD's, it is obvious that we must first integrate and extend the knowledge we have of each domain and the numerous variables contained in each. We must use a variety of sources to gain this knowledge, including cultural input from many perspectives, popular literature, feedback from clinical intervention, and research (sociological, anthropological, psychological, political, neurobiological and genetic, among others). We must then develop and/or enhance interventions for each of the domains. Such interventions might involve many different programs such as decreasing infections in and good nutrition for pregnant mothers, providing affordable low-income housing in safe neighborhoods and health care for grandparents so they are more able to provide monitoring functions when the parent figure(s) must work, and providing more police to impact crime directly "on the streets."

Of course, to some extent many activities already have been attempted, yet the problems identified at the outset of this paper continue to grow. Thus we assert the need for a next step, that of prioritization of our initiatives. The goal of this prioritization is not to denigrate some initiatives at the expense of others, but to organize what is in reality considerable competition for limited resources. This prioritization uses Positive Parenting Process as the immediate organizing principle, and asks that all proposed interventions for juvenile DBD's articulate the direct influence they will have on Positive Parenting Process. For example, a proposal for additional psychiatric inpatient procedures for referred youth, though a desirable resource, will receive a lower priority if it does not directly provide a vehicle to enhance Positive Parenting Process. Sadly, many current inpatient programs do not, or only give lip service to this variable. Likewise, a proposal for more police on the streets, though once again desirable, should be linked to facilitating Positive Parenting Process. This statement is not intended to imply that more police on the streets will not constitute a positive effect on juvenile DBD's. However, if we place our resources into alternatives other than enhancing parents' ability to parent (e.g., via education, therapeutic intervention, job skills and other avenues to economic viability and increased self worth), we will face the prospect of more and more "poorly parented" children who require more and more police to control them. If we fail to consider the relationship between the various interventions we propose and Positive Parenting Process, we run the risk of creating processes which unwittingly ignore or even serve to decrease such process. Thus we propose that all institutional (e.g., educational, legal/criminal, government and political) decisions should, ideally, be filtered through the Positive Parenting Process framework. When inconsistencies arise, for example, between what is most efficient for a school administration versus what is most efficient for enhancing parenting process, the latter must have priority. If a so-called "welfare" system is more oriented to bureaucratic efficiency or political expediency rather than to enhancing positive parenting process (not just giving birth), it needs to be revamped if we are to prioritize successfully the parenting process.

One need not be an accomplished family therapist and researcher to appreciate, prioritize, and integrate the various needs and potential resources available to families in need. However, it helps to think about families from the perspective of a therapist; at this level we are less likely to trivialize and overgeneralize the "real-life" exigencies involved in parenting. As a scientist, I can understand the effects of poverty, child abuse, gangs. As a therapist, I can feel them in the room. As a scientist, I can understand how poor family of origin experiences have rendered arcane the procedures involved in Positive Parenting Process for the offspring, who are now parents themselves. As a family therapist, I must go beyond this understanding; I must say and do what is necessary for them to be able to attain what for them may be beyond their imagination.

As we prioritize our intervention initiatives, we must be guided by the "real world" experience of family clinicians together with the data base of the social and neurobiological scientists, all of whom are informed by culture-sensitive perspectives. When we finally coordinate our efforts to prevent or intervene in juvenile DBD's, we must adopt the context sensitive family centered view of the family therapist who realizes these efforts will look very different for different families. The angry, but also frightened inner city minority youth, the lonely rural child of a farmer who has very little income, the Latino whose parent(s) are labelled "illegal," the "entitled spoiled brat" of rich parents with a well-known family name, the confused Asian child whose recently immigrated parents do not speak the dominant language, the Native American youth being bussed 40 miles to school — these and many others are all at risk, and each, in terms of their own family and parenting realities, must be the starting point for our initiatives. The "quick fix" of fences around all streams will not be the first or only choice of family-sensitive program developers attempting to prevent child drownings, because they know that for a kid, fences are an opportunity to climb! Similarly, to reverse the processes of family disintegration and resulting behavior disorders of youth, we must understand and base our interventions on what they need for positive change, not what we want them to be for our convenience or profit. The family-centered scientist and intervener usually finds this easier to facilitate than does an advocate of other perspectives, and we believe that in current times families need such advocacy!

James F. Alexander, Ph.D. *is Professor and Past Director of Clinical Training, Department of Psychology, University of Utah. Dr. Alexander has received many honors, among them Distinguished Contributor to Family Therapy Research, AFTA (1986) and Master Therapist presenter, AAMFT (1988). He* has participated in over one hundred clinical training workshops nationally and internationally and has published many refereed journal articles, a book, and numerous invited chapters. Most recent significant chapters are in the Bergin & Garfield Handbook of Psychotherapy and Behavior Change, *4th Edition (1993), and the* APA Published Family Psychology and Systems Theory: A Handbook *(1994).*

SUCCESSFUL STEPFAMILIES

JAMES H. BRAY, PH.D.
Department of Family Medicine
Baylor College of Medicine

The recent variations in marriage and family life in the United States have produced marked changes in the lives of all Americans and have implications for generations to come. The "traditional" family in which fathers work outside the home to support the family, while mothers stay home to raise the children is no longer the norm, but rather the exception. Nowadays, mothers employed outside of the home is the standard, rather than the exception. Divorce and remarriage continues to occur at a high rate. There are more children born and raised by unmarried women. Childrearing philosophies, methods, and practices have changed. Many of these changes in American family life are stressful and produce new challenges and problems for family members. However, many of these changes have increased the options for families and appear to be beneficial (Zill & Rogers, 1988). A major issue is that families are in a constant state of transition and these transitions affect most aspects of peoples' lives.

Stepfamilies are an old family form that have undergone rapid change and an increase in numbers during the past 20 years. The probability of living in a stepfamily or having a relative in a stepfamily is very high. This paper discusses factors associated with risk and resiliency in stepfamilies. The escalation in numbers of stepfamilies is the result of several demographic changes in the United States. The increased number of stepfamilies is linked to the rise in the number of children born outside of marriage, the high divorce rates, and the high remarriage rates.

CHILDREN BORN TO UNMARRIED WOMEN

There is a major change in child bearing patterns during the past 20 years (NCHS, 1991b). Each year since 1988, more than 1 million babies were born to unwed mothers. In 1991, there were over 1.2 million children born to unwed mothers. The percentage of children born outside of marriage increased during the 1980s; 18.4% of all babies born in 1980, compared to 29.5% in 1991. This is 82% more babies than born to unwed mothers in 1980 (NCHS, 1993). The increase is largely due to an increase in white women bearing more children outside of marriage. White mothers had 11% of their babies outside of marriage in 1980, and 21.8% in 1991. In comparison, black mothers had 55.2% of their babies outside of marriage in 1980, and 67.9% in 1991. In 1991, Hispanic mothers had 39%

of their children outside of marriage. There were no data available for Hispanic mothers in 1980. Although the percentages are quite different for Whites and Blacks, there are actually more White children born outside of marriage than Black children. Since most of these women eventually marry, this growth also contributes to the rising number of stepfamilies.

DIVORCE

Divorce in the United States continues to occur at a high rate. The overall rate of divorce has declined since 1979, from a high of 5.3 per thousand population to a low of 4.7 per thousand population during the three-year period of 1988 to 1990 (NCHS, 1991a). Despite this leveling of the divorce rate, it is still estimated that about half of all marriages will end in divorce (NCHS, 1991a; Norton & Moorman, 1987). In addition, recent estimates suggest that two-thirds of recent marriages are likely to experience marital disruption (Castro Martin & Bumpass, 1989). Marital separation and divorce are quickly becoming the norm, rather than the exception. There are different patterns of separation and divorce for Blacks and Whites (London, 1991). White women are more likely to divorce their husbands than Black women, 86.7% vs. 61.8%. However, Black women are more likely to separate and not divorce their husbands than White women, 32.9% vs. 8%. This pattern leads to more Black women and children living in single-parent families and experiencing a series of cohabiting partners. Following divorce, 85-90% of children live with their mothers (Glick, 1988), and have some type of access to their nonresidential fathers. In most cases, children born to unwed mothers have no formal arrangement or ties to their fathers.

REMARRIAGE

Although there is a high divorce rate in the U.S., it does not mean that people do not like marriage. It appears that Americans are in love with the institution of marriage, but with a series of partners. The divorce rate for second and subsequent marriages is higher than for first marriages (Glick, 1988). These people are also likely to divorce and remarry for a third time, thus, a common pattern for many adults is "serial monogamy" (Furstenberg, 1987).

It is estimated that between 70-75% of women and 80-85% of men will eventually remarry (Glick, 1989; Norton & Moorman, 1987). Most adults remarry quickly, within 5 years of their divorce (London, 1991; Norton & Moorman, 1987). White and Hispanic women are more likely to remarry than Black women (London, 1991). On the positive side, a study by Cherlin (1981) indicates that if the second marriage makes it through the first year, then the probability of divorce drops to that of first marriages.

STEPFAMILIES

Stepfamilies are a common family structure and will continue to be in the near future. The origin of the term "stepfamily" has an interesting history. The prefix "Step" is from the Anglo-Saxon word "Steop" which is the base of "Astypan" meaning to bereave or to make orphan (Bray, 1990). This term originated in England and was applied to children whose parents had died. The presence of a stepchild or stepparent signified a relationship established because of loss through death. Although this still occurs, it is far more common today that a stepfamily is established because of another type of loss, the death of a marriage. The original term is still used, but now it primarily describes those related by remarriage following divorce.

Stepfamilies are diverse in their structures and varied in their names (Bray & Berger, 1992). Common names for stepfamilies include remarried families, reconstituted families, REM families, blended families, bi-nuclear families, and second families. There are probably many other names, but these seem to be the most common. These names do not directly specify who lives in the family. Stepfamilies may be stepfather families, in which a man (who may or may not have been married previously) marries a woman who has children from a previous marriage who live with her. The stepfather in this case may or may not have children, but if he does, the children do not reside with him on a full-time basis. If the stepfather has children from a previous marriage, the family is called a complex stepfather family. If the stepfather does not have children from a previous marriage, the family is called a "simple" stepfather family. Stepmother families are the reverse of stepfather families. Blended stepfamilies occur when two adults marry and both bring children from a previous marriage to live together. There is currently no term for stepfamilies who procreate and have a child in the remarriage, although there is some indication that family relations are different in these families (Hetherington, 1987). In addition, these families may be created following divorce, death of a spouse, or abandonment of a previous marriage. Overall, the most common type of stepfamily is a stepfather family formed following the divorce of the mother (Glick, 1989).

Terms like "stepchild or stepparent" continue to have negative or pejorative connotations to them (Ganong, Coleman, & Mapes, 1990). There are many familiar fairy tales and folk stories of the "wicked stepparent." These images and fantasies begin to develop at an early age as children are exposed to popular fables and stories, such as Cinderella, or unrealistic depictions of stepfamily life, such as the TV series the Brady Bunch. Current films and stories are continuing this historical trend (see *The Stepfather* series or *My Stepmother is an Alien*). Because of the prevailing myths and stories about stepfamilies, family members — and especially children — often enter a remarriage with fears and anxieties unconsciously reinforced by our descriptions and names for stepfamilies.

EFFECTS ON CHILDREN

Growing up in an American family today is likely to be quite different than it was during the baby-boom years, 30 years ago. Currently, it is estimated that between 50-70% of children will spend some time in a single-parent home before they reach age 18 (Bumpass, 1984; Hofferth, 1985). This change is primarily due to the higher separation and divorce rates and because of the increase in the number of children born outside of marriage. Children born between 1950-54 were less likely to experience life in a single-parent family; with 19% of White children and 48% of Black children spending some time in a single-parent family (Hofferth, 1985). In contrast, a child born in 1980 is more likely to spend some time in a single-parent family; with 70% of White children and 90% of Black children expected to spend time in a single-parent family before they reach age 18.

Further, because of the high remarriage rates, many of these children will also experience one or more of their parents' remarriages and spend some time in a stepfamily (Moorman & Hernandez, 1989). It is estimated that up to 40% of children will live in a stepfamily before they reach age 18 (Glick, 1989). The divorce rate in stepfamilies is even higher than in first-marriages, thus, many children will experience the dissolution and reconstitution of their families two or more times.

Children's responses to their parents' marital transitions vary considerably depending on their ages, type of family, race, and socioeconomic status (Zill & Schoenborn, 1990). Children from divorced, single-parent, and remarried homes are at risk for greater morbidity and behavioral disturbances. As illustrated in Table 1, Zill and Schoenborn (1990) found that children in single-parent and stepfamily homes are about twice as likely to have developmental, learning, or emotional problems than children in nondivorced, intact families. Another study found that young children during the early months of remarriage and adolescents during later remarriage had more behavior problems than children in nuclear families (Bray, 1988b).

PERCENT OF CHILDREN AGES 3-17 WHO HAVE HAD A DELAY IN GROWTH OR DEVELOPMENT, A LEARNING DISABILITY, OR AN EMOTIONAL PROBLEM: UNITED STATES 1988

Family Structure	Delay in Growth or Development	Emotional or Learning Disability	Behavioral Problem	Any Type of Problem
Intact Family	3.8	5.5	8.3	14.6
Stepfather Family	3.7	9.1	23.6	29.6
Mother Custody	4.5	7.5	19.1	24.8
All Others	4.8	8.3	22.2	28.2

Source: Zill, N. & Schoenborn, C. A. (1990). Advanced data from Vital Health Statistics: No. 190. National Centers for Health Statistics.

It is clear from these data that not all children from divorced and remarried homes have problems, but they are at greater risk for developing psycho-social problems. The difficulty is that research has focused on problems and deficiencies, and not success and adaptation.

RISK AND RESILIENCY FACTORS FOR STEPFAMILIES

Research is beginning to identify risk and resilience factors that contribute to successful adaptation in stepfamilies. This paper draws from the results of a federally funded longitudinal study of stepfamilies, the Developmental Issues in StepFamilies (DIS) Research Project, that investigated the impact of divorce and remarriage on children's social, emotional, and cognitive development (Bray, 1988b). The DIS Research Project was initially a cross-sectional study of stepfamilies and first-marriage nuclear families. The stepfamilies were selected after 6 months, 2.5 years, and 5 years of remarriage and compared to nuclear families with comparable aged children. The families were re-interviewed 3 to 4 years later to examine longitudinal changes and predictors of adjustment and adaptation. The study was a multi-method, multi-perspective study of parents, stepparents, children, and extended family that included extensive interviews, psychological assessments, family assessments, and behavioral observations of the families.

Stepfamilies are a developing, interactional family system that evolve over time in response to the multiple demands both within and outside of the immediate family. Unique normative issues and tasks that occur during the stepfamily life cycle have been identified by research and clinical observation (Bray, Berger, Silverblatt, & Hollier, 1987; Bray & Berger, 1992, 1993a; McGoldrick & Carter, 1980; Whiteside, 1982). Relationships in stepfamilies change over time and are affected by previous individual and family experiences, developmental issues within the stepfamily, and developmental issues for individual family members. Marital and family experiences during the first marriage, separation, and divorce may have a great impact on the functioning of the stepfamily (Bray & Hetherington, 1993). Questions such as, what is the best parenting methods for stepfamilies, have to be answered in the context of how long the stepfamily has been together and the developmental stages of the children. Thus, the multiple developmental trajectories of family members and the stepfamily life cycle are important to consider in the discussion of risk and resilience factors.

MARITAL RELATIONS

Marital relations are somewhat different in stepfamilies than in first marriages or remarriages without children because of the presence of children from the beginning of the marriage (Bray, 1995). As a foundation for the stepfamily the marital relationship facilitates other aspects of family functioning, particularly parenting of children. The "honeymoon" period after remarriage is either nonexistent or quite short, in large part due to the presence of children from the beginning (Bray et al., 1987; Hetherington & Clingempeel, 1992). Thus, the typical time of childlessness in which a newly wed couple spends time alone and constructs a solid marital bond and loyalty to the marriage is compromised and complicated by the children's presence. Young children may feel a sense of abandonment or competition as their parent devotes more time and energy towards the new spouse. Consequently, remarried parents may feel guilty about their children's reactions and ignore their marriage in response to their children's demands.

The marital subsystem in stepfamilies has different effects on other family subsystems than in first-marriage families (Bray, 1988a; Bray & Berger, 1993b). Marital adjustment has little or no impact on children's behavior and adjustment during early remarriage (Bray, 1988a; Hetherington & Clingempeel, 1992). This is in contrast to first-marriage families in which marital problems are related to more adjustment difficulties for children (Emery, 1982). After several years in a stepfamily, marital relationships have more impact on children's adjustment and parent-child interactions, similar to first-marriage families (Bray & Berger, 1993b; Hetherington & Clingempeel, 1992).

PARENTING AND STEPPARENTING

From the early months through the later years of remarriage, parenting and stepparenting are the most difficult and stressful aspects of stepfamily life (Bray, 1988a, 1988b; Bray & Berger, 1992). The stepparent may have difficulty playing a parental role during the early months of remarriage. Functioning as a friend or "camp counselor," rather than a parent, can facilitate the children's acceptance of the stepparent (Bray, 1988a; Visher & Visher, 1988). Children are more likely to accept the stepparent when he/she first attempts to form a relationship with the children instead of actively trying to discipline or control the children.

A strong marital bond and minimizing conflict between stepparent and custodial parent over parental authority issues facilitates the development of a parenting coalition. The biological parent may unconsciously interfere with the stepparent's attempt to discipline out of loyalty to the children, even after a stepparent is openly asked by the custodial parent to play a parental role. Having the custodial parent remain primarily responsible for control and discipline of the children during early remarriage allows time for a relationship and bond to develop between the stepparent and children. Encouraging the stepparent to actively "monitor and be aware of" the children's behavior and activities is a beneficial parenting function that facilitates children's adjustment during both early and later remarriage (Bray, 1988b; Hetherington, 1987; Hetherington & Clingempeel, 1992). After a relationship has been formed between stepparent and children, more active authoritative parenting is beneficial. In stepfather families boys respond more quickly to this process than girls (Bray, 1988b; Hetherington & Clingempeel, 1992). This sequence facilitates both the short-term and long-term adjustment of children (Bray & Hetherington, 1993).

Since older adolescents are focused on developing their lives outside of the family they often welcome their parent's remarriage because it can assuage their sense of responsibility for their parent (Bray & Berger, 1992). Thus, stepparents need to respect adolescents' developmental stage and not attempt to over-parent. Older adolescents and younger pre-adolescent children may adjust easier to a remarriage, while younger adolescents may have more difficulty adjusting to a stepfamily (Bray 1988b; Hetherington, 1993; Hetherington & Clingempeel, 1992). These differences reflect developmental variations for children. Younger children are usually more accepting of a new adult in the family, especially when the adult has a positive influence. Older adolescents require less parenting and may have less investment in the stepfamily. In contrast, young adolescents are dealing with identity formation issues, may be oppositional, and are particularly sensitive to expressions of affection between parent and stepparent (Baumrind, 1991; Hetherington, 1993). These factors make it more difficult for young adolescents to accept a new stepparent. As rules and discipline within the stepfamily change after remarriage, an adjustment period is inevitable. It usually takes from two to four years after remarriage to adjust to a new stepparent and changes in household rules and roles, which is much longer than most people's expectations (Bray & Berger, 1992; Hetherington & Clingempeel, 1992).

STEPPARENT-CHILD RELATIONSHIPS

Stepparent-child relationships have unique characteristics and are likely to be more distant, more conflictual and negative, and involve more coalitions and triangles than parent-child relationships in nuclear families (Anderson & White, 1986; Bray, 1988b; Bray & Berger, 1993b; Hetherington & Clingempeel, 1992; Perkins & Kahan, 1979; Santrock et al., 1982). This places parents, stepparents, and children at risk for developing psychosocial problems that require professional intervention or that contribute to the breakup of the stepfamily. Educating family members about these characteristics and normalizing these differences can help stepfamilies develop realistic expectations about their family relationships that facilitate adaptation.

In most stepfamilies, parents and stepparents have an expectation for a close, cohesive family unit and the stepparent may desire to quickly form a close relationship with their stepchildren (Bray, 1988a). However, children may not be ready for this due to their developmental status, previous life experiences, or loyalty to their nonresidential parent. Younger children tend to accept a stepparent faster than young adolescents and boys appear to accept a stepfather faster than girls. The pattern for stepmothers is less clear. Children may withdraw from or even be hostile towards a stepparent who attempts to move too fast in developing a close relationship, even when the stepparent is using positive methods. When stepparents are met with this response from children, over time they may disengage from the relationship (Hetherington, 1987).

Stepparents and children may have different expectations for their relationships and may view how the relationships should develop differently. For example, in the DIS Research Project "more" adjustment problems for stepchildren were related to stepfathers' reports of "more" expression of affection towards their stepchildren, especially girls, whereas, the children's reports of the stepfathers' expression of affection were related to "fewer" adjustment problems for the children. Children and stepparents were re-interviewed and the data were re-examined to understand this apparently contradictory finding. This re-analysis indicated that stepparents and children defined affection in very different ways. Stepfathers indicated they demonstrated affection through physical contact, such as embraces or hugs, while the children, and especially the girls, were uncomfortable with such attempts. Children in stepfamilies stated that they liked verbal affection, such as praises or compliments, and this was related to better behavioral adjustment.

NONRESIDENTIAL PARENTS AND STEPFAMILIES

Nonresidential parents have quite diverse roles and levels of contact with their children following divorce and remarriage. These roles range from joint custody and frequent contact to no relationship or contact with the children and many variations between these extremes. In addition, these roles may change over the course of the family life cycle (Bray & Berger, 1993a). It is common for non-residential parents to decrease their contact with their children after divorce and remarriage, or maintain stable, but low levels of contact (Bray & Berger, 1990, 1993a; Furstenberg, Nord, Peterson, & Zill, 1983). When the nonresidential parent decreases visitation after remarriage the children may feel hurt or abandoned. In addition, children may feel resentment when the custodial parent focuses on the new spouse and directs less attention towards them.

Children and adolescents who have a better relationship and more contact with their nonresidential parents following divorce usually have better behavioral adjustment (Hetherington, 1993, 1987; Wallerstein & Kelly, 1980). After parental remarriage this pattern does not necessarily remain the same (Bray & Berger, 1990, 1993a). More contact and a better relationship between nonresidential parents and children during early remarriage is associated with better behavioral adjustment for boys and girls, but lower self-esteem for boys. The nonresidential parent-child relationship has few effects on children's adjustment during later remarriage.

With the beginning of the stepfamily, children's or adults' fantasies that the biological parents will reunite are usually ended. Never-the-less, some children still want their divorced parents to reunite, even years after the divorce and remarriage (Bray & Berger, 1992). After remarriage, anger and resentment from the divorce may re-emerge for one or more of the family members. Some children may begin to treat the stepparent with animosity and hostility, irrespective of their relationship before the remarriage. These changes may signal that there are unresolved "emotional" issues from the divorce that need attention. Resolution of these feelings contributes to successful integration of both families.

FUNCTIONAL AND DYSFUNCTIONAL STEPFAMILIES

The family characteristics and processes that contribute to problem formation in stepfamilies are not clearly understood (Bray, 1992, 1995). This deficiency is related to the lack of established norms for stepfamilies (Bray & Berger, 1992). The few studies in this area indicate that clinical or dysfunctional stepfamilies have less involvement between stepfathers and their stepchildren and stronger tendencies toward the development of parent-child coalitions (Anderson & White, 1986). Parent-child coalitions are even more extreme in dysfunctional stepfamilies than functional intact or stepfamilies or dysfunctional intact families and are related to more problematic family processes. In this common clinical problem, the stepparent is excluded while the biological parent and children side together in a coalition against the stepparent. Functional stepfamilies have better marital adjustment, more reciprocal positive involvement of stepchild and stepfather, and less exclusion of the stepfather than in dysfunctional stepfamilies.

Clinical stepfamilies report more conflict and less emotional expressiveness, less effective problem solving, less spousal individuation, poorer marital adjustment, and more negative and less positive child-parent interactions than members of nonclinical stepfamilies (Bray, 1992; Brown, Green, & Druckman, 1990). Fewer positive and more negative child to parent interactions, less effective problem solving, and less spousal individuation are related to more behavior problems and less prosocial behavior for children in stepfamilies.

There are similarities in the types of problems that may lead first-marriage families and stepfamilies to seek treatment (Bray, 1995). For example, both kinds of families may engage in family therapy because of increased conflict and communication problems. However, the qualitative issues that these families have conflict or communication difficulties over are likely to be quite different. Stepfamilies may have conflict over the parental authority of the stepparent or over loyalties to the noncustodial parent, while first-marriage families may have conflict about parenting practices or marital problems. Similarly, children's problems with emotional bonding and responsiveness in stepfamilies may be related to expectations of "instant love" and loyalty issues, but similar processes in first-marriage families may be due to rebellion or anger at parents. These qualitative differences continue to exist even after 5 years of remarriage.

The ease of obtaining a divorce in most states coupled with the social context that supports divorce and views it as a normative transition, no doubt greatly contributes to the breakup of many American families. At the basis of this is often a lack of commitment to the marriage. Research is showing that commitment is a key necessary ingredient for a successful marriage and that couples must continue to "work at" maintaining their commitment through communication, development of a shared world view, and intimacy (Renick, Blumberg, & Markman, 1992). The reasons for a lack of commitment in modern marriages are complex and not entirely clear. However, it is apparent from our long-term successful stepfamilies that an underlying process and theme is that the remarried couple makes a continued commitment to staying together and resolving problems that face the family.

There are many issues and challenges for modern American families. Marital transitions create a number of risk factors for members of stepfamilies. These include diminished parenting practices, disruptions in family roles and parent-child relationships, economic stresses, and increased risk for physical and sexual abuse of children and adolescents. Warm supportive relationships with custodial parents and stepparents, cooperative relationships between custodial and noncustodial parents, authoritative parenting by custodial parents and later by stepparents are all important factors that contribute to family members' adjustment in stepfamilies. While family transitions create significant risk factors for family members, the good news is that stepfamilies can provide positive and stable environments that support the development and adjustment of all family members.

REFERENCES

Anderson, J. Z., & White, G. D. (1986). An empirical investigation of interactional and relationship patterns in functional and dysfunctional nuclear and stepfamilies. *Family Process, 25,* 407-422.

Baumrind, D. (1991). Effective parenting during the early adolescent transition. In P. A. Cowan & E. M. Hetherington (Eds.), *Family transitions* (pp. 111-164). Hillsdale, NJ: Lawrence Erlbaum Associates.

Bray, J. H. (1988a). Children's development during early remarriage. In E. M. Hetherington & J. Arasteh (Eds.) *The impact of divorce, single-parenting and step-parenting on children* (pp. 279-298). Hillsdale, NJ: Lawrence Erlbaum Associates.

Bray, J. H. (1988b). *Developmental Issues in StepFamilies Research Project: Final Report (Grant Number RO1 HD18025)*. Bethesda, MD: National Institute of Child Health and Human Development.

Bray, J. H. (1990). Impact of divorce on the family. In R. E. Rakel (Ed.) *Textbook of family practice 4th Edition* (pp. 111-122). Philadelphia, PA: W. B. Saunders.

Bray, J. H. (1992). Family relationships and children's adjustment in clinical and nonclinical stepfather families. *Journal of Family Psychology*, 6, 60-68.

Bray, J. H. (1995). Family oriented treatment of stepfamilies. In R. Mikesell, D. D. Lusterman, & S. McDaniel (Eds.) *Family psychology and systems therapy: A handbook*. Washington, D.C.: American Psychological Association.

Bray, J. H. & Berger, S. H. (1990). Noncustodial parent and grandparent relationships in stepfamilies. *Family Relations*, 39, 414-419.

Bray, J. H. & Berger, S. H. (1992). Stepfamilies. In M. E. Procidano & C. B. Fisher (Eds.) *Contemporary families: A handbook for school professionals* (pp. 57-79). New York: Teachers College Press.

Bray, J. H. & Berger, S. H. (1993a). Nonresidential family-child relationships following divorce and remarriage. In C. E. Depner & J. H. Bray (Eds.), *Noncustodial parenting: New vistas in family living* (pp. 156-181). Newbury Park, CA: Sage Publishers.

Bray, J. H. & Berger, S. H. (1993b). Developmental issues in stepfamilies research project: Family relationships and parent-child interactions. *Journal of Family Psychology*, 7, 76-90.

Bray, J. H. & Hetherington, E. M. (1993). Families in transition: Introduction and overview. *Journal of Family Psychology*, 7, 3-8.

Brown, A. C., Green, R. J., & Druckman, J. (1990). A comparison of stepfamilies with and without child-focused problems. *American Journal of Orthopsychiatry*, 60, 556-566.

Bumpass, L. (1984). Children and marital disruption: A replication and update. *Demography*, 21, 71-82.

Castro Martin, T. & Bumpass, L. (1989). Recent trends and differentials in marital disruption. *Demography*, 26, 37-51.

Cherlin, A. J. (1981). *Marriage, divorce, remarriage.* Cambridge, MA: Harvard University Press.

Emery, R. E. (1982). Interparental conflict and the children of discord and divorce. *Psychological Bulletin*, 92, 310-330.

Furstenberg, F. F., Jr. (1987). The new extended family: the experience of parents and children after remarriage. In K. Pasley & M. Ihinger-Tallman (Eds.), *Remarriage and stepparenting: Current research and theory* (pp. 42-61). New York: Guilford.

Furstenberg, F. F., Jr., Nord, C. W., Peterson, J. L., & Zill, N. (1983). The life course of children of divorce: Marital disruption and parental contact. *American Sociological Review*, 48, 656-668.

Ganong, L. H., Coleman, M., & Mapes, D. (1990). A meta-analytic review of family structure stereotypes. *Journal of Marriage and the Family*, 52, 287-297.

Glick, P. C. (1988). The role of divorce in the changing family structure: Trends and variations. In S. A. Wolchik and P. Karoly (Eds.) *Children of divorce: Empirical perspectives on adjustment* (pp. 3-34). New York: Gardner Press.

Glick, P. C. (1989). Remarried families, stepfamilies, and stepchildren: A brief demographic profile. *Family Relations*, 38, 24-27.

Hetherington, E. M. (1987). Family relations six years after divorce. In K. Pasley & M. Ihinger-Tallman (Eds.), *Remarriage and stepparenting today: Current research and theory* (pp. 185-205). New York: Guilford Press.

Hetherington, E. M. (1993). An overview of the Virginia longitudinal study of divorce and remarriage. *Journal of Family Psychology*, 7, 39-56.

Hetherington, E. M., & Clingempeel, W. G. (1992). Coping with marital transitions: A family systems perspective. *Monographs of the Society for Research in Child Development*, 57, Nos. 2-3, Serial No. 227.

Hofferth, S. L. (1985). Updating children's life course. *Journal of Marriage and the Family*, 47, 93-115.

London, K. A. (1991). Cohabitation, marriage, marital dissolution, and remarriage: United States, 1988. *Advance data from vital and health statistics; no 194*. Hyattsville, MD: National Center for Health Statistics.

McGoldrick, M., & Carter, E. A. (1980). Forming a remarried family. In E. A. Carter & M. McGoldrick (Eds.), *The family life cycle* (pp. 265-294). New York: Gardner.

Moorman, J. E. & Hernandez, D. J. (1989). Married-couple families with step, adopted, and biological children. *Demography*, 26, 267-277.

National Center for Health Statistics (1991a). Annual summary of births, marriages, divorces, and deaths: United States, 1990. *Monthly vital statistics report; vol. 39, no 13*. Hyattsville, MD: Public Health Service.

National Center for Health Statistics (1991b). Advance report of final natality statistics, 1989. *Monthly vital statistics report; vol. 40, no 8, suppl*. Hyattsville, MD: Public Health Service.

National Center for Health Statistics (1993). Advance report of final natality statistics, 1991. *Monthly vital statistics report; vol. 42, no 3, suppl*. Hyattsville, MD: Public Health Service.

Norton, A. J. & Moorman, J. E. (1987). Marriage and divorce patterns of U.S. women. *Journal of Marriage and the Family*, 49, 3-14.

Perkins, T. F., & Kahan, J. P. (1979). An empirical comparison of natural-father and stepfather systems. *Family Process*, 18, 175-183.

Renick, M. J., Blumberg, S. L., & Markman, H. J. (1992). The prevention and relationship enhancement program (PREP): An empirically based preventive intervention program for couples. *Family Relations*, 41, 141-147.

Santrock, J. W., Warshak, R. A., Lindberg, C., & Meadows, L. (1982). Children's and parent's observed social behavior in stepfather families. *Child Development*, 53, 472-480.

Visher, E. B., & Visher, J. S. (1988). *Old loyalties, new ties: Therapeutic strategies with stepfamilies*. New York: Brunner/Mazel.

Wallerstein, J. S. & Kelly, J. (1980). *Surviving the break-up: How children and parents cope with divorce*. New York: Basic Books.

Whiteside, M. F. (1982). Remarriage: A family developmental process. *Journal of Marital and Family Therapy*, 4, 59-68.

Zill, N. & Schoenborn, C.A. (1990). Developmental, learning, and emotional problems: Health of our Nation's children, United States, 1988. *Advance data from vital and health statistics; no 190*. Hyattsville, MD: National Center for Health Statistics.

James H. Bray, Ph.D. *is Director, Family Psychology Programs and Associate Professor in the Department of Family Medicine, Baylor College of Medicine in Houston, Texas. Dr. Bray has published and presented numerous works in the areas of divorce, remarriage, custody, intergenerational family relationships, and collaboration between physicians and psychologists. He was the principal investigator of the federally funded longitudinal study, "Developmental Issues in StepFamilies Research Project," and is co-principal investigator of a federally funded project on alcohol and other drug abuse in families with adolescents. He received his Ph.D. in clinical psychology from the University of Houston in 1980.*

Family-Friendly Communities: A Movement Toward Mutual Empowerment and Strength

HELEN K. CLEMINSHAW, PH.D.
The University of Akron

Where does one begin, in an attempt to describe the symptoms related to the disintegration of the family in the United States? Within the last three decades so many social, political, economic and philosophical changes have occurred, impacting on the family, that it is truly overwhelming. Not only have the roles and functions of family members changed, but also the focus and value of family life. While many changes have been positive, providing families with new opportunities for growth and participation; others have triggered greater hardships for families. Thus, at every stage of the life cycle, women, men, and children are experiencing greater stress, yet receiving fewer supports from within and outside the family.

The purpose of my presentation is to demonstrate that there is a strong, interdependent relationship between families and community. In fact, they are completely interrelated. When the family, a major social unit, feels alienated and disconnected from its community, the larger family, the community no longer serves as its support system. The family then stands alone.

However, the community also stands alone if its schools, religious organizations, businesses, industry, voluntary and nongovernmental institutions, including transportation, etc. cannot communicate and receive their direction from families. For the community is its families.

Through a rich exchange of ideas, manpower, services, information and caring, each is critical to each others' healthy growth and survival. Unless families and communities work in unison, with respect, equality, and commitment, to design and develop healthy environments, there can be neither healthy families, nor healthy communities (Elkind, 1994; Etizioni, 1993; Kagan & Weissbourd, 1994).

Therefore, a central cause of family disintegration is the community's lack of responsibility and commitment to its families, and vice versa. This presentation will support the development of a process to share and exchange models of family-friendly programs within communities to support healthy families. To achieve this goal, I will first provide a brief review of the current status of families, focusing on elements contributing to the weakness of the family. Second, several family styles and traits of healthy families will be identified to illustrate directionality for change in the family. Third, traits of healthy communities will be described in order to provide focus for community change. Fourth, I will recommend the benefits of collaborative efforts between family and community. The conclusion will provide a process for promoting family-friendly programs to communities worldwide.

CURRENT STATUS OF FAMILIES

Today, families experience greater stress and conflict in their lives. These increased stressors and conflict come from a variety of life changes, including divorce, single parenting, increased workload and complex family-work balancing issues. To complicate the problems, there are fewer resources available to families to help them cope, such as less time, money, education and support from the family itself, as well as from the community (Hewlett,1993). For example, the divorce rate in the United States is staggering, the highest in the world. It has tripled between 1970 and 1993 (4.3 million to 16.7 million). While 79% of our children lived within two-parent households during 1990, only 58% lived with their two biological parents. Of all children under 18 years of age (17 million), 26% live with a divorced parent, a separated parent, or a step-parent; and 9.5% live with a divorced single parent. While there has been a steady increase in father custody, 90% of the single parents are mothers and 39% of them live at the poverty level. The younger the child, the more likely that the mother is poor (U.S. Census Bureau, 1993).

Gender inequity remains a problem. Studies have consistently shown that women are at risk economically following divorce, whereas men tend to recapture their earning power within several years following the marital breakup. Women are disproportionately represented in administrative positions; they lose their place in the work force due to maternal leave; and receive little emotional or task support as compared to fathers in a single parenting situation (Thompson & Walker, 1989).

Whereas only 60% of divorcing fathers have a child support agreement in place, often even the ones who do rarely maintain their legal commitment. According to a U.S. Census Report, among mothers entitled to support, only 51% received full payment, 25% received partial, and 23% received nothing. Presently, it is estimated that 4.6 billion dollars is outstanding in child support payments (Child Support and Alimony: 1987, 1990). The cause for greater alarm is the lack of time commitment between children and father following divorce. Three/fourths of the fathers of divorce spend less than two days a month in contact with their children and even this amount decreases over time according to research conducted by Furstenberg and Harris (1992). It is impossible to be a model of commitment, responsibility, and nurturance to your children, when you are not even willing to invest either time or energy into a ongoing parent-child relationship.

A recent report compiled by American Association of Retired Persons stated that there has been a 17% increase in one year alone (1992 to 1993) in the number of grandparents who are raising children with no help from the parents of the children. The primary reason given for the childrens' parents being unable to parent was drug abuse. Other issues reported include: abandonment, unemployment, teenage pregnancy, incarceration, AIDS, and death (U.S. Census, 1993). Not only are grandparents more apt to be on a fixed income, but they are also less capable of dealing with stressful situations due to their age, health, and a myriad of other issues conflicting with the parent role.

Nearly five million children (7.7%) live with a single, never-married parent. In fact, the increase in unwed mothers has escalated most rapidly, a 70% growth in one year from 1983 to 1993 (U.S. Census, 1993). While there were 3.7 million births to moms under 18 year of age in 1983, there were 6.3 million in 1993 — compare that to 243,000 in 1960. The increases are most notable in the white, younger teen population.

Lack of time remains a major problem even for those parents who have age, resources, and health on their side. Based on personal dairies collected by the sociologist, John Robinson, from the University of Maryland, parents spent 40% less time in 1985 with their children, than parents did in 1965. Thirty hours a week of "togetherness" time diminished to 17 hours a week (Mattox, 1991). Fuchs (1988) stated that the loss of potential parental time is even greater for black families with children than for white families.

In a recent survey (Gibbs, 1989), the typical work week has escalated from 4l hours (1973) to 47 hours (1989). Small business owners work the most, 57.3 hours. Stress in the workplace seems to have increased as companies size-down, reorganize, and generally convey an atmosphere of uncertainty. This upward spiraling devotion of time to earning a living, compromises the amount of time left for family relationships and the development of family identity. The time-honored family dinner for togetherness time is a luxury that is only hoped for, but not necessarily expected.

This loss of time has been blamed on longer and harder work weeks, which do not produce greater benefits. For example, over the last 25 years, increases in the cost of several major family expenses, such as housing, health care, transportation and higher education, have leaped far ahead of the general inflation rate. Whereas a young person could obtain a mortgage on a median-priced home with 21% of their gross income in 1973, ten years later it required 40%, almost double the amount (Mattox, 1991).

This has contributed to more and more families being forced into a dual-career family style. Many of these parents are truly committed to doing well, both as a parent and employee, desperately juggling it all, yet they receive little assistance in their efforts (Gilbert, 1993). Neither the workplace nor the community are family-friendly.

To further complicate matters, childcare facilities are limited, expensive, and often understaffed or inappropriate for the care of young, developing children. The problem does not lessen for school-age children, as they spend many hours as "latch-key youngsters," alone and unsupervised. The fact that in the United States children spend 25% fewer hours in school than children in Europe, illustrates our inability to recognize the void in structuring care for our children of all ages (Hewlett, 1993). Is it any wonder then that drug abuse, pregnancy, suicide, and overall violence for young people has continued to grow out of control. What child would not be filled with rage and alienation for adults who have so greatly disappointed and abandoned them.

It seems apparent that the causes of family disintegration, such as stressed parenting, career demands, etc., are very complex and that the responsibility and commitment required for roles are not well understood before being undertaken. Add to this, a extreme deficiency of critical resources such as time, education, coping strategies, communication skills, decision-making approaches, emotional, physical and social supports both from within the family itself and from the community, and it is no wonder families are hurting.

So let us now examine the traits associated with healthy, strong families. Can we see a relationship between a lack of these characteristics and the current status of families today?

TRAITS OF HEALTHY FAMILIES

Before identifying themes related to healthy families, it is important to note that a particular structure of the family does not predict the health of the family. Positive traits can be found in all family structures. The reason for making this point up front is because many experts have argued that we need to return to the "golden age" of the family, believing that there once was an ideal period for families. Certainly, families have faced challenges across time and it is only relatively recently in our history that families have become sources of emotional comfort, rather than economic units of survival. Indeed, as Fox (1994), President of the American Psychological Association stated, "It would be too simplistic to return to the traditional nuclear family, since this would ignore the richness and diversity provided by many of our newly formed family structures. Our society has changed too dramatically to go backwards in time. Our best hope then is to promote those qualities and traits which have been associated with healthy families regardless of structure."

As Elkind (1994) stated so aptly, "to be sure, a strong, emotionally healthy, financially secure nuclear family may be the least stressful arrangement for childrearing. But not all nuclear families approach that ideal. We now recognize that abuse and neglect may be as frequent in nuclear families as love, protection, and commitment are in nonnuclear families" (p.31).

Other problems inherent in the traditional family include rigid adherence to stereotypic roles which greatly restricted women and minorities. Parents were expected to stay together for the sake of the children, even it if did not serve the best interests of the children, such as in families with a history of violence or incest. There was a clear imbalance in this family form in which all was centered completely on the child. Power was unilateral and children were given great protection. Often however, adults resenting their children and blaming them for their loss of freedom, acted out in dysfunctional ways and communicated without clarity or logic.

Yet, in the present day "permeable family" structure described by Elkind (1994) there still remains an unhealthy imbalance. Contrasted to the nuclear family, this family form provides for role diffusion, wherein moms and dads can trade off roles in both the home or workplace. There is more of a mutual approach to decision-making, as compared to the traditional, unilateral authority figure. Children are perceived as more competent, and therefore provided more freedom, which they may not be appropriately prepared for. In trade, they receive less space and time as a whole. They are neither protected nor guided in a manner which helps them move from one developmental stage to the next easily. Clearly, then neither the traditional, nuclear family nor the modern, permeable family adequately meets the needs of our current times. The first overfavors children, the second, adults.

James Garbarino, President of the Erikson Institute for Child Development (1992), contends that there is a delicate balance of "all for one and one for all" coupled with "each man for himself" which aptly differentiates functional families from dysfunctional families. It seems a blend of "we" and "I" dependent upon the needs and the situation.

I believe that Elkind (1994) would agree with this concept, when he recommends a movement toward what he describes the "vital" family. This family form combines the best of both the nuclear and the permeable family. It energizes and nurtures the abilities and talents of both adults and children, while still balancing their needs. First, this is achieved by reinforcing the values of commitment and responsibility. Second, the vital family values authentic parenting. This means that both parents share caring for children and balance unilateral and mutual authority approaches. Third, the vital family is one which recognizes the need for community involvement. Elkind (1994) states that we must accept our interdependence as family members and as members of a larger community.

While several researchers (Barnhill, 1988; Fleck, 1980; Lewis, Beavers, Gossett, & Phillips, 1976) have studied strong, functional families over the last two decades, most have discovered rather similar sets of characteristics. However, for the purposes of this presentation, I will concentrate on the six traits generated by the research of Stinnett, Chesser, and DeFrain (1979). They include: 1.) appreciation — warmth, positive regard, and support given for each other; 2.) time together — frequent and enjoyable; 3.) communication — patterns are open, honest, and receptive; 4.) commitment — time and energy devoted to both "we" and "I"; 5.) religious orientation — common belief and value system; and 6.) coping strategies — to provide mutual support. Obviously, all six of these traits could be incorporated into Elkind's model of the "vital" family.

More importantly, relating each of these characteristics to the symptoms of our weakened families of today, we can clearly see a deficit in all six themes. For example, time together is a commodity rarer than a hen's tooth today. A lack of both appreciation and communication have been listed among the reasons for relationships failing. Many families have a very limited repertoire of coping strategies. Places of worship struggle continually to maintain member participation, so that we see a real decline in religious orientation. Commitment is a problem visible within families as well as outside families. According to Amitai Etzioni, family sociologist, "... young Americans expect to be tried before a jury of their peers, but are rather reluctant to serve on one," a jury, that is. We seem to have a strong sense of entitlement, a demand that our community provide services and uphold our rights, but a weak sense of commitment on our part to contribute to our local community. As shown by the research on restructured families, commitment is often not given to family members, especially to our children. This leads us to a discussion concerning the traits of a healthy community.

TRAITS OF HEALTHY COMMUNITIES

What are the themes associated with health communities? Since the community is the larger family, it seems reasonable to place the template for healthy families upon the community to learn if it matchs. Let us look at the first trait, appreciation, a warmth, positive regard and support given to the members of the community. If families perceive support from their community, then they would no longer feel disconnected or alienated.

Community activities, functions and committee work which incorporated worthwhile, meaningful time together could engender greater cooperation from families. And if patterns of communication were open, honest, and receptive, families might develop trust and openness in return towards the community. Commitment could naturally evolve if the community devoted time and energy to individual family needs as well as common overall community needs. And could we have common beliefs and values? Despite our various ethnic, racial and socioeconomic differences, we all agree on safe, healthy and enduring environments for our family members. Lastly, coping strategies that provide mutual support refer to all kinds of programming, ranging from educational to interventive. An example of programming, which could promote skills for long-term benefit to families, could include conflict resolution and mediation programs. Certainly, this brief analysis indicates that the same traits which differentiate healthy families can also be employed to assess healthy communities.

EMPOWERMENT AND STRENGTH THROUGH COLLABORATION

Families cannot function as they should, meeting both individual and total family needs, unless they receive support from their communities. No family is an island. All families are deeply embedded in environments, wherein give and take, relative to resources, is both necessary and healthy. We need to encourage communities "to recognize that their decisions and actions will usually have an impact on how families will be formed, whether they will survive or not, and how well they function as nurturers and providers" (p.13) (United Nations, 1991). Indeed, if we wish to counteract the negative effects of our rapidly changing society, it is imperative that we make changes in all institutions that affect the family, not just recommend changes to the family itself. Therefore, we must encourage ways in which to design and develop family-friendly communities.

Etzioni (1993) beautifully stated, "Neither human existence nor individual liberty can be sustained for long outside the interdependent and overlapping communities to which all of us belong. Nor can any community long survive unless its members dedicate some of their attention, energy, and resources to shared projects"(p.255).

Family-friendly communities work hard to include family members in the development of programs within all systems that affect families. They acknowledge the need for strong collaboration. What is collaboration? It is a way in which to reach mutual goals more effectively by working together rather than singly (Bruner, 1991). For example, the problems that families face today are so complex, that it is totally unrealistic to believe that they can be either studied or solved through a singular approach. No one system, no one discipline, and no one professional can propose an effective plan without input from families and multiple representation from community. More importantly, neither families nor community participants can feel commitment or responsibility, pride or disappointment, achievement or failure, unless they have undertaken the challenge together. Whereas we have traditionally responded to crises or treated existing problems, usually at the advanced stages, this new process will help families to avoid problems or to deal with them during the early stages.

We can empower families and ourselves by learning directly together, from each other, that which is truly needed to support both our families and the community. In this manner we can inspire family confidence and build upon strengths. Our responses can be relevant to family cultural preferences and values. Based upon the concrete information received from real-life family problems, our programs can be tailor-made. When families feel connected and central to the workings of their community, they want to maintain involvement (Gertz & Peck, 1994; Kagan & Weissbourd, 1994).

Our neighboring country, Canada, has already created a document called The Family-Friendly Community Checklist (Premier's Council in Support of Alberta Families, 1994). It addresses neighborhoods, schools, recreation, security, health and wellness, family serving agencies, parenting, children, teenagers and young adults, seniors, workplaces, public involvement and support. The council states that they have developed this checklist " as a tool to assist communities in reviewing those aspects of the community that can detract from, or contribute to, family well-being" (p.4). They encourage communities to be concerned about families and to consider programs broad in range, from intergenerational child-care programs, to safety measures on the playground, to family hiking trips.

When considering the cause of family disintegration as a deficit in characteristics associated with both healthy families and communities, immediately many examples of family-friendly community programs emerge. Contemplate the theme of appreciation. In order to show that both the community and its families value positive parenting, programs could be designed to show appreciation for families who demonstrate positive parenting. For example, a community in New England already awards certificates of excellence to parents signed by the mayor. Perhaps a local newspaper could feature a weekly column relating only praiseworthy news on families, rather than featuring information on the stolen bicycles or vandalism. Schools could provide "mentoring mother" programs and the hospitals could give small discounts to medical billing when new parents participate in their parent education classes. The list is endless, but communities cannot begin these positive, preventive, family-friendly programs until they first value their families enough to include them in the planning process.

In conclusion, let me inform you of the creation of a new center developed by the University of Akron in cooperation with the United Nations Secretariat for the International Year of the Family. The mission of the Center for Family-Friendly Cities is to promote the inherent strengths of families, particularly families who live in the urban centers of the world. This will be accomplished through the sharing and exchange of information on family-friendly programs worldwide. The Center has signed a Memorandum of Understanding with the U.N. Secretariat for the International Year of the Family in which we have agreed to implement an electronic communication network for cities worldwide through Internet, the information superhighway (Center for Family Studies, 1994).

The need for better urban programs for families becomes even more critical in light of the fact that urban populations are growing three times as fast as the overall population. By the year 2000, half of humanity will be urbanized. In the United States, the majority of families reside in cities. The city can be seen as that level of the government closest to families. Leaders from all sectors, including: housing, education, religion, employment, nutrition, leisure, recreation, health and medical and environment, can all work together to improve life for families. Cities will not fulfill their vital functions if they fail to provide healthy environments (Girardet, 1992; Lynn & Dennis, 1993). In this manner of sharing, urban planners, decision-makers, and families, hand-in-hand will create more family-friendly environments. Cities will be able to learn from each other's experiences. Disseminating this "know-how" helps shorten the time-lag between the emergence of innovative ideas and their implementation and diffusion.

By providing a rich database of programs supportive to families within every system of the community, the Center will contribute significantly to the lives of families and help prevent the primary symptoms which have led to the breakdown of families in our communities in the United States and throughout the world.

"Increasingly, Americans are pursuing a selfish individualism that is inconsistent with strong families and strong communities... which suggests that personal happiness is the highest good and that it can be achieved by pursuing pleasure and material goods" (p.9), states Peter Uhlenberg, a sociologist from the University of North Carolina (Mattox, 1991). Well, perhaps family-friendly programs can model a "weism" which demonstrates that personal happiness is the highest good only when it can be achieved by pursuing pleasure through commitment and responsibility to our families and our communities, as well as to ourselves.

REFERENCES

Barnhill, L. (1979). Healthy Family Systems. *Family Coordinator, 28,* 94-100.

Bruner, C. (1991). *Thinking Collaboratively: Ten Questions and Answers to help policy makers improve children's services.* Washington, D.C.: Education and Human Services Consortium.

Child Support and Alimony: 1987, (1990). U.S. Bureau of the Census, Current Population Reports, Series P-23, 67, 3-7.

Elkind, D. (1994). *Ties that Stress.* Cambridge: Harvard University Press.

Etzioni, A. (1993). *The Spirit of Community.* New York: Simon & Schuster, Inc.

Fleck, S. (1980). Family Functioning and Family Pathology. *Psychiatric Annals, 10,* 46-54.

Flynn, B. C. & Dennis, L. I. (1993). Healthy Families in Healthy Cities: A Global Responsibility. In *One World, Many Families.* Altergott, K. (Ed.). Minneapolis: National Council on Family Relations.

Fuchs, V. R. (1988). *Women's Quest for Economic Equality.* Cambridge: Harvard University Press.

Furstenberg, Jr., F. F. & Harris, K. M. (1992). The disappearing American Father? In *The Changing American Family.* S. J. South and S. E. Tolnay, (Eds.). Boulder, CO: Westview Press

Garbarino, J. (1992). *Children and Families in the Social Environment.* New York: Aldine De Gruyter.

Gibbs, N. (1989). How America has run out of Time, *Time,* 24, April, p. 59.

Gilbert, L. A. (1993). *Two careers/one family.* Newbury Park, CA.: Sage Publications.

Girardet, H. (1992). *The Gaia Atlas of Cities.* New York: Doubleday.

Goetz, K. & Peck, S. (Ed.) (1994). *The Basics of Family Support: a Guide for State Planners.* Chicago: Family Resource Coalition.

Hewlett, S. (1993). *Child Neglect in Rich Nations.* New York: United Nations Children's Fund.

Kagan, S. L. & Weissbourd, B. (Ed.) (1994). *Putting Families First.* San Francisco: Jossey-Bass Publishers.

Lewis, J. M., Beavers, W. R., Gossett, J. T., & Phillips, V. A. (1976). *No Single Thread: Psychological Health in the Family.* New York: Brunner/Mazel.

Mattox, W. R. (1991). The Parent Trap. *Policy Review, 55* Winter, 6-13.

Stinnett, N., Chesser, B. & DeFrain, J. (1979). *Building Family Strengths: Blueprints for Action.* Lincoln, NE: University of Nebraska Press.

Thompson, L., & Walker, A. J. (1989). Gender in families: Women and men in marriage, work, and parenthood. *Journal of Marriage and the Family, 51* (4), 845-871.

Helen Cleminshaw, Ph.D., *Professor of Child and Family Development at The University of Akron, is the coordinator for the United Nations 1994 International Year of the Family in Summit County. A licensed psychologist in private practice, Dr. Cleminshaw also serves as director of the University's Center for Family Studies and the Center for Family-Friendly Cities. As an educator, Dr. Cleminshaw has enriched the curriculum in the University's interdisciplinary programs in Child Life, Home-based Intervention, and Divorce Mediation. As a researcher, she has developed a national and international reputation for her expertise on family-related issues. Dr. Cleminshaw has authored numerous journal articles and is the recipient of many funded research programs. She is the producer and moderator of a television program entitled "Today's Family," which was created to address the problems currently facing families. Dr. Cleminshaw received a B.S. from Rutgers University, and an M.A. and Ph.D. from Kent State University. She and her husband live in Aurora, Ohio and are the parents of two grown children.*

THE VANISHING AMERICAN FATHER

WILLIAM J. DOHERTY, PH.D.
Department of Family Social Science
The University of Minnesota

Family life in the United States has become such a contested arena of social, political, and academic concern that it is very difficult for a diverse group of professionals to agree on language to begin a discussion of family problems. Some groups never get past the issue of defining the family. Furthermore, the term "family disintegration" strikes some professionals as an apt way to describe the state of contemporary American families, while it strikes others as at best a deficit-oriented way of viewing the pluralistic, postmodern family, and at worst an ethnocentric, rear-guard attempt to return to patriarchal family structures of the past. Another split occurs between those who stress the importance of family structure — for example, two parent versus one-parent families — and those who stress the importance of family process — how family members relate to one another irrespective of structure.

A third split is evident between those who attribute contemporary family problems nearly entirely to social, economic, and political forces, and those who point to internal family changes as the main culprit. For example, even if both sides agree that divorce is a serious problem, the first group says that divorce is mainly a problem because of its economic impact, while the second group says that divorce per se creates long-term problems for children and adults, including economic hardship. As a result of all these academic and ideological divisions, debates about family problems often devolve into accusations and acrimony, in both political and professional circles. (See, for example, the exchange between Popenoe, 1993; Glenn, 1993; Stacey, 1993). We are dealing with volatile issues here.

There is one thing, however, that practically everyone agrees on: that children today have become worse off as a group over the past 30 years or so (Horowitz & O'Brien, 1989). It is harder to be a child in America now. And most scholars and professionals who have looked at the data agree that childhood problems are disproportionately present in children in one-parent, never-married families and in families that have experienced a divorce. Children in these families are worse off, on the average, on practically every indicator of social and psychological well-being, and their future economic and educational prospects are dimmer (Angel & Angel, 1993; Dawson, 1988). These are the kinds of findings, which have been demonstrated on representative samples of children and which hold even after social class factors are controlled, that "family structure" advocates use to claim that the American family is in serious trouble.

We also know from a large quantity of research, that family conflict, particularly inter-parental conflict, is harmful to children in families of whatever structure. "Family process" advocates say that focusing on one-parent families blinds us to the everyday negative processes that are harmful to children in two-parent families as well as one-parent families (Kline, Johnston, & Tschann, 1991). Although conceding that single-parent families carry particular risks, these scholars and advocates fault lack of economic and social resources provided for single-parent families, along with gender discrimination against women and the failure of fathers to contribute economically to their children's well being after a divorce. From this point of view, if single parents were given adequate material resources and social support, there would be little or no difference for children's well being between two-parent and single-parent families. It would all come down to the quality of family process. Therefore, we should not be so concerned about high divorce rates and high non-marital births per se, but rather, should be putting our emphasis on enhancing the economic and social resources available to single parents and on promoting gender, racial, and economic equality (Stacey, 1993).

I find myself sympathetic to both arguments. I believe that family process is where the good and bad sides of family life are lived out, and that families who lack economic and social support are likely to fare more poorly no matter what their structure. In the case of divorce, recent research shows that a good portion (though not all) of the "damage" of divorce has already occurred before the marital separation, presumably because of poor family process (Cherlin et al., 1991; Doherty & Needle, 1991). I am also sympathetic to the position that an over-emphasis on family structure can lead to scapegoating single parents for their children's problems, thereby making life more difficult than it already is for these families.

On the other hand, I think that those who want to focus exclusively on family process — and want to let a thousand structures bloom — ignore the ways in which family structure shapes family process. Certain family structures make certain positive family processes far more difficult to achieve, and they make certain negative family processes more likely to take hold. In this paper, I will argue that the breakdown of father-child relationships is a central problem in contemporary American families. The disintegration of this relationship is a process issue, not a structure issue, but I will argue that it is more likely to occur when a marriage (or similarly committed relationship) between the father and mother does not occur or ends in separation or divorce.

WHAT'S HAPPENING TO FATHER-CHILD RELATIONS?

There is a terrible irony about contemporary father-child relations. On the one hand, there probably has never been a time when more fathers were involved on nurturing their children, starting from the time of delivery, that the great majority of fathers are now present for (Griswold, 1993). On the other hand, we are facing a widespread abdication of fathering by millions of fathers. I will return later to why I think these two facts are both true, but first I will briefly document my assertions.

First, in 1993 there were 6.3 million children (9.8% of all children) living with a single parent who had never married, up from 243,000 in 1960. (U.S. Bureau of the Census, 1994). In the great majority of these families, the father is not involved psychologically and socially with the child on a sustained and permanent basis throughout the child's life.

Second, an even greater number of children live in single-parent families created by divorce (about 6.6 million children). The majority of non-custodial fathers eventually move into a distant relationship with their children. One national study of school-age children found that, two years after a divorce, a majority of children had not seen their father for a year (Furstenberg & Nord, 1985). Although some fathers are quite faithful to their fathering after divorce, the predominant pattern is one of gradual withdrawal and progressively poorer relationships with their children.

A national longitudinal study by Zill, Morrison, and Coiro (1993) illustrates this sobering situation. They followed a large national probability sample of children and parents from ages 7-11 through ages 18-22. They found increasing alienation of divorced, fathers from their children, as measured by the children's reports that they had a poor relationship with the mother or father. Among the 18-22 year olds, 65% of those whose parents had divorced reported a poor relationship with their father, as compared to 29% of those whose parents did not divorce. (The comparable figures for mothers were 30% in the divorced group and 16% in the non-divorced group; all these percentages were adjusted for parent education, sex, race, age, and vocabulary tests scores of children). Thus, divorce has a powerful impact on long-term, father-child relationships, far more than on mother-child relationships. Remarriage only makes things worse, with 70% of children of divorce and remarriage reporting a poor relationship with their father.

Third, fathers in large numbers fail to provide adequate economic support for their children after a divorce. Less than half of fathers pay the full amount required by the courts, and these amounts often are insufficient to support the child anyway (Weitzman, 1985). This economic withdrawal frequently leads to a deterioration of the single parent family's living conditions and threatens their financial survival. This economic abandonment is even more true of fathers whose children are born outside of marriage. In 1993, 38.4 percent of children living with divorced mothers and 66.3 percent of those living with mothers who had never married were living below the poverty line, as compared to 10.6 percent of children living in two-parent families (U.S. Bureau of the Census, 1994).

In sum, because of large increases in divorce and in non-marital childbearing, fathers are far less involved with their children's everyday lives and far less financially supportive than they were in the recent past. Increasingly, more children do not live with their fathers, relate to their fathers on a regular basis, or enjoy the economic support of their fathers. I take this situation to be one of family disintegration. It is a rending of the moral fabric of family life and thus of society as a whole, as a generation of men fail to engage in committed generativity towards the next generation (see discussion of paternal generativity by Snarey (1993).

WHAT ARE THE ROOTS OF DISINTEGRATING FATHER-CHILD RELATIONS?

It is not enough to say that the cause of disintegration in father-child relations is the changes in family structures. Family structures have changed without a notable decline in mothers' involvement with their children, although divorce does appear to hurt that relationship as well (Zill et al. 1993). Nor is it enough to say that the cause is that fathers do not generally live with their children after divorce or when never married. Living arrangements alone cannot account for poor relationships and lack of economic support; non-custodial mothers appear to do better in both areas.

I think the root of the problem is the cultural belief that men's relations with their children are dependent to a significant extent on their relations with the child's mother. In other words, we assume culturally that a mother is committed to continual presence and support in her child's life no matter what happens to her relationship with the father. She is to act like a mother no matter what. For fathers, on the other hand, the prevailing cultural assumption in America is that fatherhood and marriage are, to use Frank Furstenberg's term, a "package deal." Even in married couple families, studies have demonstrated that fathers' nurturing involvement with their children is more dependent on the quality of the marriage than is true for mothers; mothers' relationship with their children is less contingent on the quality of their marriage (Snarey, 1993).

The upshot is that if the marital relationship is disrupted, or if a marriage partnership is never created, the father's relationship with the child becomes optional or elective, both psychologically and economically. The powerful cultural norms that bind mother-child relations, no matter what the family structure, tend to release men into a parental netherworld if he is divorced and a non-custodial parent, and especially if he is a never-married parent.

A root cause of the disintegration of father-child relations, then, is the disintegration of male-female relations in contemporary society. Marriage has become increasingly fragile in the United States over the past 30 years, with divorce rates doubling and 60% of newly married couples likely to end their marriage by divorce or permanent separation, and with far less likelihood that unmarried couples will marry because of a pregnancy (Martin & Bumpass, 1989). Intimate partnerships between men and women are far more fragile than in the past, and this fragility in turn affects the endurance of father-child relations when the mother-father relationship dissolves or is conflictual.

Taking the issue one step farther back, what historical processes have led to this situation? We know historically that until the 19th century in America, children stayed with the father in the event of a divorce (Rotundo, 1993). The father was the moral overseer and teacher of the child in these relatively patriarchal family systems. The mother's primary leadership ended when the child was weaned and could talk. A father abandoning his children, although it did occur, was held in the highest contempt. It was during the 19th century that gender roles shifts and economic shifts brought an amazing reversal of norms for post-divorce parenting. Now it was the mother who was deemed the parent most responsible for socializing children. Fathers, who by now were heavily involved in the industrial work force, were relegated to the breadwinner role. The doctrine of the "separate spheres" for men and women took hold, particularly in middle-class American life: women were to stay home and provide nurturing and socialization, while men were to work outside the home and provide economic support, disciplinary backup, and sex-role modeling for their sons (Griswold, 1993; Rotundo, 1993).

Released from the expectation that they would provide daily oversight for children, men were allowed to pursue their economic and recreational interests as the first class of liberated individuals in the modern world (Fox-Genovese, 1990). As long as they supported their families economically, men, at least in the middle classes, could pursue their own agenda in the world, whereas women were still expected to put the needs of their children and husband above all else. Families were fairly stable under this system, as long as men and women performed their prescribed roles reasonably well.

The emancipation of women, however, began to erode this arrangement in the latter part of the 19th century, the time when divorce rates began to be concerning to observers of U.S. social trends. Women began to enter the workplace and the professions in greater numbers, and women's suffrage became the political issue of the day in the early twentieth century. This period also marks the coming of age of a new norm of marriage — the companionate marriage — in which the reigning ideal called for men and women to be friends, confidants, and equals. The liberation of women from traditional constraints was leading to a revised cultural norm of male-female relations (Doherty, 1992; Rotundo, 1993). But the father's breadwinner role was still intact until later in the century.

The second wave of feminism in the late 1960s, along with major structural changes in the U.S. and world economies, brought about the most important change in the culture of fatherhood in over a hundred years. Specifically, the decline in the purchasing power of the male breadwinner's wages and the entry of mothers into the labor force meant that men could no longer claim the privilege of being the sole breadwinner in the family. As a result, women were no longer as economically dependent on men. Combined with an even stronger cultural emphasis on equal, companionate marriages, and women's increasing demands that men share household and child care responsibilities, the loss of men's unique breadwinner role represents a fundamental shift in American fatherhood (Griswold, 1993).

Historically, then, fathers moved from the primary agent of socialization and economic support for children, to a "helper" in socialization, but still the primary economic support, and finally to a "helper" with no unique role other than perhaps a sense of being a male role model for children. The "new father" of the 1980s and 1990s is expected to be a nurturing and socializing father, but expertise in childrearing was given away to mothers more than a century ago. Although many fathers are trying to embrace the nurturing role more fully than their fathers did, they have few role models and little in the way of strong incentives. The result is raised expectations for father's involvement, especially by women, but only modest behavioral changes towards more active, involved fathering (Lamb, 1987). If this confusion is true for men in marriage, men outside of marriage are bereft of cultural standards and role models for committed fathering (Seltzer & Brandreth, 1994). On the contrary, since men are still given cultural permission to "do their own thing" as individuals, and since many men experience strain in maintaining their non-custodial relationships with their children (Umberson & Williams, 1993), most of the incentives are towards letting go of these ties.

In summary, the most immediate cause of the breakdown of father-child relations is the breakdown of male-female relations in marriage, leaving non-custodial fathers (and custodial mothers) without a cultural image of involved fathering outside of a marriage-based family in which he is the main breadwinner. The breakdown in male-female relations in turn stems from new cultural expectations for marriage, new feminist-inspired expectations for equality and partnership, and economic and social changes that have taken away men's unique breadwinner role and thus women's dependence on them. We have not yet evolved a set of powerful cultural norms for how to be a good father outside of a committed partnership with the mother and outside of unique breadwinner role with live-in children.

One of the reasons we do not have a new cultural norm for fathering is that there has been a marked decline in community in America over the last century. The nation has moved increasingly in the direction of individualism and away from community expectations for private behavior (Bellah et al., 1985). Thus, fathers have been relatively free to create their own way to be a father to their non-resident children, even if the result was unconscionable neglect. Only in recent years, with feminists leading the way, have communities begun to get serious about non-resident fathers' responsibilities for the economic support of their children, as witnessed by mandatory child support collection procedures. There has been no corresponding urgency, however, about fathers' socioemotional responsibilities to their non-resident children, in part, I believe, because of a reluctance to imply that single-parent mothers cannot do an adequate job on their own. Indeed, there is a tendency for some writers to suggest that fathers are important only through their paycheck (e.g., Zinn, 1987).

This brings me back to the issue of how we can discuss difficult issues such as father-child relations outside of marriage, without lapsing into two misleading positions: either that children who grow up without a resident, involved father are doomed to serious problems, or that the life-long commitment of fathers to their children is only important in the economic arena — and that if the state did more to support single-parent mothers, even this economic support would not be that important. The first position risks elevating fathers to the status of saviors of children, and the second risks trivializing the importance of father-child relations.

We must find a different path if we are to find ways to avert the continuing disintegration of father-children relations in the United States. I believe we must elevate this problem to the highest levels of our national priorities, because we are raising millions of children with a sense of abandonment by one of the two major figures in their lives.

REFERENCES

Angel, R., & Angel, J. L. (1993). *Painful inheritance: Health and the new generation of fatherless families.* Madison, Wisconsin: University of Wisconsin Press.

Bellah, R. N., Madsen, R., Sullivan, W. M., Swidler, Tipton, S. M. (1985). *Habits of the heart: Individualism and commitment in American life.* Berkeley, Ca: University of California Press.

Cherlin, A. J., Furstenberg, F. F., Chase-Landale, P. L., Kiernan, K. E., Robins, P. K., Morrison, D. R., & Teitler, J. O. (1991). Longitudinal studies of effects of divorce on children in Great Britain and the United States. *Science, 252,* 1,386-1,389.

Dawson, D. A. (1991). Family structure and children's health and well-being: Data from the 1988 National Health Interview Survey on Child Health. *Journal of Marriage and the Family, 53,* 573-584.

Doherty, W. J., & Needle, R. (1991). Psychological adjustment and substance use before and after a parental divorce. *Child Development, 62,* 328-337.

Doherty, W. J., (1992). Private lives, public values, *Psychology Today, 25,* 32-37, 82.

Fox-Genovese, E. (1991). *Feminism without illusions: A critique of individualism.* Chapel Hill, NC: University of North Carolina Press.

Furstenberg, F. F., & Nord, C. W. (1985). Parenting apart: Patterns of childrearing after marital disruption. *Journal of Marriage and the Family, 47,* 893-904.

Glenn, N. D., (1993). A plea for objective assessment of the notion of family decline. *Journal of Marriage and the Family, 55,* 542-544.

Griswold, R. L. (1993). *Fatherhood in America: A history.* New York: Basic Books.

Horowitz, F. D., & O'Brien, M. (1989). In the interest of the nation: A reflective essay on the state of our knowledge and the challenges before us. *American Psychologist, 44,* 441-445.

Kline, M., Johnston, J. R., & Tschann, J. M. (1991). The long shadow of marital conflict: A model of children's post-divorce adjustment. *Journal of Marriage and the Family, 53,* 297-309.

Lamb, M. E. (1987). Introduction: The emergent American father. In M. E. Lamb (Ed.), *The father's role: Cross-cultural perspectives* (pp. 3-25). Hillsdale, NJ: Lawrence Erlbaum.

Martin, T. C., & Bumpass, L. L. (1989). Recent trends in marital disruption. *Demography, 26,* 37-51.

Popenoe, D. (1993). American family decline, 1960-1990: A review and appraisal. *Journal of Marriage and the Family, 55,* 527-542.

Rotundo, E. A. (1993). *American manhood: Transformations in masculinity from the revolution to the modern era.* New York: Basic Books.

Seltzer, J. A., & Brandreth, Y. (1994). What fathers say about involvement with children after separation. *Journal of Family Issues, 15,* 49-77.

Snarey, J. (1993). *How fathers care for the next generation: A four-decade study.* Cambridge, MA: Harvard University Press.

Stacey, J. (1993). Good riddance to "the family": A response to David Popenoe. *Journal of Marriage and the family, 55,* 545-547.

Umberson, D., & Williams, C. L. (1993). Divorced fathers: Parental role strain and psychological distress. *Journal of Family Issues, 14,* 378-400.

United States Bureau of the Census (1994). The diverse living arrangements of children, Summer, 1991. Washington, D.C.: U.S. Government Printing Office.

Weitzman, L. J. (1985). *The divorce revolution: The unexpected social and economic consequences for women and children in America.* New York: Free Press.

Zill, N., Morrison, D. R., & Coiro, M. J. (1993). Long-term effects of parental divorce on parent-child relationships, adjustment, and achievement in young adulthood. *Journal of Family Psychology, 7,* 91-103.

Zinn, M. B. (1987). *Diversity in American families.* New York: Harper & Row.

William J. Doherty, Ph.D. *is Professor in the Department of Family Social Science at The University of Minnesota where he is also the Director of the Marriage and Family Therapy Program. In addition to teaching and research, he is a practicing marriage and family therapist. For the past fourteen years, he has worked with physicians and other health professionals to develop practical ways to work with families outside of family therapy settings. He is co-author of seven books, mostly in the area of family-centered health care. His next book,* Soul Searching: Why Psychotherapy Must Promote Moral Responsibility *will be published in May, 1995 by Basic Books. He and wife live in Roseville, Minnesota and are the parents of two college-age children.*

Families, Institutions, and the Problem of Social Isolation

STEPHEN J. DOHNER
Catholic Charities Services Corporation
Cleveland, Ohio

As long as there have been families there have been families in distress. What is alarming about the current crisis in families is not the fact of the existence of families in crisis but the perception of its extent. This perception shapes the current debate about family well-being. Partly this perception is a byproduct of the current information age; as access to information has increased much more is known about troubled families. Partly it seems amplified by society's impatience with tenacious or complex problems that lack a quick fix. Partly it is symptomatic of a culture caught in a paradigm shift: where some perceive a breakdown in family structure and functioning, others interpret it as an evolution of social relationships away from oppressive structures and flawed expectations. Within this perspective the debate over the declining family is "often not so much about the decline of family life as about preference for a particular pattern of family and gender arrangements" (Skolnick, 1991). For others, however, the current perception of crisis is informed by a sense that much in society depends on its families being healthy, so that when they are in distress society itself seems jeopardized.

Legions of health care providers, mental health professionals, criminal justice advocates, social workers, government bureaucrats, and common folk might well argue that the crisis in families is more than mere perception, pointing to an increase in such social indicators as out-of-wedlock births, violent crime among the very young, domestic violence, gang behavior, drug and alcohol use among the young, marital breakdown, fatherless families, and elder abuse as symptomatic of an institution in distress.

An historic contribution to the discussion of families in distress has been the perspective of systems theorists who locate family disturbance within conceptualizations of family structure, homeostasis, and function. The family is not the only system open to this type of analysis; a systems approach also describes the interconnection of persons within ever larger social systems and, ultimately, within an essentially social world. Humans are embedded social beings and the process of social evolution can be understood, in part, as the construction over time of a variety of social contexts and modes of interaction.

Two perspectives underlie the discussion that follows: first, that of the family as an interconnected social system with its own idiosyncratically constructed social support network; and, second, that of the social relationship between families and elements of the larger culture that perform a supportive function for families. It assumes four things: first, that the support families receive or perceive to be available when they are faced with crisis is related to their ability to deal successfully with that crisis; second, that the function of social support is significant in understanding the effects of crisis and the disintegration of families as part of the particular issues families face, such as poverty, crime, or out-of-wedlock births. Third, the mediating support offered families by various institutions is increasingly problematic; and fourth, this lack of mediating support heightens the sense of crisis and deepens the sense of family isolation. In fact, not every family facing similar problems and stressors becomes similarly dysfunctional, stays chronically distressed, or disintegrates. Some theorists suggest that social support provides a rationale for why some people fare better than others when exposed to similar stressful situations (Brownell & Shumaker, 1984).

An explanatory note might be helpful: the task assigned to contributors to this symposium was to single out primary symptoms of family disintegration and then to articulate causal factors associated with these symptoms: effect and cause. This paper is structured somewhat differently to accomplish a similar task. It articulates what might be called "circles of support," beginning with the social relationship of members within families, extending to consider the function of social networks for families, and ending with institutional support of families within the broader culture. The most significant of these psychologically is the innermost circle where the development of personality is fostered and the socialization of family members is first shaped. Failures in bonding or nurturance at this stage have the most serious and lasting ramifications for later development and in this sense could be argued to be "ultimate causes" of later life distress. Knowing the source of a problem, however, does not necessarily lead to its solution; the systemic task is to elucidate what maintains a problem. It is argued here that a key contributing factor to the maintenance of contemporary family distress is traceable to problems with social embeddedness, and that a unique element of current distress is found in the outer circles where support for families is mediated by societal institutions.

Specifically, the issues of social embeddedness articulated here describe a problem of social isolation, which can take any of three forms. First, isolation may involve actual physical or emotional deprivation of social contact where the possibility of contact is missing, such as when literal abandonment occurs or in some extreme examples such as the milieu of infants whose primary caregiver is emotionally unavailable due to a severe drug habit. Second, social isolation may take the form of a social network being in place for the individual but providing such weak links or so lacking the provisions of support an individual seeks or needs as to result in a deprived social environment; for example, a caregiver lacking parenting skills or competencies. Third, an individual may have even an extensive social network but one that is flawed, providing modeling or encouragement that is counterproductive to healthy adjustment or that reinforces problematic behavior. The milieu of a street gang is an example of this form of social environment which isolates the individual from choices and relationships conducive to well-being.

Social support has been defined as the degree to which someone's basic social needs are gratified through interaction with others (Thoits, 1982). It may best be viewed as a metaconstruct which includes a range of social relationships (Vaux, 1988), including a person's social integration (marital status, contact with friends, membership in voluntary associations), intimate relationships (e.g., with spouse, family, close friends, confidants), and less intimate, broader social networks (e.g., with friends, co-workers, teachers, social service providers). Each individual has a salient reference group, a social network, which acts as the social field in which the individual is embedded (Mitchell & Trickett, 1980). Within this social field support is distinguishable by the type of support offered, how strong it is, whether it is positive (encouraging certain behaviors) or negative (discouraging others), its source, whether it is actually offered or potentially available, and how the individual perceives it.

SUPPORT PROVISION WITHIN FAMILIES
What distinguishes family support from other sources of support are the life-long ties and mutual obligations that is its context (Eggert, 1987). Eggert summarizes the literature on the functions family support fulfills.

"...family support functions to fulfill basic human needs for attachment (Bowlby, 1977), dampen the effect of physical illness (Gallagher, Beckman, & Cross, 1983) and depression (Lin, Dean, & Ensel, 1986), ward off stress and enhance family adaptation (McCubbin & Patterson, 1983; Pearlin, 1984), and provide cues for general social role performance (Kagan, 1977) and positive parenting (Brandt, 1984). Numerous correlational studies show a positive association between social support and mental health. Longitudinal studies demonstrate the possible predictive utility of social support and future psychosomatic symptoms, psychologic complaints, and depression (Cutrona, 1984; Holahan, 1983; Lin, Woelfel, & Light, 1986; compare Biegel, McCardle, and Mendelson, 1985). Finally, Caplan (1976) claims, based on empirical evidence, that family support functions as a feedback guidance loop, source of ideology, problem-solving guide, concrete source of aid, haven for rest, reference and control group, and validator of identity" (cited in Eggert, 1987, pp 82).

Identifying its social connections provides a way of describing the status and functions of families. Perhaps the most basic task of the family is to produce healthy members. Failures of families to support their members at this level can take several forms, the extreme of which is physical abandonment or failing to provide food or shelter. Less extreme, but no less important, are failures in parental support during the process of psychological and emotional development of children. Freudian theory locates psychological development, in part, within the framework of early social relationships. Mahler (1968) argues that childhood psychosis is rooted in failures of mother-child symbiosis. Bowlby (1969) considers early attachment, particularly between mother and infant, to be central to psychological development by creating a stable base from which the infant can explore the environment. For Bowlby, attachment develops through phases; over time the infant gains confidence in exploring the environment in relationship to the mother (approaching her, moving away from her, clinging, returning to her as a haven of safety). Whether the infant securely or anxiously attaches to the mother will affect social bonds over the entire life course. Social development begins with interactive experiences with the primary caregiver in infancy and leads to experiences with other members of the child's social world; negative experiences early in life have a critical impact on later social and emotional adjustment (Flaherty & Richman, 1986; Kahn & Antonucci, 1980).

NETWORK PROVISION OF SUPPORT

The family remains an essential part of the social network but few social networks are limited to family membership. The body of literature on social support provision tends to cluster research and theory around common themes (Sarason, Sarason, & Pierce, 1990; Vaux, 1988) that describe its scope.

Epidemiological studies suggest a robust link between provisions of support and health outcomes. Support by other persons can have an impact on the etiology of disease (Cassel, 1974) and other physical illness (Gallagher et al., 1983). This is not limited to physical symptoms, but includes psychiatric symptoms (Eaton, 1978; Lin, Ensel, Simeone, & Kuo, 1979) and depression (Cobb, 1976; Lin, Dean, & Ensel, 1986). An association has been suggested between the lack of support and mortality (Blazer, 1982). Not only do social connections help prevent illness and assist recovery; some social relationships can also prolong and reinforce physical ailments (Kaplan & Toshima, 1990) and social marginality is associated with mental and physical breakdown (Pilisuk, 1982).

Stressful life events can be ameliorated by effective support. Family support, particularly, is related to the level of stress experienced by depressed patients (Mitchell & Moos, 1984) and the onset of psychosomatic symptoms related to stress (Aro, Hanninen, & Paronen, 1989). Support from family and others can also buffer the effects of chronic everyday stress (Burks & Martin, 1985).

The effectiveness of support is linked to characteristics of the support network itself. For instance, there is a need for appropriate fit between types of stressors and support system characteristics, such as the density of the network in a given situation (Hirsch, Engel-Levy, DuBois, & Hardesty, 1990). Individuals' social adjustment may influence who in the network they turn to for support; one study showed healthy or better adjusted chronic clients accessing family or professional contacts and poorly adjusted clients turning to friends (Froland, Brodsky, Olson, & Stewart, 1979). The stage of the life cycle also influences the source of support accessed; for instance, the structure of children's social networks and the ways they relate to its members differ from those of adolescent networks (Furman & Buhrmester, 1985), and adults relate differently to various members of their social network depending on their stage in life and the type of support sought (Rook, 1990). Ineffective or deficient accessing of social support is a function of one's orientation to the support network; a negative orientation can lead members of multiproblem families to not utilize support resources because of a desire to remain independent, because of mistrust, or due to a lack of faith that others will provide help (Tolsdorf, 1976).

The support network also plays an important role in social conformity. Suttles (1972) proposes that gangs provide a substitute source of social control and socialization in otherwise deprived environments, although in a dysfunctional way, insofar as they provide standards of conduct that work within the gang world but do not prepare a member to function outside it. In this way delinquent behavior may be a result of social isolation. Krohn (1986) theorizes that delinquent behavior occurs in a social context lacking multiplexity among network members (the number of contexts or activities that two people share); since inappropriate behavior in one context tends to have an adverse effect on the relationship in other contexts, multiplexity acts as a constraint on antisocial behavior. Krohn also considers network density (in which people know and relate directly with one another) salient in the etiology of delinquency, particularly when the network includes more than immediate friends. The less opportunities there are for people to know each other personally, the weaker the social ties that inhibit delinquency.

PROVISION OF SUPPORT IN THE LARGER CULTURE

Inevitably the discussion of family support moves from the intrafamilial and subjectively constructed social network levels to the macro level of societal institutions and their relationship to families. As the discussion shifts to the level of institutions and families, it moves from one that is primarily psychological to one that is also sociological and political with psychological implications.

The idea of the larger culture supplying support to families and individuals is not novel. In his examination of diminished social ties, Durkheim (1897) considered not only the level of family support for those at risk, but also examined supportive links between the individual and the larger community and specific institutions such as the church. Caplan (1974) has delineated three different types of support systems: the first includes marital and family groups with binding kinship relationships; the second is organized support through formal groups and associations, voluntary service groups, and mutual help groups; the third is of religious denominations as organized support systems. Recent ecological models have shifted examinations of support from family and network sources to include larger environmental settings such as the nation or state (Cauce, Reid, Landesman, & Gonzales, 1990; Garbarino, 1982). Sokalski (1994), in speaking for the United Nations, claims that "the support offered to families by the society and the State are major elements in achieving both human rights and social progress."

The relationship between society and families is both complex and symbiotic; what happens in one inevitably affects the other. Families create citizens; they help shape personality development; they socialize their members; they reinforce or undermine social norms. Tocqueville (1969) recognized the mutual relationship between institutions and families, considering it a basic task of families to create productive members of society. Others have noted that when people fail to learn to build reciprocal relationships in the family they cannot act reciprocally in public (Cortes, 1991).

At the same time, social institutions have a pervasive effect on families. Relevant to an appreciation of family support are the ways institutions share the functions of families. As part of its task to assess the effectiveness of programs for children and families, a congressional task force formulated a list of family functions that are affected by social policies and programs of government and other social groups such as churches, businesses, and industry. Six such functions were identified: family formation and membership (including marriage, birth, adoption, divorce, and death); economic support and welfare (including the provision of food, shelter, clothing, and other necessities through employment or the direct provision of these services); education (including teaching competencies, socialization, and life skills); physical and mental health (including promotion of health and caring for the sick); the protection of vulnerable family members (including legislation and enforcement of safety standards and the protection of vulnerable and at-risk persons); and social responsibility (including teaching, establishing, and enforcing rules, norms, and appropriate behavior) (Family Criteria Task Force, 1988). The same report listed five family functions not normally affected by social policies or programs: affection and caring (mutual care, intimacy, affection, and affirmation); identity (family, ethnic, community, and national identity); cultural socialization (transmitting social values and traditions); religion (family spirituality and worship); and recreation (entertainment, leisure, and diversion).

The provision of support through institutions sharing in family functions has long been part of the social contract in American society and provides the philosophical justification for efforts as diverse as the development of government social policies and charitable giving to community appeals.

Institutional support for families has become increasingly formalized within a family support movement (Kagan, 1994). It includes organized efforts to improve the delivery and effectiveness of support given families by professionals (Stott & Musick, 1994); from local (Garbarino & Kostelny, 1994; Rice, 1994), state (Bruner, 1994) and federal governmental sources (Farrow, 1994); for specific populations including the elderly (Gottlieb & Gignac, 1994), those accessing the health care network (Zuckerman & Brazelton, 1994), those in the criminal justice system (Adalist-Estrin, 1994); as well as the support given to families in specific contexts such as local schools (Bowman, 1994), the workplace (Galinsky, 1994), and the neighborhood church (Caldwell, Greene, & Billingsley, 1994).

Three categories of problems adhere to attempts to support families at the institutional level. First is the problem of effectiveness, the political question of support. Senator Daniel P. Moynihan has been involved in the political question of family support for more than a generation and has summarized several arguments made against the effectiveness of social program which include the belief of some that: social programs designed to help families actually harm them, as in the view that welfare benefits act as a disincentive to work; or the attempts during the last decade to define as harmful any government activity that affects families; or the contention that the assumption upon which public education is built is wrong when it acts as an agent of the larger society instead of students' families (Moynihan, 1986). Moynihan concludes that a common fallacy among these critiques is their mistaking the correlation of social problems with causality, although as a political issue the debate on the effectiveness of institutional support of families continues.

The second category of problems associated with institutional support of families involves the limitations of institutional support. Some families may need pervasive intervention and ongoing institutional support merely to survive; many families benefit from some form of ongoing support by institutions. However, a global appreciation of the family's needs, its support network's ability to fulfill those needs, and the place of institutions in this system is sometimes lacking. Contrast this with what has been described as occurring during the transition of members of crisis-oriented families from residential care to the community; a process facilitated, in part, when families are encouraged to build supportive networks apart from the institution and its staff, and when issues of loss between helpers and families are addressed therapeutically (Kagan & Scholsberg, 1989). Not all institutions deal so effectively with issues associated with termination of services or support.

Institutional support is also undermined by the failure of institutions themselves to recognize limits to the appropriateness of their help. Loury suggests that many of the problems of African-Americans lie beyond government action to remediate, not because they are too large, but because the appropriate level of discourse is the African-American community itself (cited in Moynihan, 1986). An adaptation of the philosophical principle of subsidiarity is suggested, which states that no issue that can be addressed effectively at a lower or less complex level of organization should be addressed at a higher or more complex level.

Related to this is the issue raised by Tocqueville who warned against the tendency of institutions, particularly the state, toward being autocratic in dealing with its citizens, a warning perhaps more evident when applied to corporate than to government policies that affect family income, benefits, and the frequency with which families must move. When even well-intentioned institutions assume functions traditionally identified with families, support can be compromised. Glenn (1993) argues against the usurpation of family functions by larger institutions that have left families with only two functions: childrearing and providing affection and companionship to its members; or that Sokalski (1994) refers to as the basic societal functions of families of production, reproduction, and caring.

A final problem of limits inherent in large institutions is that social institutions change slowly (White, 1991) and norms governing social institutions change very slowly. The lack of adaptability of institutions to alter the ways they understand families or to change the ways they offer support can weaken the effectiveness of the larger support network.

The third category of problems associated with institutional support of families involves the question of mediation. Recent social theory building on Tocqueville's observations suggests that in addition to families acting as mediators on behalf of their members in society, families themselves need institutions to mediate on their behalf. Between the metastructures of society (big government, big business) and the individual family, intermediate institutions offer support for families both directly and indirectly. These intermediate structures include institutions as diverse as voluntary organizations, stable neighborhoods, strong public school systems, churches, and labor unions. In describing one type of mediating institution, Cortes (1991) says it:

...."plays a key role in the protection of private life and in the nurturing of families. It must protect the integrity of families from the penetration of modes of relationships which threaten private, intimate relationships. It both advocates for families and helps families protect themselves." (Cortes, 1991, pp. 162-163).

Increasingly, institutions that have supported families and their concerns in the larger society are themselves in crisis: for example, the loss of a sense of neighborhood and social connection (Krohn's concept of "multiplexity"); the crises associated with funding, programs, and outcomes in public education; and the decline in the size, influence, and effectiveness of labor unions are losses not only for these institutions, but for families.

As their effectiveness is compromised, the supportive network around families is weakened in three ways. First, when mediating institutions are no longer able to support families effectively, new stressors are introduced into family life directly. For instance, when a labor union is no longer strong enough to support job security, level of income, or health benefits, the family has to deal with the insecurity concerning their health, standard of living, or their future that they were previously spared. Second, when institutions cannot mediate on behalf of families in the larger society, stressors are introduced into the family's life indirectly. When social support is given or perceived to be available, a buffering effect against general life stress is made available to people. When that source of support is weakened or removed, that buffering effect of support is no longer available. The effects of other life stressors are felt more intensely by family members. Third, when nothing replaces mediating institutions in the role of articulating family needs to the larger society, the family is left standing more alone in its dealings with larger, less sensitive social institutions whose policies and programs are detrimental to family well-being. The family's sense of social isolation is increased.

As long as there have been families there have been families in distress; as part of the human condition this will likely remain true to a greater or lesser extent in the future. One important factor that differentiates families that survive crises from those that do not is the presence and perception of social support. The health of a family is related to its support network; its ability to overcome crisis, manage stress, and develop its members' potential is linked to the quality of its support. Critical problem areas that undermine families — such as poverty; violence and crime; the disempowerment of women; and the lack of access to adequate housing, education, or health care — continue to demand specific, ongoing, and sophisticated interventions by the society in which they occur; mostly they are beyond the power of individuals to remediate alone. Specific problems in families demand specific remedies, but the efficacy of any successful remediation will derive, in a fundamental way, from attending to the development, extent, and strength of the family's support resources as integral to the family's constructed solutions or society's support on the family's behalf.

REFERENCES

Adalist-Estrin, A. (1994). Family support and criminal justice. In S. L. Kagan & B. Weissbourd (Eds.) *Putting families first: America's family support movement and the challenge of change.* San Francisco: Jossey-Bass, 161-186.

Aro, H., Hanninen, V., and Paronen, O. (1989). Social support, life events, and psychosomatic symptoms among 14-16 year old adolescents. *Social science medicine, 29* (9), 1051-1056.

Blazer, D. G. (1982). Social support and mortality in an elderly community population. *American journal of epidemiology, 115* (5), 684-694.

Bowlby, J. (1969). *Attachment.* New York: Basic books.

Bowman, B. T. (1994). Home and school: The unresolved relationship. In S. L. Kagan & B. Weissbourd (Eds.) *Putting families first: America's family support movement and the challenge of change.* San Francisco: Jossey-Bass, 51-72.

Brownell, A. and Shumaker, S. A. (1984). Social support: An introduction to a complex phenomenon. *Journal of social issues, 40* (4), 1-9.

Bruner, C. (1994). State government and family support: From marginal to mainstream. In S. L. Kagan & B. Weissbourd (Eds.) *Putting families first: America's family support movement and the challenge of change,* 338-357.

Burks, N. and Martin, B. (1985). Everyday problems and life change events: Ongoing versus acute sources of stress. *Journal of human stress, 11,* 27-35.

Caldwell, C. H., Greene, A. D., & Billingsley, A. (1994). Family support programs in black churches: A new look at old functions. In S. L. Kagan & B. Weissbourd (Eds.) *Putting families first: America's family support movement and the challenge of change.* San Francisco: Jossey-Bass, 137-160.

Caplan, G. (1974). *Support systems and community mental health: Lectures on concept development.* New York: Behavioral publications.

Caplan, G. (1976). The family as a support system. In G. Caplan and M. Killilea (Eds.) *Support systems and mutual help: Multidisciplinary explorations.* New York: Grune and Stratton, 19-36

Cassel, J. (1974). An epidemiological perspective of psychosocial factors in disease etiology. *American journal of public health, 64* (11), 1040-1043.

Cauce, A. M., Reid, M., Landesman, S., & Gonzales, N. (1990). Social support in young children: Measurement, structure, and behavioral impact. In B. R. Sarason, I. G. Sarason, & G. R. Pierce (Eds.) *Social support: An interactional view.* New York: John Wiley and Sons, 64-94.

Cobb, S. (1976). Social support as a moderator of life stress. *Psychosomatic medicine, 38* (5), 300-314.

Cortes, E. (1991). Reflections on the Catholic tradition of family rights. In (J. A. Coleman, Ed.) *One hundred years of Catholic social thought.* Maryknoll, NY: Orbis, 155-173.

Durkheim, E. (1951). *Suicide: A study in sociology.* (J. A. Spaulding & G. Simpson, Trans.). New York: Free Press. (Original work published 1897).

Eaton, W. W. (1978). Life events, social supports, and psychiatric symptoms: A re-analysis of the Newhaven data. *Journal of health and social behavior, 19,* 230-234.

Eggert, L. L. (1987). Support in family ties: Stress, coping, and adaptation. In T. L. Albrecht & M. B. Adelman (Eds.) *Communicating social support.* Newbury Park: Sage Publications, 80-104.

Family Criteria Task Force (1988). *Report to the house select committee on children, youth, and families.* Washington D.C.: Government Printing Office.

Farrow, F. (1994). Family support on the federal policy agenda. In S. L. Kagan & B. Weissbourd (Eds.) *Putting families first: America's family support movement and the challenge of change.* San Francisco: Jossey-Bass, 358-372.

Flaherty, J. A., & Richman, J. A. (1986). Effects of childhood relationships on the adult's capacity to form social supports. *American journal of psychiatry, 143* (7), 851-855.

Froland, C., Brodsky, G., Olson, M., & Stewart, L. (1979). Social support and social adjustment: Implications for mental health professionals. *Community mental health journal, 15* (2), 82-93.

Furman, W. & Buhrmester, D. (1985). Children's perceptions of the personal relationships in their social networks. *Developmental psychology, 21* (6), 1016-1024.

Galinsky, E. (1994). Families and work: The importance of the quality of the work environment. In S. L. Kagan & B. Weissbourd (Eds.) *Putting families first: America's family support movement and the challenge of change*. San Francisco: Jossey-Bass, 112-136.

Garbarino, J. (1982). *Children and families in the social environment*. New York: Aldine.

Garbarino, J. & Kostelny, K. (1994). Family support and community development. In S. L. Kagan & B. Weissbourd (Eds.). *Putting families first: America's family support movement and the challenge of change*. San Francisco: Jossey-Bass, 297-320.

Glenn, N. D. (1993). A plea for objective assessment of the notion of family decline. *Journal of marriage and the family, 55*, 542-544.

Gottlieb, B. H. & Gignac, M. A. M. (1994). Family support and care of the elderly: Program and policy challenges. In S. L. Kagan & B. Weissbourd (Eds.) *Putting families first: America's family support movement and the challenge of change*. San Francisco: Jossey-Bass, 216-242.

Hirsch, B. J., Engel-Levy, A., DuBois, D. L., & Hardesty, P. H. (1990). The role of social environments in social support. In B. R. Sarason, I. G. Sarason, & G. R. Pierce (Eds.) *Social support: An interactional view*. New York: John Wiley and Sons, 367-394.

Kagan, R. & Schlosberg, S. (1989). *Families in perpetual crisis*. New York: W.W. Norton.

Kagan, S. L. (1994). Defining and achieving quality in family support. In S. L. Kagan & B. Weissbourd (Eds.) *Putting families first: America's family support movement and the challenge of change*. San Francisco: Jossey-Bass, 375-400.

Kahn, R. L., & Antonucci, T. C. (1980). Convoys over the life course: Attachment, roles, and social support. In P. B. Baltes & O. G. Brim, Jr. (Eds.) *Life span development and behavior: Volume three*. New York: Academic Press, 253-286.

Kaplan, R. M., & Toshima, M. T. (1990). The functional effects of social relationships on chronic illnesses and disability. In B. R. Sarason, I. G. Sarason, & G. R. Pierce (Eds.). *Social support: An interactional view*. New York: John Wiley and Sons, 427-453.

Krohn, M. D. (1986). The web of conformity: A network approach to the explanation of delinquent behavior. *Social problems, 33* (6), 581-593.

Lin, N., Ensel, W. M., Simeone, R. S., and Kuo, W. (1979). Social support, stressful life events, and illness: A model and an empirical test. *Journal of health and social behavior, 20,* 108-119.

Mahler, M. S. (1968). *On human symbiosis and the vicissitudes of individuation.* New York: International Universities Press.

Mitchell, R. E., & Moos, R. H. (1984). Deficiencies in social support among depressed patients: Antecedents or consequences of stress? *Journal of health and social behavior, 25,* 438-452.

Mitchell, R. E., & Trickett, E. J. (1980). Social networks as mediators of social support: An analysis of the effects and determinants of social networks. *Community mental health journal, 16* (1), 27-44.

Moynihan, D. P. (1986). *Family and nation.* New York: Harcourt, Brace, Jovanovich.

Pilisuk, M. (1982). Delivery of social support: The social inoculation. *American journal of orthopsychiatry, 52* (1), 20-31.

Rice, N. B. (1994). Local initiatives in support of families. In S. L. Kagan & B. Weissbourd (Eds.) *Putting families first: America's support movement and the challenge of change.* San Francisco: Jossey-Bass, 321-337.

Rook, K. S. (1990). Social relationships as a source of companionship: Implications for older adults' psychological well-being. In B. R. Sarason, I. G. Sarason, & G. R. Pierce (Eds.) *Social support: An interactional view.* New York: John Wiley and Sons.

Sarason, B. R., Sarason, I. G., & Pierce, G. R. (1990). Traditional views of social support and their impact on assessment. In B. R. Sarason, I. G. Sarason, & G. R. Pierce (Eds.). *Social support: An interactional view.* New York: John Wiley and Sons, 9-25.

Skolnick, A. (1991). *Embattled paradise: The American family in an age of uncertainty.* New York: Basic books.

Sokalski, H. J. (1994). Families: Smallest democracy at the heart of society. *Report of the national conference on family relations, 39* (3), 8-9.

Stott, F., & Musick, J. S. (1994). Supporting the family support worker. In S. L. Kagan & B. Weissbourd (Eds.) *Putting families first: America's family support movement and the challenge of change*. San Francisco: Jossey-Bass, 189-215.

Suttles, G. D. (1972). *The social construction of communities*. Chicago: University of Chicago Press.

Thoits, P. (1982). Conceptual, methodological, and theoretical problems in studying social support as a buffer against life stress. *Journal of health and social behavior, 23,* 145-159.

Tocqueville, A. (1969). *Democracy in America* (G. Lawrence, Trans.). New York: Doubleday.

Tolsdorf, C. C. (1976). Social networks, support, and coping: An exploratory study. *Family process, 15* (4), 407-417.

Vaux, A. (1988). *Social support: Theory, research, and intervention*. New York: Praeger.

White, J. M. (1991). *Dynamics of family development: A theoretical perspective*. New York: Guilford Press.

Zuckerman, B., & Brazelton, T. B. (1994). Strategies for a family-supportive child health care system. In S. L. Kagan & B. Weissbourd (Eds.) *Putting families first: America's family support movement and the challenge of change*. San Francisco: Jossey-Bass, 73-92.

Stephen J. Dohner *is a native of Northern Ohio, attending undergraduate and graduate programs in Cleveland. In 1976 he was ordained a Roman Catholic priest and has spent most of the past twenty years at parish churches in a variety of urban and suburban communities. Early interest in youth work and with couples led him to professional training in counseling and a doctoral program in counseling psychology at Loyola of Chicago with a focus on marital and family therapy. His current work is with Catholic Charities Services Corporation of Cleveland where he directs training for the staffs of 250 churches and agencies in areas related to marriage and family life. Father Dohner's research interests include studying the role of social support with adolescent males in residential care and their families, and support provision by churches of families.*

THE DISSOLUTION OF THE AMERICAN FAMILY

JOHN M. GOTTMAN, PH.D.
Department of Psychology
University of Washington in Seattle

OVERVIEW

The divorce rate remains extremely high in the United States of America; current estimates of the chances of first marriages ending in divorce range between 50% and 67% (Martin and Bumpass, 1989). The data suggest that failure rates for second marriages are about 10% higher than for first marriages. My laboratory has been studying marriages for the past twenty-two years, and, for the past eight years we have been studying the effects of marital conflict on children, particularly on the social-emotional life of children. What I can contribute to our discussion about the dissolution of families is an understanding of marriages and parent-child relationships.

While a great deal of research on marriages is based on survey methods that are broad, based only on what people say, my understanding of marriages is based on very detailed, in-depth observation of what couples actually do, how they think, and the study of people's physiology during marital interaction. At the University of Washington, we have constructed an apartment laboratory in which couples live for 24 hours as they go about their normal everyday activities. My colleagues and I have studied couples from the newlywed phase through old age, and we have systematically compared couples who differ in social class. We are now planning to study couples who vary widely in ethnicity and race.

There is a great deal of research on divorce and marital separation, perhaps over 2,000 studies. However, it may surprise you that when we began our research, only about six of these studies were longitudinal, prospective studies of divorce. The rest were about how people adjusted to divorce, on the effects of divorce. The area of divorce prediction, that is, trying to predict and understand who divorces and why, did not really exist before my colleagues and I began our research. Furthermore, the studies that had been conducted showed no ability to predict, or very low ability to predict, and there was no theoretical understanding of what did predict and why.

Now, after more than a decade of research on divorce prediction, we can predict with over 94% accuracy who will divorce and who will stay married in a short-term, longitudinal study of 3 to 8 years. Not only can we predict, but we have a theoretical understanding of what predicts and why. This understanding was recently published in some scientific papers and in two books, an academic book called *What Predicts Divorce?*, and a popular book called *Why Marriages Succeed or Fail.* I will summarize the major results in this brief paper.

At the present time, I am writing a research monograph that also bears on this question of the stability of families, but expands the arena to include the parent-child relationship as well as the marital relationship, and the longitudinal effects on children as they develop. This book will be titled *Meta-Emotion: How Families Communicate Emotionally.* We have discovered a new dimension of families' emotional lives, which is how parents feel about anger and sadness. Parents feelings about feelings (which we call "meta-emotion") varies widely, and it turns out to be related to almost every important aspect of the family's patterns of communication (particularly emotional communication). It also is highly predictive of the child's development. From how the parents feel about anger and sadness we are able to predict the child's academic achievement in school, even controlling for the child's initial intelligence; we can predict what the child's relationships with other children will be like, how the teacher will view the child, whether the child has behavior problems, and the child's physical health as well. Many of these relationships are mediated through the parents' marriage, but meta-emotion has the potential to buffer the child from bad marital relationships, to some degree. Also, the parents' meta-emotion is strongly related to the way they deal with emotions and resolve conflict in their marriage, so it is likely to be a basic, fundamental aspect of marital relationships.

BASIC FINDINGS ABOUT MARRIAGE

There have been many speculations about what is "dysfunctional" in marriages and what is "functional." All of these speculations have sounded quite reasonable, and they have been backed by the authority of the writers who proposed them. Unfortunately, they have been based on no data, and, also unfortunately, all of them have been totally wrong in terms of their ability to predict marital stability. However, they still live on as folklore about marriages, and they keep being repeated and perpetuated in the popular media. They have led to myths about marriages and marital stability.

The Marriage Myths. Here are a few of the myths that have been proposed about what makes marriages succeed or fail:

1. Couples who avoid conflict and sweep problems under the rug, who are not very psychologically minded, are at risk for marital dissolution. In fact, these were among the most stable couples.

2. Couples who continually bicker over trivia, who go at it tooth and nail, who are terrible listeners and try immediately to persuade one another and argue for their own point of view, will be at risk for marital dissolution. False. Not only were these marriages stable, they were the only marriages that maintained a romantic relationship after being married a long time.

3. An inability to negotiate reciprocal giving to one another is indicative of a marriage at risk. False. In fact, having a sense of reciprocity of giving is associated with unhappy marriages.

What the Truth Is. Interestingly enough, the truth about what makes for stable or unstable marriages is really a lot simpler than the myths. As I mentioned, there have only been a handful of prospective studies on divorce prediction. They are reviewed in Gottman (1993) and Gottman (1994). The most consistent discriminator between happy and unhappy couples during marital conflict is the response to negative emotions of one person with negative emotions expressed by the other person. This is probably most likely to be due to the inability to accept repair attempts to improve the interaction as it unfolds. Gottman and Levenson (1992) observed couples discussing an area of disagreement in their marriage, video taped them, and classified each message using both verbal and nonverbal information. We created one variable, which was kind of like a Dow-Jones average for the marital interaction: If the cumulated curve was going up it was a good interaction, otherwise it was not so good. We computed the slope of this cumulated curve that plotted positive minus negative behaviors using our observational coding system. The slope of these curves was used to classify couples into two groups: "Regulated" if there was a positive slope indicating more negative than positive interaction for both spouses, and "Dysregulated" for any other shape curve. This distinction made it possible to predict marital dissolution with 75% accuracy in a short-term longitudinal study of 4 years. If one computes the ratio of positive to negative interaction, the ratio is 0.8 for couples headed for divorce and 5.0 for all types of stable couples.

I added to the accuracy of this prediction (Gottman, 1994) by first proposing that not all negative behaviors are equally corrosive; I identified four behaviors that form a Cascade I call the "Four Horsemen of the Apocalypse": Criticism, Contempt, Defensiveness, and Stonewalling. These variables improve the prediction to 85%. I also discovered another cascade toward marital dissolution I call the "Distance and Isolation Cascade." This a set of the following events: Emotional Flooding (feeling overwhelmed by the way your partner expresses negative things), Viewing Your Marital Problems as Severe, Not Wanting to Work Out Marital Problems with the Spouse, Setting Up Parallel Lives, and Loneliness. These variables increased the prediction to 90%. An Oral History interview we designed coded for thoughts and attributions about the marriage alone had a prediction rate of 94% for divorce. Thus, what I discovered is that marital dissolution is accompanied by a distinct process of two cascades, the "Four Horsemen of the Apocalypse" and the "Distance and Isolation Cascade."

Not only can our laboratory predict divorce, but we have developed a distinct theory based on the balance a couple creates between positivity and negativity in their marriage. This theory is now being used to conduct a series of experiments to change marriages. Despite the grim divorce statistics in the United States, marital therapy is at a practical and theoretical impasse. The outcome results suggest that: (a) most couples (75%) report improvement in marital satisfaction immediately following marital therapy; (b) all therapies are about equally effective in this regard, regardless of the "school" of therapy, once replication studies have been done; (c) there is a strange effect that separate "components" of an intervention are often equally effective, and about as effective as the combined treatment; thus, it has proven difficult to build a theory of change based on dismantling a complex intervention; (d) there is a large relapse effect: In general, after long-term follow-up only between 30 and 50% of couples stay improved. In fact, the relapse data are probably much more grim than these conclusions suggest. Longer term follow-up is likely to yield evidence of greater relapse, and, if more stringent measures than self-reports of marital satisfaction are employed, the results on relapse are likely to be far worse. The series of studies we are conducting plans basic research in changing marital interaction, particularly those longitudinal predictors of marital dissolution that have been identified in previous research, and then to combine this knowledge into an intervention trial, in which the control group is the best marital intervention program to date.

BASIC FINDINGS ABOUT PARENTING AND META-EMOTIONS

For the past decade we have been studying the relationship between the parents' marriage and the emotional and social development of children. We have suggested that this relationship is mediated through the development of emotion-regulation abilities in the child (Gottman and Fainsilber, 1989). By emotion-regulation abilities we meant the ability to inhibit inappropriate negativity, the ability to self-soothe, and the ability to focus attention in the service of an external goal.

In pilot work for our first study of the effects of the parents' marriage on children, we discovered a great variety in the experiences, philosophies, and attitudes that parents had about their own emotions and the emotions of their children. One pair of parents said that they viewed anger as "from the devil," and that they would not permit themselves or their children to express anger. A similar negative view toward anger was echoed by other parents. Other parents felt that anger was natural, but ignored the experience of anger in their children. Other parents encouraged the expression and exploration of anger. There was similar variety with respect to sadness. Some parents minimized sadness in themselves and in their children, saying such things as, "I can't afford to be sad," and "What does a kid have to be sad about?" Other parents thought that emotions like sadness in themselves and in their children were important and viewed themselves as emotion coaches of their children about the world of emotion. In our pilot work there also appeared to be gender differences: Fathers seemed less likely to be aware of their own sadness or to assist when their children were sad; fathers who were oriented toward emotion seemed more interested in their children's anger than in their sadness. Mothers seemed to be more concerned with their children's sadness than fathers. These were our initial impressions.

To explore this area of family life, we designed a "meta-emotion interview" (Katz and Gottman, 1986). Each parent was separately interviewed about their own experience of sadness and anger, their philosophy of emotional expression and control, and their attitudes and behavior about their children's anger and sadness. Their behavior during this interview was audio taped and later coded with the Hooven meta-emotion coding system. Similar concepts have been discussed by Hochschild (1983) in her book, *The managed heart*, and by Salovey and Mayer (1990) in their discussion of emotional intelligence, and by Mayer and Gaschke (1988) in their state and trait meta-mood scales.

We decided that we were studying parents' feelings about feelings, which we called their meta-emotion structure. The notion we had in mind parallels metacognition, which refers to the executive functions of cognition (Allen an Armour, 1993; Bvinelli, 1993; Flavell, 1979; Fodor, 1992; Oson and Astington, 1993). We use the term "meta-emotion structure" to refer broadly to similar executive functions of emotion. What we mean by this construct, specifically, is the parents' awareness of specific emotions, their awareness and acceptance of these emotions in their child, and their coaching of the emotion in their child. Coaching refers to talking to the child about the emotion, the conditions that elicited it, and strategies for coping with it. If this construct is to be useful, it ought to relate to how the family actually functions.

We found that the meta-emotion variables were related to the parents' social skill at resolving their marital conflict, particularly in terms of overall hostility. The meta-emotion variables were also predictive of the stability of the marriage. They were also related to their views of their history together: Parents who were aware of their own sadness and coached their children about their anger, tended to emphasize we-ness in their marriage, and had a philosophy of marriage that involved emotional expression and facing marital conflict rather than avoiding it. They tended to view conflict engagement as worth the struggle and as a way of avoiding chaos. Their marital interactions were less contemptuous, less belligerent, and less defensive than that of parents with a different meta-emotion structure. The slope of their Dow-Jones-like point graphs was more positive, also a predictor of marital stability.

We have developed the following theory. We propose that having a coaching meta-emotion structure is related to the parents' actual social skill in emotion regulation, that is, in managing negative affect. In particular, we have found that there is a positive relationship between having a coaching meta-emotion structure and the parents' emotion regulation skills during our standard laboratory discussion of their own marital conflicts. We have found that this skill will also be reflected in an emotion-oriented view of marital conflict and their philosophy of their marriage, as measured by our Oral History Interview (Buehlman, Gottman, and Katz, 1992). This skill is reflected in our prospective longitudinal design in greater marital satisfaction and greater marital stability.

We propose that part of the role of a coaching meta-emotion structure is a superior ability in the regulation of emotion in the service of the management of stress (Fox, 1982; Fox, 1989). Because of the connection between the management and stress and physical health (e.g., see Barnett, Biener, and Baruch, 1987), we have found that this emotion-regulation ability is reflected longitudinally in higher parental physical health.

We also have found that the parents' emotion-regulation abilities are related to similar abilities in the child. The coaching meta-emotion structure was related to more positive and less negative parent-child interaction. More positive and less negative parent-child interaction was reflected in lower levels of child stress as displayed by the child's physiology, particularly a lower baseline heart rate, a higher child vagal tone, which is an index of the tonus of the parasympathetic branch of the autonomic nervous system (Porges, 1984; Izard, Porges, Simons, and Haynes, 1991), and lower levels of stress-related hormones (both catecholamines and cortisol) in a 24-hour urine sample. The meta-emotion variables were related to child physical health.

We posit that through the mechanism of lower levels of physiological stress in the child, the child will be better at focusing attention and self-soothing. Toward this end, we examined the child's performance on the Stroop Interference Test, which assesses attentional competence and the ability to inhibit impulsive responses (e.g., see Lufi, Cohen, and Parish, 1990) and attention deficit disorder (e.g., see Grodzinsky and Diamond, 1992). Children whose parents coached them with respect to their emotions had greater abilities at focusing attention than other children. We also found that there was a relationship between the parents' emotion coaching and the child's developing social competence with other children. The children whose parents coached their emotions were better in the inhibition of negative affect (Guralnick, 1981), particularly aggression, whining, oppositional behavior, fighting requiring parental intervention, sadness, and anxiety with peers.

The emotion coaching of the parents was also a buffer against the development of child psychopathology. Finally, we found that emotion coaching parents had children superior in the development of cognitive skills (operating through superior vagal tone and greater ability to focus attention). Since we think that this superior cognitive performance is mediated by the parents' meta-emotion structure, we predicted that the relationship between the parents' meta-emotion structure and the child's achievement at age 8 would hold over and above pre-school measures of intelligence, and this was indeed the case. Thus, we predicted that two preschool children of equal intelligence will differ, in part, in their ultimate achievement in school as a function of the parents' meta-emotion structure. This was indeed the case.

The Importance of Fathers. Our data have been suggesting to us an increasing awareness of the father's role in the emotional life of his children, and the impact of this involvement on the marriage, as well as the children. The father's involvement with his child's emotions has turned out to be very important in our data. The importance of fathers has been pointed out for some time by several writers, most notably Parke (1981). Recently, we were struck by an example from

Schwartz's (1994) book about peer marriages, in which she compared a father who was emotionally involved with his children to a more traditional father. The traditional father typically asked the children about their day at dinner, saying, "Children, how was your day?" and they answered in chorus, "Fine." That was the end of the conversation, and the wife quietly fumed about how little her husband knew about his children's lives. In contrast, an involved father's question was specific and detailed, revealing his knowledge of his children's everyday life, names of their friends, their immediate thoughts and concerns. The involved father knew the names of his children's friends, what the children did every day, what their concerns were, and so on. In short, he knew quite a lot about his children's social and emotional worlds. Fathers of this sort do not get their knowledge of their children's emotional worlds without quite a lot of time and active involvement with them when they are having emotions. As Schwartz (1994) has suggested, the father's active involvement with his children's daily lives and emotions is related to the quality of his involvement in the marriage as well. Hence, we were not surprised to discover that parental meta-emotion structure was related to the parents' marriage as well.

Summary. We now have evidence that the emotional life of families, the kinds of emotional connections people make or fail to make with one another, the very way they feel about emotions is strongly related to the stability of the marriage, the quality of parent-child relationships, and to child outcome itself.

SPECULATIONS ABOUT SOCIOLOGY AND TRENDS OVER TIME

We know that the divorce rate has been increasing at alarming rates all over the world. In the United States, in fact, the rate has been exponential. Why is this the case, and how does it relate to what we have discovered about the processes at work in families that spell their eventual dissolution? This section of my paper is based on speculation, but speculation that is informed by data. Let us briefly examine the sociological research attempting to account for variation in the divorce rate across countries.

Sociological Studies of Divorce and Separation Rates

As an example of these studies, consider Trent and South (1989), who used 1983 data on 66 countries and attempted to account for variance in the crude divorce rate, which is the number of divorces per 1,000 population. These authors admit that the crude divorce rate is only a rough estimate of actual divorce rates, since it is influenced by such factors as the age and the marital composition of the population. Trent and South used the following indices to account for variation in the divorce rate: (1) an index of socioeconomic development (a factor made up of the log of gross national product per capita, the infant mortality rate, life expectancy at birth, and the percentage of the population that is urban), as well as the square of this index, (2) the female average age at marriage, (3) the sex ratio (number of males per 100 females at ages 15 to 49), (4) the female labor force participation (percentage of adult women defined as economically active) and the square of this variable, (5) the percentage Catholic, and (6) whether the country was predominately Muslim. The explored 3 equations, and the second of these accounted for 43.9% of the variance in divorce rates. Based upon beta weights, the divorce rate increased with development, decreased with female age at marriage, decreased with sex ratio, and decreased with female labor force participation, decreased with percent Catholic, and increased with whether the country was Muslim. They also found a linear and a curvilinear relationship between the divorce rate and the development index, and between the divorce rate and female labor force participation rate; this turned out to be a curvilinear interaction. When the economic development index is low, women's participation in the labor force has a buffering effect on the divorce rate (i.e., it lowers it), whereas when countries are more developed, the reverse is true, women's labor force participation increases the divorce rate. They offer no explanation for this curvilinear interaction effect. However, many hypotheses can be proposed for their results. For example, it is likely that when societies are at a low level of development, women's entry into the labor force reflects some liberalization of attitudes towards women, but the jobs women obtain are likely to be fairly routine, low-status jobs. At higher levels of development, on the other hand, women may have access to jobs that are more interesting and professional; these jobs may provide both significantly more income and self-esteem. These more prestigious jobs may give women the freedom to leave a failing marriage that they do not have in countries at a lower level of development.

The Trent and South study illustrates advantages and disadvantages of a traditional sociological approach to the study of divorce. First, it is remarkable that so much of the variance is accounted for in the cross-national statistics by these variables. Second, it is clear that the regression models do not explain the phenomenon, nor do they come anywhere close to suggesting theory that might account for variation in divorce rates across countries. This is quite unfortunate.

Would models indexing development and female labor participation also hold in a country that had a high divorce rate such as the USA?

A study by Yang and Lester (1991) attempted to account for the statewide variation in the crude divorce rate and separation rate within the United States of America (using 1980 Census data). They used a Principal Components analysis with a varimax rotation of 36 variables designed to measure "social instability," obtaining 7 non-orthogonal factors. Factor III correlated very highly with the separation rate (r = 0.71), while factor IV correlated very highly with the divorce rate (r = -0.82). Correlated with separation rate were the variables that loaded highly on factor III, which were: % in poverty, latitude (negative loading), % Black, homicide rate, southern-ness, % Roman Catholic (negative loading), and infant mortality. Correlated with the divorce rate were the variables that loaded highly on Factor IV (recall the negative correlation of this factor with the divorce rate), which were: Suicide rate (negative loading), interstate migration (negative loading), church attendance (positive loading), alcohol consumption (negative loading), longitude (negative loading), the reciprocal of the sex ratio (positive loading), the % born in state (positive loading), and the strictness of the gun control laws (positive loading). Individual variables also were highly correlated with the divorce rate; for example, the correlation with suicide rate was 0.78, the correlation with the rate of interstate migration was 0.74, the correlation with church attendance was -0.49, and the correlation with alcohol consumption was 0.40. This pattern of results portrays quite a different picture from the cross-national results of Trent and South.

Variations across samples, and age at marriage. It is important to realize that a clear and replicable pattern of factors at a macro-level associated with divorce may be difficult to obtain from any one study or group of studies. For example, an interesting retrospective study of divorce by Thornes and Collard (1979) obtained a random sample of people divorcing in England, in the West Midlands, and a sample of intact marriages from the same geographic region. On the basis of interviews and questionnaires, these investigators found that the couples who divorce differed from the intact marriage in some very dramatic ways. In particular, the divorcing couples had married quite young; in 44% the bride was under 20 years old, compared to a 28% figure for the intact marriages, that 32% of the brides from the divorcing group were pregnant at the time of marriage, compared to 19% of the intact marriages, and that of the divorcing women, 51% reported that their parents were opposed to the marriage at its outset, compared to 13% of the intact marriages. This sample reveals one dramatic sample of failed marriages; those couples who married very young, were likely to be pregnant, and married despite parental disapproval. Despite the fact that this study highlights one set of risk variables for marital instability, the high risk pattern they identified is probably a very general pattern across countries, in the sense that there may be some generality in the fact that an early age at marriage can be a risk factor for dissolution; for example, a similar finding was reported by Wong and Kuo (1983) for divorce among Muslims in Singapore (see also Broel-Plateris, 1961 for the USA). This factor of age at marriage and unplanned premarital pregnancy, has been identified as a consistent high-risk factor for marital dissolution. It can be found quite pervasively in the countries in Europe described in the book, *Divorce in Europe*, edited by Chester (1977). In fact, the factors that accompany marrying at a young age may underly another consistently observed relationship between lower socioeconomic status (SES) and divorce. The pattern was well described by Rubin (1978): One common way for a teenage girl to get out of a difficult conflict-ridden lower SES family is to marry. Teenage pregnancy may be more of a high-risk factor for Whites in the USA, and not for African-Americans, due to a different culture surrounding extended intergenerational families among Blacks.

SPECULATIONS

Speculation #1. We are in the midst of a long-needed worldwide movement in equal rights for women, and this movement spells increasing economic power for women, and increasing psychological power as well. My guess is that only about 25% of all marriages, throughout the ages, were probably good marriages, satisfying to both men and women. In past eras women put up with these bad marriages, but, increasingly, as women gain economic and psychological power, they will not put up with these bad marriages. I would predict that the divorce rate will stabilize at about 75%. The increasing displays of contempt we see in dissolving marriages are a reflection of expressions that would have been stifled in the past, as women suffered quietly with inadequate marriages.

Speculation #2. The roots of the problems between men and women lie in the way men and women are socialized. Young boys are either socialized or have been biologically selected to accept very little influence from girls, and this fact has been suggested by E. Maccoby (1990) as the basis of the world-wide sex segregation effect (young boys and young girls stop playing with one another almost entirely by age 7).

This sex segregation effect is accompanied by entirely different socialization of the sexes with respect to emotion. Boys become socialized to not express emotions, to minimize emotions in their play so that the game will go on in spite of how the children feel. Girls, on the other hand, are socialized to attend to emotions, particularly sadness, and the more nuturant emotions (affection, sympathy, empathy). Girls become the caretakers of relationships in our world, and they are raised to become the emotional managers of the families. Upon reaching puberty and young adulthood, boys, who have avoided girls for the childhood years, now become very interested in girls. Eventually boys and girls marry. However, boys are still not used to accepting influence from girls. In families, women are the experts about emotion. Here is my speculation: Marriages will succeed to the extent that men can accept influence from women in the area of emotion in families, or to the extent that they are already oriented positively toward the importance of emotions.

Speculation #3. I believe that our data about meta-emotion suggests that fathers who have an awareness of their own sadness and anger, who value the world of emotions, who can accept their children's emotions, consider them important, and who act as emotion coaches to their children, will be in families that are rewarding, will have marriages that are stable and satisfying, and will have children who do well in the world.

Speculation #4. What is the major effect on children of dissolving marriages, and of the processes that lead to divorce? It is to make the children more aggressive, antisocial, and out of control. Hence, the problem of violence in the United States is tightly linked with the problems of marital dissolution.

RECENT FINDING FROM OUR LABORATORY ABOUT VIOLENT MARRIAGES

For the past 5 years Neil Jacobson and I have been studying violent marriages. We have discovered that the current view of violent men as being out of control with respect to anger is not true. Also, the view of the abused women as being passive in their marriages is also not true. The women are as angry, contemptuous, and belligerent as their husbands. Women in violent marriages are not that different from women in distressed but nonviolent marriages. I believe that what makes the difference between violent and nonviolent men is that the violent men cannot accept influence from women; in fact, I would speculate that it is a point of honor or face-saving for them to not accept influence from their women.

Speculation #5. What has to change to make these problems improve is a two-pronged initiative: (1) we need to change the way boys are socializing with respect to emotion, and (2) we need to change how husbands and fathers feel about the world of emotion.

I suggest that what is needed is more research on these specific ideas. There needs to be a National Research Center on Family Dissolution established that will be dedicated to a laboratory-based empirical program of research on the dissolution of families, whose goal it is to specify the salient processes that spell the dissolution of families, and whose goal it will be to devise preventive interventions to alter the dangerous course of destruction of the American Family, and its terrifying consequences of increased child violence in which we currently find ourselves.

 **John M. Gottman, Ph.D.** *is a Professor in the Department of Psychology at the University of Washington in Seattle. He has received the prestigious Research Science Award from the National Institute of Mental Health, renewed every 5 years since 1979 and was awarded the Distinguished Scientist Award from the American Association of Marriage and Family Therapists. He has written a book,* Why Marriages Succeed or Fail: What You Can Learn from the Breakthrough Research to Make Your Marriage Last *(New York: Simon & Schuster, 1994). He lives with his wife and their daughter in Seattle.*

STEMMING FAMILY DISINTEGRATION: CAUSES, SYMPTOMS, AND THE ROLE OF PSYCHOSOCIAL SKILL-TRAINING

BERNARD C. GUERNEY, JR., PH.D.
Director, National Institute of Relationship Enhancement
Bethesda, Maryland

Clearly, the disintegration of the family is one of the greatest problems facing our society today. Seeking to determine what factors lie high in the causal chain of this disintegration is an excellent conceptual strategy for designing and evaluating plans for effective interventions to stem it. And the Conceptual Approach diagram drawn up by William J. O'Neill, Jr. and reproduced here as Figure 1, also is an inspired and inspiring stimulus to creative thinking about intervention. Figure 2 summarizes the author's thoughts in response to that stimulus, showing another version of cause-effect chains pertinent to the disintegration of the family. (When effects are undesirable, they may be labeled symptoms, as has been done in these diagrams.)

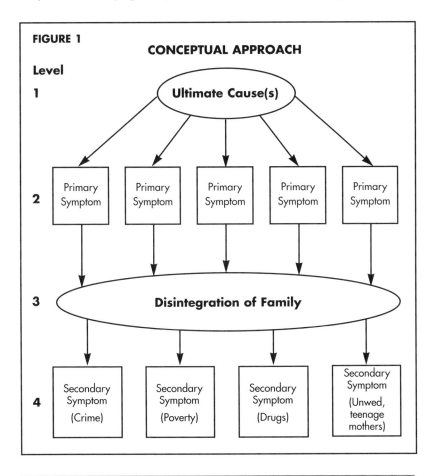

FIGURE 1

CONCEPTUAL APPROACH

Level

1 — Ultimate Cause(s)

2 — Primary Symptom | Primary Symptom | Primary Symptom | Primary Symptom | Primary Symptom

3 — Disintegration of Family

4 — Secondary Symptom (Crime) | Secondary Symptom (Poverty) | Secondary Symptom (Drugs) | Secondary Symptom (Unwed, teenage mothers)

FIGURE 2

PSYCHOLOGICAL AND FAMILY DISINTEGRATION: A PARTIAL, TENTATIVE CHART OF INTERACTIVE SYMPTOM-CAUSE LEVELS AND INTERACTIONS

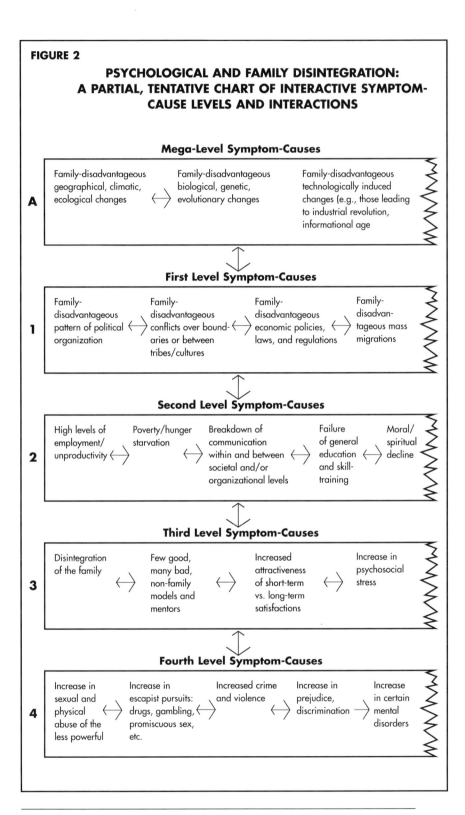

Mega-Level Symptom-Causes

A

Family-disadvantageous geographical, climatic, ecological changes ⟨→⟩ Family-disadvantageous biological, genetic, evolutionary changes   Family-disadvantageous technologically induced changes (e.g., those leading to industrial revolution, informational age

First Level Symptom-Causes

1

Family-disadvantageous pattern of political organization ⟨→⟩ Family-disadvantageous conflicts over boundaries or between tribes/cultures ⟨→⟩ Family-disadvantageous economic policies, laws, and regulations ⟨→⟩ Family-disadvantageous mass migrations

Second Level Symptom-Causes

2

High levels of employment/ unproductivity ⟨→⟩ Poverty/hunger starvation ⟨→⟩ Breakdown of communication within and between societal and/or organizational levels ⟨→⟩ Failure of general education and skill-training ⟨→⟩ Moral/ spiritual decline

Third Level Symptom-Causes

3

Disintegration of the family ⟨→⟩ Few good, many bad, non-family models and mentors ⟨→⟩ Increased attractiveness of short-term vs. long-term satisfactions ⟨→⟩ Increase in psychosocial stress

Fourth Level Symptom-Causes

4

Increase in sexual and physical abuse of the less powerful ⟨→⟩ Increase in escapist pursuits: drugs, gambling, promiscuous sex, etc. ⟨→⟩ Increased crime and violence ⟨→⟩ Increase in prejudice, discrimination →⟩ Increase in certain mental disorders

Like O'Neill's diagram, Figure 2 should be viewed not as a finished product, but as a heuristic device. Its tentativeness and incompleteness is conveyed by the jagged lines that run at the right side of the boxes. Doubtless each box should contain more items than it does, and very likely the lower down the level in the diagram, the less complete is each box.

In presenting Figure 1, O'Neill suggested that a more circular view of causality than the diagram conveys probably would be desirable. As reflected by the upward and backward pointing arrows, Figure 2 takes a step in that direction. That is, nearly all of the arrows are bidirectional. The bidirection of the arrows indicates that while it is appropriate to think of some forces as preceding others and as being more powerful than others and, hence, to consider them more primal or causal than others, their effects very often have what might be called a "return-causal" effect or a "flow-back" effect. That is, the effects come to exert a causal effect on the very causes responsible for their own creation. (These would include, but would not be limited to what are called "feedback" effects in systems theory.) For example, if the FDA allows a drug to be marketed, and it is later discovered that the drug is having unanticipated negative side-effects that outweigh its benefits, to redress the balance the approval may be withdrawn, or specific, narrower limits placed on its use. Thus, the effects of the policy changed the policy; they changed the nature of the force that created them.

It is possible to very roughly estimate the relative strength of the more primary cause on the one hand and the flow-back effects that influence the primary cause on the other hand. In Figure 2, such crude estimates have been indicated by the width of the arrowheads.

Another difference between Figure 1 and Figure 2 is that whereas Figure 1 separated out levels as either a cause or an effect, Figure 2 shows each level of effect or symptom as being also a cause for phenomena at the next lower level. In other words, effects or symptoms are here viewed as operating in chains: one level's symptoms act as a cause for the symptoms at the next lower level. Therefore, in Figure 2, except for the highest and lowest levels, each level instead of being depicted as either a cause or effect level is depicted as being both a cause and an effect (symptom) level.

A further difference between Figure 1 and Figure 2 is the grouping of a number of cause-effects into a single box as opposed to having a separate box for every cause. In this manner, the diagram reflects the view that — in the realm of psychosocial behavior — causes and effects tend to be multiple in nature rather than being easily isolated as pure and independent phenomena. It seems more realistic, at least at this stage of psychosocial science, to work with families of cause-effects than to try to isolate them and pinpoint each effect as having only one cause.

But, as in Figure 1, it did seem reasonable and feasible to put cause-effects in an hierarchical order. Thus, in Figure 2, the more powerful and the earlier in the causal chain a family of cause-effects is considered to be, the higher its place in the diagram and the lower the number it is assigned. These numbers were made to correspond to the numbers in Figure 1. But we brought in an additional level, at the top, the primal end of the diagram, and labeled the new level as the "A" level.

Finally, it should be pointed out that there are cause-effect relationships, again usually with flow-back effects, within each level of cause-effects as well as between levels. In fact, the flow-back effects are viewed as stronger within levels than between levels. The horizontal arrows within boxed levels indicate the relative strengths of causality within pairs of interactive variables in the same manner as do the arrowheads between levels of cause-effects.

The top level in Figure 2 was designated by a letter "A" rather than a number not only to keep the numbers of the other levels matching those in Figure 1, but for another reason. The second reason is that the forces at level A are immense and elemental in nature. These are forces such as the effects of the movement of tectonic plates on continental climates; of eons of interactions between humans and their environment creating certain genetic patterns through survival of the most adaptive; massive shifts in cultural beliefs such as shift from pantheism to monotheism, or technological mega-changes such as those brought about by the discovery of fire, the development of metals, the wheel, gunpowder, the machine, and the computer. Such changes can have powerful effects on family structure and function, both short term or long term. But any person seeking to counter such effects, no matter how powerful that person (or group) by human standards, would, in comparison, make King Canute look deficient in chutzpa.

One might try to *decipher* the effects of such forces on the family. For example, it is of value to try to understand the effects on the extended family as technology led to vastly greater mobility, or the effects of industrialization on the nuclear family as families left the farms for cities and men, women, and children, went to work in factories outside the home. But any group attempting to *change* forces at the A-level seems certain to be as ineffective as were the Luddites.

These megaforces lead to shifts in the way humans think, what they can understand, and above all, how they organize their society — their relationships to one another, including family structure and function. Depending on their differing structures and functions, different cultures attempt different adaptations to the new megaforces. For that reason, and because such forces do not necessarily come into being at the same time in different parts of the world, the new societies between themselves, and between them and societies not yet experiencing these new forces, often will compete. Because of the way it has shrunk the world, new transportation and communication technologies have rapidly accelerated such competition. And the survival of a society, along with its values, mores, and family structures, is determined by its relative adaptive and/or competitive superiority.

In other words, the megaforces of the A level may lead to new political and/or social, and/or familial organizations. Those societies or forms of organizations that adapt well survive, those that do not may be overtaken through powerful peaceful modeling or destructive wars by those societies that have better adapted. Sometimes different social and familial patterns may adapt equally well and co-exist. Or the same pattern in different stages of its development may co-exist in different parts of the world. Thus, we have the tremendous array of cultural and familial patterns that co-exist today.

The fall of communism directly and forcefully illustrated — amazingly within the tiny time-frame of a few generations — how one economic-spiritual-political culture that is not well-adapted to the times collapses and must reorganize itself. To a large extent it collapsed under its own weight — that is, its collapse and reorganization probably would eventually have taken place even if no other societies existed. But, on the other hand, the collapse seems to have occurred earlier than it otherwise might have because of between-society competition. Both the collapse and the reorganization-in-process seems to have been facilitated by the presence of an alternative model (the industrialized free world) — in much the same way that the French revolution was facilitated by the ideals and the success of the American revolution.

Today's ecological movement provides some hope that humans can consciously influence megaforces (e.g., the control of fluorocarbons to help heal the hole in the ozone layer). But since family-related effects of mega-forces are not nearly so direct and visible as they recently have become in the ecological area, we won't do more here than briefly explain what we mean by some of the items listed. Geographic and ecologic conditions and changes determine, for example, whether farming, hunting, fishing, gathering, herding, or agriculture is possible, and how easy or difficult it is to survive, how much leisure time is available for spiritual and intellectual pursuits; and whether people are going to be nomadic or stationary. Such variables, in turn, can have a major impact on family structure.

Technologically induced changes, such as the invention of the machinery creating the Industrial Revolution, gave birth to a variety of Level I effect-causes. First, it gave rise to capitalism and eventually to fascism and communism as alternatives to industrial democracy. In turn, the new forms of political-social-spiritual organization gave rise to certain shifts in cultural values such as, under communism, the decline of the work-ethic. It also can lead to radical shifts in the realm of the family. For example, policies of divorce and of abortion virtually on demand were an integral part of the Russian revolution.

The lower-numbered cause-effect levels in Figure 2 are much more susceptible to conscious and deliberate influence. They are the levels better suited for individuals not seeking to become, or groups not actively seeking to find or follow, a society-shaping leader — a Washington, a Ghandi, a Lenin or a Hitler — but rather, to make a contribution as much as they can within the sociopolitical organization that prevails as they find it. Those fortunate enough to live in a democratic society are not unreasonable in having aspirations to change things without having to create or support a revolution.

That thought leads us to a consideration of Level 1 cause-effects. It seems clear that varying governmental policies can and regularly do lead to results that at least relative to megalevel effects are easy to understand and predict. It is perfectly obvious that the laws and judicial decisions permitting slavery caused wholesale disintegration of the families of slaves. The case has been made that New Deal policies saved us from more radical changes, that could have had very negative consequences on our political structure and policies. Even those who believe that the New Deal had negative effects, believe that it had a powerful influence. So either way, the New Deal stands as an example of Level 1 changes influencing such level 2 variables as employment, productivity, hunger, education, etc. which could be expected to affect, at very least, the size and mobility of families.

One could even make the case that something as "far afield" from the family as banking deregulation can, though very indirectly, affect families. Had adequate safeguards been put in place along with the deregulation, at least some of the hundred and fifty billion, or whatever the savings and loan and bank failures cost taxpayers, might have been available for better prenatal or child health care, subsidization of day care, or other family-related expenditures. A more direct example is Welfare policy. Many believe that policies denying aid to women and children with a breadwinning husband has greatly contributed to the disintegration of the family among the underprivileged. The current debate on health policy as it relates to abortion clearly shows that people recognize the impact of a wide range of public policy and family-related variables.

It will be helpful at this point in the analysis to choose one specific mini-theory concerning a particular aspect of public policy for consideration. Most psychologists and social workers would agree that when young people cannot anticipate gainful employment, and see large numbers of the adults with whom they identify lacking jobs, certain effects are very likely. Among these are loss of hope, of goal setting, of planning, and of a willingness to postpone immediate satisfactions in the pursuit of long-term goals. Motivation for learning drops. Short-term and immediate gratifications tend to be the only kinds viewed as reality-based. These are the kinds of satisfactions that can most readily be found through drug use and promiscuous, unprotected sex. As living for the moment comes to be the only thing one can rely on, there generally is a loss of respect for oneself, for others like oneself, and even of life itself. Such attitudes promote exploitation of others, crime, and violence.

These factors lead to an unwillingness to take on commitments and responsibilities such as those involved in family life. Needs to intimately give and receive respect, security and loyalty that usually are met through true families are then attained, as best they can be, through gang membership. In communities where gainful employment is generally unavailable, role models for establishing and maintaining good marriages and for good parenting are more and more difficult to find and bad ones are everywhere. All of these things obviously tend to promote family disintegration.

This mini-theory is certainly not presented as the only cause of family disintegration. Far from it. However, the linkage seems generally consistent with economic, psychological, sociological, interpersonal and family theory and research. And it is helpful in that it clearly points to a specific public policy goal: Establish full employment. The theory helps make our next point in another way: it provides a policy objective of which almost everyone would approve, and very few would disapprove.

Then what is the problem? The problem comes with knowing how to do that — what specifically to support to establish full employment. Is full employment best attained by supporting legislation designed to energize entrepreneurs by minimizing government involvement and regulations? Or should one take the opposite tack and support legislation that would make federal and/or state governments the employer of last resort? Should the minimum wage be increased to provide greater incentive for working? Or should it be abolished so that more youngsters will be hired and thus more will find easier access to the world of work?

And there is another problem of which there has been growing awareness over the last decade or so: we humans have hardly begun to even try to develop expertise in looking at problems in a holistic, systemic fashion. We have seldom even attempted to anticipate the circle of ripples and cross-currents that will emanate from any piece of social engineering. Environmental Impact Studies are now beginning to attempt this type of task, but with a rather narrow focus and only in the limited realm of construction projects. How successful such efforts will be in balancing economic and ecological factors, and how effective they will prove to be, is yet to be decided. Certainties — like margarine is much better for you than butter — seem to have a way of becoming uncertainties with great rapidity these days. Seems like it took only years for margarine to fall from grace, while in the past it took decades before the desirability of meat and the undesirability of carbohydrates turned into its opposite. If anything, we seem more eager than ever to take a quick look at a single variable, and jump into strong intervention efforts. If "wolf" is cried too often people will stop listening by the time we really know what we are doing.

Finally, with respect to the point now being made, one has to wonder whether unintended consequences may be the rule rather than the exception. You work hard to eliminate pesky and potentially disease carrying mosquitos only to find out 40 years later that in the areas in which you massively sprayed the DDT to do that, you caused breast cancer in epidemic proportions — and who knows what else? (Another sobering fact about this particular issue, for those of us concerned with planning intervention strategies and studying their effects, is that no scientists or health experts or planners or legislators were even looking for such effects — it took a dedicated, concerned lay person to uncover the facts.)

More to the point with respect to unintended consequences as that phenomenon pertains to social issues: you try hard to help mothers and children through a welfare program, only to find out decades later that in doing so you have unwittingly set up regulations which abetted the destruction of the nuclear family among those you attempted to help, and perhaps also created a huge surge in teenage, unwed motherhood.

If none of the above depresses the appetite for doing so, at least the way to go about seeking to influence public policy is much more clear than most other choices in life. As the efforts toward health-care reform recently made clear, nothing beats establishing a PAC. But it may be that the biggest problem of all in promoting policies that help the family (e.g., perhaps universal health coverage for children and free prenatal care) is the power of PACs. And it may be that the single most important thing that could be done at the policy level to weaken the super-power of special interest organizations that care little about the welfare of the family would be to eliminate the power of PACs by establishing public funding of campaigns. Therefore, establishing a PAC instead of working to eliminate the basis of their power may make a would-be reformer part of the problem rather than part of the solution.

Despite the tremendous appeal of working at the highest levels of causality, it seems from the above considerations, that there is an a cruel catch to doing so: The more basic, primal, powerful, and far-reaching the effort to produce positive change, the broader and more revolutionary the effects — i.e., the higher up one goes in the causal chain — the more difficult it is to accurately predict side-effects and long-term effects, and the more likely it is that one will unwittingly trigger undesirable, unintended consequences. Many revolutions eat their fathers, and some their children. The more circumspect, limited, clearly defined, and limited the goal, the more likely one can achieve the intended effects and at the same time do no harm. (And it is perhaps worth noting that the health professions have traditionally adhered to the primary dictum of the Hippocratic oath: Do no harm.)

So, does all of that mean that would-be well-doers should stick only to modest ambitions and avoid the highest levels of the causal chain? Not at all. One thing it does mean is that individuals and organizations should carefully consider the level of risk-to-reward ratio with which they feel most comfortable. It seems that the analysis undertaken here says that investing in social change is not unlike financial investing. The highest potential gains entail the highest level of potential error and loss. Investors who do not understand that, or who do not understand how they will react to emotional strains, risks, mistakes, and losses are likely to end up being disappointed and frustrated. This analysis suggests that the same is true for those who seek positive social change.

The other major conclusion that might be drawn from this analysis is that one need not feel foolish, weak, or ineffectual in choosing goals and projects that are not at the very highest levels of the causal chain. At lower levels what is lost in terms of breadth and power is very largely compensated for by the greater certainty that something will in fact really be accomplished and that one will not end up having unwittingly done serious harm. If lower levels of reward were not often compensated for in ways that are meaningful, sensible, and satisfying, God would not have made so many bank CDs.

Thus, with an awareness that we are not descending from being a lion to being a dog, but simply becoming a lion that would choose two sure-thing antelopes to one iffy Zebra, it is time now to proceed to Level 2 of Figure 2, Second Level Symptom-Causes. And it is time also to become more specific. So we will develop one example of a Level 2 intervention designed to stem family disintegration.

The type of intervention we have chosen is sometimes thought of as a "primary-prevention" program. The idea is that one is intervening before any serious problem has developed in the population one is trying to reach. This is the type of program in which one may either target a population that is at high risk of developing problems, or attempt to reach as many of the members of the general population as possible. The example we will use here will be so aimed at the general population rather than directed only toward high risk or problematic families. (However, dysfunctional families would not be excluded and should greatly benefit from the program — so, the program also would be a "secondary" and "tertiary" prevention program.) This type of labeling and thinking is derived from the Medical Model. That is, it is based on taking medical practices as a model for dealing with psychosocial problems. Since the mode of service delivery and the objectives are psychoeducational in nature, and do not involve the administration of drugs or other medical procedures, we prefer to use the Educational Model in thinking about how the problem should be approached and the service delivered. Hence, although preventing dysfunction is certainly one of the goals of this program, it is only a part of the goal. Also, we prefer to talk about positive goals rather than ones that seek to have something not happen. Hence, we prefer to think about and to describe the program in terms of family enrichment, or family-strengthening rather than prevention.

Unlike what is typically the case at higher levels, at Level 2 there often are research findings to guide one's choices. Research has indicated the types of characteristics that typify strong families, and those that, in contrast, typify families that are prone to divorce, and violence and that tend to rear children who are emotionally disturbed or delinquent. This research is consistent with the insights of family therapists. Key variables that strengthen family coherence, harmony, and satisfaction and which diminish the likelihood of unhappiness, divorce, and maladjusted children are the ability to deal successfully with feelings, to be open with one another, to be understanding and supportive of one another, to face problems and conflicts between members, and to be able to resolve the problems constructively and creatively.

There is also research on the effectiveness of interventions designed to increase these qualities in marital partners and in families. It indicates that psychoeducational programs designed to teach the above mentioned positive qualities are effective — if they use behavioral skill training to do so.

The specific illustrative program chosen here is picked for a number of reasons. One is that the author originated the program and therefor knows it better than any other. But again, research plays a major role in the choice: an award-winning meta-analytic study conducted at Purdue University involving data from many thousands of subjects found it to have by far the most powerful statistical effects in improving relationships of any of the dozen or so major approaches included in the study. This was true for both marital couples and families.

The name of the program is Relationship Enhancement (RE). It is used for families with children over 10 years of age. It, and another RE-based program originated by Dr. Louise Guerney, for families with children under 10, called the Parenting Skills Training Program, were chosen, after a five-year government sponsored review of the research and writing in the field of family intervention programs conducted at Utah State University, as being among the best 25 in the country.

After controlled research showed RE to be more effective in many ways than the Marriage Encounter program sometimes used as part of the Catholic Church's Pre-Cana program, an adaptation of the program by Dr. William Nordling, called To Love and to Cherish has been included as a Pre-Cana option in the Washington D.C. archdiocese. The program has been running successfully in D.C. for several years now. The methods used to implement that program in D.C. will serve as our model for our Level 2 illustrative program. But the participant-unit in the illustrative program is the family rather than the couple. The D.C. program is chosen as a model for the illustrative program not only because of its successful track record, but because the model is highly cost-effective.

The cost-effectiveness is high because the program is based on volunteers. In the present illustration, professionals certified to train people in the RE Family Relationship Enhancement Program would train volunteers first to conduct the program, and then to train other volunteers also to conduct the program. Thereafter the program is largely self-sufficient and self-perpetuating.

Because of the interest in churches in strengthening the family and the trust and prestige enjoyed by churches and clergy, the church is an ideal medium for spreading a family-strengthening program around the country, and perhaps beyond. (In fact, the RE Program Manual, although not yet the Leader's Manual, has been translated into Spanish and several other languages and there is some interest in the Catholic hierarchy in trying the program in other countries.)

A program such as this, then, exemplifies what can be done to strengthen the family at relatively low cost, with confidence that it will yield the expected positive results, that it will do so with very little chance that it will engender negative side-effects, and with potential for mass dissemination. The impact is likely to be greater at this high level on the causal chain than interventions lower down, and to yield more certain results than interventions at higher causal levels. It is doubtless true, and very desirable — because work is needed at all levels — that some people would prefer to take a greater risk for a potentially greater reward and some people would prefer to take less risk in exchange for more certainty. But a Level 2 program risk-reward ratio, such as the one just illustrated, is likely to appeal to a great many.

 **Bernard C. Guerney, Ph.D.** *is Professor Emeritus of Counseling Psychology and founded and directed the Individual and Family Consultation Center at Penn State University. Alone and with others he has produced over 80 articles and chapters, four books, and numerous manuals, training tapes and films in the areas of individual, marital and family therapy. Together with his wife, Dr. Louise Guerney, he has won several national awards for developing RE marital and family therapy and enrichment methods. He is a diplomate in Clinical Psychology, Counseling and Psychotherapy, Behavior Medicine, and Marital/Family Therapy, and is an Approved Supervisor for AAMFT and IDEALS. Currently, as Training Director of the National Institute of Relationship Enhancement, Bethesda, Maryland, Dr. Guerney conducts demonstrations, workshops and oversees the supervision of RE therapists nationwide.*

Putting Families First: Creating the Leaders of the Next Generation

DOROTHY V. HARRIS
Past President,
National Association of Social Workers

JULIE N. JAKOPIC
Research Analyst

As we examine families and recent trends toward a non-traditional family structure, we should keep in mind why families are important. Talcott Parsons described the family as a factory for the next generation of society (1955). They are charged with the responsibility to provide food and shelter for children, to protect the health of children and to provide values and serve as role models for children as they grow to adulthood. The children of today will be the leaders of tomorrow. They will be our parents, teachers, doctors, and legislators.

In 1991, more than 20 percent of these future leaders — children in the United States — lived in families whose income fell below the poverty line (Lugaila 1992); 56 percent of children in mother-only families were poor (Bianchi 1991). Family disintegration is frequently cited as the root of such current social problems in the United States as child poverty, violent crime, drug abuse, and teenage pregnancy. As we work to protect tomorrow's leaders, we need to understand the forces that put children at risk and to develop strategies to reduce this risk.

RECENT CHANGES IN AMERICAN FAMILY STRUCTURE

Families are not the same in 1994 as they were in 1954. There have been major changes in family structure in the United States. The economic circumstances of families has also changed dramatically. In one study on race, family structure, and child poverty, Eggebeen and Lichter (1991) found that child poverty rates would have been one-third less in 1988 if family structure had not changed since 1960, and that changing family structure accounted for nearly 50 percent of the increase in child poverty rates since 1980.

There are several recent changes in family structure that have had a particularly significant impact on American society. These include: (1) a decrease in the marriage rate; (2) an increase in the rate of marital dissolution; (3) differing trends in childbearing; (4) teenage childbearing; and (5) decreased father involvement.

Decreased Marriage

While it is estimated that most people will eventually marry, the average age at first marriage has risen in recent years. The rate of cohabitation has also increased; it is estimated that the majority of the children of the baby boom generation are likely to live with a partner before marrying. Reasons posited for the delay of marriage include: (1) greater economic opportunities for women and increased labor force participation (resulting in a lessened need for marriage as an economic partnership); (2) an increase in the number of women who are postponing marriage until they complete their education and establish their careers; and (3) an increased acceptance of non-marital sexual relations (Cherlin 1992).

These trends, as with most recent demographic trends, have moved in the same direction for Blacks and Whites, but at different rates. In 1990, for example, 60 percent of White women age 20-24 years had never been married, but 76 percent of Black women the same age had never been married. Further, it is estimated that, while 91 percent of White women born in the 1950s will eventually marry, only 75 percent of Black women from this cohort will do so (Bennett, Bloom and Craig 1989). A variety of reasons have been suggested to explain the lower marriage rates of Black women, including: (1) increased economic opportunities for Black women; (2) increased incarceration rates of Black men; (3) increases in the number of Black men who form interracial marriages (as compared to women); and (4) the relative lower earnings of Black men when compared to earlier eras. In one study, Wilson and Neckerman (1986) found that the ratio of employed young adult men per 100 women were similar for Blacks and Whites in the 1960s; in recent decades, however, the employment rate for young Black men has declined dramatically. Wilson and Neckerman suggest that this decrease in employment is due in large part to the decrease in high-wage, low-skill blue collar jobs; the increase in low paying service sector jobs that are perceived to be "women's work"; and the movement of employment centers from cities to the suburbs.

Black women are also likely to spend less time in marriage than White women. Black marriages are almost twice as likely to end in separation or divorce than White marriages. For example, divorce rates from 1965 to 1979 indicated that 47 percent of all Black married women were separated or divorced within 10 years of marriage, while the same was true of only 28 percent of non-Hispanic Whites and 26 percent of Mexican-Americans. Further, only 32 percent of Black women were remarried within 10 years of separation, compared to 72 percent of non-Hispanic Whites (Sweet and Bumpass 1987). Again, the reason for these differences appears to be largely economic. Poverty adds stress to family relationships, making separation and divorce more likely. The costs of formal divorce, however, are too high for many poor people. This means that fewer poorer people legalize their separations through divorce and, as a result, fewer remarry.

Marital Dissolution

Between 1860 and 1970, the rate of marital dissolution was largely constant, with a rate of 33.2 dissolutions per 1,000 marriages between 1860-1864, and a rate of 34.5 in 1970. Nearly 20 years later, in 1989, the dissolution rate was 38.7 per 1,000 marriages. While the rate of dissolutions has been largely constant over the past century, their cause has changed significantly. In 1860, the major reason for dissolution was the death of a spouse; by the mid-1970s, the major cause was divorce (Cherlin 1992, 25).

The consequences of this change has a major impact on families. Divorce usually occurs earlier in family life than a death and therefore has a more direct impact on children. It is estimated that 40 to 50 percent of children born in the last 15 years will experience a marital disruption by the time they turn 16 years of age (Cherlin 1992, 26; Bumpass 1984). The majority of these children (79 percent) go on to live with their mothers in single, female-headed households. In 1992, 54 percent of Black children and 17.6 percent of White children in the United States resided in mother-child families without a father present (Bianchi 1992).

Not only are children more likely to spend some time in mother-child families, but they are also likely to spend a substantial amount of time in this family form. It is estimated that children in single-parent families will stay in this family form for an average of five years before either their mother remarries or they turn 18 years of age (Cherlin 1992; Bumpass 1984).

A variety of explanations have been put forth to account for the increase in divorce. One explanation is the development of no-fault divorce laws that minimize the stigma once attached to divorce. However, when you compare the divorce rates in States with no-fault laws to those without, the rates are not significantly different.

Another explanation for the change in divorce rates has been the decline in the earnings of men since 1960, compared to that of their fathers. The theory is that this reduction in male earnings has resulted in more women being employed outside the home to supplement their family's income. A related explanation is the increase in women's labor force participation, particularly after marriage. In 1940, 14.3 percent of married women were employed or looking for work, while in 1989, 58 percent of married women were employed or seeking employment. It is unlikely, however, that the fact of women's employment causes divorce. Rather, the opportunities for women to participate in the labor force make it possible for a woman to leave an unhappy marriage and still survive economically (Cherlin 1992, 52-3).

Divorce usually leads to a sharp decrease in father involvement. Furstenberg, Nord, Peterson and Zill (1983) found that only 17 percent of fathers absent by divorce maintained regular contact with their children. Experiences in father-absent families are likely to have some consequences for children, both during childhood and as adults. Women raised in father-absent families are more likely to have premarital births, early marriages, and divorces than their counterparts who have been raised exclusively in intact families (McLanahan and Bumpass 1988). It is also more likely that women raised in father-absent families will raise their own children in father-absent families.

There are social/psychological consequences of divorce as well. While it is difficult to separate whether these consequences are a result of the family structure itself or the economic consequences of the family structure, McLanahan and Bumpass (1988) estimate that the economic consequences explain only 50 percent of the social/psychological consequences. Several previous studies have found differences in the behavior and experience of women raised in two-parent families and those raised, for at least some period of time, in father-absent families. McLanahan and Bumpass found that women from divorced or mother-only families are "53 percent more likely to have teenage marriages, 111 percent more likely to have teenage births, 164 percent more likely to have premarital births, and 92 percent more likely to experience marital disruptions than are daughters who grew up in two-parent families" (1988, 142). Keith and Finlay (1988) found that, for White women, growing up in a divorced family is associated with a higher rate of divorce and lower educational attainment. This finding was also supported by the research by Li and Wojtkiewicz (1992), who found that the length of time spent living in a mother-only family or a mother-step family, living in a non-intact family at age 15, and experiencing a greater number of family structure changes were all associated with lower educational attainment. Amato and Keith (1991) found that, for Black and White women, and to a lesser extent Hispanic women, father-absence is associated with decreases in adult socio-economic attainment.

Krein and Beller explored the relationship between family structure and educational attainment for children from single-parent families. They found that the negative effect of living in a single-parent family: "(1) increases with the number of years spent in this type of family; (2) is greatest during the pre-school years; and (3) is larger for boys than girls" (1988, 221). According to Amato, "Children in divorced families, on average, experience more problems and have a lower level of well-being than do children in continuously intact two-parent families" (1994, 145). Allison and Furstenberg (1989) find that marital disruption has extensive and long-lasting effects for children in the areas of problem behavior, psychological distress, and academic performance, with larger significant effects for girls — particularly when children are very young at the time of separation. Kulka and Weingarten (1979) found that when socio-economic status is controlled, adolescents who have experienced parental divorce have lower levels of adult adjustment, though only slightly. The women studied by Wallerstein and Blakeslee (1989) in their ten-year study of the children of divorce reported significant difficulties in adolescence that are connected to relationships with men, such as idealization of the absent father, early marriage, early childbearing, and promiscuity.

Divorce was the major reason for the increase in single female heads of households from 1960 to 1970 in the United States. From 1970 to the present, there have been two trends leading to increases in the number of single female-headed households. For White families, divorce continued to be the primary cause of single female-headed families. For Black families, while divorce continued to be a factor, the major source of growth was an increase in the number of never-married mothers. This resulted from both a decrease in the number of marriages and increased childbearing among non-married women (Wojtkiewicz et al. 1990).

Trends in Childbearing

Black and White women have similar numbers of children; however, the timing of these births is very different. In the last decade, the average age at first birth for White women was about 3 years older than the average age of Black women. The average age at last birth is also younger for Black women than for White women (Rindfuss et al. 1988). In comparing rates of marriage and childbearing for Black and White women, White women have postponed marriage and childbearing over the last few decades, while Blacks have postponed marriage but not childbearing. Hence, the increase in young, single Black mothers.

The increase in proportion of unmarried to married Black mothers is not the result of an increase in actual childbearing of unmarried Black women; unmarried Black women between 20-24 were no more likely to give birth in the late 1980s than they were in the 1960s (Smith and Cutright 1988). The reason for the higher proportion of births to unmarried Black women is the result of a decrease in births among married Black women, coupled with a decrease in marriage for Black women (Cherlin 1992). The consequences of this, according to Cherlin, are that "Black children are about half as likely as White children to be living with both parents or with one parent and a stepparent (41 percent versus 81 percent); they are about eight times more likely to be living with a never-married parent (31 percent versus 4 percent); and they are more than half again as likely to be living with a separated or divorced parent (25 percent versus 14 percent)" (Cherlin 1992, 98-99).

Teenage Childbearing

While birth rates have been decreasing in recent years, there has been a dramatic increase in the proportion of all children that are born to unmarried teenagers in the United States. According to the Center for Social Policy (1993), almost 9 percent of all babies born in the U.S. in 1990 were born to single teenage mothers — an increase of 16 percent between 1985 and 1990. Early childbearing is associated directly and indirectly with a variety of outcomes, including lower educational attainment (Card and Wise 1978; Koo and Bilsborrow 1979; Hofferth and Moore 1979; Marini 1984; Furstenberg and Brooks-Gunn 1985; Rindfuss et al. 1980; Li and Wojtkiewicz 1992), larger families with children closer together (Presser 1980; Bumpass et al. 1978), lower occupational status, lower economic well-being, and greater poverty (Hofferth et al. 1979; Koo and Bilsborrow 1979; Furstenberg and Brooks-Gunn 1985).

Approximately 20 percent of girls who have babies drop out of high school and of these, 47 percent never return to school. The drop-out rates are similar for pregnant Black and White girls, but are considerably higher for Hispanic girls (Schorr 1989, 12). The effect here is lower educational attainment, which in turn affects long-term income and employment opportunities and leads to a continued cycle of poverty.

Upchurch and McCarthy (1990) found that women who have their first child while a teenager are less likely to graduate from high school. This is particularly true for those who drop out of school before having a child (as opposed to having the child and then dropping out of school). This led the authors to conclude that teen childbearing may be one of the many outcomes of lower socio-economic status, educational aspirations, and educational attainment, rather than a cause of lower attainment.

This is a point of much debate in recent research. Geronimus and Korenman (1992) studied pairs of sisters in examining the precursors and outcomes of teenage childbearing, which made it possible to control for family background characteristics. Their study suggested that the majority of the effects of teenage childbearing were the result of these background characteristics, not maternal age at first birth. Furstenberg (1991) suggests that both factors contribute. For teens who are already disadvantaged, the cost of childbearing may be considerably lower. There is little reason to postpone childbearing if one believes that the chances of getting a good education, getting married, and improving one's socio-economic status are slim. Once a teenager has a child, the chances for these things happening are further reduced. Furstenberg points out, however, that there is a lack of research connecting "perceived life chances and subsequent responses to childbearing" (1991, 134).

Hoffman, Foster and Furstenberg (1993), building on the work by Upchurch and McCarthy, used the sibling model technique with three additional sources of data. They found that background characteristics did account for more of the outcomes of teenage childbearing than previously thought. However, there were still significant, important effects of teenage parenthood on high school graduation, family size, and economic well-being.

The percent of unmarried teen mothers in 1984 was three times that of 25 years earlier. "Children of unmarried teenage mothers are four times as likely as children in other families to be poor, and likely to remain poor for a long time" (Schorr 1989, 13). Before they reach the age of nine, 70 percent of children born to mothers under eighteen have spent part of their childhoods in single-parent households, (regardless of the mother's marital status at the time the child is born) (Schorr 1989, 13). Girls most likely to have teenage first births are those who have experienced emotional and/or economic deprivation. According to Schorr, "For Blacks, the high incidence of poverty combined with dismal future economic prospects account for high rates of teenage childbearing. Although birth rates in the United States among Black teenagers have been going down steadily since 1970, they are still twice as high as among White teens" (Schorr 1989, 60). This difference is due in part to the earlier age at which Black teenagers become sexually active (Miller and Moore 1990).

One purported cause of increased non-marital childbearing is the availability of welfare benefits; however, research has not supported this claim. Contrary to public opinion, the average number of children in families receiving AFDC in 1991 was two (U.S. Department of Health and Human Services 1992). Duncan and Hoffman (1990) studied the relationship between welfare benefits, economic opportunities, and non-marital births among Black teenage girls. They found that the impact of AFDC benefits levels on the rate of non-marital teen childbearing was insignificant. They did find a strong relationship between economic opportunities and the rate of out-of-wedlock teen births.

Father Involvement

Children in mother-child or step-parent families often have little on-going contact with their fathers. Seltzer and Bianchi (1988) found that only 59 percent of non-resident fathers see their children once a month. Yet Thompson (1994) found that between 15 percent and 25 percent maintain weekly visits, and that proportion seems to be growing. King (1994) found evidence that non-resident father involvement has some positive effects on child well-being. She found stronger evidence for the effect of child support payments by non-resident fathers on child well-being. Unfortunately, Teachman and Paasch (1994) reported that, in 1989, only 72 percent of ever-married mothers received child support awards and only 75 percent of these women actually received payments. For never-married mothers, these figures were even lower.

Teachman also found that "a majority of noncustodial fathers seldom or never made contributions to their children. Among fathers who contributed, the most frequent ways were through child support, medical insurance, and dental care. Fathers were more likely to provide contributions requiring outlays of money rather than time. Very few fathers performed time-intensive activities, such as helping their children with home work or attending school events, which may be influenced by custody arrangements" (Teachman 1994, 76-77). When a mother remarries, participation is further complicated by fathers feeling that they no longer have a role to play (Thompson 1994; Wallerstein and Blakeslee 1989).

Even more than family structure, current social concerns are associated with a lack of economic resources. Hernandez identified two
major factors in family disruption: low income and unemployment.
Two-parent families who were below the poverty line were more than
twice as likely as those above the poverty line to separate and/or
divorce within 2 years (U.S. Bureau of the Census 1993).

Schorr sees poverty as the greatest risk factor of all. She points out
that "family poverty is relentlessly correlated with high rates of
school-age childbearing, school failure, and violent crime — and with
all their antecedents. Low income is an important risk factor in itself,
and so is relative poverty — having significantly less income than
the norm, especially in a society that places such a high value on economic success. Virtually all the other risk factors that make rotten
outcomes more likely are also found disproportionately among poor
children: bad health during infancy and childhood, malnutrition,
having an isolated or impaired mother, being abused or neglected,
not having a decent place to live, and lacking access to the services
that would protect against the effects of these conditions" (Schorr
1989, xxii-xxiii). While certainly there have been changes in family
structure, these changes have not occurred in a vacuum. There have
been significant economic changes for families as well.

Overall Changes in Family Income
While family income increased rapidly following World War II, the
pace has not continued throughout the post-war period. In constant
1990 dollars, the median family income in 1947 was $17,689; that
doubled to $35,379 in 1973, largely due to increased productivity.
From 1973 to 1984, however, median family income fell to $33,162
(in 1990 dollars) — a decrease of 6 percent (Cherlin 1989, 127-8).
This decrease occurred even with an increase in the labor force participation of women, from 28 percent in 1940 to 58 percent in 1990
(Blau and Ferber 1992). More and more, two incomes are required
to maintain a constant level of family income.

As the American economy has moved away from manufacturing
toward services and high technology, a major change has occurred in
employment opportunities. A significant split has evolved, resulting
in new jobs either being high education, high wage, high technology,
or low skill, low wage, service jobs. "Starting in 1973, recessions
occurred every few years and each cycle of boom and bust created
higher levels of joblessness, which depressed wages. Low wages and
high joblessness increased poverty and such related problems as fami-

ly dissolution and welfare receipt. Moreover, minority workers, especially in the rust-belt cities, have been particularly vulnerable to the structural economic changes of the past two decades because of their disproportionate concentration in industries with the largest number of layoffs due to economic cutbacks, plant closings, and the relocation of firms to cheaper labor sites and to the suburbs..." (William Julius Wilson, in the Foreword to Schorr 1989, ix-xi).

The impact of this change on families has been enormous. According to Schorr (1989, 18), young men who are unemployed or working at below-poverty wages are only one-third as likely to marry as their peers, regardless of race. She reports that 60 percent of young men were able to earn enough to keep a family of three out of poverty in 1973, but only 42 percent were able to do so in 1984. This was particularly true for Black families, which have less access to the education required for high-skill jobs and more competition for the low-skill, high-wage manufacturing jobs. We often hear that the answer to the problem of poverty is jobs. Yet half of poor family householders in 1991 were employed for at least part of the year, and 15.8 percent worked year-round, full-time. The answer is not jobs alone, but full-time jobs with benefits and livable wages.

Minimum Wage Stagnation

In 1992, 16 percent of full-time workers earned incomes that were at or below the poverty line. This is a one-third increase over the 12 percent in 1979 (U.S. Bureau of the Census 1994). Further, of those who receive hourly wages, 6.6 percent make at or less than the minimum wage (U.S. Department of Labor 1994). A major contributor to the poverty of working families is the decreased value of the minimum wage. In constant 1994 dollars, the minimum wage declined 25 percent between 1981 and 1994, from a value of $5.67 to $4.25 (Luttner 1994).

Gender-Poverty Gap

Women are particularly hard hit by poverty. Female heads of households in 1993 were almost three times more likely than male heads of households to earn minimum wage or less (U.S. Department of Labor 1994). Further, "one-third (33 percent) of families maintained by women with no spouse present had incomes below the poverty level" (U.S. Bureau of the Census 1993, 28). This is particularly high when compared with 11.5 percent of all families and 6 percent for married-couple families. Further, female heads of households earn a median income of $17,961, only 60 percent of the amount ($30,126) earned by all households (U.S. Bureau of the Census 1993).

There is an extensive body of research on the economic consequences of divorce that suggests three results: (1) women and children experience large decreases in their standard of living following divorce; (2) men are most likely to maintain or increase their standard of living; and (3) the most likely way for women and children to increase their economic well-being is through the mother's remarriage. Teachman and Paasch (1994) revealed that, in 1991, 39 percent of all divorced women with children and 55 percent of those with children under six had incomes below the poverty threshold established by the U.S. Bureau of the Census.

Not only are single women with children more likely to be poor, they are also likely to remain poor longer. Bane and Elwood (1986) found that female-headed families are likely to spend a period of seven years in poverty, compared to an average of less than two years for all families.

Regarding relative earnings, a statistic frequently used to describe income differences between the genders is the median earnings ratio of women to men. Over the last century, women have come much closer to making the same wages as men. In 1990, their median earnings were 71 percent of that of men (O'Neill and Polachek 1993). Women have increased their wages by investing in more education and acquiring more experience in the labor force. The level of education and workforce experience of women has almost reached that of men. At the same time, men's wages have fallen as the country has moved from a manufacturing to an information and service economy. O'Neill and Polachek (1993) find that women's greater educational investment and labor market experience explain only one-third of the narrowing of the difference between women's and men's earnings. The remainder is attributable to other factors such as the decline of men's wages with the decline of blue-collar work.

Child Support

The low incomes of single mothers make child support an important source of income. Teachman and Paasch (1994) report that, according to the 1989 Current Population Survey, child support payments provided 17 percent of the income of divorced mothers who received support; for women below the poverty line, these payments made up 38 percent of their income. Clearly child support is an important contribution when it is available, despite the low average amount of awards ($3,138 per year) (Teachman and Paasch 1994, 73). Yet only about 48 percent of single mothers receive child support payments.

In a study of non-custodial fathers and the factors that influence payment of child support, Ferguson (1990) finds that the major factor is fathers' employment. However, all fathers who are employed do not pay. Ferguson goes on to explore what other factors are important in determining payment of child support. These include the age at which the father first had sexual intercourse (the earlier the less chance of payment); the number of children not living with them (the more non-resident children, the greater the likelihood of payment); marital status (divorced fathers are more likely to pay); and weekly earnings (higher wages increase likelihood of payment).

A LOOK AT POTENTIAL INTERVENTIONS

We have identified some of the problems or risk factors which arise out of the changing demographics of the family, which tend to have an adverse impact on their social, emotional, and economic well-being. One common thread underlying all of the risk factors discussed is their role in undermining the future of our children. Can we reverse the trend in teenage childbearing? Can our society make it possible for satisfying and productive employment to become the norm for all those able and willing to work? Can a different interaction of demographics and economic conditions result in fewer at-risk children? Can we shift our resources and re-organize our system of social services delivery to treat causes instead of symptoms?

No single service program will solve all of the problems related to family well-being. The aforementioned statistics graphically support the need for concerted family preservation efforts. Yet preserving the "family" as we have known it is a formidable task. We can no longer define the family as a solitary structure consisting of a father, mother, and their children living in the same household. Today, there is a plethora of family structures that demand our attention. Some are a result of the breakup of the family, as described in this paper; others are brought on by the prevailing lifestyles in a changing society.

In addition, as statistics show, many of these families are minorities, poor, and headed by single mothers. While the current situation calls for creative efforts in dealing with family problems, there is a part of the equation that may have greater impact on solving these problems than any other single factor — i.e., societal attitudes toward minorities and the poor. In our search for solutions, we cannot ignore the fact that the more affluent segments of our society remain largely intolerant of the poor and at-risk populations that are the concern of this paper.

A review of the literature and the types of demonstration projects being funded by public agencies, foundations, and private entities indicate that, across the country, groups are engaged in developing and delivering services and materials to help meet and/or anticipate family needs. Discussed below are several intervention efforts that we feel hold promise for helping to strengthen, support, and enhance family functioning, thereby improving the chances for a better future for children.

Family Strengthening and Support Services

Most service providers suggest that family-focused delivery systems which provide universal access to comprehensive services and are neighborhood-based, comprehensive, and staffed by a competent and multidisciplinary work force must be created to meet the complex needs of today's families. Our own practice experience in the settlement houses a few decades ago suggest that such an approach had much that could inform today's practice with families. The planned Settlement Houses and Community Centers of old were neighborhood-based agencies that provided, on a universal basis, comprehensive services to families in their geographic area. They were usually staffed by professionals who developed, administered, and provided the direct services.

These neighborhood agencies provided a wide variety of services, activities, and self-improvement classes for children, youth, and adults. Services included child care, preschool and adult education, after-school activities for school-age children, outings and summer camps, counselling for parents and at-risk teens, and a variety of other activities, all geared to help those involved live more satisfying and productive lives. In addition, there were literacy, English, cooking, sewing and homemaker classes, and arts, crafts, music and dancing lessons. In those instances where the centers were not suited for providing a needed service (e.g., health care), they provided the leadership to mobilize services on behalf of their "program participants." We feel that one of the most important contributions of the settlement house was to give people the tools to be in control of their lives and participate fully in the affairs of their community. A family or individual did not have to be dysfunctional in order to be welcomed as a program participant.

It is possible today to develop family service centers patterned after the settlement house programs of past decades. We need service centers in the neighborhoods where people live that are committed to innovative delivery systems, providing services directly in the home, where necessary, and adapted to each family's circumstances. The goal of these centers should be to serve all families — those in trouble, those at risk, and those who want to extend their potential. As was our experience with the settlement house, it appears that informal service delivery programs that are culturally sensitive enjoy great receptiveness from families and individuals served and therefore are very effective.

The role of government, at some level, should be to integrate the different funding sources so that a group opting to develop a comprehensive family service delivery system would not spend an inordinate amount of time accessing resources from multiple funding streams. An example of a successful approach to serving families is the Family Support Network developed by Maryland's Friends of the Family (FOF) in Baltimore. The network is comprised of 15 community-based Family Support Centers (FSC) whose target population is young-parent families with very young children who live in low-income neighborhoods. These FSCs provide comprehensive, culturally-sensitive, community-based, preventive services to families who live in neighborhoods that show high concentrations of a variety of risk factors known to be predictive of long-term welfare dependency and poverty.

Addressing Inadequate Economic Resources
While employment used to be a route out of poverty for many families, we have seen that it offers no sure escape from poverty today, nor does it ensure a constant level of family income. The linkage between female-headed households and poverty is clear, and this poverty gap cannot be defined in strictly economic terms. We also find that many children live in poverty because of the lack of consistency in the enforcement of child support payments.

Therefore, in addition to social service programs that strengthen, support, and preserve families, we agree there exists a need for the implementation of policies that provide for a nationwide investment in the economic prosperity of families. The following are important principles:

1) Access to meaningful employment and the earning of a livable income ought to be the cornerstone of efforts to improve the economic well-being of families. Work provides a number of benefits to individuals, among them increased potential for economic self-sufficiency and increased self-esteem. Economic self-sufficiency, however, requires more than a job. It requires the kind of education, training,

and preparation that enhances opportunities for long-term employ-ment in jobs that pay a living wage, and provide benefits such as health insurance for the whole family, access to quality childcare, and care for elderly dependents. There needs to be a concerted effort toward expansion of employment and training programs, and for better targeting of those programs so that women are served equi-tably. If employment is to be the road out of poverty, then there are serious arguments for increasing the minimum wage, the stagnation of which is a major contributor to poverty among working families.

2) The government should give serious consideration to utilizing different approaches in subsidizing the income of the working poor, in order to assure a measure of economic security to all families. Options include the creation of family allowances, which are quite common in many other countries, or a guaranteed annual wage (which implies government subsidy in low-paying jobs). Subsidies could also be in the form of access to health care and good nutrition, quality child care, dependable transportation, preschool education, and adult care services. Recent changes in tax policies which lowered the tax liability for poor families is a step in the right direction. Society has a responsibility, as well as a vested interest, in fostering conditions where families are able to maintain a decent standard of living. They can then improve the present well-being of their children and assure their growing into healthy and productive adulthood. Employment for parents should never have the effect of making children worse off than if they were welfare recipients.

More sensitive government policies will help, but by themselves they are not enough. The private sector also needs to help support families through greater use of human resource development programs for employees. Companies need to allow more flexible work schedules, and fringe benefit packages that can be adapted to the particular situation of employees who may be responsible for young children, elderly parents, or a handicapped family member.

3) Children should not be allowed to grow up in poverty because one parent fails to meet their support responsibilities. One means of supporting many single-parent families and keeping them intact is to better enforce laws governing child support payments. The government should utilize every opportunity to emphasize parental responsibility for their children. Child support must be seen as a fundamental obligation — one which cannot be abandoned because of separation and/or subsequent marriages.

We know firsthand the critical importance of a strong family life for fostering the successful growth and development of children. We know some families need help with education or with child-rearing and parenting skills, while other families may require health insurance, or job training, or assistance in obtaining their high school diploma, or some form of income subsidy. We know that unemployment, underemployment, and fear of job loss can take a heavy toll on families. We know there is no single solution, nor one right approach to improving family well-being. We know it is not the job of government alone. Nor of the private sector alone.

One of the most effective means of protecting our children from debilitating social and economic handicaps is a strong, healthy family life. It is within the family that individuals develop a set of values, a culture, and a perspective on the future. It is as members of a family that children learn about and come to appreciate religion, education, a sense of community, and of social responsibility. And family experiences, to a very large extent, shape an individual's sense of self-worth and their ability to cope with the stresses and difficulties of life in our times. Therefore, the way the family performs its vital role of educating and socializing children today will determine to a very large degree the capabilities and values of tomorrow's workers and leaders. Viewed in this context, today's families represent our collective future. Therefore, it is in our best interests to do everything possible to assure a strong and healthy family life for every child in our society.

REFERENCES

Allison, P. and F. Furstenberg, Jr. 1989. How Marital Dissolution Affects Children: Variations by Age and Sex. *Developmental Psychology* 25, 4:540-549.

Amato, P. R. 1987. Family Processes in One-Parent, Step-Parent, and Intact Families: The Child's Point of View. *Journal of Marriage and the Family* 49:327-37.

Amato, P. R., and B. Keith. 1991. Separation from a Parent during Childhood and Adult Socioeconomic Attainment. *Social Forces* 70, 1:187-206.

Amato, P. 1994. Life-Span Adjustment of Children to Their Parents' Divorce. *The Future of Children*, Vol. 4, 1:4-14.

Bane, M. J. and D. Elwood. 1986. Slipping into and out of Poverty: The dynamics of spells. *Journal of Human Resources* 21:1-23.

Behrman, R. and L. Quinn. 1994. Children and Divorce: Overview and Analysis. *The Future of Children*, Vol. 4, 1:4-14.

Bennett, N., D. Bloom, and P. Craig. 1989. The Divergence of Black and White Marriage Patterns. *American Journal of Sociology* 95:692-722.

Bianchi, S. and E. McArthur. 1991. *Family Disruption and Economic Hardship: The short-run picture for children*. U.S. Bureau of the Census, Current Population Reports, Series P-70, No. 23. Washington, D.C.: U.S. Government Printing Office.

Bianchi, S. 1992. The Changing Demographic and Socioeconomic Characteristics of Single-Parent Families. Forthcoming.

Blau, F. and M. Ferber. 1992. *The Economics of Women, Men and Work*. Englewood Cliffs, NJ: Prentice-Hall.

Bumpass, L. 1984. Children and Marital Disruption: A replication and update. *Demography* 21:71-82.

Bumpass, L., R. R. Rindfuss, and R. Janosik. 1978. Age and Marital Status at First Birth and the Pace of Subsequent Fertility. *Demography* 15:75-86.

Card, J. J. and L. L. Wise. 1978. Teenage Mothers and Teenage Fathers: The impact of early childbearing on the parent's personal and professional lives. *Family Planning Perspectives* 10 (July/August): 199-207.

Casper, L., S. McLanahan and I. Garfinkel. 1993. The Gender Poverty Gap: What we can learn from other countries. Paper prepared for the Annual Meetings of the Population Association of America, Cincinnati, OH.

Center for Social Policy. 1993. *Kids Count Data Book: State profiles of Child Well Being*. Greenwich, CT: Annie Casey Foundation.

Cherlin, A. 1992. *Marriage, Divorce, Remarriage*. Cambridge, MA: Harvard University Press.

Demo, D. H. and A. C. Acock. 1988. The Impact of Divorce on Children. *Journal of Marriage and the Family* 50:619-648.

Duncan, G. and S. Hoffman. 1990. Welfare Benefits, Economic Opportunities, and Out-of-Wedlock Births Among Black Teenage Girls. *Demography*, Vol. 27, 4:519.

Eggebeen, D. and D. Lichter. 1991. Race, Family Structure, and Changing Poverty Among American Children. *American Sociological Review* 56:801-817.

Ferguson, R. F. 1990. Non-Custodial Fathers: Factors that Influence Payment of Child Support. Preliminary summary of empirical results and implications for the Manpower Demonstration Research Corporation.

Furstenberg, F. F., Jr. and J. Brooks-Gunn. 1985. Adolescent Mothers in Later Life. Final report to the Commonwealth Fund. Philadelphia, PA: University of Pennsylvania.

Furstenberg, F., Jr., C. Nord, J. Peterson, and N. Zill. 1983. The Life Course of Children of Divorce: Marital Disruption and Parental Contact. American *Sociological Review* 48:656-668.

Furstenberg, F., Jr. 1991. As the Pendulum Swings: Teenage Childbearing and Social Concern. *Family Relations* April: 127-138.

Furstenberg, F. 1994. History and Current Status of Divorce in the United States. *The Future of Children*, Vol. 4, 1:29-43.

Geronimus, A. and S. Korenman. 1992. The Socioeconomic Costs of Teen Childbearing Reconsidered. *Quarterly Journal of Economics* 107: 1187-1214.

Geronimus, A. and S. Korenman. 1993. The Socioeconomic Costs of Teenage Childbearing: Evidence and Interpretation. *Demography* 30:281-296.

Guidubaldi, J. and H. K. Cleminshaw, J. D. Perry, B. K. Nastasi, and J. Lightel. 1986. The role of selected family environment factors in children's post-divorce adjustment. *Family Relations* 35: 141-151.

Hofferth, S. L. and K. A. Moore. 1979. Early Childbearing and Later Economic Well-Being. *American Sociological Review* 44:784-815.

Hoffman, S., E. Foster and F. Furstenberg, Jr. 1993. Reevaluating the Costs of Teenage Childbearing. *Demography* 30:1-13.

Keith, V. M. and B. Finlay. 1988. The Impact of Parental Divorce on Children's Educational Attainment, Marital Timing, and Likelihood of Divorce. *Journal of Marriage and the Family* 50:797-809.

King, V. 1994. Non-resident Father Involvement and Child Well-Being: Can Dads make a difference? *Journal of Family Issues* 15, 1:78-96.

Koo, H. P., and R. E. Bilsborrow. 1979. Multivariate Analyses of Effects of Age at First Birth: Results from the 1973 National Survey of Family Growth and 1975 Current Population Survey. Final report to National Institute of Child Health and Development.

Krein, S. and A. Beller, 1988. Educational Attainment of Children from Single-Parent Families: Differences by Exposure, Gender and Race. *Demography* 25:221-343.

Kulka, R. and H. Weingarten. 1979. The long-term effects of parental divorce in childhood. *Journal of Social Issues* 35: 50-78.

Lowenstein J. and E. Koopman. 1978. A comparison of the self-esteem of boys living with single-parent mothers and single-parent fathers. *Journal of Divorce* 2:195-208.

Lugaila, T. 1992. U.S. Bureau of the Census, Current Population Reports, Series P23-181, Households, Families and Children. Washington, D.C.: U.S. Government Printing Office.

Li, J. and R. Wojtkiewicz. 1992. A New Look at the Effects of Family Structure on Status Attainment. *Social Science Quarterly* 73, 3:581-595.

Luttner, Steve. 1994. Running a family of 4 on $14,350 a year. *Cleveland Plain Dealer*, August 7, 1994.

Marini, M. M. 1984. Women's Educational Attainment and the Timing of Entry into Parenthood. *American Sociological Review* 49:491-493.

McLanahan, S. and L. Bumpass. 1988. Intergenerational Consequences of Family Disruption. *American Journal of Sociology* 94:130-152.

Miller, B. C. and K. Moore. 1990. Adolescent Sexual Behavior, Pregnancy, and Parenting: Research through the 1980s. *Journal of Marriage and the Family* 52:1025-1044.

O'Neill, J. and S. Polachek. 1993. Why the Gender Gap in Wages Narrowed in the 1980s. *Journal of Labor Economics*, Vol. 11, 1:205-228.

Parsons, T. and R. Bales. 1955. *Family Socialization and Interaction Process.* Glencoe: Free Press.

Presser, H. 1980. Social Consequences of Teenage Childbearing. In Catherine S. Chilman, ed., *Adolescent Pregnancy and Childbearing: Findings from Research.* National Institutes of Health Publication No. 80-2077. Washington, D.C.: U.S. Government Printing Office.

Raschke, H. J., and V. Raschke. 1979. Family Conflict and Children's Self-Concepts. *Journal of Marriage and Family* 41:367-374.

Rindfuss, R., S. P. Morgan, and G. Swicegood. 1988. *First Births in America: Changes in the Timing of Parenthood.* Berkeley, CA: University of California Press.

Rindfuss, R. R., C. St. John, and L. Bumpass. 1980. Education and Fertility: Roles women occupy. *American Sociological Review* 45:431-447.

Rosen, R. 1979. Some Crucial Issues Concerning Children of Divorce. *Journal of Divorce* 3:19-25.

Schorr, L. B. and D. Schorr. 1989. *Within Our Reach: Breaking the Cycle of Disadvantage.* New York, NY: Anchor Books.

Seltzer, J. and S. Bianchi. 1988. Children's Contact with Absent Parents. *Journal of Marriage and the Family* 50:633-677.

Smith, H. and P. Cutright. 1988. Thinking about Change in Illegitimacy Ratios: United States, 1963-1983. *Demography* 25:235-247.

Sweet, J. and L. Bumpass. 1987. *American Families and Households.* New York, NY: Russell Sage Foundation.

Teachman, J. and K. Paasch. 1994. Financial Impact of Divorce on Children and Their Families. *The Future of Children,* Vol. 4, 1:63-83.

Thompson, R. 1994. The Role of Father After Divorce. *The Future of Children,* Vol. 4, 1:210-235.

U.S. Bureau of the Census. 1993. Current Population Reports, Series P23-185. *Population Profile of the United States: 1993.* Washington, D.C., U.S. Government Printing Office.

U.S. Bureau of the Census. 1994. The Earnings Ladder. A statistical brief.

U.S. Department of Health and Human Services, Administration for Children and Families, Office of Family Assistance. 1992. *Characteristics and Financial Circumstances of AFDC Recipients FY 1991.*

U.S. Department of Labor, Bureau of Labor Statistics. 1994. Unpublished tabulations from the Current Population Survey, 1993 annual averages.

Upchurch, D. M. and J. McCarthy. 1990. The Timing of a First Birth and High School Completion. *American Sociological Review* 55:224-234.

Wallerstein, J. S. and S. Blakeslee. 1989. *Second Chances: Men, Women and Children a Decade After Divorce.* New York, NY: Ticknor and Fields.

Weiss, R. 1979. *Growing Up Fast: Unexpected Social and Economic Consequences for Women and Children in America.* New York, NY: Free Press.

Wilson, W. J. and K. Neckerman. 1986. Poverty and Family Structure the Widening Gap Between Evidence and Public Policy Issues. In S. H. Danziger and D. H. Weinberg, *Fighting Poverty: What works and What Doesn't,* 232-259, Cambridge, MA: Harvard University Press.

Wojtkiewicz, R., S. McLanahan, and I. Garfinkel. 1990. The Growth of Families Headed by Women: 1950-1980. *Demography,* Vol. 27, 1:19-30.

Dorothy V. Harris, *ACSW, LCSW-C, is currently Conference Director for the National Conference on Child Abuse and Neglect. She previously served as Director of the Office for Children and Youth for the State of Maryland and as Consultant to the Commissioner on Child Care Issues for the Social Security Administration. Ms. Harris has published articles and lectured widely on issues related to the well-being of children and families. She was a "Fellow" at the U.S. Department of Health and Human Services and served as National President of the National Association of Social Workers from 1985 to 1987.*

Julie N. Jakopic, *is a sociology graduate student at the University of Maryland with concentrations in family demography and social psychology. Professionally, she is the Research Analyst for a national association of state directors of anti-poverty programs. Ms. Jakopic previously served as the Program Director for crisis and child abuse and neglect programs for D.C. Hotline, Inc., and as the Program Director of Job Connection, an employment project for people with disabilities of the Epilepsy Foundation for the National Capitol Area.*

The authors wish to thank Jean Swift, MSW, who provided editorial assistance, Carol Hanrahan and Kristen Hagy for overall proofing for accuracy.

POVERTY IN THE AFRICAN-AMERICAN COMMUNITY: PERSPECTIVES AND APPROACHES

RICHARD L. JONES, PH.D.
President & Chief Executive Officer
Center for Families and Children

The family, it is agreed, has enormous potential for affecting the quality of life for its members. However, if its members are caught in the grips of poverty and are also African-American, the family faces incredible challenges in attempting to carry out its roles and responsibilities. The question which will be explored in this discussion is, "How can our society increase the urban poor African-American family's capacity for effectively carrying out its role, while concurrently aiding in its efforts to become a self-sufficient and productive social unit?"

Three basic assumptions will guide this discussion. First, it is recognized that many conditions faced by urban poor African-Americans are less a function of personality traits and group membership, and more a direct result of a rapidly changing economy, the continual presence of institutionalized racism, ineffective and inadequate social policies, and an urban educational system which is in desperate need of total reform. Second, while many African-American families are struggling, and some are failing in their attempts to carry out their roles, resulting in a generation of children and youth who are ill prepared to assume their future roles as contributing and productive citizens of our society, there are still many African-Americans who are succeeding and successfully overcoming the odds. Third, many poor African-American families can achieve positive outcomes in their lives through appropriate governmental participation, or social policy initiatives and other forms of family intervention.

THE IMPACT OF POVERTY ON FAMILIES

Poverty continues to place great restrictions on the lives of many African-Americans and is showing signs of growth. Though African-Americans represent 31 million individuals, or 12% of the total U.S. population, they tend to be disproportionately represented on measures which suggest that a large percentage of this population is facing precarious social and economic conditions. Thirty-three percent (33%) of all African-Americans are affected by poverty, while that rate remains 11.6% for the majority group.[1] For children, that rate is much higher. In 1970, one in five children, or 20% of all children were growing up in poor families. In 1991, this number had climbed to one in four, while if these children are minority, the rate is one in two or fifty (50) percent. Reflecting the low earnings and income of their families, in 1991 more children under six lived in families receiving food stamps, unemployment insurance, and welfare benefits, than in 1990.[2] Poverty is continuing to grow and showing no signs of abatement. Recently, *The Cleveland Plain Dealer* reported that the percentage of people living in poverty in 1993 climbed to 16%, up from 15.4% in the previous year. Poverty was higher among racial minorities, single-parent households and the less educated.[3]

Though the African-American family continues to restructure itself in the face of rapidly changing economic and social conditions, particular family structures seem to increase the likelihood of some families slipping into poverty. The bread winner-homemaker model of the family with husband and wife raising their own biological or adopted children was once the dominant family pattern, but now represents fewer than 12% of all families in the United States today. While the vast majority of African-American households are family households (that is, the household members are related by birth, marriage, or adoption), only about half the families were headed by a married couple in 1990, down from 68 percent in 1970 and 56 percent in 1980. These trends profoundly affect all members of the urban African-American community: men, women, youth, and the elderly, and most dramatically, children. The population of African-American children living with two parents declined from 58 percent in 1970 to 38% in 1990.[4]

Family structure is an important determinant of economic status and quality of life, although different factors influence the economic well-being of some families as opposed to others. Married couples and male maintained families are more likely to become poor as the result of factors associated with business cycles, where as the higher poverty rate among households maintained by women is affected by economic conditions.[5] Family structure becomes significant because of its association with poverty. Families headed by single parents are more likely to be poor. The poverty rate for female headed households is 44%, more than six times the rate for married couple households (7.2%). For African-American female household heads the rate increases to 61.5%.[6]

Poverty in and of itself can have a devastating impact on the life of every family member because of its high correlation with poor health, limited education, homelessness and hopelessness. In other words, poverty can result in the generation of a number of factors which can place members of the family "at risk." Poor children are at greater risk of negative lifetime outcomes than are those in more affluent families. Abundant evidence documents that poor children are at greater risk for health problems, school failure, delinquency, early child-bearing, and adult poverty. Most poor households are not very good nurturing, protecting, and learning systems. When parents are unable to respond sensitively to their infants' needs because of such factors as marital conflicts, depression, or their own history of abuse, the infant develops feelings of helplessness that lead to later difficulties. When children had two or more risk factors, they were four times as likely to develop social and academic problems.[7]

Communities with high concentrations of the poor are also struggling with other social issues, including community and family violence, social isolation, alcohol and chemical dependency, and high rates of unemployment. Murders and other violent crimes rose 16% in 1990 in cities with populations greater than 500,000. Factors contributing to the nation's high homicide rate include the drug epidemic, poverty, and the rising level of violence on television. While criminal gang membership is growing, gang growth is spreading by gender with more, larger and increasingly violent female gangs.[8] Violence continues to grow in our communities at an alarming rate, taking a significant toll on the lives of many of our future leaders, teachers, and civil rights advocates. In 1990, African-Americans were 41% and Hispanic-Americans 32% more likely than Whites to be victims of violent crime.[9]

PERSPECTIVES ON POVERTY

Many writers have offered their analysis and/or perspective accounting for those factors which result in high concentrations of chronic and persistent poverty in many parts of the African-American community. There are as many theories as there are social issues, each offering some insight into our understanding of the various dimensions of poverty.

Cornell West, in his book *Race Matters*, argues "the major enemy of blacksurvival in America has been the threat of nihilism," which he defines as loss of hope and the absence of meaning.[10] Others argue that many of these problems are directly attributable to internalized oppression and institutionalized racism. Derrick Bell suggests that a crucial part of each of us, White and Black, will be lost at the bottom of the well as long as racism remains a pillar of American society.[11] There are many who would argue that we know what to do, while others argue that poverty can be explained by inadequate parenting and broken families. More recently, there are renewed attempts to account for the "so called broken family" in terms of the collapse of "community" and the very institutions which are designed to serve families.

STRATEGIES FOR APPROACHING POVERTY

It's argued that chronic and persistent poverty can be addressed through the implementation of a comprehensive multi-faceted strategy which: (1) supports and strengthens the natural helping systems existing in all communities; (2) sustains effective family intervention strategies which have been validated through research; (3) and finally encompasses and implements social policies which are supportive of family centered communities. Each of these strategies working as a collective whole can help increase the likelihood of "protective factors" that help children and families to achieve positive outcomes in their lives. Each of these will be explored in the following material.

A) Community Empowerment

In approaching the resolution of poverty, it is important that we fully recognize that "the community" in which people live offers tremendous potential for serving as one of the key protective factors which can limit risks and influence the difference between good and poor outcomes. Self-help and other forms of community initiatives represent important traditions which have played key roles in the survival of the African-American community both past and present. Until the 1960's, African-American families depended almost exclusively on informal social-support systems or mutual-aid networks for primary and secondary goods and services. According to McCray, it was this "sense of caring and social responsibility in the African-American community, plus strong kinship bonds and other reinforcements that kept Black families together and strengthened their functioning."[12] Jewell argues that many enacted social policies diminished the important role which mutual-aid networks assumed and therefore weakened an important aspect of the African-American community.[13] Though there often appears to be a significant focus on the challenges facing African-American communities, self-development efforts have been underway for years in African-American communities and have shown signs of accelerating in the 1990s.[14] The loss of hope and absence of meaning in life described by West can be rekindled when the institutions which constitute the infrastructure of a community are valued, supported and nurtured in a way which allows them to respond to the needs of the very people they are designed to serve.

The Cleveland Community Building Initiative has used the "community" or community empowerment model as an organizing framework for the creation of approaches to geographical areas which are characterized by high concentrations of poverty in many of Cleveland central city areas.[15] Two of the underlying principles of this approach, which is often referred to as "village based development," are the recognition that low-income or at-risk communities offer assets and capacities which can be utilized for the benefit of the total community; and furthermore, that many of the problems generated by poverty are interlocking or interrelated, thus necessitating a strategy which is broad based and inclusive of many systems such as economic development, education, and health care. Similar models are emerging throughout the country. For example, in Boston, Massachusetts, the Urban League is working with the Efficacy Institute to develop and implement the African American Self-Development program.[16] Many social scientists have contributed to the development of this revised community framework, including William Julius Wilson, John McKnight, and Jeffery Howard, to name a few. It is agreed, however, that "a sense of community" has represented an important survival mechanism in the African-American community and again is being rediscovered as renewed efforts are made to find new ways of nurturing and strengthening indigenous resources like churches, schools, and local businesses to not only support the family, but also to serve as a key strategy in the fight against poverty.

When a sense of community is absent, many factors associated with poverty can be observed, including the absence of social cohesion, the prevalence of social isolation for many poor communities, and all too often a higher incidence of crime and other non-productive activities which only serve to further place the community in at-risk conditions. Far too often many of the poor find themselves isolated from other economic groups who could potentially serve as important role models and contributors to a community's tax base. Though the absence of social cohesion can have a devastating effect on the entire community, the youngest members of the community are particularly hard hit. Social disorganization with urban poverty can lead to low birth weight, child abuse and neglect among children. Researchers have found that social isolation not only deprives parents of crucial resources, it also limits access to the kinds of cultural learning and positive role models that can help them cope better at home and in school.

The erosion of community organizations has left children more vulnerable to a variety of hazards, including drug and alcohol addiction, violence, crime, and teen pregnancy. Of course, the erosion of a sense of community is not restricted to low-income or African-American families. The dispersal of the extended family, greater geographic mobility, smaller family sizes, and the increased labor-force participation of women, have all reduced the amount of time that women and other family members have to participate in the community organizations that once helped parents develop their children and themselves.

According to Wilson's research cited in the Cleveland Community Building Initiative Report, there is a strong correlation between the weakening of neighborhood-based institutions and the rise of neighborhood crime and other social problems.[17] However, the converse is also true based on preliminary findings of behaviors observed in communities which have adopted a village development program. Recently, one of the principal investigators for the Commission reported that crime had been reduced by as much as 30% in neighborhoods embracing the village concept. This was very encouraging news.

Other research can also be cited further supporting the notion that when a greater sense of community is achieved, positive changes can result in many parts of the community. For example, a family's effectiveness as a child-rearing system is bolstered by the existence of a supportive social network. A study conducted by the Child and Family Neighborhood Program provided a variety of resources that supported parents' child-rearing efforts. When parents are more connected to other families in the community, network resources reduced the probability of certain mental and physical illnesses and larger networks had a positive effect on parents' ability to deal with stress, or mothers' perception of themselves and their children, or fathers' involvement in child-rearing, and on children's self-esteem and school success.[18]

B) Economic Development and Self Help
Though strengthened community networks represent an integral component of any comprehensive approach directed toward poverty, this strategy must be further enhanced with the adoption of social policies which lead to economic development and job training and employment opportunities for neighborhood residents. Since poverty is clearly in a long-range upward trend, particularly in African-American communities, breaking that trend will take concerted efforts at both the national and local level. The negative poverty trend is supported by state cutbacks in assistance to the poor, eroding wages and blue-collar job opportunities, and limited work opportunities for single-parent family heads.[19]

Public policy in the 1990's should focus on the economic revitalization of inner cities and the provision of training and employment opportunities. Trends around the country are suggesting that economic revitalization efforts are concentrated on regional targets, many of which are missing serving the residents of inner city neighborhoods grappling with chronic poverty. This trend is corroborated by the Cleveland Community Building Initiative Report which noted that between the first quarter of 1989 and the first quarter of 1991, Cleveland was to lose some 18,500 jobs, while suburban areas of Cuyahoga County gained 7,100 jobs and nearby Lake and Geauga Counties, more than 10,000 jobs and approximately 500 business establishments. Of the 980 jobs to be created in Cleveland 730 will be created in the suburbs.[20]

Social policy development must also complement the self-help efforts underway throughout African-American communities across the country. Building on a long-standing tradition in the African-American community, though self-help efforts are accelerating, they will require additional funding if they are to be sustained. In Oakland, California, Safe Streets Now! is an innovative, low-cost and efficient program designed to eliminate drug houses. In Pittsburgh, Pennsylvania, Crawford Square is a new housing development located in a historically African-American neighborhood known as "the Hill." To date, more than 140 rental units have been built, while many single-family, detached homes are also under construction.[21] Developments such as these can be found in many urban centers like Cleveland, Ohio and Washington, D.C. Community investment initiatives should take the form of financing worker-owned businesses and self-help activities undertaken by the church. The African-American church represents another significant institution which has also taken a very active role in the self-help movement. *The Wall Street Journal* featured a number of church-sponsored initiatives in a January 1993 article entitled, *More Black Churches Go Into Business*. One of the most successful projects was undertaken by the Greater Christ Temple Church in Meridian, Mississippi. Ninety-six (96%) of the congregation was on public welfare before the start of an ambitious program launched by the church minister. A food co-op was organized among the church membership, which eventually began running a grocery store out of the basement auditorium of the church. After four months, the members had earned enough money to purchase a supermarket. Today, the church owns a 4,000-acre farm, seven tractors, and an auto repair shop. More importantly, none of its members are on welfare because of employment opportunities which have been generated through the church.

The national Urban League has proposed that because of the seriousness of the "economic depression" which is currently facing the

African-American community that job creation must become a top national priority in 1994. In fact, the Urban League has gone a step further and proposed the development of a Marshall Plan which would include an annual investment of 50 billion dollars to revitalize and develop urban communities.

Government participation in the development, funding, and enforcement of social and economic programs is not only important, but essential if African-American families are to successfully move out of poverty. There is a clear need for more urban policies, such as the commitment which is being made to the creation of Enterprise and Empowerment Zones. The argument is made that there are many hopeful signs of positive developments occurring in urban centers struggling with poverty across the country.

These developments must be supported through public and private expenditures and public policies, which can do much to help strengthen families and to help families become self-supporting and self-sufficient.

C) Family Intervention Programs

The third strategy proposed for addressing poverty includes the continuation and expansion of programs which have demonstrated positive effects in reversing some of the negative behaviors observed in parent-child interactions. Social scientists have validated the fact that the quality of interaction occurring between parents and their children can make the difference between good and poor outcomes. A well-functioning family during the first few years provides a particularly important building block for healthy development. There is clear evidence that well-designed childhood education programs can produce positive results. The best-known study, the Perry Project, which has tracked a group of children for over 20 years, clearly documents the kinds of success which can be made by children if they are given appropriate support, learning opportunities, and interventions. After completing a specialized program, the research shows that these children performed better in classrooms, were less likely to be retained a grade, and were less likely to be placed in special education classes than were similar students who did not participate in the preschool programs. More than 67% of program participants graduated from high school compared with 49% of the control group.[22] Careful evaluation of the benefits of the Perry Pre-School Project indicated that benefits outweighed costs by 7 to 1.[23] Well-planned interventions to help poor children and their parents cope with developmental problems can produce positive outcomes. These interventions can help overcome a cluster of factors associated with severely disadvantaged parents, including "a sense that one has little capacity to shape the events in one's life, low self-esteem, and little perception of opportunities."[24]

In summary, though poverty creates multiple-risk factors which can lead to negative outcomes for parents and children, it is important to recognize that these outcomes are not inevitable and can be overcome by parental actions and constructive social and economic policies. Poverty in the African-American community can be reduced through the development and implementation of a three-prong strategy, which includes initiatives which strengthen institutions comprising the social and economic infrastructure; the implementation of social policies which are supportive of family-centered communities and result in the generation of jobs and training programs; and finally, sustaining effective family intervention strategies which have been validated by research.

FOOTNOTES

[1] The National Black Child Development Institute, *The National Black Child Advocate*, (1994), Volume 21, No. 1, p. 13.

[2] The National Center for Children in Poverty, *News and Issues*, Fall 1993, Vol. 3, p. 1.

[3] *The Cleveland Plain Dealer*, "Number of Ohioans in Poverty Climbs On," July 26, 1994, p. 1.

[4] Henderson, Leneal S., *African Americans in the Urban Milieu: Conditions, Trends, and Development Needs* in the State of Black America 1994, Tidwell, Billy (Ed) New York, New York: National Urban League, p. 17.

[5] Marshall, Ray. *The State of Families, 3: Losing Direction, Families, Human Resource Department, and Economic Performance*, Milwaukee, WI: Family Service America, 1991, p. 28.

[6] *Ibid*, p. 31.

[7] *Starting Points, Meeting the Needs of Our Youngest Children*, Carnegie Corporation of New York, April 1994, p. 14.

[8] *1994 Environmental Scan*, Strategic Planning Process, Milwaukee, WI: Family Service America, 1994, p. 8.

[9] *Youth Violence Prevention: A Review of the Literature*, Cleveland, Ohio; Center for Families and Children, 1994, p. 2.

[10] West, Cornell. *Race Matters*, Boston: Beacon Press, 1993.

[11] Bell, Derrick. *Faces at the Bottom of the Well,* New York: Basic Book, 1992.

[12] McCray, Carrie Allen. "The Black Woman and Family Roles" in *the Black Woman in LA Frances Rodgers* - Rose (Ed.) Beverly Hills, California: Sage Publications, p. 17.

[13] Jewell, K. Sue. *Survival of the Black Family,* New York: Praeger Press, 1988.

[14] *Ibid,* National Urban League, *State of Black America,* 1994, p. 7.

[15] *The Cleveland Community - Building Initiative, the Report and Recommendations of the Cleveland Foundation Commission Poverty,* Cleveland, Ohio: Mandel School of Applied Social Sciences, Case Western Reserve University, 1992.

[16] Wallace-Benjamin, Joan. *Organizing African-American Self Development: the Role of Community-Based Organizations, in the State of Black America,* 1994, Tidwell, Billy Ph.D (Ed) New York, New York: National Urban League, p. 189.

[17] *Ibid, Cleveland Community Building Initiative Report,* p. 19.

[18] *Ibid, Starting Points: Meeting the Needs of Our Youngest Children,* p. 17.

[19] *Ibid, State of Black America,* 1994, p. 4.

[20] *Ibid, Cleveland Community Building Initiative Report,* p. 16.

[21] *Ibid, State of Black America,* 1994, p. 22.

[22] Berruetta-Clement, John R.; Schweinhart, Lawrence J.; Barnett, W. Steven; Epstein, Ann S.; and Weikart, David. *Changed Lives: the Effect of the Perry Pre-School Program on Youth through age 19,* (Ypisilanti, MI: High/ Scope Press, 1984).

[23] Barnett, Steven. *The Perry Preschool Program and its Long-Term Effects: A Benefit-Cost Analysis, High/Scope Early Childhood Policy Papers,* No. 2, Ypsilanti, Michigan, 1985.

[24] Hamburg, David. *Early Intervention to Prevent Life Long Damage: Lessons from Current Research,* testimony before the Senate Committee on Labor and Human Resources and the House Committee on Education and Labor, September 9, 1987, p. 16.

 **Richard L. Jones, Ph.D.** *currently serves as President and Chief Executive Officer for the Center for Families and Children, one of the largest private human service agencies in Cleveland, Ohio. Prior to returning to Cleveland in 1991, Dr. Jones served as Senior Vice President of Planning for the United Way of Boston and Executive Director of Boston Children's Services. He currently serves on the board of directors for Leadership Cleveland, American Red Cross, and the Business Volunteerism Council. He also serves as a member of the Visiting Committee for Case Western Reserve University, Co-Chair of the Cleveland 1994 International Year of the Family Committee, and a member of the United Way Services Commission. Dr. Jones completed his M.A. and Ph.D. in social work administration at the Mandel School of Applied Social Sciences at Case Western Reserve University.*

NOBODY'S CHILDREN OR EVERYBODY'S CHILDREN

FLORENCE W. KASLOW, PH.D.
Independent therapist, mediator and family business consultant
West Palm Beach, Florida

"And a woman who held a babe against her bosom said, Speak to us of Children. And he said: Your children are not your children. They are the sons and daughters of Life's longing for itself. They come through you but not from you, And though they are with you yet they belong not to you.

You may give them your love but not your thoughts, For they have their own thoughts. You may house their bodies but not their souls, For their souls dwell in the house of tomorrow, which you cannot visit, not even in your dreams. You may strive to be like them, but seek not to make them like you. For life goes not backward nor tarries with yesterday. You are the bows from which your children as living arrows are sent forth. The archer sees the mark upon the path of the infinite, and He bends you with His might that His arrows may go swift and far. Let your bending in the archer's hand be for gladness; For even as He loves the arrow that flies, so He loves also the bow that is stable."

CHILDREN WHO ARE WANTED AND LOVED

Gibran's (1923) beautiful, sensitive and still timely philosophic poem seems predicated on the assumption that parents naturally may want to be over-protective and over-possessive. Profound phrases like "and though they are with you yet they belong not to you" imply that many adults have difficulty letting their children feel their own feelings and think their own thoughts. The process of individuation may be much harder for children with loving parents who believe they know what's best for their offspring — even when the children become adolescents and young adults ready and willing to make their own decisions and take the risk of making mistakes as part of their own life journey of learning through personal experiences — including trial and error. This Persian poet portrays an image of parents who care a great deal about their children and who may be extremely attached to them as a very central focus of their lives, and therefore may feel rejected or torn asunder when their youngsters are ready to leave home (Haley, 1980). In a few short stanzas, he eloquently conveys the strength and longevity of the parent/child bond and cautions parents not to cling to their children, perhaps even implying they should not live vicariously through them.

There is a supposition that runs throughout all forms of art and literature, across time from Biblical days to the present, and across space — as it seems to be incorporated in all cultures, that a primary function of the family is to bear and rear children. In Ecclesiastes it is said that, "To everything there is a season and a time to every purpose under the heaven." (Holy Bible, 1934, p. 582). That includes "a time to be born" and by implication, to have and raise one's offspring. The Bible also directs readers "to be fruitful and multiply." In popular literature — both fiction and non-fiction, having children is spoken of as a blessed event, eagerly awaited by many couples. Many couples who cannot conceive for a host of physiological and/or psychological reasons go to great lengths and great cost to have their coveted child, including but not limited to: surgery to open blocked tubes, drugs to increase sperm counts and fertility, artificial insemination, use of a surrogate, and adoption (Schwartz, 1991). They cannot bear the idea of going through life without children, and literally will do whatever they must to build a family. The wished for child, when acquired, is perceived as precious and often adored and treated as extra special. This great love and appreciation is what all children are entitled to and need (short of being over-indulged) to develop into loveable human beings with good self esteem. Unfortunately, all too few children in this world have such emotional entitlements bestowed upon them lavishly and lovingly.

Thousands of professional books have been written devoted to parent/child relationships, and many parents take courses to enhance their parenting skills. In the contemporary family literature, theorists/therapists like Bowen (1978) stress the importance of children individuating from their family of origin, while still seeking to maintain ties and rework problems; and Boszormenyi-Nagy & Spark (1973; 1984) stress the importance of family loyalties and childrens' indebtedness to parents. Carter & McGoldrick (1980, page 17) depict six stages in the family life cycle, three of which distinctly center around children: Stage 3 — the family with young children; Stage 4 — the family with adolescents; and Stage 5 — launching children and moving on. Clearly being productive through conceiving, bearing or adopting, loving and raising children is considered by many to be a part of adult healthy generativity and activity.

The parental role and function is also celebrated and glorified in works of art — like madonna and child paintings, and sculptures of families in which members affectionately hold onto one another. Such attention to parenting is lauded with political pronouncements and interventions in numerous countries that provide for social supports when children are born and growing up. The forms vary, and may include paid maternity and sometimes paternity leave; tax deductions for each dependent, or some direct incentive to have children; and the provision of free or very low-cost nurseries and day-care centers. Such programs highlight the avowed importance various societies place on the institution of the family and its continuity for passing on of a positive family legacy and myriad societal, religious and cultural mores and values. Adults whose children do well in school, interpersonal relations and extracurricular activities feel they have "done a good job" in this important arena of their lives, and when their children turn out to be reasonably confident, content and productive members of society, the parents justly feel proud of themselves as well as of the children.

Today, many social analysts and family theoreticians are redefining the family much more broadly than encompassing just the nuclear, two (heterosexual) parents and child unit to include also: single parent families by choice or life circumstance, bi-nuclear post-divorce families (Ahrons & Rodgers, 1987; Kaslow & Schwartz, 1987), remarriage (Sager, et al, 1983) or stepfamilies (Visher & Visher, 1979), extended three or four generation families, and gay or lesbian couples with children from prior relationships or through adoption (Kaslow, 1995). All definitions include some semblance of relationships that entail ongoing commitment, living together in a shared residence, some stability and predictability, and a sense of connectedness to and responsibility for one another. None sanction neglect of the children involved in the family.

Where modern societies, like that in Israel, have experimented with children being reared in a Kibbutz, living in a Gan (nursery or group home) either all day or day and night, the parents are still integrally involved in some daily activities with their children, and they are entrusted to the loving care of a mothering person — the "metapelet." A sibling relationship is fostered between the youngsters in the peer group, and warm, reciprocal bonds encouraged. In the United States, with the proliferation of day-care centers, we are also now seeing an emphasis on peer interaction and as much family involvement as possible.

All societies seem to accept or arrive at the same conclusion — a family environment created by loving parent(s) who have or adopt children because they want them, and who continue to nurture, protect and guide them for as long as necessary is vital to the continuity of the species and of society (Kaslow, 1981; Walsh, 1982). Healthy families are perceived as being cohesive, adaptable and cooperative (Olson, Russell & Sprenkle, 1983) and as not erring too much on the side of being either enmeshed or disengaged/detached (Minuchin, 1974).

UNWANTED CHILDREN

If these are the spoken and written-about objectives and ideals of societies around the world, how strange that what is happening in many countries diverges substantially in reality from these purported ideals and expectations. Given that "children are our future," how did the contemporaneous situation of hordes of "throw away children" emerge? A closer look is warranted. In this section, which takes a global view of the problem, issues are highlighted and short-term as well as long-term "solutions" and pathways are suggested.

BORN UNPLANNED, UNWANTED, AND OFTEN "OUT OF WEDLOCK"

Unfortunately, there are many situations in which children who are unplanned and unwanted are conceived. Their parents, all too often young teenagers, do not think in terms of intercourse as an act of making love and/or that through this activity they are voluntarily bestowing upon an innocent unborn infant "the gift of life," thereby undertaking the responsibilities inherent in parenting as an outcome of their behavior. Rather they act impulsively because of either seeming hormonal imperatives, curiosity, peer pressure, desire to be popular or cool, or a combination of the foregoing. Often no birth control is used and there is either a lack of awareness of the possibility of "having sex" leading to pregnancy or of acquiring a sexually transmitted disease (STD), or the belief in one's invincibility and that "nothing awful will happen to me." If the adolescent girl becomes pregnant from her sexual adventures and she, her parent(s) and/or the putative father is opposed to abortion, she often goes full term and delivers a baby she may be too young, too poor and/or too unwilling or unable to care for. For her parent(s) the baby may be welcome or may constitute an additional unwanted burden. Thousands of the babies born out of such scenarios are either kept and raised unwillingly or haphazardly, and all too often become victims of emotional neglect, physical and/or sexual abuse (Walker, 1988). They may or may not know who their real daddy is. Scores of youngsters are born to moms who have different children with different men so that the half siblings each have a different father. Partially rejected and abandoned by one parent, and often inadequately cared for by the other, ordinarily such children grow up with low self esteem ("If I were more worthwhile, my daddy would not have left;

or my mommy wouldn't have to hit me," etc.) since they are led to believe that whatever is wrong is their fault. They have a continual identity crisis regarding, "Where do I come from and who am I?" and may become so angry and hurt because they are emotionally deprived and/or physically abused that they act out against themselves, their parent(s), and the society that they rightly perceive has been unwelcoming, rejecting and mean to them. Realizing they are unwanted and unloved, they do not become trusting or trustworthy (Erickson, 1963) and often develop various kinds of character disorders, like anti-social and borderline personalities (APA, 1994).

POVERTY

There are a cluster of factors that are intertwined — sometimes all in the same package, simultaneously, sometimes more sequentially, and at times some but not all are present. When a baby is not only unplanned and unwanted, but is conceived by an adolescent, young adult or older woman, who lives at the bottom rung of the socioeconomic scale, poverty and disillusionment can add to her woes, and her anxiety and pessimism can be transmitted to the fetus en utero and/or during the early formative years of the baby's life (Sullivan, 1953). Often the mother has little, if any, pre-natal care and that which she receives can be terribly inadequate. Her baby can be delivered under far below standard conditions, may receive improper medical care and nutrition, and may have an above average risk of birth complications, or of serious illnesses during the first few years of life. To the extent that poverty is often coupled with overcrowded housing, crime-ridden communities, and unsanitary conditions, the child often does not get the consistent loving care in a safe environment that he or she needs to experience a sense of object constancy (Mahler, 1967; Slipp, 1988) and stability.

NEGLECT, ABUSE AND INCEST

Many children born into two-parent intact families, or residing in stepfamilies or families headed by grandparents, or that are not in the lower socioeconomic strata, are also abused. No one group has a monopoly on this behavior. Being treated as if one is invisible or just doesn't matter is devastating for a child's sense of security and confidence and constitutes emotional abuse. If the parenting figure(s) leave a child alone untended, with a very young sibling, or incompetent and disdainful sitter as a caretaker, or disappears when an infant or young child is sleeping and they wake up to find no one there, the worst abandonment fears are not only triggered, but experienced as all too real. No matter how much one can understand a parent's need to go to work or go out and have a good time, it is the belief of this author that when the fundamental needs of the child conflict with the wants of the parent, that the adult must place the child's needs first and arrange for a competent, honest and concerned caretaker before departing. Parenthood entails not only rights, but also myriad responsibilities — and this is certainly one of them. A child's well being, and sometimes even very survival, may be at stake.

Other forms of emotional abuse include constant criticism, put downs, being screamed at, being humiliated, and being told "You can't do anything right," "You'll never amount to anything," "You're stupid," and even "You're nothing but a piece of s---." How distressing it is when we see clients/patients raised with vivid memories of such pejorative statements; for the vast majority these ideas become internalized as negative self statements that they have come to believe and act out. It takes a great deal of contradictory, more positive input from teachers, clergy, scout leaders, therapists and others with whom the child comes in contact for these horrific, demeaning scripts and prophecies to be reversed, and that can only occur if one can dare to be vulnerable to the risk of trusting that they won't be embarrassed, exploited and ultimately rejected.

Incest is another intra-familial degrading violation of babies, young children and adolescents. To some, such behavior is so taboo that it is incomprehensible. And yet, the number of reported cases continues to mount in each decade. Incest occurs whenever one member of the family sexually molests another; the perpetrator may be the mother, father, grandmother or grandfather, aunt or uncle, cousin or sibling. Although sexual activity that crosses generational boundaries is the form most frequently described, sibling and cousin incest, both heterosexual and homosexual occur (Kaslow, Arce, et. al., 1981), and also have devastating and long lasting sequelae and scars (Courtois, 1988; Kirschner, Kirschner & Rappaport, 1993). The exploitation of a youngster to satisfy an older child's sexual curiosity and desires, or an adult's lust, need for power, release, or misguided sexuality is untenable — from the position of the child and of society. It is a noxious and destructive influence on the sanity and sanctity of the family.

Other forms of sexual and physical abuse of children also constitute dysfunctional, even pathological, behaviors and contribute to children becoming deeply distressed (MacFarlane, Waterman, et. al., 1986; Everstine & Everstine, 1989). Over time they may become symptomatic, exhibiting all kinds of fears, anxiety, depression, withdrawal, school failure and/or truancy, anti-social/delinquent and violent behavior in which they have identified with the aggressor(s) and become abusive like him or her (Freud, 1971). As part of a children's bill of rights, being conceptualized and recommended throughout this paper, little ones have a right to be raised free of emotional, physical and sexual abuse, with respect accorded to their need for love, affection, guidance and privacy, and to be given rationally set limits. Erratic, irrational spankings, and other forms of intrusive behavior on a child's body and spirit have no place in a civilized world. And it is abundantly clear that violence begets violence, and the time is now for all concerned professionals, parents and politicians to intercept the vicious cycle of violence (Steinmetz, 1977) so it does not continue to be passed on to successive generations.

While we are doing this, there need to be sufficient 1) "safe houses" and shelters in which abused adults and children can reside until they can live unafraid in the outside world, and 2) programs in which abusers can receive treatment and confront their responsibility for their own explosiveness and how to channel it differently.

ADDICTIVE BEHAVIORS

All too often children are born to parents who are addicted to drugs, alcohol, gambling and other forms of behavior that some hold to be beyond their control (Orford, 1985). These addictions or extreme using behaviors dissipate parents' financial resources (if they have them), consume inordinate amounts of time and energy, divert people from their spousal and parenting roles, and contribute to their acting in inappropriate, ineffective, and often damaging ways. When someone is inebriated or stoned, they may be more prone to uncontrollable violence, and their children may be the innocent victims of their volatility and/or witness it being inflicted on the other parent or a sibling — also a devastating event. Such parents generally instill dread and shame in children (Fossum & Mason, 1986), and are poor role models. When poverty, addiction, and violence all characterize the family, and are also combined with other forms of anti-social and criminal behavior, the child's right to "life, liberty and the pursuit of happiness" is sharply curtailed. His or her behavior must become self-protective for survival. Often the youngster becomes either alienated and detached (turning inward) from other family members and the surrounding neighbors, as interpersonal interactions can be too risky, or, driven by anger and the need to retaliate against those who have been negligent or cruel to him/her and others who have permitted it, the child acts out by either harming self (such as self mutilation, school failure, attempted or completed suicide, their own addictive behaviors, or in anti-social behaviors — such as stealing, rape, car jacking, intimidation, gang warfare, and other forms of delinquent actions). Some of the youngsters respond quite differently and become parentified caretakers who look after their parent(s) and younger siblings. Frequently in an effort to keep peace they become "people pleasers" and sacrifice their right to be a playful child and to be unruly or recalcitrant at times.

THROW AWAY CHILDREN

Throw away children is the term being utilized here to encompass such groups as those children who are left out on the streets to fend for and raise themselves, or die, in cities like Rio de Janeiro, Brazil. These little ones "hang out" together in bands of street urchins, fighting amongst themselves and yet protective of each other to the larger world that has been hostile to them. They scrounge for food, shelter, and everything else — becoming street wise while very young — just to survive. With no one to care for, nurture, or protect them they become tough and hardened. The police often chase them for loitering, preying on passerbys or disturbing the peace. Several years ago U.S. television channels carried stories documenting such children being shot on the streets.

Perhaps the counterpart to the street urchins of Rio in the United States are the myriads of homeless children. Despite the efforts of many homeless parents to maintain some semblance of family life and values in shelters, in underground sewer systems, and on the streets, it is exceedingly difficult to do so over time. In the immediate present we must provide decent housing, job counselling and placement, education, medical care and the economic support necessary to make at least a minimal standard of living, at a safe and stable address, possible.

Another high risk group are children in two kinds of "war zones." One is those in the vast and numerous urban ghettos where gang warfare, rape and sexual molestation, and violent shootings are legion. Children living in such communities often fear going to school or going out to play, and do not experience childhood as a happy time of exploring a safe and beckoning world. Every day may be fraught with fear about their ability and that of their loved ones to survive unharmed. Seeing people they know killed needlessly is tragic and traumatic (Ochberg, 1988). The torturous drama seems never ending.

The other war zones, during the past five years, have been in places like Rowanda, Haiti, Bosnia and Croatia. Children see people brutally beaten and shot in the streets by the police and the military; they themselves may be the recipients of brutality. Not only do they witness there terrible occurrences on the streets where they live, but often they lose one or both parents in the street fighting or in their active duty role in the armed forces. Sadly, not only do those children living in countries torn by civil strife and efforts at "ethnic cleansing" or war with other countries have to contend with the shock and dehumanization of viewing this dark side of human beings en vivo, they often are further traumatized by the maiming or loss of significant extended family members, and seeing their whole personal world disintegrate. This is a shock from which it is difficult to recuperate. And who is there to help them make sense of what seems inexplicable, barbaric, and totally disruptive — particularly if their parents are taken as prisoners of war or killed?

Although the actual impact on youngsters who see wartime violence that occurs in distant countries only on the TV screens in their living rooms daily — as during the Persian Gulf War— may not be as great as it is on those who live through it daily, the fact of exposure to such brutal killing fields, and that it enters their own homes via TV, can still be devastating. With continued exposure to such behavior, the sense of fear and revulsion may diminish and the child may build up an indifference as he or she comes to see murder as an everyday occurrence over which he or she has no control and to which adults seem indifferent. This dissipates one's willingness and ability to get involved in causes and efforts designed to end street crime, domestic violence and war.

Although there are numerous other trends that merit inclusion, space constraints limit the extent of this descriptive analysis of forces that produce neglected, rejected, and abandoned children. But three other compelling situations demand inclusion. In countries as distant as Peru and Poland, Bosnia and Rumania, hordes of children end up in orphanages, either because their parents have voluntarily disappeared or been abducted, because they have given up all parenting endeavors, or because they have died. Many of these children are adoptable and we, as responsible professionals in the family sphere, need to see that placements for adoption are expedited. One can make a case, as has been done by some, that children should be placed with parents of similar racial, ethnic, cultural and religious background. However, when potential parents who match on all of these demographic variables are not available for the surfeit of children requiring homes, then one can make a compelling argument that any reasonably mentally healthy, physically and financially capable and emotionally willing couple or individual should be able to adopt into biracial, multicultural, and interfaith families. It is this author's belief that the ability to love and care on a sustained basis is the overriding variable to be considered.

Each year a number of infanticides occur in the United States probably mostly because a mother is suffering from post-partum depression and cannot tolerate her baby's cries and demands, and in some other lands where female babies are devalued and therefore killed so that the couple can try again to have a boy child. We must all cooperate to see that killing of babies after birth does not loom as the only viable option for despairing women.

MORE INNOCENT VICTIMS

One more exigency that merits attention is that of disasters such as floods, massive fires, earthquakes, hurricanes, and airplane crashes. When parent(s) are killed suddenly by such occurrences, children are inundated by grief, loss and other traumatic shock reactions (Saylor, 1993). Each local, state and national government needs to have emergency procedures and personnel ready in case of such disasters, so the wounds to the children are minimized and they do not become long-term casualties.

SUMMATION

All of the foregoing has been written from the perspective that:

• Needs of children are paramount;

• Since infants are born not only as citizens of their country of origin, but of the entire world, we are all intertwined in our collective responsibility;

• When the needs of children and parents conflict and are deemed "irreconcilable" by the parent(s) or by knowledgeable and sensitive, concerned representatives of society, the needs and rights of children take precedence over those of the adults — particularly when their behaviors have violated doctrines of the "best interest of the child";

• That all health professionals and school personnel, social welfare agency staff members, as well as attorneys and judges involved in child abuse and neglect cases and child custody imbroglios have a child protection and advocacy function to perform;

• That we actively promote family planning activities and parenting classes;

• That we help solicit high quality foster and adoptive homes and provide financial incentives to those who need the remuneration and higher status to take on these difficult roles so quality placements are available when needed;

- That we create child friendly and safe communities and school systems;

- That we open our hearts and homes to those who have been "nobody's children"

Such situations as those alluded to above are appalling and incomprehensible — yet they do exist. When we stop closing our eyes and denying the reality of such untenable situations as this, we are compelled to address such questions as:

- How do we change social systems — including the families and schools that comprise them — to socialize their young people in ways that would mitigate against irresponsible sexual behavior and to realize the long-term consequences and responsibilities inherent in the act of conception?

- Why do people who are either unwilling and/or unable to take care of children have them?

- What are the social and family policy implications of anti-abortion positions? How do we hold those who take the stance that one must give the unborn fetus the right to life accountable for their stance by making certain that once these unwanted children are born, these right-to-lifers help provide the homes, parenting and financial wherewithal to raise these children? The life to be protected is also after delivery and this should not be left to vague platitudes such as 'God will provide," and move rapidly toward ensuring:

- That all communities and the larger states/nations they comprise make and fulfill a commitment to take care of the children nobody wants as well as those, who because of dire circumstances, such as war and other disasters, are orphaned. Instead of there being "nobody's children" anywhere, they must become everybody's children everywhere. Individuals and couples wanting children should be screened and "ready," and then tapped to adopt such children as soon as they become available, and procedures should be simplified to speed the process and not add any additional trauma to the child's life. When this is not possible, top quality foster homes for children should be ready as reception centers, and the transition into such small group residences made as easy and pleasant as possible. The third option is a larger institutional setting or, for older children who need it, a residential treatment center, boarding or military school. In all of these settings, children need to have their basic needs for food, clothing, shelter, affection, individualization, emotional and physical health care met. They need to be provided with a good education, good study and work habits, treated respectfully and taught to respect and be considerate of peers and adults. They should be taught and expected to engage in age appropriate tasks of self care and contributing to family or group living activities and responsibilities. But, they should not be abused, exploited, humiliated or demeaned.

Only when all societies accept as urgent to all of our humanity and to the fostering of world peace that at the most profound level "all children are everybody's children" when they are cast out and in need of loving care, can we consider ourselves capable of making heart connections and worthy of being considered civilized. We must try to ensure that all children receive at least some of the emotional, educational, social and financial benefits that the fortunate children described in the first part of this chapter do, as each one is precious and "deserving."

REFERENCES

Ahrons, C. R. & Rodgers, R. H. (1987). *Divorced families: A multi-disciplinary developmental view.* New York: W. W. Norton.

American Psychiatric Association (1994). *Diagnostic & Statistical Manual of Mental Disorders IV.* Washington, D.C.: APA.

Boszormenyi-Nagy, I. & Spark, G. (1973). *Invisible loyalties.* New York: Harper & Row. (Reprinted 1984 – New York: Brunner/Mazel).

Bowen, M. (1978). *Family therapy in clinical practice.* New York: Aronson.

Carter, E. & McGoldrick, M. (Eds.) (1980). *The family life cycle.* New York: Gardner Press.

Courtois, C. A. (1988). *Healing the incest wounds: Adult survivors in therapy.* New York: Norton.

Erikson, E. H. (1963). *Childhood and society* (2nd edition). New York: Norton.

Everstine, D. S. & Everstine, L. (1989). *Sexual trauma in children and adolescents.* New York: Brunner/Mazel.

Fossum, M. A. & Mason, M. J. (1986). *Facing shame: Families in recovery.* New York: Norton.

Freud, A. (1971). *The ego and the mechanisms of defense.* New York: International Universities Press. (Revised Edition of Writings of Anna Freud, Vol. II, 1936).

Gibran, K. (1923). *The prophet*. New York: Knopf. (1975 edition), 15-16.

Haley, J. (1980). *Leaving home: The therapy of disturbed young people*. New York: McGraw Hill.

Holy Bible (1934). King James Version. Edinburgh: William Collins, Sons & Co., Ltd.

Kaslow, F. W. (1981). Profile of the healthy family. *Interaction, 4,* (1/2), 1-15; and in *The Relationship,* (1982), 8, (1), 9-24.

Kaslow, F. W. (1995). *Families and family psychology in the 21st century*. Submitted for publication.

Kaslow, F. W., Haupt, D., Arce, A. A. & Werblowsky, J. (1981). Homosexual incest. *Psychiatric Quarterly, 53,* (3), 184-193.

Kirschner, S., Kirschner, D. A. & Rappapor, R. (1993). *Working with adult incest survivors*. New York: Brunner/Mazel.

MacFarlane, K., Waterman, J., with Conerly, S., Damon, L., Durfee, M. & Long, S. (1986). *Sexual abuse of young children*. New York: Guilford.

Mahler, M. (1967). On human symbiosis and the vicissitudes of individuation. *Journal of the American Psychoanalytic Association, 15,* 10-67.

Minuchin, S. (1974). *Families and family therapy*. Cambridge: Harvard University Press.

Ochberg, F. W. (Ed.) (1988). *Post traumatic therapy and victims of violence*. New York: Brunner/Mazel.

Olson, D. H., Russell, C. & Sprenkle, D. H. (1983). Circumplex model VI: Theoretical update. *Family Process, 22,* 69-83.

Sager, C. J., Brown, H. S., Crohn, H., Engel, T., Rodstein, E. & Walker, L. (1983). *Treating the remarried family*. New York: Brunner/Mazel.

Saylor, C. F. (1993). *Children and disasters*. New York: Plenum.

Schwartz, L. L. (1991). *Alternatives to infertility: Is surrogacy the answer?* New York: Brunner/Mazel.

Slipp, S. (1988). *The technique and practice of object relations family therapy*. New York: Jason Aronson.

Steinmetz, S. K. (1977). *The cycle of violence: Assertive, aggressive and abusive family interaction*. New York: Praeger.

Sullivan, H. S. (1953). *The interpersonal theory of psychiatry.* New York: Norton.

Visher, E. B. & Visher, J. S. (1979). *Stepfamilies: A guide to working with stepparents and stepchildren.* New York: Brunner/Mazel.

Walker, L. E. A. (1988). *Handbook of sexual abuse of children.* New York: Springer.

Walsh, F. (1982). *Normal family processes.* New York: Guilford.

Florence W. Kaslow, Ph.D. *is in independent practice as a therapist, mediator and family business consultant in West Palm Beach, Florida. She is a Director of the Florida Couples and Family Institute; an Adjunct Professor of Medical Psychology, Department of Psychiatry at Duke University Medical School in North Carolina, and a Visiting Professor of Psychology at Florida Institute of Technology in Melbourne, Florida. Dr. Kaslow is a past Editor of the Journal of Marital and Family Therapy and is currently on the editorial board of JMFT, as well as almost two dozen other journals. She is editor of the Family Law Issues in Family Therapy Practice section of the American Journal of Family Therapy. Since 1973 Dr. Kaslow has been a consultant to various Departments of Psychiatry of the U.S. Navy and Air Force, training residents and other mental health personnel in understanding and treating military families. Some of this work is reflected in her books, "Military Family Dynamics and Treatment," co-edited with Admiral Richard Ridenour, M.D. (1984), and "The Military Family in Peace and War" (1993). She has a Ph.D. from Bryn Mawr College.*

Low-Income African-American Families: A Child's Perspective

NADINE J. KASLOW, PH.D.
Emory University School of Medicine

SONYA BURGESS ROWLAND
Georgia State University

SUSAN ELLIS CHANCE
Georgia State University

We are child-oriented family therapists and researchers working in the Southeast, in an urban, general hospital that serves a primarily low socioeconomic status, African-American population. In being charged with the task of articulating the root causes of the disintegration of the American family, we decided to focus upon the families with whom we work most closely. We realized that our views are biased by our cultural and socioeconomic status, which differentiate us in key ways from the families who are the focus of this chapter. Specifically, the first author was raised in an upper middle class, Caucasian Jewish family in the Northeast; the second author, who was raised in a low-income housing project, is a well-educated African American whose husband is a successful professional and a minister and whose children attend private school; and, the third author grew up in an upper middle class, traditional, southern White Anglo Saxon Protestant (WASP) family. Thus, despite our commitment to providing quality mental health services to underserved and underprivileged African-American families, our experiential understanding of their lives is limited. Given our limitations, we decided that rather than review the literature regarding the complex interplay of factors associated with the disintegration of low-income African-American families, we would offer the perspective of the children.

Children are our focus, as their well-being is central to the development of the family and the survival of the culture (Wilson, 1989) and they are the family members whose development is impeded most by the stresses associated with urban poverty and racial oppression. To glean the perspective of children, we conducted semi-structured interviews with youth receiving services at the hospital. Twenty-five 7-16 year olds, including 15 females and 10 males, were in the sample. These youth assumed a systemic, rather than linear, perspective in understanding those factors associated with family disintegration. They appreciated the variability of African-American families, both within a particular social strata and across socioeconomic classes (e.g., Coner-Edwards & Spurlock, 1988). This paper shares the children's comments and quotes, and integrates their thoughts and feelings with the relevant clinical and theoretical literature and burgeoning and increasingly sophisticated body of empirical work (Taylor, Chatters, Tucker, & Lewis, 1990).

FAMILY STRENGTHS

Prominent writers underscore the importance of attending to the strengths of African-American families, assets crucial in the struggle for survival and that must be built upon to improve the quality of family life (e.g., Billingsley, 1968; Boyd-Franklin, 1989; Farley & Allen, 1987; Gibbs & Huang, 1989; Hill, 1972; McAdoo, 1988; Staples & Johnson, 1993; Wilson & Tolson, 1990). Typical family strengths enumerated in the literature include: kin-structure network, strong work and achievement orientations, adaptability of family roles, strong religious and moral values, a sense of optimism and determination, and resilient children. Attention to these characteristic African-American family strengths has led to the development of nondeficit models that emphasize resilient and adaptive family features and culturally relativistic views regarding the functioning of African-American families.

The youth interviewed were articulate and proud as they portrayed the strengths of their families. In answer to the question, what do you like best about your family, the children responded with pride, "all of the people in the family who give me lots of love." One 13-year-old female remarked, "we love each other, we go places, we have fun." Another 8-year-old female commented, "when I get hurt, they always come to see about me." Children indicated that they liked "doing things together and playing together," "going places together," and "having fun times." They appreciate when their family members do not argue and fight and when they get along well.

Kinship network. Many children spoke about the availability of their extended family network and the importance of kinship support. They underscored the complicated arrangements and cooperation that enable relatives and friends to share resources and responsibilities. A 12-year-old male who lives with his "grandparents, mother, uncle, and uncle's girlfriend" and holds a part-time job at a neighborhood grocery store, reported that he and his grandfather are responsible for family chores. A 9-year-old male, who lives with his grandmother, two aunts, cousin, four brothers, and one sister indicated that everyone who resides in the apartment helps with chores.

These children's appreciation of kinship relations is consistent with the literature that highlights the importance of blood kin and non-blood kin in providing support and help (e.g., Billingsley, 1968; Hill, 1972; Shimkin, Shimkin, & Frate, 1978; Wilson, 1989; Wilson & Tolson, 1990), and the high incidence of co-residential arrangements among African-American families, particularly low-income and single-parent families (Wilson & Tolson, 1990). Additionally, research reveals an association between strong kinship support, psychosocial adjustment, and adaptive coping with stress in adolescents (Taylor, Casten, & Flickinger, 1993). Similarly, African-American teenage mothers who receive help and support from extended family members exhibit more effective parenting behavior and more adaptive psychosocial adjustment (e.g., Crockenberg, 1981; Stevens, 1984). Further, data suggest that grandmothers' involvement in childcare may influence positively the socialization of the developing child of a teenage mother (Tinsley & Parke, 1984). Despite the fact that not all studies find positive effects of multigenerational households for the parenting of children (Chase-Lansdale, Brooks-Gunn, & Zamsky, 1994), taken together it appears that the extended network helping system, with its origins in the helping tradition dating back to times in Africa and American slavery, enhances the quality of African-American life (e.g., Martin & Martin, 1985).

Work ethic, optimism, and determination. Many children interviewed were cognizant of how hard family members work to accomplish all requisite tasks, underscoring the legacy of family members evidencing courage in overcoming obstacles. They indicated that their families were skilled in handling adversity. This is consistent with data indicating that African-American families appear better able than their European-American counterparts to deal with hardship due to higher self-worth and lower depression levels (Pickett, Vraniak, Cook, & Cohler, 1993).

Education and employment. Although the literature emphasizes the importance placed upon education, this was not directly noted by the children. However, implicit in their wishes for the future were desires to achieve goals requiring education. Many identified the college they wished to attend. One 16-year-old ninth grader stated that one of his wishes was for a "high school education." He did not want a Graduate Equivalency Diploma (GED), wanting to attend a reputable college and become a "writer, and if not, a basketball player." Many youth noted the careers they were interested in pursuing, such as law, medicine, nursing, education, hair and clothes design, sports, and music. Most of these careers involve advanced training, and the majority of the youth were confident they could achieve their career aspirations. Although the children and adolescents plan to continue their education, some expressed concern about doing so. A 14-year-old claimed, "I want to finish school without getting pregnant."

Religious and moral values. A high value is placed upon spirituality, religion, and morals. The Church and its members are important elements of the support network and a resource to children and families (Gillum, Gomez-Marin, & Prineas, 1984; Taylor & Chatters, 1988). Unfortunately, no direct questions were asked regarding the children's view of the role of the Church in family life. However, some children commenting on solutions to family problems, felt that prayer would be helpful. One 8-year-old girl said, "we prayed and our family got better."

FACTORS ASSOCIATED WITH FAMILY DISINTEGRATION

According to the children and adolescents, family disintegration is interwoven inextricably with a number of familial and sociocultural difficulties. Primary family problems noted were communication difficulties, concerns about the well-being of parental figures, and fears about separation of family members. The sociocultural issues the youth expressed most concern about were safety and violence, substance abuse, poverty, and the consequences of high-risk sexual behavior. These variables will be discussed in a manner consistent with the priorities articulated by the youth. Certain variables noted in the literature (e.g., racism) were not directly considered problems by the children interviewed, and thus are not discussed in detail.

FAMILY CONCERNS

Many of the children indicated that their primary caretaker was either their mother or their grandmother and that they had limited contact with their biological father. Some expressed significant concern regarding their mother's or grandmother's well-being. One 14-year-old female remarked, "I worry about my Mom when she doesn't come home when she's supposed to and doesn't call." An 8-year-old female stated, "I worry about my grandmother because she had a stroke." As one child poignantly stated and expressed the sentiment for many of the children, "I worry that my mother will die." Some youth expressed dissatisfaction with residing in environments without their father. One 9-year-old female said, "My wish is to live with my Dad. I want my entire family to live together." A lot of the children expressed concerns about their family breaking up. Some feared being separated from their siblings, others feared placement in foster homes or group homes.

The children felt that good communication was a requirement of healthy family functioning. One 9-year-old girl commented that family problems are attributable to the fact that "they don't talk about their feelings." Another 13-year-old female said family problems were due to "lots of fights and arguments and they can't settle them." Her solution was to "help them straighten out their problems and to settle all family problems when they happen." Similarly, an 11-year-old male, in response to the question, "Why are there problems in families?" commented, "somebody be trying to straighten something out and somebody else jump in to it." His solution was "tell other people not to jump into it." A 16-year-old, recently placed in a Group Home because his family was unable to care for him, remarked that family problems are due to "animosity and hatred."

The changing social and economic structures and conditions have strained African-American families, threatened family resources, impeded these families ability to cope and respond effectively, and may impair the psychological development of children (Wilson & Tolson, 1990). These changes are associated with the changing composition of family networks, the increased rates of unemployment for men and the associated decrease in their desirability as marriage partners, and the increased number of single-mother families dependent upon welfare (Wilson & Tolson, 1990).

All families face multiple challenges in raising their children and socializing them to participate successfully as citizens of the broad community. The task of childrearing for low-income, African-American families is more complex, as families are coping with poverty and racism and need to socialize their children to develop a positive racial self-esteem, learn skills to live effectively in two cultures, and cope with racial oppression. The lack of existing services in low-income minority communities that emphasize strengthening families and address the needs of troubled children, combined with high rates of child abuse and parental difficulties (e.g., substance abuse, incarceration) and economic instability, has made it difficult for many adults to commit to raising a family and has disrupted family unity for many minority children. This has resulted in disproportionately high numbers of children being raised by relatives other than their parents and out-of-home placements (Stenho, 1990).

The extended family organization, historically the dominant cultural norm in the African-American community, partially functions as a family coping strategy for addressing sociocultural problems (e.g., poverty, unemployment, single-parenthood, extramarital births) (Wilson, 1989). The practice of intergenerational childrearing has increased recently in some communities, largely in response to problems associated with the crack-cocaine epidemic (e.g., Burton, 1992; Minkler, Roe, Robertson-Beckley, 1994). Thus, many grandmothers and other kin are forced to care for other family members' children, and cope with the strains of having the children's mother involved with drugs and the effects of prenatal drug exposure on children's emotional and physical development.

SOCIOCULTURAL CONCERNS

Safety and violence. All of the children listed safety concerns as the primary factor associated with family disintegration. They spoke poignantly of their fears regarding the lack of safety in their neighborhood and at school. Very few expressed concerns about family violence, despite the fact that in all cultural groups, many children fear physical and sexual abuse.

The children we interviewed spoke about how frightened they are of the violence, guns, and fighting in the neighborhood. The following answers were received in response to the question, "What scares you?" One 16-year-old male stated, "they was always shooting and I was always ducking." An 8-year-old girl said, "when I hear shooting around our neighborhood at night." Others said, "violence in the neighborhood," "when the police and Red Dogs come," and "being out on the street because anything could happen, people are crazy." One 14-year-old female summed it up by saying, "the killing in the world today scares me." Many of these children live in housing projects, and often are eye witnesses to violent interactions and deaths. The violence interferes with involvement in age-appropriate activities that could improve the quality of life. One child claimed, "people be shooting and I have to stay in the house," and another 14-year-old female stated, "last year someone got shot at school, I don't know about this year. I feel like dropping out and not going to school to avoid all of that." Often in response to witnessing an acute traumatic event or a series of frightening events in the neighborhood, children exhibit post-traumatic stress disorder symptoms (Boyd-Franklin, 1993).

Research reveals that African-American adolescents, particularly males, are at high risk to be the victims of assaultive violence. Victimization statistics reveal that African-American youth are at higher risk than youth from all other ethnic groups for nonfatal and fatal interpersonal violence (for reviews see, Hammond & Yung, 1993; Rosenberg & Mercy, 1991). Homicide has been the primary cause of death for 15-34 year-old African-Americans since 1978. Recently, homicide rates for 15-19 year-old African-American males increased 55%. Assaultive violence not associated with mortality manifests similar patterns, with African-American male adolescents from inner-city, low-income families being the subpopulation at greatest risk. More than 90% of these murder victims are killed by other African-Americans from similar demographic backgrounds.

Drug use and abuse. Substance abuse is the third major mental health problem for African-Americans. In response to the question, why are there problems in families, one of the most frequently cited responses was "drugs." Youth expressed concerns regarding drug usage and selling. Walking through drug infested areas, passing by crack houses, and stepping over needles, frightened and angered many of the children.

There is a strong correlation between substance abuse and violence. Thus, many of the youth acknowledged concerns about excessive drug use in their family and the community, particularly vis-a-vis interpersonal violence. A 16-year-old female asserted that her gravest safety concerns were the "violence, shootings, and killings in the neighborhood, that was mostly related to drugs." The participants were aware that their families often feel helpless in preventing the rampant drug-related violence from negatively influencing them (Boyd-Franklin, 1993).

Substance abuse, a serious problem among low-income minority youth, is associated with elevated rates of high school dropouts, unemployment, crime, incarceration, and acquired immunodeficiency syndrome virus (AIDS) (e.g., Oyemade & Washington, 1990). Although physiological, psychodynamic, and environmental factors are major reasons for the disproportionately high rates of alcohol and drug abuse in low income African-American youth, it has been asserted that family dynamics are the primary causal motivating factor of substance abusing behaviors (Oyemade & Washington, 1990). Historically, African-American family values on kinship networks, responsibility and flexibility, the work ethic and religion may have mitigated against substance abuse. Unfortunately, the recent erosion of these values in the low-income African-American urban community and their replacement with an increased emphasis on individualism, materialism, and entitlement may account for the increased rates of substance abuse (Oyemade & Washington, 1990).

Poverty. Being raised in conditions of poverty and economic hardship is a major stress for all the children interviewed. For them, poverty is associated with violence and crime, drugs, inadequate housing and transportation, and fears about going homeless and hungry. Implicit in their comments was the limitations that poverty places upon their family's capacity to feel safe, spend time together, and accomplish their life's goals (Parnell & Vanderkloot, 1989).

The aspect of poverty of greatest concern related to shelter. The youth complained about living in overcrowded and roach infested environments. Overcrowding referred to "four aunts, two uncles, my grandmother, my mother, two brothers, two sisters, and me all living in three rooms." One 10-year-old felt that the best way to help families would be to "clean up all the roaches and the community." As one of their three wishes many of the youth desired better housing. One child wished that "my family could live in a big house and not in the projects," another desired that "my mom and I could have our own place," and another said, "I wish we could change from living in an apartment to living in a house." Some of the children also were fearful of becoming homeless.

The youth focused on their lack of basic necessities. Two wished for "shoes and clothes" and another wanted "enough food for my whole family." Transportation was of particular concern. Many wished for a car, and others complained about the transportation system. In sum, these youth were troubled by the effects of poverty on themselves and their family, and felt that more financial resources would improve their family's situation. I wish: "we were rich," "for all of the money in the world," and "for a million dollars for myself and money for my family."

Issues of social class and race are difficult to disentangle, particularly for those in impoverished urban environments (e.g., Boyd-Franklin, 1993; Parnell & Vanderkloot, 1989). Low socioeconomic status African-Americans are oppressed by virtue of both their race and class. Low socioeconomic status excludes many youth from access to activities and resources associated with effective functioning and success (Oyemade & Washington, 1990). Much of this exclusion is associated with racial and class discrimination (Oyemade & Washington, 1990).

It has been posited that multigenerations of poverty characterize many African-American families, who feel overburdened by the stresses associated with economic deprivation, and helpless to alter their situation. They become inextricably bound up in a victimization cycle (e.g., Pinderhughes, 1989). Pinderhughes (1989) suggested that poverty leads to stress in interpersonal relationships, which impedes adequate role performance, resulting in lowered self-esteem and rage, feelings of powerlessness, and more dysfunctional interactions and communication patterns. Many African-American children and families feel helpless and rageful in the face of poverty, and powerless against high rates of unemployment, high school drop-outs, substance abuse, violence, and homelessness (Boyd-Franklin, 1993). These psychological and social difficulties interfere further with an individual's capacity to maximize the relatively limited opportunities for achievement and advancement, which sustains the family's impoverished conditions.

Sexual behavior. The two major concerns expressed by the youth that may be categorized under the rubric of sexual behavior relate to teenage pregnancy and sexually transmitted diseases, particularly the HIV virus. When asked about the school environment, one 14-year-old female stated, "every time I turn around someone's pregnant. My friend is 15 and has two kids." When given three wishes, one of this youth's wishes was, "that I can finish school without getting pregnant." Another 14-year-old female admitted that she worries "about STDs, crabs and AIDS."

Low socioeconomic status African-American youth reportedly engage in high rates of sexual activity, including high-risk sexual behaviors (Harrison, 1990) and the failure to utilize contraceptives (Hayes, 1987). The outcome of these behaviors has been an increased incidence and disproportionately high rate of births to teenage mothers and unmarried women (Farley & Allen, 1987). Statistics indicate that: (1) among mothers 15 to 19 years of age, 87% of African-American births are outside of marriage; (2) birth rates for 15-19 year-old unmarried African-American females are 90%; (3) 32% of the births to African-American women are to unmarried 15-19 year olds; and (4) 43% of African-American males ages 15-19 are fathers (Harrison, 1990; U.S. Bureau of the Census, 1987). Having a child while unmarried and still an adolescent increases the likelihood of dropping out of high school and thus interferes with educational advancement (e.g., Furstenberg, Brooks-Gunn, & Morgan, 1987) and access to job opportunities, is associated with welfare dependency and the feminization of poverty (Pearce & McAdoo, 1981), and is associated with high rates of physical, psychological and family problems (Gibbs, 1990). Since the majority (e.g., 90%) of African-American unwed teenage mothers keep and raise their children, they are vulnerable to many of the negative sequelae associated with this choice. Both family legacy of teenage pregnancy and peer pressure may perpetuate the high rates of African-American babies being born to teenage parents, despite the potentially negative consequences of giving birth during adolescence.

Elevated rates of high-risk sexual activity in African-American adolescents residing in impoverished environments, combined with elevated rates of substance abuse (notably crack, intravenous drug use) reveals high rates of sexually transmitted diseases (e.g., Bowser, Fullilove, & Fullilove, 1990), including AIDS (e.g., Petersen & Marin, 1988). Explanations for the rates of high-risk sexual behavior among low-income African-American youth have focused on issues related to social systems and to the sexual ideology of the community (Harrison, 1990).

CONCLUDING COMMENTS

Despite the stresses associated with racial prejudice and poverty, most low-income African-American youth and families manifest adaptive social and psychological functioning. Thus, many do not require traditional psychotherapeutic services. For troubled children for whom psychotherapeutic services are indicated, the interventions must be conducted in a culturally responsive fashion (for review, see Vargas & Koss-Chioino, 1992). Similarly, many of these families do not require family therapy. However, for families who may benefit from family therapy, a multisystems approach that addresses individual, family, and community issues and examines the impact of social, political, and economic factors on the family is recommended (e.g., Boyd-Franklin, 1989; Ho, 1987). Family interventions should empower the executive subsystem to parent effectively and in a developmentally sensitive fashion, and empower all family members to intervene in the multiple systems in which they interact (e.g., Boyd-Franklin, 1989). Additionally, since the African-American family unit possesses considerable strength and potential that serves as the building blocks for the African-American community, effective intervention must be culturally sensitive in enhancing assets and positive attributes (Wilson & Tolson, 1990). The children with whom we spoke articulated that individual and/or family counseling would be helpful if it taught them self-respect, helped their family to communicate more effectively and engage in more effective problem-resolution and conflict negotiation, and offered less verbally and physically aggressive and violent ways to express feelings and provide discipline.

In addition to clinic-based individual and family therapy or counseling approaches to address family problems and the sociocultural context within which they are embedded, a variety of national and community-based organizations actively are implementing programs to combat the problem of the deterioration of the African-American family and to enhance family unity, adaptive family functioning, and effective childrearing. Many of these programs are psychoeducational and strive to improve family unity by offering marriage preparation and enrichment and sex education, and providing literacy training and career and guidance counseling (Abatso & Abatso, 1991). There are a growing number of programs designed to teach parenting skills and books have been written to provide information to adults regarding raising African-American children and preparing them to handle racial matters in a manner that enhances their psychological growth and development (Comer & Poussaint, 1992). To combat the massive problems of African-American youth, programs that provide alternative secondary education, employment, sex education and family planning, comprehensive services and child care for teenage parents, and violence and drug intervention and prevention urgently are needed (e.g., Gibbs, 1990; Hammond & Yung, 1993). In developing preventive programming for children and adolescents, it is essential that the programs and their staff be sensitive to the race, ethnicity, culture, socioeconomic status, and developmental stage of the population being served. This often necessitates adapting educational methods that are accepted widely in the culture, such as the implementation of home- or church-based therapy or education and the use of role models or mentors similar to the target population as demonstrators and supporters of adaptive behavior and functioning (e.g., Bobo, Cvetkovich, Gilchrist, Trimle, & Schinke, 1988).

To provide low-income African-American children, adolescents, and their families hope for a better future and the competencies and opportunities associated with adaptive functioning, it is essential that resources be devoted to designing and implementing culturally sensitive preventive interventions that address those familial and sociocultural issues of particular concern to the children. These preventive interventions must build upon the strengths and resiliencies of the youth and families for whom they are developed and must take into account the perspective of the children.

REFERENCES

Abatso, G., & Abatso, Y. (1990). *How to equip the African-American family.* Chicago: Urban Ministries, Inc.

Billingsley, A. (1968). *Black families in White America.* Englewood Cliffs, NJ: Prentice-Hall.

Bobo, J., Cvetkovich, G., Gilchrist, L., Trimble, J., & Schinke, S. (1988). Cross-cultural service delivery to minority communities. *Journal of Community Psychology, 16,* 263-272.

Bowser, B. P., Fullilove, M. T., & Fullilove, R. E. (1990). African-American youth and AIDS high-risk behavior: The social context and barriers to prevention. *Youth and Society, 22,* 54-66.

Boyd-Franklin, N. (1989). *Black families in therapy: A multisystems approach.* New York: Guilford Press.

Boyd-Franklin, N. (1993). Race, class, and poverty In F. Walsh (Ed.). *Normal family processes* (Second edition) (pp. 361-376). New York: Guilford.

Burton, L. M. (1992). Black grandparents rearing children of drug-addicted parents: Stressors, outcomes, and social service needs. *The Gerontologist, 32,* 744-751.

Chase-Lansdale, P. L., Brooks-Gunn, J., & Zamsky, E. S. (1994). Young African-American multigenerational families on poverty: Quality of mothering and grandmothering. *Child Development, 65,* 373-393.

Comer, J. P., & Poussaint, A. F. (1992). *Raising black children.* New York: Plume.

Coner-Edwards, A. F. & Spurlock, J. (Eds.) (1988). *Black families in crisis: The middle class.* New York: Brunner/Mazel.

Crockenberg, S. V. (1981). Infant irritability, mother responsiveness, and social support influences on the security of infant-mother attachment. *Child Development, 52,* 857-865.

Farley, R., & Allen, W. R. (1987). *The color line and the quality of life in America.* New York: Russell Sage Foundation.

Furstenberg, F. F., Brooks-Gunn, J., & Morgan, S. P. (1987). *Adolescent mothers in later life.* Cambridge: Cambridge University Press.

Gibbs, J. T., & Huang, L. N. (Eds.) (1989). *Children of color: Psychological interventions with minority youth.* San Francisco: Jossey-Bass.

Gibbs, J. T. (1990). Mental health issues of Black adolescents: Implications for policy and practice. In A. R. Stiffman and L. E. Davis (Eds.), *Ethnic issues in adolescent mental health* (pp. 21-52). Newbury Park: Sage.

Gillum, R., Gomez-Marin, O. & Prineas, R. (1984). Racial differences in personality, behavior and family environment in Minneapolis school children. *Journal of the National Medical Association, 76,* 1097-1105.

Hammond, W. R. & Yung, B. (1993). Psychology's role in the public health response to assaultive violence among young African-American men. *American Psychologist, 48,* 142-154.

Harrison, A. (1990). High-risk sexual behavior among Black adolescents. In A. R. Stiffman and L. E. Davis (Eds.), *Ethnic issues in adolescent mental health* (pp. 175-188). Newbury Park: Sage.

Hayes, C. D. (Ed.) (1987). *Risking the future: Adolescent sexuality, pregnancy and childbearing (Volume 1).* Washington D.C.: National Academy Press.

Hill, R. (1972). *The strengths of Black families.* New York: Emerson Hall.

Ho, M. K. (1987). *Family therapy with minorities.* Newbury Park: Sage.

Martin, J. M. & Martin, E. P. (1985). *The helping tradition in the Black family and community.* Silver Springs, MD: National Association of Social Work.

McAdoo, H. P. (Ed.) (1988). *Black families* (Second edition). Newbury Park: Sage.

Minkler, M., Roe, K. M., & Robertson-Beckley, R. J. (1994). Raising grandchildren from crack-cocaine households: Effects on family and friendship ties of African-American women. *American Journal of Orthopsychiatry, 64,* 20-29.

Oyemade, U. J., & Washington, V. (1990). The role of family factors in the primary prevention of substance abuse among high-risk Black youth. In A. R. Stiffman and L. E. Davis (Eds.), *Ethnic issues in adolescent mental health* (pp. 267-284). Newbury Park: Sage.

Parnell, M., & Vanderkloot, J., (1989). Ghetto children: Children growing up in poverty. In L. Combrinck-Graham (Ed.), *Children in family contexts: Perspectives on treatment* (pp.437-462). New York: Guilford.

Pearce, D., & McAdoo, H. (1981). *Women and children: Alone and in poverty.* Washington, D.C.: National Advisory Council on Economic Opportunity.

Peterson, J. L., & Marin, G. (1988). Issues in the prevention of AIDS among Black and Hispanic men. *American Psychologist, 43,* 871-877.

Pickett, S. A., Vraniak, D. A., Cook, J. A., & Cohler, B. J. (1993). Strengths in adversity: Blacks bear burden better than whites. *Professional Psychology: Research and Practice, 24,* 460-467.

Pinderhughes, E. (1989). *Understanding race, ethnicity, and power: The key to efficacy in clinical practice.* New York: The Free Press.

Rosenberg, M. & Mercy, J. (Eds.) (1991). *Violence in America: A public health approach.* New York: Oxford University Press.

Shimkin, D., Shimkin, E. & Frate, D. (Eds.) (1978). *The extended family in Black societies.* Chicago: Aldine.

Staples, R., & Johnson, L. B. (1993). *Black families at the crossroads: Challenges and prospects.* San Francisco: Jossey-Bass.

Stenho, S. (1990). The elusive continuum of child welfare services: Implications for minority children and youth. *Child Welfare, 69,* 551-562.

Stevens, J. H. Jr. (1984). Black grandmothers and Black adolescent mothers' knowledge about parenting. *Developmental Psychology, 20,* 1017-1025.

Taylor, R. D, Casten, R., & Flickinger, S. M. (1993). Influence of kinship social support on the parenting experiences and psychosocial adjustment of African-American adolescents. *Developmental Psychology, 29,* 382-388.

Taylor, R. J., & Chatters, L. M. (1988). Church members as a source of informal social support. *Review of Religious Research, 30,* 114-125.

Taylor, R. J., Chatters, L. M., Tucker, M. B., & Lewis, E. (1990). Developments in research on Black families: A decade review. *Journal of Marriage and the Family, 52,* 993-1014.

Tinley, B. R. & Parke, R. D. (1984). Grandparents as support and socialization agents. In M. Lewis (Ed.). *Beyond the dyad* (pp. 161-195). New York: Plenum.

U.S. Bureau of the Census (1987). Statistical Abstracts of the United States: 1988 (108th edition): Table 1-32, No. 87. Washington, D.C.

Vargas, L. A., & Koss-Chioino, J. D. (1992). *Working with culture: Psychotherapeutic interventions with ethnic minority children.* San Francisco: Jossey-Bass.

Wilson, M. N. (1989). Child development in the context of the Black extended family. *American Psychologist, 44,* 380-385.

Wilson, M. N., & Tolson, T. F. J. (1990). Family support in the Black community. *Journal of Clinical Child Psychology, 19,* 347-355.

Nadine J. Kaslow, Ph.D. *is Associate Professor at Emory University School of Medicine, Department of Psychiatry and Behavioral Sciences. She holds joint appointments in the Departments of Pediatrics and Psychology. Additionally, she is the Chief Psychologist at Grady Health System. Dr. Kaslow is the 1994 recipient of the American Psychological Association, Division 29 (Psychotherapy) Jack Krasner award for early career contribution to psychotherapy. She received her doctoral degree in clinical psychology from the University of Houston and completed her predoctoral internship training and postdoctoral fellowship at the University of Wisconsin — Madison. From 1984-1990 she was on the faculty at Yale University in the Departments of Psychiatry, Child Study Center, and Psychology.*

REDESIGNING SERVICES USING AN ASSETS APPROACH

NINA MCLELLAN
Senior Planning Associate
The Federation for Community Planning
Cleveland, Ohio

The charge to Symposium participants is to identify and analyze symptoms and the "root causes" of symptoms which cause families to fail. The conceptual framework which has been suggested assumes a hierarchy of problems, of deficits.

This paper will depart from a deficit approach. Rather than trying to analyze factors which cause families to fail and which seem to be both cause and effect of family breakdown, it will take an asset approach to assisting families. It will argue that a deficit approach has led to a service system which is failing.

The paper will delineate a framework for redesigning services which is organized around three interlinked components: neighborhood resources, safety net services, and public systems. It is a model based on family strengths, neighborhood assets, and linkages between formal and informal services.

A NATIONAL AND HISTORICAL PERSPECTIVE

There is a strong theme in the history of social assistance in America which views poverty and the need for assistance as weakness and failure. In reviewing the history of assistance for children and families in her keynote address to the Federation for Community Planning's 1994 Health and Human Services Institute, Sharon Lynn Kagan stated, "to be poor in a great land that offered untold opportunity was regarded as either a sign of moral indecency or human ineptitude." Only when families fail, is government intervention felt to be legitimate.

Social programs tend, therefore, to be suspect. Funding must be justified by sufficient crisis, family breakdown, and widespread social problems. Solutions are framed in terms of fixing the deficiencies displayed by families and communities. People qualify for assistance by having sufficient amounts of specific problems.

This history has created a national perspective in which social policy, legislation, funding, and service delivery focus on analysis and remediation of various specific problems at any given time. Funding and services come and go depending on which problems are receiving national attention. This deficit approach helps to explain the absence of a coherent national family policy and universally available family services. We simply move from fixing or attempting to fix one deficit after another.

There are significant exceptions (e.g. public education, social security) where there has been sufficient national consensus to maintain universal supportive services available without stigma. But in comparison to other industrialized countries, USA has far fewer universally accessible supports for families.[1]

EFFECT OF A DEFICIT APPROACH
On Service Delivery and System of Services

At the service delivery level, the service system presents formidable obstacles, particularly for families with multiple stressors. Despite our understanding that individuals and families have multiple and interrelated problems, the deficit approach has created separate bureaucracies and services systems — for income support, employment, substance abuse, mental health, juvenile justice, child protection, and mental retardation.[2]

Even prevention programs are categorical with separate funding for preventing teen pregnancy, juvenile delinquency, substance abuse, infant mortality and so on. As the effectiveness of outreach workers and home visitors in reaching stressed families has been demonstrated, we find specialized outreach workers knocking on the same doors, some focused on getting pregnant women to prenatal care, others looking for people with Alzheimer's Disease, others with information on substance abuse.

The deficit approach has thus resulted in a daunting array of multiple public and private agencies, each dependent on funds which determine their scope, setting requirements which limit the ability of staff to be flexible and responsive to the multiplicity of individual and family needs. All too often, agency staff cannot help with urgent family issues because they fall outside of the responsibility of the particular agency. The needs of family members, other than the identified client, are ignored. Schools, social and health services operate in isolation from one another. And, when a family must become involved with new workers each time it needs a service, the development of strong relationships and the development of trust is undermined.

Worse than the fact that formal services are fragmented, is that a family or individual must be in deep and serious crisis to qualify for assistance. The result is labeling and treating people as dependent clients and patients.

Formal services are usually short term and isolated from the family's informal helping networks and organizations which could, with better linkages to formal services, provide long-term supports. Formal services typically ignore the interrelatedness of family and community.

And finally, any list of system ills resulting from a deficit model, must include the financial waste in running separate service bureaucracies, the turf issues and competition for funds.

Case managers have been one solution to trying to manage our complex and fragmented service system. But too often, families have multiple case managers who do not communicate with one another and whose multiple, sometimes conflicting expectations, put stressed families under even more stress. Local agencies can provide examples of families having 10 or more workers.

In large and complex service delivery areas, such as Cuyahoga County, there are multiple planning bodies and interagency teams trying to develop better coordination and to assure needed collaboration, often now required by funders. These separate bodies involve many of the same agencies and themselves overlap and require coordination.

Professionals within different service systems and agencies are increasingly frustrated with service fragmentation and deficit-based approaches that impede their efforts and do not lead to long-term family stability and strengthening. They recognize that having to label people in terms of particular problems for which they must be assessed and "case managed" reinforces dependency and does not build capacity. Professionals are overwhelmed by the crises and stressors faced by many families which they feel helpless to change.

As a result, attention is turning to capacity building approaches. Ted Bowman has contrasted deficit and empowerment approaches in work with individuals, illustrating how a deficit approach results in negative reinforcement.

In a problem approach: assessment is based on problems, strengths are minimized and the person/family is viewed as deficient or incompetent; the "client/patient" is treated as recipient of services, undermining skills and resourcefulness; self-identification as sick, inadequate, or weak, is reinforced.

In a strengths-based or empowerment approach: assessment is based on strengths and identified stresses, resourcefulness is affirmed, susceptibility to stress is reduced, collaboration and interdependence is emphasized, a self-view of being effective and in control is internalized with buildup of coping capacity.[3]

Current thinking about system reform has developed from both a recognition of the ills of the current service system and the characteristics of programs which have been successful in helping families, including Head Start, a variety of prevention and early intervention programs (many of them grass roots, small scale programs), and community development efforts. The settlement house experience has been rediscovered and revisited. Common elements of a myriad of successful programs have been identified and expressed as core family support principles and approaches.[4]

These principles include the following elements for effective services:

• strengthen family functioning, responding to all family members and interrelated family issues;

• build on family strengths, assisting families to set their own priorities in a partnership approach;

• respond flexibly and comprehensively to family needs;

• value and strengthen personal and cultural values and informal supports;

• enhance a sense of community, responding to local needs and resources, and facilitating community action, informal supports, and mutual helping among families;

• share responsibility and develop collaboration, involving families in planning and evaluating services, as well as developing collaboration among service providers;

• mobilize resources and supports, identifying and building on the talents and capacities of neighborhood residents and other community assets;

• better integrate formal services and link them to informal and neighborhood-based supports and services.

Taken as a whole, these principles contrast with the deficit approach in a commitment to a universal approach which assumes all families have strengths and all families need support. While families with special problems should not be neglected, they must be served within a more universal framework for all families and children.

As the above list of principles indicates, the family support movement is firmly based on a social ecological model, commitment to empowerment,[5] and the necessity for increased integration of services. There is a growing literature on collaboration and service integration and a

National Resource Center For Service Integration has been established with federal funds.

These principles have been applied, not only to social services, but to community development, and more cooperative, decentralized business management models. They are summarized in the following chart.

THE PROCESS IS THE KEY . . .
MODELS FOR CHANGE IN HOW WE DO BUSINESS:
THE PROCESS OF EMPOWERMENT[7]

Paradigms

Building on Family Strengths	Building on Community Strengths	Building on Cultural Diversity/the Workplace
Old Paradigm: (Deficit Model)	Old Paradigm: (Deficit Model)	Old Paradigm: (Deficit Model)

Building on Family Strengths

Old Paradigm: (Deficit Model)

1. Serves only dysfunctional families through formal social services system.

2. Fixes "people's problems" by isolating the problem and labelling individual.

3. Defines and funds programs to address a single problem area: substance abuse, lack of housing, youth gangs. (as examples)

4. Looks for answers by asking the professionals.

New Paradigm: (Asset Model)

1. Serves all families holistically.

2. Lets families define their needs and goals with the professionals as partners in the process. (reciprocity),

3. Builds on the basic value that all families have strengths and these may differ culturally.

4. Recognizes and helps build personal support systems. (relationships)

5. Funds programs by encouraging integration of resources and services. (responsibility)

6. Shares accountability. (responsibility)

Similarities in the new paradigm:

• Acknowledges diversity and change and views them as assets

• De-centralizes decision making

• Builds on the integration of individual and institutional differences; not on fragmentation, factiousness and competition

Building on Community Strengths

Old Paradigm: (Deficit Model)

1. Uses needs assessments to identify problems and dysfunctions.

2. Operates from a belief in a resource scarce environment, systems are in competition for these resources.

3. Defines empowerment as implying someone else is disempowered.

4. Has professionals conduct surveys.

New Paradigm: (Asset Model)

1. Emphasizes resources and the identification and maximization of assets.

2. Acknowledges that assets differ by community, based on its cultural attributes and values, geographic location, etc.

3. Has a community define its assets.

4. Defines empowerment as capacity-building, localizes decision making, shares information; is inclusive.

5. Develops programs, services and supports, as identified by community and not by professional institutions.

6. Supports cooperation and collaboration, rather than competition; responsibility for sharing resources includes total community.

Building on Cultural Diversity/the Workplace

Old Paradigm: (Deficit Model)

1. Sees individual as an employee who is separated from his or her other roles, ignores cultural attributes.

2. Sees diversity as achieved in the workplace by two basic policies:

a. EO — equal opportunity; selection based on merit; ignores other differences as relevant.

b. affirmative action — categorization of individuals, usually by race, created "in groups" and factions among people, fear of quotas create dissension; labels people by limited categories.

New Paradigm: (Asset Model)

1. Sees a diverse work force as giving a company a marketing edge because it can respond to and be sensitive to diversity of marketplace; helps find new audiences.

2. Defines cultural diversity by race, economic status, region, marital status, family status, physical and mental differences, education, gender and age. Considers these aspects of individuals as attributes that can enrich the work place.

3. Realizes that productive employees are those that are viewed and treated holistically by their employers.

4. Helps companies look at diversity of experience of employees as assets; manage this diversity by tapping cultural richness of its employees and inclusion in decision making.

National organizations representing different professional disciplines and service systems, are recognizing and applying family support principles and perspectives in calling for system reform. The American Psychological Association, for example, is developing a paper which calls for psychological services for children to be "integrated with a broad range of related services and driven by concern for the needs and desires of families."[7]

There are calls for social work to move from its current emphasis on office-based clinical treatment to more community-based services and generic social and environmental support for children and families.[8]

While none of the family support principles is a new concept, their application as an integrated framework for change in the current social service context presents enormous challenges, new commitments, new service delivery models, and the integration of family services with community revitalization redevelopment initiatives.

The challenge is not more programs. The challenge of family support is to make all services, public and private, more family supportive. The challenge is to reform the service delivery and funding system so that services are more integrated, coherent, and accessible. The challenge is to develop feasible linkages between social services, health services and schools. The challenge is to link family services and community revitalization. Ultimately, the family support movement asks "...what will it take for America in its commitment to families and children to have thus become a normative system, one that lives in neighborhoods and in communities...embedded into the fabric of America..."[9]

The following sections of this paper go beyond recommendations for planning and process, to present some emerging ideas for redesigning the service system based on family support principles and a commitment to an integrated and comprehensive approach. These concepts are being developed and tested in Cuyahoga County through the efforts of the Federation for Community Planning, the County's Family and Children First Council, Neighborhood Centers Association, The Cleveland Community Building Initiative, a number of children's mental health agencies, and other service providers.

We recognize that redesigning social services is just one part of the equation. Healthy families require national commitments to adequate housing, income, public transportation, health care, excellent schools. In poverty neighborhoods, communities must implement comprehensive approaches which include economic reinvestment and jobs.

A redesigned system of services should provide comprehensive and integrated services for families in their own neighborhoods, with an emphasis on primary prevention and development of family and community capacity. The system should have the following overall characteristics:

1. It should respond comprehensively and flexibly to the needs of all children and families, building on existing resources and strengthening both families and their communities and neighborhoods.

2. It should effectively mobilize, strengthen, and link existing informal and formal resources in order to respond to locally defined needs and priorities, with particular attention to linkages between social services and education.

3. It should provide access points for all families for positive and non-stigmatizing activities and services, including activities which strengthen family-to-family connections and build strong communities.

4. It should assure that children and families involved with public systems are systematically connected with on-going supports and positive opportunities in their neighborhood or through their cultural group.

5. The system should be evaluated on the basis of long-term normative outcomes for families and communities.

As a first step to developing a comprehensive approach which integrates existing resources, three interrelated components are proposed:[11] 1) Neighborhood,[12] 2) Safety-net, and 3) Public systems.

The neighborhood component broadly supports all families, offering opportunities for families voluntarily seeking services and support, as well as for those involved with public systems such as natural, foster and adoptive families. This component focuses on strengthening family functioning and neighborhood/cultural supports to families. This component should coordinate and strengthen natural support networks and existing neighborhood-based resources. It does not assume a problem. Rather, it assumes opportunities for families to address their interests, their concerns, their objectives.

The safety-net component develops linkages and partnerships between the neighborhood service network and treatment and crisis services, providing support and back-up to the neighborhood organizations through training and consultation, and services to families who want and need additional assistance.

The public systems come into play when neighborhood and safety-net component resources are unable to meet the presenting needs because of severity or complexity of the problems and refer the child/family for intake to a public system. This stage coordinates intake, assessment and case planning for multi-need children and families, and provides access to designated services paid for only by public systems.

Individuals and families may be involved with activities and services in more than one component at a time. Furthermore, since it is at the neighborhood level that on-going support is possible, all other services must coordinate with neighborhood level services and supports.

An overview of this system is depicted in the diagram below. The following sections provide more detail on each component.

FAMILY RESOURCE NETWORK FLOW CHART

• Point of entry for services can be accessed at any neighborhood resource network organization. Families should be informed of all resources in the network by staff/volunteers of any network organization.

• The Flexible Response Team can be utilized by all network members for training, consultation to staff, participate in planning for individual families, and provide specific services. For additional support and service, the team refers the family to the neighborhood organization.

• Public systems refer to lead neighborhood organization for access to all neighborhood resources and receive referrals of families from the flexible response team.

This component offers support to all families through multiple activities and services which are easily accessible close to home, which are not stigmatizing, and which offer positive opportunities for family members. The key structural elements at the neighborhood level are the neighborhood family center[13] and the family resource network.

1. The neighborhood family center

The family center approach is embodied in hundreds of organizations which have developed from grassroots efforts and through state initiatives.[14]

A "family center" is both a concept and a place.

As a place, a family center is accessible and welcoming of community children and families. It can be an extension of a school, community center, child care program or other neighborhood organization with a commitment to the neighborhood and the trust and involvement of neighborhood residents. Family centers provide a place where family members can drop in, meet in groups, participate in positive activities, find direct assistance and referral, and move toward individual, family, and neighborhood goals. Family centers should have the capacity to reach some families in their own homes.

As a concept, a family center means 1) the integration and coordination in a single delivery system, activities and services needed by families, and 2) the enabling of neighborhood families for mutual help and community action.

While family centers look different from neighborhood to neighborhood, they should embody the same family support principles. They provide multiple activities and services in response to family and community needs.

Family centers respond to families as a unit and to individuals as functioning within their family and informal support system. Persons are also viewed as having skills and competencies, not as passive recipients of services. Participants are neighbors and citizens who can make contributions to the program, to other families and to their communities. A key aspect of the family center approach is involving participants and community residents in planning, governance, and as volunteers and employees.

2. Family resource network

The second structural element in developing a service system at the neighborhood level is the concept of the family resource network.

Members of a neighborhood family resource network could include a wide range of neighborhood-based organizations, including schools, Head Start Center, day care center, churches, youth/recreation center, library, street clubs, associations, municipal government.

The goal of the network is to mobilize and expand neighborhood assets to strengthen families and the community. This can include collaborative arrangements and working agreements among organizations to make best use of existing resources, agreement on unmet needs, and cooperative action. At minimum, families coming to any of the organizations in the network should be able to communicate their needs and obtain information about activities and services throughout the network. For example, staff at the day care center would be available to hear about other family needs and could direct a mother concerned about an aging parent to appropriate resources.

Whether through a neighborhood family center or family resource network, capacity should be developed which fulfills three key functions: access, group activities, and family assistance. These three functional areas provide a structural framework which can assist individual programs, or collaborative networks, assess their programming.

• Access: How do individuals and families know about and access services and activities? Activities and services which relate to access, include newsletters, public information, outreach to family homes, and hospitality and information at one or more sites.

• Group activities: What activities and services are offered and how do they respond to family and community interests and priorities? How do they strengthen families and build community? Group activities can include family fun activities, parent/child activity drop-in programs, parent education classes, interest groups, programs to meet the needs of specific age/interest groups, mutual helping and cooperative efforts, community organizing. A key service is short-term child care while parents/caretakers are involved in activities.

• Family assistance: How are families with particular needs assisted? Family assistance can include help in meeting emergency needs, information and referral, service coordination and family development services. The capacity to meet with families in their own homes is essential for reaching stressed families who may not come to a center.

Families seeking assistance may or may not have a social worker or case manager in another agency or public system. For families who do not have a case manager, family assistance staff should provide the following services:

- respond to immediate needs;

- help families identify their needs/goals, strengths/resources;

- provide information, referral, advocacy (including referral to activities and services within the neighborhood family resource network, as well as to outside resources);

- provide ongoing assistance and support for families to achieve their goals and strengthen support systems;

- assure service coordination for children/families without other lead case manager (identify all service providers involved with the family and work with providers to assure an integrated, accessible approach);

- make home and school visits;

- develop positive activities, support groups, and on-site services to meet the needs of families and individuals (with assistance of other staff and through partnerships with other organizations);

- involve flexible response team (see Component II) to consult with staff, assist children/families who are in crisis or need early intervention.

For children/families with a lead case manager, the family assistance staff can:

- assist the case manager and participate on case team;

- assist in strengthening neighborhood supports for the child/family, including informal support network, involvement in positive activities;

- assist case manager and family to solve problems around service access and coordination by finding ways to decentralize and integrate services, e.g., bringing some specialized services to the neighborhood site(s).

It is important to note that a formal intake and assessment should not be a part of the neighborhood component. Families may provide non-intrusive family information as part of registering or enrolling in the neighborhood family center or in particular programs. Family members may give more information about their needs and resources if they request assistance. Family members and staff should also have sufficient information on children's developmental stages to identify need for more formal screening for early intervention. Staff should be trained to respond knowledgeably to families expressing concerns, and to recognize obvious safety and health risk factors.

Neighborhood family centers generally have both professional and paraprofessional staff. Particularly in low-income and minority neighborhoods, it is essential to recruit family support workers and other staff from the neighborhood and to create staff teams in which the knowledge and experience of the indigenous workers is valued. Paraprofessional family support workers can provide outreach and home visiting, assistance with family activities and mutual helping among families.

The ideal of partnership and shared responsibility between staff and participants presents additional challenges. Empowerment of families raises questions about their access to "case" information. Social workers and other professionals are likely to need training in interdisciplinary team practice in community settings. Family centers require staff with a broad range of knowledge, including child development, adult and family development, group work and community organizing. We do not yet have paraprofessional and professional training curriculum that integrates these areas.

COMPONENT II: SAFETY NET

Safety net services provide time-limited and more specialized services, including crisis services, more focused assessment, and interventions which help stabilize children and families with more serious needs. The key elements of the safety net component are a "flexible response team," and county-wide services which back up and supplement the neighborhood system.

1. Flexible Response Team[15]

The flexible response team concept was developed and has been implemented by Parmadale, a Cleveland children's treatment agency working with a number of neighborhood centers. Its thrust is to get mental health services out of the office and into the neighborhoods as a backup to natural supports and neighborhood-based services.

Social workers with clinical experience are employed by a child/family mental health agency which provides supervision. The team responds to requests by neighborhood staff and families including: training and consultation; participation in family assistance meetings; additional assessment and case planning, including specialized mental health assessment; group counseling; crisis intervention; in-home intervention/family preservation; referral for treatment services (substance abuse, child/family counseling, home-based intensive treatment) and to public systems for designated services (such as residential treatment, specialized/treatment foster care).

Funds should be available to purchase individualized goods and services. The Alaska Youth Initiative developed this flexible "wraparound" approach which has been shown to be successful in keeping families intact and returning children to the community from out-of-home placements.

Integrating "wrap-around" into a comprehensive systems approach, links it to both on-going informal supports at the neighborhood level, and with a gate-keeping function for referral to public systems for deep-end services when these are appropriate.

2. Area-wide resources

Communities have a variety of area-wide resources which can provide back-up support, and which have contact with neighborhood children and families in crisis. These include: telephone assistance (hot lines, warm-lines, resource and referral services); emergency shelters; police departments; health providers; and a variety of organizations offering time-limited special services.

These resources should be included in developing a comprehensive system. Some resources can be co-located, or provided at neighborhood sites. Some resources can provide information, training, and consultation. New communication and referral procedures may emerge, for example, with police departments and health providers.

COMPONENT III: PUBLIC SYSTEM SERVICES

Particularly in low-income neighborhoods, families are likely to have multiple involvements with public systems. Public systems must be part of any comprehensive plan.

There are a number of ways that public systems can improve their accessibility to their customers through collaboration with neighborhood sites.

Where information systems can be adapted, eligibility specialists for public entitlement programs may come on site to qualify people. In addition to income maintenance staff, neighborhood agencies strongly recommend that JOBS workers come to neighborhood sites, particularly for discouraged, long-term unemployed persons.

Because computer programs are now available for screening families for public entitlements, neighborhood staff can do preliminary screenings so that potential clients are identified and informed ahead when they can be assisted in their neighborhood.

A partnership between public systems and neighborhood family centers/networks can strengthen prevention efforts. Public agencies such as drug/alcohol, mental health, mental retardation/developmental disabilities, and child welfare, can use neighborhood networks to distribute information, and can train neighborhood staff in early identification and referral procedures.

A primary purpose of a pro-family system is to assure positive and on-going opportunities and supports are available in their neighborhood for children and families involved with public systems, particularly children's services and juvenile court. These connections will work more effectively if case workers and probation officers are assigned cases on a geographic basis and are familiar with what family centers/resource networks offer and establish working relationships with neighborhood staff to assure that children and families are connected to neighborhood supports. This will require joint training and procedures.

For example, foster, adoptive families and biological families can participate in many activities the neighborhood family center/resource network offer. They build on-going informal support systems in a "least restrictive" or normative environment with many good role models.

Family assistance workers or designated neighborhood contacts who know the child and family might be helpful members of public system case planning.

All too often, public systems pay for intensive family preservation and reunification services, but do not provide long-term, less intensive follow-up. The use of neighborhood outreach workers/home visitors to follow-up families leaving intensive in-home family preservation should be evaluated.

Public systems contract with a variety of organizations to provide family preservation and treatment services. Typically, stressed family members have to travel to sites outside their neighborhood to participate. If these classes, treatment and support groups, were held at neighborhood sites, it would help families and strengthen local family-to-family informal supports.

Finally, the multiple public systems must make it easier for children and families who are involved with more than one public agency through development of integrated intake, assessment, and case planning with access to designated continuum of publicly contracted services. These should include day treatment, treatment and specialized foster care, specialized respite, crisis beds, and residential treatment.

In conclusion, this model organizes services in a linked, three-component system which first broadly supports all families, second, provides back-up support and more intensive intervention for families in need, and lastly, coordinates the key public systems, particularly to insure improved assistance for the most troubled families.

Instead of stressed families traveling outside their neighborhood to services, they will participate in treatment and support groups with other neighborhood families, strengthening, rather than weakening their informal support networks.

There is no example of a completely integrated system. However, there are numerous examples of exemplary programs which illustrate some of the components and possible linkages. Some examples are included as an appendix.

There are many challenges to moving in the direction this paper outlines, including:

• family support policies at the federal, state, and county levels, with changes in funding to support emerging directions;[16]

• increased collaboration among public and private agencies;

• new training at paraprofessional and professional levels in community-based family development;[17]

• public education in the importance of family support.

Added to these challenges, family support initiatives are opposed by religious fundamentalist groups as interference in the family by government.

Assets which are helping to move this agenda ahead, include the hundreds of successful local family support/family center programs.

National Foundations have been a force for conceptualizing and funding pilot system change initiatives. A number of national organizations are taking leading roles in moving system change through policy development, advocacy, technical assistance, and information.[18]

Federal Funding through the Family Preservation and Support Act, passed as part of the Budget Reconciliation Act of 1993, provides a flow of federal funds for family support services, and encourages states to redesign their service system.

Numerous states have initiated interdepartmental planning for system reform and, in some cases, are funding state-wide family support services. Ohio's Family and Children First Initiative, for example, created a cabinet-level council of departmental directors, Family and Children First Councils at the county level, and is funding family center approaches in selected communities.

Despite these initiatives, fundamental change is yet to come. Americans have yet to agree that all families need and deserve support. We have yet to agree that, as a nation, we should invest in strengthening families and communities, not just in treatment or punishment for those who fail.

PROGRAM EXAMPLES

Lafayette Courts Family Development Center, Baltimore, Maryland
Lafayette Courts is a project of the City of Baltimore which has brought together separate federal dollars for job training and community development, Community Development Block Grant funding, health and education resources. A public housing project was chosen as the site and residents recruited to survey their neighborhoods about what services they wanted. A core staff, responsible for coordinating and brokering services, are the entry point for families who will be "members" of the center. Offerings include a drop-in center with children's play area where families and youth gather to chat, watch TV, do laundry, make food in the kitchen. The center also includes a day care center (newborn to 5 years and before and after school program), Head Start, on-site health services, adult education and training, including computerized literacy lab, pre-GED and GED classes. A youth group meets weekly for workshops and field trips. An initial evaluation found that family center members were far more likely to be in job training and education programs than residents in other housing developments, reported feeling better about themselves and their lives.

Walbridge Caring Communities, St. Louis, Missouri
A school-based program in a poverty neighborhood, Walbridge Caring Communities met with teachers, canvassed the neighborhood for input and held community meetings. It is meeting the following needs: early screening and parent education for families with children birth to 3, youth center for evening recreational and educational activities, health services, tutoring, intensive intervention for families in crisis, day treatment for referred students, case management, community action against drugs. Impact includes at least a doubling of parent involvement at the school.

Decker Family Development Center, Barberton, Ohio

This program is a collaboration of the Barberton Schools and the Children's Hospital Medical Center of Akron, the Summit County Department of Human Services and the University of Akron. Built around an array of early childhood programs, the Decker Center offers an integrated array of services to families with preschool children. These include parent/child interaction classes (parents and children birth to 3 years), parent education, nutrition education, adult education, health screening and nursing services, home visits, and family activities. Income maintenance workers qualify families on site and there is close collaboration with county child welfare services.

Heights Parent Center, Cleveland Heights, Ohio

HPC is an example of the many programs serving suburban communities. Located in a public school building now used as an early childhood center, HPC offers parent/child drop-in, parent education and support groups, toy lending, developmental screening, family nights and special events. At the request of the Cuyahoga County Early Intervention Local Collaborative Group, HPC is now specially contacting families from the Heights area, who have been identified as at-risk by a maternity hospital and who requested follow-up contact.

Neighborhood Centers Association

The twenty-one neighborhood centers in Greater Cleveland provide examples of agencies in the settlement house tradition. In addition to offering basic programming for seniors, youth and young children, they provide a wide variety of classes, interest groups, and family activities. They have partnerships with neighborhood schools, often sending staff into the schools to run support groups, make home visits and coordinate tutoring and after-school activities. Community organizing and citizen action is a major focus. Many have partnerships with community/housing development organizations and the surrounding business community. They work cooperatively with other neighborhood-based service providers and many deliver services to persons involved with public systems through contracts with the Juvenile Court, Children and Family Services, and the JOBS program.

FOOTNOTES

[1] Kahn, A. J., and Kamerman, S. B. (1977). *Not for the Poor Alone: European Social Services.* New York: Harper and Row.

[2] While the poor are most affected by the fragmentation of public system services, middle-class families with multiple and severe problems, also have difficulty negotiating these systems, a family with a low functioning child suffering mental health and substance abuse problems, school problems, and in trouble with juvenile court.

[3] Figure III, A Problem Paradigm, Training materials developed by Ted Bowman, Associate Director, Community Care Resources, a program of the Wilder Foundation, St. Paul, MN.

[4] For example: Kagan, S. L., Powell, Douglas R., Weissbourd, Bernice, Zigler, Edward F., *America's Family Support Programs*, Yale University Press, New Haven, 1987; Schorr, Lizbeth, *Within Our Reach, Breaking the Cycle of Disadvantage*, Anchor Press Doubleday, New York, 1988; U.S. Department of Education, U.S. Department of Health and Human Services, *Together We Can, A Guide for Crafting A Profamily System of Education and Human Services;* National Governor's Association, *Changing Systems for Children and Families*, Washington D.C. 1993; Dunst, Carl J., Trivetter, Carol M., Deal, Angela G., *Enabling and Empowering Families: Principles and Guidelines for Practice*, Brookline Books, Cambridge, MA, 1988.

[5] In fact, the family support movement has spawned new efforts to clarify ideas about empowerment and applications in local communities. The university-based Cornell empowerment Group, was initiated in 1989 with funding by the Ford Foundation. This project published, *"Networking Bulletin, Empowerment and Family Support"*.

[6] Family Center Program of the Hawaii Community Services Council, *"Family Strengths, Community Strengths: Collected Wisdoms, A Resource Manual."*

[7] The Task Force on Comprehensive and Coordinated Psychological Services for Children (Ages 0-10), *"Comprehensive and Coordinated Psychological Services for Children: A Call for Service Integration,"* Board of Professional Affairs and the Psychology in the Schools Program, American Psychological Association, Fifth draft: February 18, 1994.

[8] Richman, Harold A., Stagner, Matthew W., Social Services for Children: Recent Trends and Implications, Chapin Hall Center For Children, Chicago, February 1987.

[9] Kagan, Sharon Lynn, Keynote Address, *Families: Redefining, Reinforcing, Revitalizing*, Health and Human Services Institute, 1994.

[10] The term "Profamily" is taken from the term used in *"Together We Can: A Guide for Crafting a Profamily System of Education and Human Services,"* U.S. Department of Education, U.S. Department of Health and Human Services, Washington D.C., April 1993.

[11] This conceptual framework is consistent with the recommendations of the National Commission on Child Welfare and Family Preservation of the American Public Welfare Association, published in a paper entitled, *"A Commitment To Change,"* adopted December 1990.

[12] "Neighborhood" can be either a recognized geographic area, or a collection of institutions serving a particular cultural group; the issue is the existence of informal support networks, easy accessibility of activities and services, and sense of identification and ownership by residents or participants.

[13] The following description of the family center approach is excerpted from *"Guide To Developing Neighborhood Family Centers: Strategies for Service Integration and Community Building,"* Nina McLellan et al, Federation for Community Planning, Cleveland, Ohio, 1992.

[14] Goetz, Kathryn, Editor, *Programs to Strengthen Families, Family Resource Coalition: A Resource Guide,* Third Edition, Chicago, 1992.

[15] *"Specialized Clinical Services: The Flexible Clinical Response Team,"* Guide To Developing Neighborhood Family Centers, Federation for Community Planning, 1992, p. 80-81.

[16] Progress is being made in the financing arena through the efforts of some national organizations and consultants. See for example: Farrow, F., Bruner, C., *Getting to the Bottom Line: State and Community Strategies for Financing Comprehensive Community Service Systems,* Resource Brief 4; National Center For Service Integration, 1993.

[17] The Kellogg Foundation recently funded a number of initiatives, including one in Cleveland, to develop new curricula and training in community-based family development.

[18] Examples include Family Resource Coalition, National Center for Services Integration, Council of Governors' Policy Advisors, Center for the Study of Social Policy, National League of Cities, American Public Welfare Association.

 **Nina McLellan, M.A.,** *is a senior planning associate with the Federation for Community Planning in Cleveland, Ohio. She began working in the area of social services planning in 1980, after six years as director of the Child Study Center at Cleveland Metropolitan General Hospital, and prior to that, lead teacher at Hanna Perkins School, both programs serving emotionally disturbed, developmentally impaired pre-school children. At Federation for Community Planning, Ms. McLellan has been director of the Council on Children, Youth and Families, staff to the Day Care Planning Project, and is currently Director of the Family Center Planning Project. She provides consultation, technical assistance, and training to community organizations and planning bodies. She is the primary author of "Guide to Developing Neighborhood Family Centers: Strategies for Service Integration and Community Building," as well as other publications and articles.*

The Individual Within the Family Unit: Genetic Input and Behavioral Dynamics

SHERROD D. MOREHEAD, PH.D.
Clinical Psychologist
University Suburban Health Center
Cleveland, Ohio

This paper will address several dimensions of the family structure that might shed light on the question of success and failure of the family. I will address initially, genetic contributions to individual characteristics and how these factors could play a role in family function. I will then explore coping styles of individuals within the family, styles which arise as a combination of personality factors and learned approaches of functioning within the group. Finally, I will discuss some of the ills that attack the family and their impact which can change the dynamic composition of the family.

Lyken, et al., (1992) reported a study of behavioral characteristics of identical twins, fraternal twins, and siblings. Their findings indicate a significant influence of genetic factors reflected in the attitudes, thought processes, behavioral preferences, and behavioral patterns of identical twins. Fraternal twins and siblings data reflect no evidence for behavioral concordance compared to identical twins. Some identical twin pairs were raised apart from infancy. Yet many of their idiosyncratic behaviors were perfectly matched.

In families where members are rather dissimilar in genetic influence, for example, in temperament, personality style, conflict resolution, sociability, and interpersonal preferences, leadership in the family has a special challenge to understand and manage these differences to maximize personal development and effective family identifications. Individuals in whom genetic influences are quite similar experience almost spontaneous empathy, similar thought processes — how they assess and perceive the world — and other behavioral characteristics which result in a strong sense of compatibility. These factors are often conducive to the development of positive rapport and good working relationships. The trite sayings, such as "they are so similar that they do not get along," or "opposites attract," is viewed with great skepticism. When individuals are similar in basic ways, factors such as inclusion, identification, and predictability are relevant to good and effective interpersonal relationships within the family.

At this level, perhaps a family with reduced effectiveness in terms of installation of ego strength, self-worth, and personal growth within individual family members is a consequence of a core incompatibility, a basic sense of being different as compared with being very similar. Identification within the family is incomplete; interpersonal distance and a reduced sense of compatibility results. To a minor degree, this is a house divided — a basic weakness in the foundation of the family. When these differences are misunderstood by the family leadership, feelings of guilt, shame, and inadequacy might arise. Avoidance behavior, tension, and conflict can result within and between group members. For young family members there can be a modification or fixation of mental and emotional development. An unevenness in emotional profile and an exacerbation of normal developmental stages can effect the child's thought processes, attitudes, and behavioral patterns. As maturation continues, coping patterns and skills are usually less effective and not conducive to rewarding interpersonal relationships.

If the family managers are more aware of the common effects of genetic influences within the group, efforts are made to accept differences, build on individual strengths, create a sense of belonging, and family identification. The managers can encourage environmental mastery in ways that relate to the aptitudes of each individual family member.

How do family managers learn and develop effective approaches to work with individual family members? And, is a team approach necessary? Data derived from the United Nations Statistical Chart on Families (1993) indicates the following characteristics:

	U.S.	U.K.
1) Total # of families	95,619,000	19,949,000
2) Total # in family	2.6	2.8
3) Family headed by females	33.4%	25.2%
4) Own residence	64.2%	55.6%

To compare the United States with a similar country, the United Kingdom, the U.S. has a larger number of families. However, other comparisons are very similar. In both countries the family size is small. At least 50% of families own the place where they live. And one-third to one-fourth of the families have female leadership. What is new! So, we can see that the family leaders have on average a relatively small number of people to manage. The team is usually comprised of family identifications. The managers are often individuals within the small group.

In an article by Stagdill, (1948), several leadership factors were described:

1) dominance
2) extroversion
3) sociability
4) ambition or achievement
5) responsibility

6) integrity
7) self-confidence
8) mood and emotional control
9) diplomacy
10) cooperativeness

A more modern version of similar dimensions is reported by Digman (1990), R. Hogan (1992), and Goldberg (1993), who describe factors such as:

1) sergeancy
2) agreeableness
3) conscientiousness

4) emotional stability
5) intellect

In group observations, leadership factors are described by J. Hogan (1978), Gough (1990), Rueb and Foti (1990), and Zaccaro, Foti, and Kehay (1991) as:

1) dominance
2) capacity for status
3) sociability
4) social pressure

5) self-acceptance
6) achievement via independence
   (emotional stability)
7) empathy (agreeableness)

The most often cited reasons for failure by these authors is the leader's inability to work through others to be successful. They are unable to build a team. They produce alienation and exclusion, rather than inclusion.

In terms of team building, Hallam and Campbell (1992) describe several factors:

1) communicate a clear mission or sense of purpose
2) identify available resources and talent
3) develop talent
4) plan and organize
5) coordinate work activities
6) acquire needed resources
7) minimize or resolve conflict among group members
8) ensure members understand the team's goals, constraints, and resources

The success of family leaders is dependent in part on the leader's capability, including a high capacity to communicate, developing a sense of cohesiveness in the family, and developing an effective division of labor. As stated before, the manager's ability to understand the unique personal characteristics of each group member and to develop a sense in the group of acceptance and inclusion is fundamental to success in the family.

Part of success in the family is associated with the health status of family members. To a large extent, health-related behaviors are associated with socioeconomic status. Socioeconomic status is well defined by Dulton and Levine (1989) as economic status measured by income, social status measured by education, and work status measured by occupation.

In an article by Adler, et al (1994), the author points out that socioeconomic status has a potent and pervasive effect on biological outcomes. Adler, et al (1994), Adelstein (1980), and Marnot, et al (1991) concur that there is evidence that the association of socioeconomic status and health occurs at every level of the socioeconomic hierarchy, not only below the poverty line. Those in unfavored circumstances have poorer health than those at the highest levels. It seems those at lowest levels of socioeconomic status engage in a greater number of illness-related behaviors as compared to families at higher socioeconomic levels. These health risk behaviors include cigarette smoking, physical inactivity, poor diet, and substance abuse, particularly abuse of alcohol.

In addition to these health-risk factors, psychological characteristics are of vital importance to the health of the family. First is depression. Depression has been studied both as a pathological state of major depression, and in terms of general depressive symptoms. Socioeconomic status is inversely related to both major depression and depressive symptoms. In a Canadian sample, the prevalence of depression was 1.9%, 4.5%, and 12.4% in high, average, and low socioeconomic groups. In a sixteen year follow-up, the inverse gradient repeated itself in annual incidence of new depression. Murphy, et al (1991) and Kaplan, et al (1987), found higher rates of new depression over a nine-year period among those of lower income and education.

Of major importance is the fact that depression is linked to health outcomes, particularly coronary artery disease. Of patients with coronary artery disease, twice as many of those with a major depression experienced at least one major cardiac event, e.g., myocardial infarction, bypass surgery, in the subsequent year compared to non-depressed patients (77.8% vs 34.9% p < .02, Carney, et al, 1988).

Another major contributor to the psychological illness of the family member is hostility. A disposition reflecting anger proneness, a cynical, distrusting view of others, and antagonistic behavior comprise the profile. These factors also seem to relate to socioeconomic status with disease risk. In a national sample in the United States, hostility was inversely related to five levels of education ($p < .001$), occupational status ($p < .001$), and income ($p < .003$; Barefoot, et al, 1991).

Several prospective studies linked hostility to risk of coronary heart disease (CHD) and premature mortality. Some reports indicated that among men under age 47, greater hostility measured on entry into the multiple risk factor intervention trial conferred an adjusted relative risk of 2.1 for coronary heart disease or both. ($p = .001$; Dembroski, et al, 1989). Shekel, et al, (1983) found the relative odds of an initial CHD event to be .68 for low versus high hostility groups after adjustment for age, systolic blood pressure, serum cholesterol, cigarette smoking, and alcohol intake ($p < .01$). Also, cross-sectional studies show associations between hostility and peripheral arterial disease (Joesoef, et al, 1989).

Life events precipitate another significant relationship between the health of the family and negative emotion. Such perceptions are known to alter neuroendocrine responses and immune responses that may put individual family members at greater risk for a range of illnesses. Family members experiencing recent stressful life events have been found to be at greater risk for gastrointestinal disorders (Harris, 1991), menorrhagia and secondary amenorrhea, and heart attack (Theoral, 1974). Perceptions of stress and negative affect have been similarly linked to heart disease (Byrne & Whyte, 1980), stroke (Harmea, et al, 1990), and infection (Cohen, et al, 1991, 1993).

These data suggest that family managers in average to low socioeconomic families have a very significant challenge in terms of maintaining the health status of the family, and to perhaps elevate the socioeconomic status of the family by encouraging fewer health risk behaviors, increasing earning power, and providing educational opportunities for each family member.

In more advantaged families, managers must recognize the strong potential for personal growth, good health, and higher education available to individual family members. To overlook these factors or minimize their importance is to strike at the core of the family.

How do families cope with all the many pressures brought about by challenge and disadvantage? What is possible in terms of the range of usual human personality and character development? First of all, genetic influences of personality and character style are considered, at least in a clinical setting, to be apparent and factual. In infancy, caretakers can differentiate various dissimilar personality styles and central aspects of temperament. Early on, most young children respond in a pervasive fashion to various stimuli, e.g., physically, emotionally, and vocally. Later in life, certain biologic systems seem to dominate over others in response to stimulation. One might develop as a gastrointestinal responder, a headache responder, or an anxiety responder. Some people will be loquacious, while others might be withholding and not forthcoming.

We have reviewed earlier some of the known effects of context and experience on behavior and biologic outcomes. In some combination, one's genetic and experiential history blends to characterize personality and temperament, two vital parts of coping. Intellectual capacity, use of fantasy, imagination, and inherent problem-solving facility all contribute to coping capacity.

What are the favored coping styles, perhaps in terms of object relationships, communication and task-effective behaviors? In terms of a division of labor, managers and team players possibly have somewhat of a different blend of personality characteristics. As stated previously, most managers succeed because they find success through others. We said an effective leader is empathetic, socially dominant, recognizes and develops talent and communicates goals in a clear-cut fashion. What about the team players? With the early development of family identification, a sense of inclusion, and basic opportunity to thrive, the team forms into a family process.

In families I have seen through the years, both in family distress, or in family business, the following personality features I think are effective to the managers. Males or females with a basic obsessive-compulsive personality style are often conscientious, punctual, detail oriented, caring, subject to guilt—which keeps us close to the standard—informed, and appreciate issues of control. If the family manager happens to have such features as these, their effectiveness seems likely to be in place. But if the manager has a propensity for impulse-control issues, or is subject to harsh and rigid controls of superego, then managerial effectiveness is likely reduced. Family members respond differently to these types of leaders.

The obsessive-compulsive type instills pride, mastery, a tendency to have a game plan, self-control, and strength. In these terms, the family can give and accept guidance, correct errors, and be supportive.

With the other scenario, there is often disruption, a sense of shame, reduced self-esteem, and lack of mastery.

Obviously, with the presence of physical or psychological illness, even the best of family circumstances is compromised and limited. Hope or future opportunity is clouded. Family resources are strained. At these times, support and intervention might be best achieved from resources outside the family. Individual as well as family treatment is a major resource for the family.

I have attempted to address an unwieldy, somewhat amorphous, mega-large topic. My thoughts are entirely unexhaustive. Yet there are major themes presented about the role of genetics in personality and family style, some ideas are explained about family managers and why they are or are not successful. Personality style and temperament are considered as a viable segment of the total picture. Coping capacity and style are central to maintain integrity of the family core against illness as well as life experiences.

Overall, the family is the strength that individuals need. And this effect generalizes into the fabric of our society. To some extent, as the family goes, so goes the individual and our society at large.

REFERENCES

Barefoot, J. D., et al. "Hostility Patterns and Health Implications: Correlates of Cook-Medley Hostility Scale Scores in a National Survey." *Health Psychology* 10 (1991): 18-24.

Byrne, D. G. and Whyte, H. M. "Life Events and Myocardial Infarction Revisited: The Role of Measures of Individual Impact." *Psychosomatic Medicine* 42, (1991): 1-10.

Carney, R. M., et al. "Major Depressive Disorder Predicts Cardiac Events in Patients with Coronary Artery Disease." *Psychosomatic Medicine* 50, (1988): 627-633.

Cohen, S., Tyrrell, D. A. J., and Smith, A. P. "Psychological Stress in Humans and Susceptibility to the Common Cold." *New England Journal of Medicine* 325, (1991): 606-612.

Cohen, S., Tyrrell, D. A. J., and Smith, A. P. "Negative Life Events, Perceived Stress, Negative Affect, and Susceptibility to the Common Cold." *Journal of Personality and Social Psychology* 64 (1993): 131-140.

Dembroski, T. M., et al. "Components of Hostility as predictors of Sudden Death and Myocardial Infarction in the Multiple Risk Factor Intervention Trial." *Psychosomatic Medicine* 51 (1989): 514-522.

Digman, J. M. "Personality Structure: Emergence of the Five Factor Model." Palo Alto: Annual Reviews. *Annual Review of Psychology* Vol. 41 (1990): 417-440.

Goldberg, L. R. "The Structure of Phenotypic Personality Traits." *American Psychologists* 48 (1993): 26-34.

Gough, H. G. "Testing for Leadership with the California Psychological Inventory." In K. E. Clark and M. B. Clark (Eds.) *Measures of Leadership*. (West Orange: Leadership Library of America 1990): 355-379.

Hallam, G. L. and Campbell, D. P. "Selecting Team Members — Start With a Theory of Team Effectiveness." Paper presented at the 7th Annual Meeting of the Society of Industrial and Organizational Psychology. Montreal, Quebec, Canada.

Harmsen, P., et al. "Risk Factors for Stroke in Middle-Aged Men in Goteborg, Sweden." *Stroke* 21 (1990): 23-29.

Harris, T. O. "Physical Illness: An Introduction." In G.W. Brown and T. O. Harris (Eds.) *Life Events and Illness*. (New York: Guilford, 1989) 199-212.

Harris T. O. "Life Stress and Illness: The Question of Specificity." *Annals of Behavioral Medicine* 13 (1991): 211-219.

Hogan, J. "Personalogical Dynamics of Leadership." *Journal of Research in Personality* 12 (1978): 390-395.

Hogan R. and Hogan, J. *Hogan Personality Inventory Manual*. Tulsa: Hogan Assessment Systems.

Joesoef, M. R., et al. "The Association of Peripheral Arterial Disease with Hostility in a Young Healthy Veteran Population." *Psychosomatic Medicine* 51 (1989): 285-289.

Kaplan, G. A., et al. "Psychological Predictions of Depression: Prospective Evidence from the Human Population Laboratory Studies." *American Journal of Epidemiology* 125 (1987): 206-220.

Murphy, J. M., et al. "Depression and Anxiety in Relation to Social Status." *Archives of General Psychiatry* 48 (1991): 223-229.

Rueb, J. D. and Foti, R. J. "Traits Self-Monitoring, and Leadership Emergence." Paper presented at the Fifth Annual Conference of the Society for Industrial and Organizational Psychology, Miami, FL.

Shekelle, R. B., et al. "Hostility, Risk of Coronary Heart Disease, and Mortality." *Psychosomatic Medicine* 45 (1983): 109-114.

Stogdill, R. M. "Personal Factors Associated with Leadership: A Survey of the Literature." *Journal of Personality* 25 (1948): 35-71.

Theorell, T. "Life Events Before and After the Onset of a Premature Myocardial Infarction." B. S. Dohrenwend and B. P. Dohrenwend (Eds.) *Stressful Life Events: Their Nature and Effects* (New York: Wiley, 1974) 101-117.

United Nations Publication Sales, Statistical Division. (New York: United Nations) No. E 93. XVII 9.

Zaccaro, S. J., Foti, R. J., and Kenny, D. A. "Self-Monitoring and Trait-Based Variance in Leadership: An Investigation of Leader Flexibility Across Multiple Group Situations." *Journal of Applied Psychology* 76 (1991): 308-315.

Sherrod D. Morehead, Ph.D. *is a clinical psychologist in full-time private practice at the University Suburban Health Center in suburban Cleveland, Ohio. He is an Assistant Clinical Professor of Psychology at Case Western Reserve University Medical School, and on the staff at University Hospitals of Cleveland and St. Luke's Hospital, Cleveland, Ohio. Dr. Morehead specializes in psychodynamics in terms of the individual and groups. His extensive teaching extends into both clinical and scientific areas. For the past ten years, he has also been a consultant focusing on family-owned and closely held businesses. He received his Ph.D. from the University of Houston in 1966 and acquired further training in psychoanalysis after coming to Cleveland in 1967.*

COMMUNITY VIRTUES:
THE IMPACT ON FAMILIES

ARTHUR J. NAPARSTEK, PH.D.
Grace Longwell Coyle Professor
Mandel School of Applied Social Sciences
Case Western Reserve University
Senior Fellow Cleveland Foundation

During the past three decades, debate about the welfare of family and children has focused on family economics or family structure. Liberals argue that families with children are hurt by declining wages, while conservatives point to family disintegration as the primary problem. Statistics support both perspectives, as more and more we find troubled children who are raised in financially squeezed homes and/or a "non-traditional family." Clearly, increasing rates of divorce, out-of-wedlock childbirth and co-habitation have changed the meaning of family.

David Popenoe writes that throughout its history this country has depended heavily, for both social order and economic success, on the relatively self-sufficient, nurturing family unit — a childrearing unit that is crucial to the survival and development of its children; a social unit that attends to its members' socioemotional needs; an economic unit that efficiently specializes its work and consumption roles; and a welfare unit that cares for the sick, injured, handicapped and elderly. Many scholars are now concluding that in each of these functions, the modern American family is failing.[1]

What has been missing from the debate is the relationship between the family and the larger community. If the family is the basic unit and key mechanism of community, it requires the support of the larger community. And conversely, when that support falls short or disappears, the family has trouble fulfilling its basic functions. When the family fails to function as it should, the community suffers.

In recent years, this fundamental truth has become clearer than ever. The community and the family are inextricably intertwined: What hurts one, hurts the other; what strengthens one, strengthens the other.

This paper identifies community-based factors which can be singled out as critical to support of the family. The paper is based on the assumption that to understand the interrelationship between community and family, we must extrapolate lessons from culture and religion. In this context, we will also identify how intertwined religious and civic virtues are with the functioning of family life.

John Gardner states, "Families and communities are the ground-level generators and preservers of values and ethical systems. No society can remain vital or even survive without a reasonable base of shared values — and such values are not established by edict from lofty levels of the society. They are generated chiefly in the family, school, church, and other intimate settings in which people deal with one another face to face. The ideals of justice and compassion are nurtured in communities."[2]

Yet, modernity has promoted a new and radical form of "individualism," that, in turn, has weakened the traditional groupings that make up society — the neighborhoods, local communities, volunteering associations, and religious organizations. This "New Individualism" encourages narcissistic, hedonistic, and self-oriented behavior in what otherwise might be socially motivated and responsible family members. Popenoe notes that this new individualism eroding the family is in part the result of affluence. Oddly enough, it is not economic insecurity that is the main cause of family decline, but the relative economic security that produces increasing rates of marital dissolution, co-habitation without marriage, single-parent families, voluntary step families, single-person households and non-marital births.[3]

Modernity has its costs. Yet, we cannot turn the clock back, nor is it desirable to do so. The challenge is to develop strategies that can lead to strong communities for us now, communities that will bring about a natural shift away from radical individualism.

In the past and the present there have been and continue to be communities rooted in different cultures and religions that utilize a variety of mechanisms (rituals, associations, organizations), which transmit virtues and values that support family life. Two good examples are the religious communities of the eastern European shtetl and the West African village.

By revisiting these two communities that so strongly support family life, we can identify and build on what is positive for families now.

A RELIGIOUS COMMUNITY: THE EASTERN EUROPEAN SHTETL

During the 19th and 20th centuries, European Jewry experienced significant persecution. As a means of coping with anti-semitism, Jews settled in small villages often found in the outer fringes of urban centers. These villages were called shtetls and the people were extremely poor.

Was there any sort of family preservation or family support program in the shtetl? Were there mental health services? How were the poor and homeless taken care of? What did people do about domestic violence, mental illness, serious family problems, retardation, unemployment?

When we look at the shtetl, the first thing that impresses us is how intertwined religious values and institutions are with social services. There is no separation. The shelter for the homeless and the soup kitchen are usually in the Bet Midrash, the study house, where children and adults went to learn Torah.

The voluntary associations that rendered charitable services were named for Biblical Mitzvot:

"Visiting the Sick"
"The Burial Society"
"Welcoming Visitors"
"Redeeming the Captives"
"The Free-Loan Association"

The official minutes of these societies were considered holy objects with special protective powers for those that kept them. They were written by a professional Torah scribe and decorated with Biblical mottos.

So, too, with the minutes of the workers' societies — the tailors, cobblers, hatmakers, and tanners groups — that cared for the social and material needs of their own when the Torah portion of the week related to one particular craft, it was those craftsmen that were called up in synagogue for special honors.

The integration was total, and the shtetl's powerful family therapist/ mental health counselor/ad hoc ombudsman was usually the Rebbe. Now, the Rebbe was usually not the same as the rav, the Rabbinic authority in the community based on the age-old Talmudic hierarchy, who decided on matters of life and death, sacredness and profanity. Usually the rav was seen as removed and above-it-all, narrow and legalistic in his focus. The Rebbe, on the other hand, was a spontaneous, natural leader, sometimes quite knowledgeable in the traditional ways, but coming to his position due to some remarkable natural gift — force of intellect, healing power, spiritual discernment or sheer charisma. He related to the common person and gave hope, comfort, kindness, and inspiration at a time when Jews were demoralized and hopeless in a hostile Gentile world.

The Rebbe provided advice on child-rearing, healing of illness (using special rituals, life-style advice, herbs, laying on of hands, prayer), mediation in personal conflict (between spouses, parent/kids, in-laws, business partners), and emotional counseling for "spiritual imbalances." He even had his own methods of securing money to ransom Jews in jail for non-payment of rents (a common occurrence) or for needy families.

Anyone familiar with the work of Isaac Bashevis Singer also knows that Rebbes were also seen as providing a paranormal service or two: exorcism of evil spirits; clairvoyant location of deserting husbands and missing people; interventions with troublesome dead relatives; and miraculous protection from Gentiles and their army drafts and forced conversions.

Needless to say, with a leadership style that touched everyone with a powerful and personal compassion, the Rebbe had an exalted position of tremendous authority in his milieu, and was a great catalyzer of growth among his followers. People followed his instructions for change, believed in their power, and changed. Families felt secure.

The Rebbe did not function alone. He had a circle of followers, apprentice rebbes-in-training and helpers. He usually had a "Gabbai" or secretary, who wrote up requests for help and agendas for formal individual meetings, called "yehidut," and prioritized the day's or night's appointments. The Gabbai would identify problems of families and locate the support that was needed. Often that support came from the "Haver" or "Friend." The Haver was a special ally to the family seeking help, and assisted them in planning their meetings with the rebbe, was informed of the Rebbe's Counsel, and became a daily support in the struggle for a new direction.

The Rebbe was also surrounded by a ritual structure that assisted him in his work with the family, particularly the father or grandfather, and promoting his effectiveness. People not only came to the Rebbe for the "yehidut" at times of trouble, but at significant junctures in their lives — before a Bar Mitzvah or wedding.

The actual meeting was extremely intense, but usually rather brief — about a half hour — usually at night (when the Hasid's soul was more accessible) and in the Rabbi's inner chamber. (To give some idea of the Rebbe's clout, this inner chamber was sometimes called the Holy of Holies.)

Once inside, the expectation was of intense and complete union with the Rebbe. One could speak of anything, and many cathartic outpourings occurred. The Rebbe used his diagnostic skill, his empathy, his intellect, and his intuition to listen and prescribe a remedy or course of action. Always the goal was the same: To help the person harmonize his or her life, balance the material and the spiritual world.

The problems he dealt with included substance abuse, spousal abuse, and various problems with children and finances.

The intertwining of Jewish values and such interventions is very strong and the connections are very powerful ones. For instance, Judaism puts a very high value on "awareness." According to the Talmud, it is essential that we not just exist, but that we observe ourselves in our existence, and try to frame it and evaluate it in the light of a higher purpose. But first we must be willing and able to observe ourselves.

Judah Ha Nasi in Pirkay Avot said, "Know what is above you — a seeing eye, and a hearing ear and all your deeds are written in a book." Now I'll admit that the book part is a bit concrete, but the essential message is clear: We are to see ourselves being seen.

Maimonides says, "Man needs to direct every single one of his deeds solely toward attaining knowledge of the Name, blessed be He." Again, the idea of self-awareness, at all times.

The community correlate — not as lofty, but a definite cousin of awareness — is the notion of being seen by "the observing neighbor." The observing neighbor is essential to community accountability and such community virtues as commitment and discipline. We behave better when we behave as if we were being watched.

The overriding value to family came from the importance given to community by the great Rabbis and in the prayer books. For example, Rabbi Hillel said, "Do not separate yourself from the community" (Pirke Avot 2:5). In the same book, *The Ethics of the Fathers,* there is only one thing we are enjoined to do "for the sake of heaven" — work on behalf of the community.

Roughly translated it says, "All who work for the community work for the sake of Heaven, for then the merit of their parents sustains them, and their righteousness endures forever" (Pirke Avot 2:2). And of course we have the most famous quote of all, the terse but profound words from Hillel: "If I am not for myself, who will be for me? and if I am only for myself, what am I? And if not now, when?"

Clearly, from a community-building perspective, Hillel was putting forth both values of self-esteem and virtues which rely upon faith and obligation to others in the family and community.

We all know that self-esteem, obligation and faith, are the sine qua non of strong community and family. We must have it to be able to care for others, maintain relationships, give love. It provides the reserves that allow us to tolerate frustration, roll with the punches, contribute, create, hope, get up and try again. It's the difference between the parent who wants to kill his kid for crying all night and the one that actually does. It is the nourishment that staves off evil.

What we hope for in our work with families and individuals always is that self-esteem, faith and obligation, will be experienced in a new way or a stronger way, or re-learned the original old way. Living ourselves, after all, and we need to learn how to love our neighbor.

The community offered associations which transmitted such virtues as faith, obligation, commitment, and a sense of self-esteem throughout the entire shtetl population.

THE COVENANT OF THE TRIBE: STRONG COMMUNITY/STRONG FAMILIES

It is clear that the European shtetl and Hassidic communities in America have put forth values and virtues which reinforce family life through community associations. However, the shtetl is not alone in putting forth such virtues. If one were to examine an African tribal village, we would find the same values placed on virtues such as (a) a sense of responsibility leading towards being obligated toward other members of one's family and village; b) courage which leads to behaviors like telling the truth or advocacy in the village; c) honesty which leads to trustworthy behavior; d) discipline, which leads to working hard for self and others; e) commitment, leading to cooperation and mutual accountability; and f) faith, which gives over-arching hope and meaning to it all.

The following will excerpt several passages from Malidoma Patrice Somé's book, *Of Water and the Spirit*, which offers vivid descriptions of village life. In fact, it is uncanny how close to the Hassidic community of eastern Europe is the Dagara Village of West Africa. For example, the role of Rebbe is played by Malidoma's grandfather on the use of ritual to celebrate life events, and integrate the spiritual with everyday functioning in the community.

Consider the following passages from *Of Water and The Spirit*:

> "Grandfather's respect and love for children was universal in the tribe. To the Dagara, children are the most important members of society, the community's most precious treasures. We have a saying that it takes the whole tribe to raise a child. Homes have

doorless entrances to allow children to go in and out wherever they want, and it is common for a mother to not see her child for days and nights because he or she is enjoying the care and love of other people. When the mother really needs to be with her child, she will go from home to home searching for it.

When a child grows into an adolescent, he or she must be initiated into adulthood. A person who doesn't get initiated will remain an adolescent for the rest of his/her life, and this is a frightening, dangerous, and unnatural situation. After initiation, the elders will pick a partner for the young person, someone who is selected for their ability to team up with you in the fulfillment of your life purpose. If one obediently walks their life path, they will become an elder somewhere in their late forties or early fifties. Graduating to this new status, however, depends on one's good track record.

A male elder is the head of his family. He has the power to bless, and the power to withhold blessing. This ability comes to him from his ancestors, to whom he is very close, and he follows their wisdom in counseling his large family.

Wealth among the Dagara is determined not by how many things you have, but by how many people you have around you. A person's happiness is directly linked to the amount of attention and love coming to him or her from other people. In this, the elder is the most blessed because he is in the most visible position to receive a lot of attention. The child is, too, because it "belongs" to the whole community.

Some elders are chosen to sit on the village council. There they participate in decision making that affects the entire village. Women have their council separate from men because of their unique roles and responsibilities. Dagara culture is matrilineal — everybody in the village carries the name of their mother. The family is feminine, the house where the family lives is kept by a male. The male is in charge of the family security. The female is in charge of the continuity of life. She rules the kitchen, the granaries where food is stored, and the space where meals are taken. The male is in charge of the medicine shrine and of the family's connection with the ancestors. He brings the things that nourish the family, like food.

For a full 50 years, my grandfather had been the priest, the leader, and the counselor of a family of over 50 souls. Faced with domestic problems of all kinds, he had had to be tough.

Judging from his physical appearance—muscles still protruding from tired biceps, square shoulders that looked as if they could still carry weight, big chest that seemed to hide massive lungs—one could see that he had been a robust young man capable of sustaining long hours of demanding physical labor. Grandfather's greatest fame, however, came from his spiritual accomplishments. In the village, everyone knew him as the "upside-down arrow shooter." He was one of the people in the tribe whose name made people shudder, for if he wished to destroy an enemy, he would retire to the quiet of his chambers, place an arrow upside down on his bow, and magically hit his target. The arrow would kill whomever or whatever he named, then rematerialize in his chamber ready for more. The slightest scratch from such a weapon is mortal.

Grandfather's magical guardianship had enabled our family to always have enough food to eat. Two-thirds of the tribe did not share our surplus and could never put aside enough extra food to avoid the hardship of the hunger season, which ran every year from July to September, when stored food ran out. During this time, a mild famine visited many compounds. Children would stop singing and laughter would vanish from the houses at night. Every morning during that time, a long line of people stood at the door of the Birifor house, waiting for a calabash of grain. Distributing food to all these needy people was another of grand-father's tasks. So, every morning of those misty days of July and August, after he had given orders to the men and women of the family regarding their daily assignments, Grandfather would drag himself to the door of his room. There, he would take all the time he needed to be seated comfortably. I would wait calmly until he was settled, then I would sit on his bony lap. Aided by a woman whose charge it was to measure up the proper amount of millet to be distributed to each of the needy, Grandfather would dispatch his task until shortly after noontime when the heat became unbearable.

Grandfather's space housed the pharmacy of the entire Birifor clan — an array of roots, daily collected, nightly prepared, to face emergencies of all sorts. These little dwellings contained the prosperity — spiritual, material, and magical — of the Birifor. Some of these roots were good for physical illness, but most of them were good for illness of the soul. These little buildings held the spiritual destiny of every member of the family. There, each one of us existed in the form of a stone, silent, docile, available.

The stones represented the birth certificate of every person in the clan. This is where Grandfather went to examine the physical and spiritual energy fields of the people under his care. Through this magical means, Grandfather could check on each of us at his leisure.

He took care of people outside the family, too. Strangers used to come now and then to seek medical help, and Grandfather would begin long ceremonial rites that took most of the day. Sometimes the strangers would bring chickens and, speaking breathlessly in an unintelligible magical language, he would cut their throats and direct the spurting blood onto some statues, representing different spirits, carved out of wood or built against the wall. He never tired of rituals. It took me many years to understand the reasons behind these visits and how Grandfather was able to help these strangers."[4]

THE VILLAGE AS A BASIS FOR COMMUNITY BUILDING

It is clear that we cannot emulate an African village or an eastern European shtetl in an American city. Instead, we can learn from such experiences and extrapolate principles that offer guidance in support of modern community building and family development.

The eastern European shtetl and the West African Dagara village provide a feeling of belonging among the residents. Village-based development in American cities offers the opportunity to reconfigure how neighborhoods function. This concept implies a fresh start and connotes the interdependence of residents with local associations and new governance/service delivery structures.

It is in the neighborhoods where people live, among familiar faces and relatively accessible institutions that people most easily become involved and accountable, and where they stand the best chance of regaining some measure of control over their own destiny. Village-based development is, in brief, an organized effort to make older and lower-income neighborhoods self-sustaining. The process seeks to acquire, develop and use resources for the benefit of families. Several principles should guide in village-based development in American cities.

1) Work in support of families must be comprehensive and integrated.
The eastern European shtetl and the West African village represented natural communities that were characterized by a complex web of relationships. Each community had a certain sense of connectedness and a feeling of belonging. The integration was total.

Why a holistic approach to needs? The mistake made by contemporary attempts to strengthen families was isolating specific problems for intensive intervention — such as enhancing basic family and parenting skills, helping families interact through crisis, building economic opportunities for families, housing or job training, or getting people to jobs. The trouble is that these things are all tangled up with other factors that can undermine the best efforts if they aren't also taken into consideration.

In American cities, we now know that there's an interrelationship between female-headed households, the persistence of poverty over two or more generations, the concentration of poor households in the inner city — and quality of life issues like health and poor outcomes for school-age children.

And to deal with these issues, we must deal with unemployment — particularly male unemployment, because the shortage of "marriageable males" — that is, employed males — in the inner city is a major factor here. But, at the same time, existing transportation systems aren't getting inner-city residents to where the work is; and the available jobs require a different level of skills than what people in the community have.

If we don't acknowledge these linkages, and act with the big picture in mind, our so-called "solutions" can end up doing more harm than good. We have seen this. Housing projects become prisons for the poor and the elderly when issues of crime and security, or city services, also aren't dealt with. And what good is offering a young inner-city mother a job if she doesn't have a way of getting to it, or lacks proper daycare for her kids, or has to deal with other problems in her family that continually drag her down?

But our whole system of human services is set up in such a way as to separate all these issues — children's needs from the needs of their parents, health care from job training, food stamps from completing an education. And each of them has evolved with its own separate bureaucracy and set of hoops that people are required to jump through, all of it quite well meaning.

In many ways, the biggest challenge is going to be to change the whole culture of how all these issues are currently addressed. It's an essential piece. Because we have to start looking at the family's life as a whole, and finding ways to tie all of these services together so they make the family more able to cope — instead of adding to its stress.

2) Village-based development should be based on assets. When we look at the shtetl and West African village, we are struck with the integration of all aspects of the community. And every association or network is thought of clearly as an asset.

On a more contemporary basis, the Cleveland Foundation Commission on Poverty adopted a strong conviction that development should focus on assets, not deficits.[5] The report noted that in the past, the tendency of social welfare practices aimed at families, has been to take a deficit or need-based approach to those being served, focusing on what is lacking. John L. McKnight of Chicago, has developed an exciting new strategy for empowering low-income communities, which starts with the idea that they too have assets. It is a matter of viewing the glass as half full, says McKnight, instead of half empty.[6]

Operating from the "half empty" perspective, he argues, has had the unintended but very deleterious results of sapping individual initiative, diminishing community control, and draining the public coffers for programs and services of questionable effectiveness. Clients are led into working the system instead of working for themselves in the marketplace.

This asset approach has been used with individuals working in program areas such as health or family development. In Tupelo, Mississippi, building on the work of Michael Sherraden in this regard, participants in a family development program are given the equivalent of "seed" money. These funds, which are under the joint control of client and sponsoring agency, can be used for investments toward agreed upon goals, such as books to complete a college degree, or may simply be placed in a savings account to appreciate until the participant completes whatever developmental milestones have been agreed upon, such as graduation from college, at which time the appreciated funds may be used as seed money for a new business.

With middle-class families, this sense of a "life course" in which each stage builds on one's preceding accomplishments is a normal part of life. But for most middle-class families, the process does not begin anew with each generation, because families pass along certain assets. The challenge is to build an opportunity structure where none now exists, to create a "ladder of hope," as it were, by which individuals and families can climb out of poverty.

The Commission Report goes on to identify village assets that are important to families. Consider the following:

• Centralized facilities to house support network services and provide a communal place for family-oriented programs and activities, such as an existing community-based neighborhood center or settlement house

• Library where residents have access to public records

• Child-care facilities: infant, toddler, and after-school care

• Educational facilities

• Churches

• Financial services

• Village shopping areas

• Merchants' association able to help fledgling businesses

• Communal associations: churches, block clubs, parent groups, play groups which are involved in and support family activities

• Safehouses and emergency shelters for women and children who are victims of abuse or who are homeless

• Hotlines and other over-the-phone counseling and emergency referral services

• A community board of parents, residents, service professionals, educators, and business people to guide and design the ongoing development of a basic "family center," a constellation of activities for all village families without categorical identification of specific problems

• A support network of resources facilitating family cohesion and parenting: these may include family life counseling, child developmental screening, temporary child care, mentoring, family recreational/social activities.

• A family network of parents and village organizations to foster peer support and informal community programs

• Coordinated outreach and family assistance services by a team of professionals and trained residents who contact isolated families and identify family needs, initiate family center participation, and facilitate access to services in and out of the center

- Advocacy at the state level for programs for families and children to be integrated from the ground up which will entail their decentralization to the neighborhood level. In Ohio, this will involve broadbanding of funding and regulations and overall missions among the departments of Human Services, Education, and Labor

A focal point of family development is the Neighborhood Family Center which is a mechanism for family service integration. There are various options for how a Center may be structured, where it could be housed in a community, and what services it will offer. Those options selected depend upon the neighborhood, its particular strengths and needs and the overall strategy of the planning initiative it devises to address those needs. For example, a neighborhood may decide to locate such a center within an existing organization or facility: a neighborhood school, an existing neighborhood center, a recreation center. Or, the community may decide to construct a new facility. There may be one lead agency or a consortium to implement and administer the services provided within the center.[7]

3) Village-based development must actively involve the local people in shaping family development strategies. Village-based development involves many intangible forces such as the informal networks of support and leadership that are critical to any long-term effort. Such relationships need to be nurtured and encouraged as part of the process. In the shtetl, the voluntary associations that rendered charitable services were utilized as support for families and those in need. The worker societies that linked tailors, cobblers, etc., to the synagogue were also utilized. In fact, the integration between work, service and spirituality was complete through such associations and networks. It is through these networks that people of a local community become engaged in controlling their lives and community.

We now have empirical evidence which supports the efficacy of community-based networks. Robert Putnam's comparative study of northern and southern Italy has revealed that where there were networks of civic engagement such as guilds, religious fraternities, cooperatives, mutual aid societies and neighborhood associations, people influenced one another to act fairly, families were supported and public institutions worked.

Putnam compared the northern and southern regional governments of Italy. Beginning in 1970, Italians established a nationwide set of regional governments. They were identical in form, but the social, economic, political and cultural contexts were dramatically different.

Some of the new governments were dismal failures, while others were remarkably successful.

Putnam's research suggests that strong traditions of civic engagement made the difference. He noted that networks of civic engagement facilitated coordination and communication and amplify information about the trustworthiness of other individuals. Networks of civic engagement embody past success at collaboration and Putnam concludes that they can even serve as preconditions for economic development.[8] The relevance to contemporary communities in American cities has also been established. Professor William Julius Wilson of the University of Chicago has shown that it is much harder for people living in neighborhoods where that whole network of supports has broken down to escape poverty. Strengthen a neighborhood's fabric and you strengthen the ability of its families to manage their own needs.[9] As noted by Putnam, Anne Case and Lawrence Katz have shown that regardless of race, inner-city youth living in neighborhoods blessed with high levels of civic engagement are more likely to finish school, have a job, and avoid drugs and crime, controlling for the individual characteristics of the youth. He states, "...two identical youths, the one unfortunate enough to live in neighborhoods whose 'networks' have eroded is more likely to end up hooked, booked or dead."[10]

In 1973 Margaret Mead told a Senate Committee, "As families go, so goes the nation."[11] David Papenoe notes that a symbiotic relationship exists between the family and civil society.[12] Growing out of this relationship are community virtues — faith, commitment, obligation, honesty, trust, personal responsibility. Such virtues are taught in the home, but reinforced and transmitted by community-based associations, networks or institutions. McKnight has labeled these entities as assets; Putnam as social capital.

Finding ways to promote and support the health of natural communities through village-based development may be an important key to building strong families. Insights from the eastern European shtetl or the West African village suggest that "top-down" solutions do not work in the long run. The assets and associations of social capital cannot be run roughshod over by programs imposed from above. Indeed, ways must be found to nurture and strengthen those indigenous resources. Churches, schools, neighborhood centers, local banks or credit unions, along with programs that support civic and religious engagement — choral societies, community organizational processes that lead to voter turnout and newspaper readership, fraternal and burial societies are the hallmarks of a neighborhood which will have the support necessary for individual and family life. Experience has shown the folly of failing to build on and support the indigenous life of a community.

FOOTNOTES

[1]David Popenoe (1994). *The family condition, Values and Public Policy.* Washington, D.C.: Brookings Institute, 81.

[2]John W. Gardner (1991). *Building community.* Washington, D.C.: Independent Sector, 5.

[3]David Popenoe, op. cit., 86.

[4]Malidoma Patrice Somé (1994). *Of water and the spirit.* New York, NY: G. P. Putnam's Sons, 23-25. Reprinted by permission of A. Jeremy P. Tarcher/Putnam Books.

[5]*The Cleveland Community Building Initiative: The report and recommendation of the Cleveland Foundation Commission on Poverty* (1992). Cleveland, OH: Case Western Reserve University.

[6]John P. Kretzmann, John L. McKnight (1993). *Building communities from the inside out: A path toward finding and mobilizing a community's assets.* Evanston, IL: Northwestern University.

[7]*The Cleveland Community Building Initiative*, Ibid, 100-101.

[8]Robert D. Putnam (1993). *The prosperous community: Social capital and public life.* Cambridge, MA: The American Prospect, 36-37.

[9]James L. Wilson (1991). Public policy research and the truly disadvantaged. In Christopher Jensles, & Paul Peterson (Eds.), *The urban underclass* (pp. 460-483). Washington, D.C.

[10]Ibid, 39.

[11]Popenoe, op. cit., 95.

[12]Ibid, 95.

 **Arthur J. Naparstek, Ph.D.** *is Professor of Social Work and former Dean (1983-1988) of Case Western Reserve University's Mandel School of Applied Social Sciences. In 1990, in addition to his position as the Grace Longwell Coyle Professor of Social Work, Dr. Naparstek was appointed by the Cleveland Foundation as Director of the Foundation's Commission on Poverty. He is now a Senior Fellow for the Cleveland Foundation. In 1994, President Clinton appointed Dr. Naparstek to the 14-member Board of Directors of the Corporation for National Service. Dr. Naparstek has devoted more than 25 years to working for urban policy and change, especially at the neighborhood level. He has worked with several Congressional committees and assisted in the drafting of Congressional legislation for the reinvestment of neighborhood funds. His applied and theoretical research in urban and neighborhood policy has resulted in additional legislation aimed at improving conditions in American cities. He received his B.S. degree from Illinois Wesleyan, his M.S.W. from New York University and his Ph.D. from the Florence Heller School for Advanced Studies at Brandeis University.*

HUMAN SERVICE AGENCIES AND FAMILIES: WHAT THEY'VE DONE. WHAT THEY CAN DO.

DAVID R. REINES
Deputy County Administrator
Health and Human Services
Cleveland, Ohio

In most urban areas 20% to 25% of all families are impacted, in some way, by the local Department of Human Services. This is certainly the case in Cuyahoga County where one in five residents receive some form of aid through the entitlement programs. Historically public human service agencies have focused on eligibility determination for categorical programs with little effort made to address in any holistic way the typical problems and prevalent risk factors a family seeking public assistance brings to the initial intake process. Existing policies and procedures have, in many ways, actually forced the disintegration of existing family units or delayed the formation of new ones. This does not have to be the case. By refocusing program missions and pursuing a broader, family-based set of outcomes, the public human services agencies can change the impact of their involvement and provide positive support.

To begin the process of designing a system that works to keep families together, an understanding of the demographics and risk factors faced by families in general and those living in poverty in particular, is essential. The most telling of these factors is that only 50% of all family units include a mother and father residing under the same roof. This single statistic mandates that any discussion of families must accept that children, in fully half of the families, are being raised by one parent, grandparents or other adults. Recommendations to improve family life must anticipate only one parent (in 25% of households) being available to carry them out.

The second most telling statistic is that 20% of all children live below the poverty line. This rate rises to 25% for children under six and to 43% for children under 18 living in the City of Cleveland. This is a chilling statistic. Research identifies child poverty as one of the most powerful risk factors leading to negative outcomes in people's lives. Long-term solutions must include economic as well as social interventions to be successful.

To begin to structure service delivery systems to holistically address the multiple socio-economic issues any given family on public assistance is trying to grapple with, some understanding of the presenting secondary symptoms and the less obvious primary symptoms must be reached. Because more than one of these symptoms tend to be present in all families on public assistance, only by developing long-term, coordinated approaches can realistic, lasting solutions be realized. The significance of the two factors already identified can't be ignored. Children growing up in single-parent households typically do not have the same economic, housing, or human resources available as those growing up in two-parent families. This is magnified when the family is located in a community where other risk factors are prevalent. Public assistance families are almost exclusively single-parent families with a higher than average likelihood of high school dropouts, long-term unemployment, or no history of employment. There also is a tendency towards periodic to long-term reliance on welfare. Many of these families are clustered in large numbers in five neighborhoods in Greater Cleveland. When whole communities have these risk factors, specialized service initiatives must target the whole community. Public assistance programs are designed to determine individual program eligibility and offer individual support with little effort to involve the community in efforts to make a family self-sufficient. This approach is not conducive to maintaining the family structure and stemming the breakdown of the family and the surrounding community.

Prevalent risk factors and their impact on a family's prospect of providing an economically stable and nurturing family environment, and a child's chances to grow up to be a contributing adult, must be considered in any effort to develop solutions. The county, for example, has the state's worst rate of out-of-wedlock births to teens and third worst rate of repeat teen births. Of the 2,971 babies born to Cuyahoga County teens in 1992, nearly 68% of these parents depended on public programs. The number of these teen parents dependent on public assistance makes the likelihood of poor physical care of these children high.

Often poor physical care of children between birth to five predicts later delinquency and adult criminality, factors that tear at the fabric of a struggling family and hurt the chances of that child becoming a successful parent. The same is true of children mistreated or abused and the prospect of later delinquency, including violent behavior. In a similar study, 17 of 22 cases analyzed found a significant association between marital discord and child delinquency and aggression. A separate study showed that in families in which parents divorced or separated, the prevalence of antisocial behavior was twice as great in children whose families remained discordant, even following the divorce or separation compared with those whose families became harmonious.

These statistics are relevant in this discussion since the majority of heads of households in ADC families are single women who have experienced the familial discord these studies suggest result in future problems. They become more alarming when educational issues are considered. Nearly 20% of all teens in the City of Cleveland between the ages of 16 and 19 years of age are not in school and don't have a diploma. The long-term impact of limited education is substantial. The unemployment rate for those who drop out of school is nearly twice that of those who graduated from high school but did not go on to college. Among those employed, full-time median income of high school dropouts was only half that of high school graduates. Clearly, education plays a major role in determining the probable success of an individual and that individual's ability to provide for a family. One in five of all teens in the city have dug a significant hole for themselves unless they re-enroll or pursue their high school diploma through other means.

Families on public assistance typically include at least two and often more of these risk factors. A recently released report prepared by Congress provides a synopsis of the typical Aid to Families with Dependent Children (AFDC) Family. In 72% of AFDC families there are two or fewer children. Parents are absent due to divorce or separation 30% of the time, while 53% had no marriage ties with the absent parent. Only 6.8% had some college while less than 1% actually graduated from college. Only 7.4% had any earnings to report. These statistics are consistent with or more conservative than Cuyahoga County's experience.

To begin to effectively address all of the prevalent problems existing when the initial application for assistance is made and start the family on the road to self-sufficiency, a comprehensive assessment which goes beyond the determination of eligibility needs to take place. Other disciplines, which could team to insure timely service provision for identified areas of need, have to be present or involved early on. Policies and regulations need to be designed to encourage the family to stay together and provide support during the transition period.

Unfortunately, the human service system, in many ways, has done the exact opposite. Initial eligibility determination focuses almost entirely on whether the applicant is qualified for the categorical program applied for. There is no discussion of other issues or problems which may have played a major role in bringing the person to apply in the first place. A check, food stamps and medical coverage is provided if eligibility criteria are met. No assessment of what services might be required to assist the individual or family with substance abuse, locating adequate housing, or developing parenting skills which emphasize the importance of spending time with children to prepare them for success in school, is provided. Specific regulations go a long way towards discouraging dad from staying in the home. His presence may in fact jeopardize the family unit's prospect of being determined eligible. The rule requiring a male residing in the home to have worked 100 hours during the most recent four quarters to be eligible for assistance is an example. It is an unrealistic regulation in areas of high unemployment for groups of people without education or marketable job skills. Most fathers don't meet the criteria and the result is, if dad was in the home, he leaves.

The initial application process also fails to emphasize the importance of identifying the children's father for the purpose of collecting child support. A simple statement of "whereabouts unknown" is accepted with little explanation of the importance of children having access to the absent parent and of equal and sometimes greater importance, benefiting from steady and adequate support. A reexamination of the risk factors related to growing in poverty should help to underline the importance of pursuing child support aggressively.

Once on assistance, a person is eligible to receive job training and educational supplements, as well as day care and other supportive services. Initially, this program was set up to emphasize participation as a measure of success. The creation of and retention of actual jobs received less emphasis and as a result remains the weakest, but most important component of the jobs program. For those who do find employment, the gains realized by accepting a minimum wage, full- or part-time job, are minimal and offer little incentive. In many ways, work is not better than welfare for under-educated public assistance recipients in areas of high unemployment.

The Child Support Program does attempt to locate absent parents when identified and when adequate information becomes available. However, an ADC mother who assists in locating an absent father is only entitled to the first $50 dollars of any support received each month. The remainder goes to offset the cost to the state of providing the grant. Clearly, this is inadequate incentive. Custodial parents who know the whereabouts of the absent parent are unlikely to cooperate if the disregard amount can be surpassed by a payment made directly by the absent parent. Mom is better off not cooperating with the Child Support Agency and not impacting her ADC grant in any way, while accepting support under the table. Typically, she receives less than the court determined amount, but more than the $50 she would receive if the support payment was reported.

Other factors work to make the child support system less than efficient. Inconsistent state support guidelines and cumbersome enforcement procedures make the collection of support particularly difficult if the absent parent has relocated to another state, even if avoidance of payment is not an issue. Information that would make parent location efforts more effective and increase the likelihood of support collections is not universally available and when it is, is often through slow, paper-intensive manual processes, as opposed to being accessed through an on-line automated system. The same is true of efforts to establish paternity, although some creative ways are being tried to improve success in this area.

When the by-product of the presence of multiple-risk factors is the abuse or neglect of a child, local child welfare agencies must intervene. In Cuyahoga County, the local Department of Children and Family Services is involved with over 12,000 children, with approximately 3,800 of those children in the custody of the agency. Past practices resulted in many of these children being placed in foster homes or institutions located some distance away from the child's neighborhood. Of the 3,800 children in custody in 1993, at least 60 were placed out of state and 1,050 placed outside of Cuyahoga County. Almost 70% of the children in custody currently come from eight zip code areas in the county, while only 30% of agency foster homes are located within those zip codes. The median length of stay in substitute care was 45.5 months, almost four years. Given these statistics the likelihood reuniting the family and avoiding the impact long-term, out-of-home placement has on a child's chances of becoming a successful adult and parent is remote.

The presence of multiple-risk factors in public assistance families and the failure of public welfare agencies to consider these factors when implementing programs, has had a significant negative impact on poor people. By not coordinating the service delivery system and developing rules and regulations consistent with a mission to keep families together while helping them become self-sufficient, public agencies have actually contributed to the demise of families in the welfare system. Because twenty to twenty-five percent of the residents in a typical urban county are in the system at any given time, the ongoing effect could be disastrous.

This does not have to be the case. Welfare reform is now a national issue and intelligent reform in four key areas could begin a positive turnaround in the public agencies relationship with the families they serve. These areas are the initial intake process, earned income disregards and subsidized employment, the child support system and community-based delivery of social and child welfare services.

The place to begin system reform is when a family first walks through the door. Initial intake needs to take on a broader scope than simple eligibility determination. It must be viewed as an assessment process designed to identify barriers which could undermine the families prospects of staying together, and moving towards a better life. Problems like substance abuse and limited education need to be identified early on and included in a case plan that is developed with input and participation by the family. The importance of paternity being established and financial support for children needs to be emphasized. Finally, rules which cause dad to leave home for a family to become eligible for benefits must be changed. Efforts need to be directed to helping dad and mom accept their responsibility towards their children and become better parents.

The second, and perhaps more important reform which needs to take place, is in the woefully inadequate income received by a typical welfare family, and the failure of the system to effectively support the transition from assistance to self-sufficiency. Currently, an ADC grant for a family of three is $341 per month, with an additional $300 in food stamps. Annualized, this is significantly below the poverty level. Existing regulations governing the amount of earned income, or child support a family can retain while receiving assistance, provide little incentive to seek employment, or cooperate in the location of absent parents. By raising the disregard amount to $500, a parent could work a part-time job, continue to receive benefits and retain medical coverage. The job market in Greater Cleveland has seen its growth, to the extent there has been any, in the service industry, an industry characterized by part-time, low-paying, limited benefit positions. Current regulations inhibit access to these jobs by welfare recipients. Full-time minimum wage earnings would make a family of three ineligible for benefits. Part-time earnings under current regulations would result in a reduction of the grant and food stamps. If such a position does not include medical coverage and requires mom to pay for day care out of net earnings, work of this type is not better than welfare. However, a part-time position of twenty to thirty hours per week, with relaxed earned income disregard amounts of up to $500 that allows continued eligibility for assistance, would actually make work better than simple welfare. Such a position, paying minimum wage with a $500 earned income disregard, would bring the average-sized family's available income near the poverty level. The impact on the family of mom or dad going to work each day, in the area of self-esteem, development of a work ethic and as a role model for children is an additional, and very important benefit to be realized from employment.

A program which would subsidize employment, in the amount of the grant, for a defined period could have a similar positive impact on available job opportunities. Such a program would benefit both the welfare recipient/employee and the employer. By implementing both reforms, increased earned income disregard and subsidized employment, work becomes better than welfare. Low-wage jobs and part-time positions, where most of the job growth is occurring, become much more accessible and the benefit realized by the welfare recipient significantly greater.

Revamping the child support system could also improve the level of financial support realized by families, move more of them off public assistance and significantly improve their chances of long-term success by reducing the number of risk factors the family has to deal with. Child support must become nationalized, with consistent policies across state lines, and collections enhanced by automated access to income tax information. Serious consideration should be given to turning the responsibility over to the Internal Revenue Service. This would place the systems emphasis back where it belongs, on the collection of court-ordered support. Finally, child welfare must focus on developing neighborhood-based, foster homes for those children who require temporary placement, while working with the natural family to address problems which caused removal of the child(ren). When the prospect of family reunification is real, all efforts must be made to move the child back into the home. When a return to the home cannot happen and a child is taken into permanent custody, a plan to move that child into a stable, long-term family placement must be enacted as quickly as possible. Decisions cannot wait four years while a child grows old in the system.

Human service agencies touch the lives of 20% to 25% of the families in urban areas. These agencies may be in the best position to help a family below the poverty level begin the difficult process of dealing with those prevalent second-level symptoms, which often dictate their need for public assistance. Human service agencies cannot help families the way they are currently structured. Changes in the way agen-

cies assess a family's needs at initial intake, improvements in the child
support collection system, increased income disregard levels and
subsidized employment, and child welfare systems which emphasize
neighborhood-based, family reunification whenever possible, and
move quickly to find a permanent home when a child's future
is placed permanently into the hands of the public agency, must be
initiated. Clearly, this approach will not impact all families, but it
could begin to change things in a positive way for those most vulnerable. Failure to make changes will insure the continuation of minimal
support for families receiving assistance, but will not provide the
opportunity for a better life to those most in need.

REFERENCES

A Higher Price to Pay; Teenage Pregnancy in Ohio, 1994. Volume
    Two: County Profiles. p. 7, p. 21. Children's Defense
    Fund-Ohio Association of Ohio Children's Hospitals.

Early Determinants of Delinquency and Violence by Stephen Buka
    and Felton Earls; Health Affairs Volume 12, Number 4.
    Winter 1993. pp. 54, 55.

Home Again. Volume 1. July 1994. No. 3. Newsletter of the
    Homeless Families Program. p. 2.

Keeping the Trust, Summer 1994. A Quarterly Report from the
    Cleveland Foundation.

Kids Count Data Book, 1994; *State Profiles of Child Well Being.*
    The Annie E. Casey Foundation. pp. 14, 16.

McGowan, Brenda G. with Alfred J. Kahn and Sheila B. Kamerman
    (1990). *Social Services for Children, Youth and Families:
    The New York City Study.* Columbia University School
    of Social Work, New York. p. 6.

Overview of Entitlement Programs, 1994. Released by the House
    Ways and Means Committee, July 26. Special Report:
    AFDC Characteristics, 1969-1992.

Statistics from Cuyahoga County Department of Children and
    Family Services Family to Family Proposal, June 1993.

 **David R. Reines** *is Deputy County Administrator of Health and Human Services for Cuyahoga County, Ohio. His main objectives have been the reorganization of the Department of Human Services and improving services to the County's client population. He is charged with oversight responsibilities for five departments, which provide public assistance, child welfare services, employment services, child support enforcement, and services to seniors and adults. Combined staff for the five departments total about 3,000, with combined budgets of $210 million, not including public assistance grants. Prior to becoming Deputy County Administrator, Mr. Reines was Director of the Cuyahoga County (Ohio) Support Enforcement Agency. He is a graduate of Cleveland State University, with an M.B.A. and a B.A. in Political Science. He is a graduate of Harvard University's Program for Senior Executives in State and Local Government and a Leadership Cleveland alumni.*

REDEFINING FAMILIES: A LOOK AT ROLES AND RULES

LYNNE BRAVO ROSEWATER, PH.D.
Cleveland, Ohio

This paper focuses on one root cause of family disintegration as being violence in the home. Such violence includes wife-battering, marital rape, child abuse and incest. Domestic violence, as used in this paper, is defined as the misuse of power by one individual to achieve and maintain control over another individual in an intimate or family relationship. The tendency toward violence is exacerbated by many other problems in the culture, especially lack of financial resources or a lack of power and control in their work-a-day life. While the premise of this symposium is that family disintegration is accelerating, this paper postulates two premises which may seem at odds with other presentations: families have been in trouble for a very long period of time; and that an alleged "intact" family is not necessarily a healthy or desirable one.

Dealing with the disintegration of families implies that families were once healthier than they presently are. I respectfully disagree with this presumption. The problems of families may be more public today, but I believe these problems have always existed. The so-called disintegration may be an indication that the very structure on which we've based family life needs to be changed. The root cause of family dysfunction is, I believe, an unequal distribution of power resulting from a hierarchical, "power-over" model, based on sex-role stereotypes. The qualities we need to form a healthy family — mutual respect, mutual empowerment and mutual empathy — are more likely created in an egalitarian, "power-with" model.

In order to define the root causes of the disintegration of families, we have first to address what assumptions we make about what is a healthy family. It is erroneous, I believe, to equate "intact" with "healthy." Many women remain in abusive relationships in order to keep the family together. The ironic legacy of this effort is that violence becomes "normalized."

FAMILIES: WHERE WE COME FROM

Family has traditionally been defined as a unit consisting of a father, a mother and one or more children. This nuclear family was charged with providing food and shelter, emotional support, spiritual guidance and education. Most families were built on sex-role stereotypes: the father being the breadwinner and disciplinarian and the mother being the nurturer and caretaker. This family unit functioned on the father's working for pay outside the home and the mother's working without pay inside the home. When women did work, it was to provide a "second income," extra spending money to make ends meet. This is the family from the situation comedies of the fifties — Father Knows Best, Ozzie and Harriet. In many respects we have come a long way from that stereotypic family — and in others we've made little progress. For while our roles for women and men have changed greatly, the rules that underlie relationships have not (Rosewater, 1992). It is the premise of this paper that we need to change those rules, both the ones that define who woman and men are and who they can be and the basic way we define families.

WHAT IS A FAMILY?

While the focus of this conference is on the causes of family disintegration, it seems equally important to focus on what traits create successful families. These traits, from my clinical and personal experience, are unconditional love and concern for the best interest of the child. While we have based our definition of families on who is a member, I would propose that we define family by the presence of these traits — that any combination of individuals who can provide these qualities can be parents. In addition I would propose that we need to redefine the model on which families function. The existing model is based on "power over," a belief that "might makes right." In order to assess the future directions families need to take, we need to take a critical look at this model, which, in my clinical opinion, leads to interpersonal violence in the home, commonly called domestic violence. I would propose the need to create a different model, based on "power with" rather than "power over." The cornerstones of such a model would be based on mutual respect, mutual empowerment and mutual empathy. These qualities foster unconditional love and concern for the best interest of the child.

SEX-ROLE STEREOTYPES: THE SEQUELLAE

The ultimate cause of the primary symptom of domestic violence is, in my opinion, unequal power in relationships. This power imbalance is a sequellae of sex-role stereotyped rules, which assign men the roles of provider and decision-maker and prohibit their displaying vulnerability and assign women the roles of caretaker and nurturer and place ultimate responsibility for the success or failure of a relationship (Rosewater, 1992). The dynamics of violent relationships reflect these rules: an abusive man feels justified in his controlling his partners and, in fact, blames her for the violence that occurs; a battered woman feels personally responsible for the violence, because it indicates her personal failure as a wife/partner. This sense of personal responsibility is the reason many battered women stay in abusive relationships. These rules form the basis for the fertile soil from which domestic violence springs.

DOMESTIC VIOLENCE

Domestic violence occurs among all races and socioeconomic groups. As stated earlier, domestic violence, as used in this paper, is defined as the misuse of power by one individual to achieve and maintain control over another individual in an intimate or family relationship. The key words in this definition are "misuse of power" and "achieve and maintain control." It is not difficult to deduce that expecting men to be the "boss" in the family leads to the misuse of power.

Marriage is a formalized means of entrenching the dynamics of power imbalance. It is not coincidence that marriage vows once compelled women to promise to "love, honor and obey." Two respected researchers on domestic violence (Dobash & Dobash, 1977), who write about the connection between power and battering, entitled one article, "Love, Honor and Obey: Institutional Ideologies and the Struggle for battered Women." Straus (1980) labeled a marriage license as a "hitting license." Good (1971) believes that force and violence are the foundations on which the family rest.

One out every two couples have experienced at least one instance of interpersonal violence (Walker, 1979). Status differential between husbands and wives, especially higher occupational status for the wife than the husband, lead to a higher possibility of spouse abuse, particularly life-threatening violence (Hornung, McCullough & Sugimoto, 1980, Walker, 1984). An estimated 3 to 4 million women are battered each year by husbands or partners. More than one million women a year seek medical assistance for injuries caused by abuse; abused women represent 20% of all women seeking hospital emergency services (NCADV, 1990). These frightening statistics make evident the problems of such a power imbalance.

Interpersonal violence is the result of the expectation that men be dominant in a relationship with the subsequent prohibition of displaying vulnerability. Men who are physically abusive believe they have the right to control their women. This need for control stems from their own insecurity and fear of being abandoned. Batterers are men whose dependency needs are ego alien. They hate their women precisely because they need them. The way they quell these fears is to isolate their women from family and friends and hold them accountable for any time away from home that is not spent on the job. Their fear of rejection is so great that anticipate it, formulating the pathological jealousy and accusations of sexual infidelity. These misogynist men are blamers of the highest order. Their denial is so entrenched that they fail to see that they have a problem, but rather attribute the blame to his woman who "made me do it" (Sonkin, 1987). Not surprisingly, fifty percent of these men abuse alcohol or other drugs. Physically abusive men take the expectation of being boss quite literally. They see their women as their possessions: "If I can't have her, no one can."

It is this possessiveness that leads to violence. Wives once were considered property; many men still consider women a type of property. This belief justifies their right to control and dominate (Martin, 1976). The key variable in domestic violence is intimidation, which constant presence is emotionally depleting. After a batterer has demonstrated his propensity for violence, his threats often suffice to keep his women "in line." Fear is an effective means of creating compliance.

Women, who have been raised to "take care of their men," feel personally responsible for the violence that occurs (Rosewater, 1985). Constantly bombarded by the criticism rained on them by their mates, they feel they ought to be able to — and soon will — find a way to end the violence in their relationships. The most common phrase I've heard from battered women is "I thought I could get him to change." This belief is fortified by the loving/contrite stage (Stage 3) that follows an incident of violence. The remorse is all too real as are the promises that "it will never happen again." This "honeymoon" phase provides relief and hope. All too soon the inevitable tension building stage begins (Stage 1) leading to the inevitable eruption of violence (Stage 2), which, of course, is followed by the begging of forgiveness in Stage 3 (Walker, 1984).

In trainings I do about diagnostic, forensic and treatment issues with battered women, I sometimes refer to them as "hostages in their own homes." The dynamics found with battered women (Walker, 1989) and those found with hostages (Hatcher, 1981) are similar: isolation, threats to injure or kill, psychological torture and degradations, occasional indulgences and induced debility.

Leaving a battering relationship does not mean that violence ends. Women are most at risk to be killed when they end violent relationships (Browne, 1987). This fear is one reason women stay in abusive relationships. Their fears about economic security are also valid: batterers are not easy men to leave; the abuse continues in the courtroom over custody and financial arrangements. Battered women are often re-victimized by the divorce process. Their personality assessments may make them look "disturbed," while their abusive husbands look "normal." The statistics about how many battered women have lost custody of their children has not been compiled, but I, along with my colleagues around the country with expertise on domestic violence, have seen numerous instances when this loss of custody has occurred.

The most important role parents provide for their children is as role models. So what are we teaching our children? Do they obey out of respect or out of fear? What is happening in our families today? Domestic violence begets domestic violence. Unfortunately, boys who grow up with fathers who batter their mothers become husbands who batter their wives; girls who witness their mother beaten are more likely to become battered women (Walker, 1984). And in this senseless maze of family violence the best interest of children is nowhere to be seen.

As a culture we constantly ask, "Why don't battered women leave?" This victim-blaming question places the focus in the wrong place. What we should ask is, "Why do we allow men to get away with violence in their home?" Why is it more permissible to assault your wife than a stranger? Why have we only legally recognized in the past decade that a man can rape his wife? Our society condones violence against women. We cannot create a stable family as long as we allow domestic violence to be an issue to which we only pay lip service.

Placing the sole or majority responsibility for the success of relationship, and by extension, families on women allows men to be irresponsible. This irresponsibility is apparent on several levels. Most men who are physically abusive to their mates do not accept that they have a problem and hence these men are resistant to seeking psychological help. When wife-beating is treated as it should be as a criminal offense, battered men are more likely to seek help if it is an alternative to going to jail (Sonkin, 1987). Men more easily abandon their families because they do not feel the same sense of responsibilities their wives do. This lack of responsibility on fathers is most clearly evident in our statistics regarding child support payment. Of all court-awarded child support, only 50% is paid in full. Twenty-five percent is partially paid and twenty-five percent is never paid. (Congressional Record, 1987).

SEXUAL ASSAULT IN THE FAMILY

Interpersonal violence is based on a perpetrator's abusing his power or privilege. The use of the male pronoun reflects the fact that 94-97% of all interpersonal violence is male-perpetrated against women and children (Walker, 1988). I believe that our current model for relationships is a hierarchical, "power over" model, based on the premise that "might makes right." Ironically, it is this very model, on which the traditional family has been based, that is, in my clinical opinion, one of the major factors for the disintegration of families — or at least of what a family should represent: a safe, supportive place to exist.

The statistics on intrafamilial child sexual assault confirm that families are often not safe places. In a survey of 930 women, Russell (1988) found that 16% of her sample reported at least one incident of intrafamial sexual abuse before the age of 18. Finklehoar (1979), in a survey of 796 New England college students found that 19.2% of the women and 8.6% of the men had been sexually victimized, 43% of the females and 33% of the males by a family member. The National Center on Child Abuse and Neglect estimates there are 100,000 cases of child sexual abuse each year (Justice & Justice, 1977). In discussing treatment approaches for nonoffending mothers, Cammaert (1988) found "two major overbearing factors" to explain the behavior of non-offending mothers: the status of women and the status of the marital relationship, both built on women's inferior status (pp. 315-318).

While statistics on marital rape are almost non-existent, it is significant that until 15 years ago there were no statutes on marital rape, the presumption being that a married man, who had the "right" to sex from his wife, could not rape her. Currently, thirty-six states have marital rape statutes, but often these statutes apply only if the husband and wife are living separately.

A NEW MODEL

The new model I propose is an egalitarian, "power with" model, based on respecting all members of the family as having valid contributions to make. It is my contention that the traits that make for healthy families more closely follow this egalitarian model. A healthy family, this author believes, is comprised of the following traits: unconditional love, mutual respect, mutual empowerment, mutual empathy, shared values and a belief that the whole is greater than the sum of its parts.

UNCONDITIONAL LOVE

The hardest work I do as a therapist is with adults who are survivors of childhood violence: their ability to trust has been seriously eroded. After all, if your own parents don't care about what happens to you, why would you believe anyone else would? This is the work I do — assuring individuals that others do care, that I care, that not everyone will hurt you and that you can learn to tell the difference. The most important variable we therapists offer clients is unconditional caring. It is in learning to trust me that my clients learn to trust themselves (Rosewater, 1987). Congruence — the matching of our words and actions — is the balm for emotionally shattered lives. It is also the glue for emotionally healthy children.

My first five years as a professional was working at a short-term psychiatric hospital working on a locked ward with teenagers. Amidst barred windows, locked doors and the dull green paint that graces the walls of most institutional settings, we had a caring and committed staff. Years later, I would receive occasional phone calls, the message of which was similar: "Are you the Rosewater that worked at CPI?" the caller would ask. "Yes," I'd reply. My name is Mary Smith. Do you remember me?" "Yes," I'd reply. "I just called to tell you the three months I spent at CPI were the best three months of my life. So I called to thank you." My first reaction always was, "How pathetic! The best three months of your life were on a locked psychiatric ward." But in retrospect, I've changed my mind. I see now that where these kids were didn't matter, but what they were receiving did: they were being genuinely cared about, perhaps for the first time in their lives.

Loving unconditionally does not forsake discipline. Structure is an essential ingredient for all children; they need predictability. It is vital that families have rules and consequences. However, in order to be healthy, rules have to based on the best interest of the child and enforced in a manner that maintains a child's emotional well-being. Families in trouble tend to fall into two polar problems: a lack of structure and consistence, or an overly rigid structure based less on the child's best interest than on the pursuit of power for it's own sake ("You'll do it cause I told you to.") Effective discipline never needs to be physical. Parents have ample power to deprive their children of a long list of privileges: use of telephone or television, the right to have friends over, visiting and/or sleeping over at friends, etc. Effective discipline is based on caring and concern. Here's a personal story I often share with my clients:

When my daughter, Alysse, was in forth grade she cheated on a math exam by giving the answers to her two friends so they could proceed to recess. Called by her teacher, her father and I felt that cheating was an unexceptable behavior. We therefore took away Alysse's birthday presents for a month and canceled her party which was a trip to a local amusement park with the two girls to whom she given the answers. The next day following the incident and our punishment, my daughter told me when I returned from work, "What do you think happened to the other two girls?" I replied, "I don't really care. We're not their parents, but you can tell me if you want to." "Well," my daughter answered, "nothing happened to them." "How does that make you feel?" I questioned. "After all, we gave you a big punishment." Alysse, to her credit, responded, "You must really care about me, because you think I did something very wrong and that's why you gave me such a big punishment."

THE BEST INTEREST OF THE CHILD

As a culture, we give a lot of lip service to the phrase, "the best interest of the child." The problem I have encountered as a professional, is that there are a lot of assumptions made about what is in a child's best interest that are not based on reliable data. For instance, there have been numerable court cases in which a lesbian mother was denied custody of her child(ren) because the court ruled that the mother's sexual identity would harm the development of her child's sexual identity, would cause her child to be rejected by peers and would adversely affect the child's psychological development (Chessler, 1986). The Committee on Women and the Committee on Gay and Lesbian Concerns of the American Psychological Association (1991) did a literature review to see what psychological research had shown about any differences that may exist between children raised by heterosexual mothers and children raised by lesbian mothers. An extensive literature review found that there was no difference between these children save for one variable: children raised by lesbian mothers were more tolerant of differences. Was the best interest of the child or societal fear and prejudice best served by denying lesbian mothers custody based solely on their sexual identity?

We are a society that professes to deal with the best interest of the child, but in reality the child's best interest is often lost in the power struggles of the courtroom where adversaries in custody battles are far more interested in hurting one another than considering the welfare of their children. Children in so-called "intact" homes may fare no better.

When my son, Mark, went to college, he was bothered by the animosity many of his peers had toward their parents. Towards the end of his freshman year, some of these other freshman criticized Mark for "always listening to your parents." Mark's response to this criticism was succinct and sage: "You don't seem to understand that my parents always give advice with my best interest in mind. That's why I listen to them."

In order to create healthier families, we need to address the question of what makes healthy relationships and hence healthy families. A healthy family, as I define it, is one where each member is respected and treated with dignity. It is my belief that we need to change the rules that govern relationships, as following the sex-role stereotypes creates dysfunctional relationships. The problem with these outdated rules is that power in relationships is imbalanced, and this very imbalance is what leads to abuse. We can no longer hold women solely responsible to make relationships work, and we can no longer deny men the right to both feel and to express their dependency needs. The model I have developed for a healthy relationship is an equilateral triangle composed of three equal sides, a "me," a "you" and an "us." This model allows both for independence (the "me" and the "you") and interdependence. The "me" and the "you" form individual boundaries which are comprised of non-negotiables — those things necessary to maintain personal integrity and self-respect. The "us" is formed of negotiables — those concessions individuals are willing to make in order to have a productive relationship.

In the work I have done with couples, both violent and non-violent, the problems with relationships are similar: Women have difficulty maintaining a sense of self, the "me," in a relationship. Because they feel responsible to make the relationship work, they sacrifice their own needs towards this end. This sense of personal responsibility is what keeps battered women in abusive relationships. Feeling that they are at fault for the violence that is happening, these women struggle to figure out how to make the violence end. Men have difficulty maintaining an "us," fearful that being interdependent will rob them of their independence. Men who beat women hate the women precisely because they need them. Rather than seeing this need as healthy and normal, they perceive it as emasculating.

Healthy families, like healthy relationships, need to be built on respecting personal boundaries. Parents are role models who teach their children by the way they interact with one another, as well as with their children. The root problem in many families today is a lack of basic respect, both of parents toward their children and children toward their parents. Disrespect, as I see it from a clinical and personal perspective, is based on unequal power. The model presented in this chapter is an egalitarian one based on equal power and privilege. The challenge to this model is how to deal with children, who are by law less empowered. The solution to this enigma is one I think feminist therapists such as myself have addressed. Feminist therapy is built on the construct that therapy should be based on an egalitarian relationship. However, the therapist both by training and by providing a service for a fee, usually has greater power and privilege than the client (Douglas, 1985). Feminist therapists have both an obligation to use their power and privilege for the client's welfare (Brown 1985) and to regard an egalitarian relationship as one equal in respect (Rosewater, 1984). Good parenting is based on these same imperatives: mutual respect for your children and using your power and privilege on their behalf. It is the premise of this chapter that healthy family relationships need to be based on a healthy partnering relationship.

TRANSFORMING RELATIONSHIPS: A NEW MODEL

The relationship model proposed in this book moves from a "power over" hierarchical one to a "power with" egalitarian one — mutual empowerment. In a two-way, rather than one-way relationship, personal growth is a result of such empowering, allowing the relationship to foster growth for both individuals. Mutual empowerment is based on the notion that each partner can contribute to a growth-promoting, life-enhancing, interactive process. Relationships do not have to exist at the expense of one partner but rather can be mutually beneficial. Such a relationship has been described in the following way:

Neither person is in control; instead each is enlarged and feels empowered, energized and more real. Empowerment is based on the capacity to turn toward and trust in the relationship, to provide the on-going context for interaction (Surrey, 1987).

Mutual empathy is based on both partners being tuned into and caring about the other's feelings. There is a difference between caring about someone's feelings and feeling responsible for someone's feelings. It is this sense of feeling personally responsible that keeps battered women in abusive relationships. The most common dynamic I see with the couples I counsel, is an insistence that in a disagreement someone is "right" and someone is "wrong." In the attempt to "win" the argument neither person really hears the other. Mutual empathy is based on an inherent belief that someone is feeling whatever they are and a commitment to respect that feeling whether or not it "makes sense." Mutual respect is impossible without mutual empathy.

WHAT DO WE LEARN FROM VIOLENT HOMES?

In trying to understand the problems of family dysfunction, violent homes provide a clear model from which to learn. The first thing violent homes teach us is that mutual respect is non-existent. One cannot misuse power to achieve and maintain control and have any respect for those individuals he or she is controlling. In violent homes this misuse of power and privilege is apparent. I believe that this same dynamic, misuse of power and privilege, exists in all dysfunctional families.

When the first data was being collected on family violence, researchers tried to define "appropriate hitting" (Straus, Gelles & Steinmetz, 1980). This term seems to be an oxymoron. "Appropriate hitting" implies that violence is sometimes acceptable, like spanking a child. The problem that develops is that sanctioned hitting supports that notion that violence is an acceptable means of controlling another individual.

The problem in our culture is that sanctioned violence is epidemic: on the football field, in the hockey rink, under the basketball boards. It is any wonder that a disproportionate amount of date rape occurs with college athletes as the perpetrators?

Violent families teach us that violence begets violence. Power is defined by physical might, interestingly, leading to an increase in what has been labeled elder abuse. When adult children can physically dominate their parents, they may feel it is now their right. This hierarchical, "power over" model is the basis of violence in the family: physical, sexual and psychological.

A "power with" model is based on mutual respect, mutual empowerment and mutual empathy. These qualities allow for family interaction based on utilizing the collective resources of the family. This egalitarian model facilitates unconditional love and a predisposition to operate according to the best interests of each member of the family. In this manner families become a collaborative effort where the whole is greater than the sum of its parts. This kind of healthy family is, and always has been, rare. To create more families like this will take a pro-active approach and systemic change. The question is: Are we willing to do the work to make this transition?

REFERENCES

Brown, L. S. (1985). Ethics and business practices in feminist therapy. In L. B. Rosewater & L. E. Walker (Eds.), *Handbook of Feminist Therapy: Women's Issues in Psychotherapy*, pp. 297-304. New York: Springer.

Browne, A. (1987). *When battered women kill*. New York: The Free Press.

Cammaert, L. A. (1988). Nonoffending mothers: A new conceptualization. In L. E. A. Walker (Ed.), *Handbook on sexual abuse of children*, (pp. 309-325). New York: Springer.

Chessler, P. (1986). *Mothers on trial: The battle for children and custody.* Seattle: Seal Press.

Committee on Women in Psychology & Committee on Gay and Lesbian Concerns. (1991). Lesbian parents and their children: A resource paper for psychologists. Washington, D.C.: American Psychological Association.

Congressional Record. (1987). S10400-S10435. July 21. Washington, D.C.: U.S. Government Printing Office.

Dobash, R. E. & Dobash, R. P. (1977). Love, honor and obey: Institutional ideologies and the struggle for battered women. *Contemporary Crisis, 42* (1), 71-80.

Douglas, M. A. (1985). The role of power in feminist therapy. In L. B. Rosewater & L. E. A. Walker (Eds.), *Handbook of feminist therapy: Women's issues in psychotherapy*, pp. 241-249.

Finklehoar, D. (1979). *Sexually victimized children.* New York: Free Press.

Horung, C. A., McCollough, C. & Sugimoto, T. (1980). Status relationships in Marriage: Risk Factors in Spouse Abuse. A paper presented at the Annual Meeting of the American Sociological Association, New York, August.

Justice, B. & Justice, R. (1979). *The broken taboo: Sex in the family.* New York: Human Sciences Press.

Martin, D. (1976). *Battered Wives.* New York: Pocket Books.

NCADV Statistics. (1990). National Coalition Against Domestic Violence Newsletter 1 (February), citing Bureau of Justice Statistics, *Preventing Domestic Violence Against Women.*

Rosewater, L. B. (1992). *New Roles/New Rules: A guide to transforming relationships between women and men.* Pasadena: Trilogy Books.

Rosewater, L. B. (1987). *Changing Through Therapy.* New York: Dodd, Mead & Co.

Rosewater, L. B. (1985). Schizophrenic, borderline or battered? In L. B. Rosewater & L. E. A. Walker (Eds.), *Handbook of feminist therapy: Women's issues in psychotherapy*, pp. 215-225. New York: Springer.

Rosewater, L. B. (1984). Feminist therapy: Implications for practicioners. In L. E. Walker (Ed.), *Women and mental health*, pp. 267-279. Beverly Hills: Sage.

Russel, D. (1988). The incidence and prevalence of intrafamial and extrafamial sexual abuse of female children. In L. E. A. Walker (Ed.), *Handbook on sexual abuse of children.* (pp. 19-36). New York: Springer.

Sonkin, D. J. (Ed). (1987). *Domestic Violence on Trial.* New York: Springer.

Straus, M. (1980). Victims and aggressors in marital violence. *American Behavioral Scientist, 23* (5), 681-704.

Straus, M. A., Gelles, R. & Steinmetz, S. (1980). *Behind closed doors: Violence in the American family.* New York; Anchor Books.

Surrey, J. (1985). Relationship and empowerment. Work in progress #30. Wellsley, MA.: Stone Center for Developmental Services and Studies.

Walker, L. E. (1989). *Terrifying love: Why battered women kill and how society responds.* New York: Harper Perennial.

Lynne Bravo Rosewater, Ph.D. *is a licensed psychologist in private practice in Cleveland, Ohio. She is a national expert on both domestic violence and the Minnesota Multiphasic Personality Inventory (MMPI) profile for battered women, as well as an expert witness on the use of the battered women's syndrome in the self- defense cases of battered women who kill their abusers. Dr. Rosewater is the author of* New Roles/New Rules, Changing Through Therapy, *co-editor of* Handbook of Feminist Therapy: Women's Issues in Psychotherapy *and author of numerous chapters on feminist therapy and test interpretation.*

On the Disintegration of Social Institutions: The Fate of Marriage and Family

JETSE SPREY, PH.D.
Emeritus Professor of Sociology
Case Western Reserve University

Toto, I have the feeling we are not in Kansas anymore.
Dorothy, in *The Wizard of Oz*

The purpose of this brief essay is to make a case rather than to prove one. Throughout the discussion I use persuasive citations and, at times, descriptive statistical information to construct my argument. No attempt is made to cover the family field and the only references listed are those that are directly relevant to the text. As indicated in the title, my focus is on the institutional realities of contemporary marital and family phenomena in Western and, specifically, North American societies. This does not mean that people who actually live in marriages and families are ignored. Far from it, but their "individuality" is treated as a function of their ongoing participation in these two social institutions.

PRELIMINARIES

To avoid ambiguities and conceptual confusion, some preliminary observations are in order. I first will clarify my use of the ideas of "family" and "marriage," and then specify the way I interpret and approach the "charge" that is presented in the "Background Statement" formulated by the planners of this symposium.

The family institution can be viewed as socially responsible for the care and rearing of newly born and young human beings. Its actual form, as manifested in the many different cultures that make up humanity, varies a great deal but its social task of caring for the young and other dependents seems universal. As a so called "primary group," it usually contains one or more related adults, one or more children and, depending on the circumstances, other designated relatives. This broad definition covers, among other things, one-parent households, polygamous ones, and those in which the adults are of the same sex. It excludes groups such as fraternities, gangs, and cohabiting and/or married childfree couples.

The family's raison d'être is caring, rather than reproduction per se and status ascription. As a functioning behavioral system, it is not limited to human societies. Most nonhuman primates, many bird species, and several kinds of fish, also engage in forms of family behavior. Without it, they might not have evolved at all.

Marriage, in its turn, institutionalizes the legitimation of offspring in all known human societies. Children born within it, regardless of its culturally prescribed form, are considered "legitimate." They belong to a clearly defined network of ancestors, siblings, cousins, and the like. Of course, so called "illegitimate" children also have ancestors and blood relatives, but their networks tend to be smaller, narrower, and less privileged.

Contrary to popular belief, the institution of marriage does not control human sexuality and is, sociologically speaking, not designed or suited to do so. Instead, it has a clear stake in its procreative consequences, as is well illustrated by its only truly universal rule, the so called "incest taboo." The "invention" of this taboo forbidding procreation among perceived blood relatives did attach an additional and crucial social function to marriage, namely, its ability to create and maintain lasting alliances between networks of families.

Unlike family, marriage is a uniquely human sociocultural invention. Only the fully evolved human brain seems capable of constructing and dealing with the complex and sophisticated kinship systems that are found in even the least technologically developed, human cultures. The family, on the other hand, is the only human institution whose genesis actually predates the birth of humankind. Its basic structure, caregiving units consisting of adults and their surviving offspring, is found among most primates and, in all likelihood, also existed among Homo sapiens' prehuman ancestors.

At this point one might ask, why bother with such seemingly "academic" distinctions? After all, in common parlance, and in much of the professional discourse, the terms "marriage" and "family" often are used interchangeably. This may well echo the fact that in our current society most families still are sanctioned by marriage or remarriage. Nevertheless, I would argue that a clear conceptual distinction between these two institutions and an awareness of their roots is necessary before we can engage in any meaningful discussion of their current problematics and future course. Not doing this will result in analytical confusion and, in practice, in wasted and potentially misdirected efforts. A concern about the growing proportion of unwed teenage mothers, for example, essentially pertains to the current functioning of marriage. Of course, the young mothers involved grew up in families, of a kind, but that only adds proximate and/or correlational explanatory factors. It behooves us to keep the latter separate in any search for more "ultimate" causal structures. Child abuse and neglect, on the other hand, basically are family problems, and should be analyzed as such.

My comments on the above referred to "Background Statement" are twofold. In that document, all participants are asked to prepare a short paper focusing on "one or more of the primary symptoms which cause families to disintegrate" and on what they see as "the ultimate cause(s)" of the former. Let me repeat, then, that I plan to focus on the social institutions of marriage and family and raise, among else, the possibility of their decline but also that of their continuation into the future. Obviously, the phenomena of dissolving families and marriages through divorce, desertion, or by other means, are linked to what happens on the institutional level, but that connection is not yet understood and certainly not "linear" in any causal sense. One of the premises of the mathematical theory of groups is that a "set" cannot be a member of itself. By defining the family as the "set containing all individual family networks," we also assign its analysis to a "level" that is different from that of its parts. The same holds for the study of the institution of marriage. Social researchers and practitioners, in their eagerness to move from the specific to the general, at times tend to overlook such elementary points of logic.

My second comment follows from the previous one. It raises the question, how do we link symptoms and causes? How do we really know, for example, that premarital teenage pregnancies are "symptomatic" of marital decline? If so, why? Because former Vice President Quale or the leaders of certain religious denominations say so? I think we need more than that. Actually, however, the answer to the general question is deceptively simple. All we need to link symptoms to their presumed "underlying causes" is a sound logical foundation and a degree of empirical evidence, whether it be quantitative, qualitative, or both. Regrettably, these two preconditions rarely are fulfilled in the study of humans and their societies. This means that in our explanatory practice we often need more than mere "models" and the assorted bits and pieces that pass for empirical evidence in the so called human sciences. What is meant by "more" is well formulated in the following comment by a prominent philosopher of science: "In seeking its goal science repeatedly runs into difficulties. Many of these difficulties are physical in nature and call for the design of new and more powerful instruments. Others are psychological and call for the invention of devices that supplement our memory and our computational powers. Still others, and those are the ones that are relevant here, are intellectual and pertain to our ability to conceive, formulate, consider, connect, and assess answers. These sorts of difficulties often call for inspiration and creative intelligence. Careful observation and description are not enough" (Bromberger,

1992, p. 2). I suggest that in our joint attempts to understand what may be wrong with contemporary marriages and families, we take the above to heart.

THE STATUS QUO

What has happened to the institutions of marriage and family since the waning years of the 1950s seems of growing concern to many academics, policy makers, and lay persons. The interpretation and evaluation of what can be observed, however, remain sources of disagreement and debate among those involved with the fate of marriages and families. The same is true for the varying prognoses of their future. Given the importance of these institutions, it is not surprising that the controversy is scholarly as well as ideological. Most often it is both. In this brief section, I offer some descriptive information to put it in a realistic perspective, but make no attempt to settle it. When ideology becomes an integral part of the way in which humans construct, rather than just define reality, facts become "loaded" and rational solutions unlikely.

In view of the above, let me begin with the presentation of a sketchy and relatively undisputed overview of what seems to be happening to contemporary marriage and family. Over the past decades, the average age at first marriage increased, but the marriage rate went down. The average family size declined and many more mothers of minor children are working fulltime. The divorce rate has climbed steadily, so that more children are reared, at least during part of their youth, in so called incomplete families. And, finally, due to the steady increase in our life expectancy, the average duration of marriage almost doubled, as compared to that in the 17th century. The presence of older persons in family networks has increased dramatically.

To illustrate and further focus the above, two quotes from a recent report follow: "The 1990 decennial census counted nearly 92 million households in the United States, containing over 97 percent of the U.S. population. Approximately 70 percent of these...consisted of two or more persons who were related to each other by marriage, birth, or adoption. However, only 34 percent of all households consisted of parents and their children under 18 years of age. An even smaller fraction, 26 percent, consisted of married couples with their dependent children. In fact, there were nearly as many nonfamily households as households with children and more nonfamily households than married couple households with children. In 1990, 30 percent of all households consisted of persons who were not related to others in the household" (Zill & Nord, 1994, pp. 5960).

And, illustrating some of the presumed "risk factors" in the current situation: "Analyses of birth certificate data show that 45 percent of all first births in the U.S. in 1990 were to a mother who had not finished high school, or to an unmarried mother, or to a woman who was under 20 years of age. Eleven percent of all new families had all three of these risk factors...Among African-American first births, more than a quarter (26 percent) were handicapped by having all three risk factors; i.e., being born to unmarried teenagers with less than 12 years of schooling. Among Hispanics, the proportion was 16 percent, and among White nonHispanics, 7 percent" (ibid., p. 26).

As stated earlier, the above "factual" information is open to a range of interpretations. It is not clear, for example, to what extent children born to married teenage couples are at risk, and if so, if such risks also vary with the ethnicity of their parents. And so forth.

What the above figures do show is that the "traditional" family, consisting of married parents, a male breadwinner, a female homemaker, and their children, no longer constitutes the "normal," or statistically "modal," family form in American society. Instead, we see many children growing up in reconstituted or singleparent families, the latter most often being headed by a female. It is this break with the past that worries some family scholars and lay persons alike. Consider, for example, the following observation by an established student of the family: "In some sense...the family has been declining since the beginning of recorded history yet we've survived. But often overlooked in the current debate is the fact that recent family decline is unlike historical family change. It is something unique, and much more serious" (Popenoe, 1993, p. 527).

What the author believes to be serious is evident below:

There are two dimensions of today's family decline that make it both unique and alarming. The first is that it is not the extended family that is breaking up but the nuclear family. The nuclear family can be thought of as the last vestige of the traditional family unit; all other adult members have been stripped away, leaving but two — the husband and the wife...The second dimension of real concern regards what has been happening to the two principal functions childrearing, and the provision to its members of affection and companionship (ibid., p. 539). Other family scholars disagree with Popenoe's assessment. They see some of the current changes as positive or liberating (cf. Cowan, 1993, and Stacey, 1993). Regrettably, lack of space prevents me from delving deeper into the above debate. A brief comment, however, does seem warranted.

Frankly, I see a debate on the potential total demise of either marriage or family institutions as somewhat irrelevant. Of course, we are observing major changes, some of which have possibly negative and/or costly social consequences. It is possible, for example, that both institutions are growing apart to a degree not yet experienced in human societies. Clearly, marriage per se increasingly is becoming an arrangement that sanctions and protects sexual intimacy as an end in itself, rather than a means of procreation. Some people see this as a form of "liberation," a judgement I agree with. If such a trend also will lead to a complete separation of marriage and family, however, remains to be seen.

A total disappearance of either family as the main caring institution or marriage as the cultural sanctioning of procreative sexuality and other forms of intimate arrangements would mean the end of human societies as more or less orderly, integrated, and self-replacing social systems. I would stress again that families, in their most basic form, existed before humanity emerged from the evolutionary twilight zone that separates Homo sapiens from their protohominid ancestors. It seems highly unlikely that even they would have evolved to their evolutionary stage without some form of family.

In other words, I agree with Popenoe and others like him about the fact that "we are not in Kansas anymore." Moreover, I see no real possibility of a return to the past regardless of how we feel about the present. I disagree, however, with the somewhat conservative assumption that the so called "nuclear family" can be seen as "the last vestige" or the "core" of the family. To me, as evident from my definition, a functioning family unit consists of one or more caring adults and children. It may well be possible that families, on the average, will function best if both parents are of different genders and if the children are their biological offspring. But that is something that must be demonstrated empirically, rather than assumed on the grounds of past experience, faith, or ideology.

A concern about status quo, then, should lead us to a search for those structural conditions and potential "ultimate" causes which, at this writing, still remain hidden below the surface of our immediate experience. Such a search is risky because it leads to answers that, because they can be verified by implication only, remain open to the challenge that they are "unscientific," political, and/or ideological. They most certainly may lead to explanations that challenge the status quo, and, as such, are unacceptable to those who have a vested interest in it. One feminist reaction to Popenoe's article may illustrate this point: "If, as many feminists have begun to suspect, a stable marriage system depends on systemic forms of inequality, it will take more than thought reform or moralistic jeremiads about family decline to stanch our contemporary marital hemorrhage. Recent proposals...to restrict access to divorce implicitly recognize, but fail to address, this unpleasant contradiction, one which poses a serious dilemma for a democracy" (Stacey, 1993, p. 547).

I agree with the author's contention, but it does not take a feminist to do so. Nor is it necessary, logically speaking, to eliminate family as an institutional reality in order to come to grips with its traditional asymmetrical power structure. Stacey for example, argues that "the family is not an institution, but an ideological, symbolic construct that has a history and a politics" (ibid., p. 545). Of course, it has a "history" and a "politics." All social institutions do. But this does not prevent me from using the concept of "institution" to describe the present, the past, and the dynamics of what we label "family." I do so in more detail in this essay's next section.

DIAGNOSIS

Twenty-five years ago I wrote an article titled, "The Family as a System in Conflict" (Sprey, 1969). Its argument has been repeated over the years and elaborated (cf. Sprey, 1979; Sprey, forthcoming), but in essence my position has remained unchanged. So I quote from it: "Conceptualizing the family as a system in conflict means to see its process as an ongoing confrontation between its members, a confrontation between individuals with conflicting interests in their common situation. The institutional arrangement called a family does not result from some kind of preconceived consensus, but from what Irving Horowitz (1967) calls, 'the contradictory yet interrelated needs and designs of men'...the position of family members may be seen as analogous to that of players in a game. The nature of their conflict of interest thus changes with the societal definition of the game, for example, the degree to which its players can all win or lose" (1969, p. 702).

First, let me pick up briefly on the game analogy alluded to above. In a two-person game, such as chess, one player may be far better than the other one so that he/she usually controls the outcome as well as the course of each match. If the second player improves, however, and the two become equally skilled the situation changes qualitatively. Neither party can control either the outcome or the course of any given match. If, therefore, for any reason, the game gets out of hand no one has the power to restore a normal state of affairs without the collaboration of the other. This, then, may help to understand one major family change, namely that from the past single provider to its current dual earner form. In it, the established balance of power between the spouses did shift drastically. A similar, yet less dramatic change is beginning to affect the balance between the generations.

This means, then, that because of the gains in power by two member categories — wives and offspring — the control over the course and outcomes of family processes by any member, or member category, is diminished. Of course, this does not necessarily lead to anarchy. After all, new and more egalitarian rules may be contracted, but this means that negotiating skills and a joint recognition of the need to compromise become essential to collective family survival. So far, the history of marriage and family does not provide too many models or recipes to help play this new "game."

I wish, for a moment, to return to the above twenty-five year old statement and juxtapose it to a few citations from Ulrich Beck's recent remarkable book, *Risk Society*. In it, the author points at "the deep insecurity and hurt with which men and women confront each other in the everyday reality of marriage and family" (1992, p. 103). He sees such daily confrontations as unique to the marital and familial arenas, as is clear in the following comment: "Class antagonisms ignited on the material immiseration of large parts of the working population. They were fought out in public. The antagonisms that emerge with the detraditionalization of the family erupted mainly in private relationships, and they are fought out in the kitchen, the bedroom and the nursery (1992, p. 106).

While on the institutional level, the 'central conflicts,' which discharge themselves in personal guilt feelings and disappointments within the relations of the sexes, also have a basis in the fact that an attempt is still being made to practice the liberation from gender stereotypes (almost) solely through the private confrontation of men and women, within the framework of the nuclear family, while keeping the institutional structures constant. This is tantamount to the attempt to accomplish a change in society with social structures in the family remaining the same. What remains is an exchange of inequalities. The liberation of women from housework and marital support is to be forced by the regression of men into this 'modern feudal existence' which is exactly what women reject for themselves...But men are no more willing than women to follow the call 'back to the kitchen!'...What remains central is that the equalization of men and women cannot be created in institutional structures that presuppose their inequality (1992, p. 109).

In the previous paragraph, the author links the problematics and contradictions that characterize modern societies to the quite personal problems that people in families, perhaps without proper comprehension or outside help, must cope with in their day-to-day collective existence. He sees the presumed indications of "decline," such as divorce, domestic strife, and child neglect, as symptomatic of an institution that no longer can deal with the traditional expectations assigned to it. I share this point of view. In fact, I believe that many contemporary families and marriages lack even the potential jointly to decide what their problems are. They do not have the skills and knowledge to diagnose or prioritize the contingencies they must deal with. Sources of the not too distant past, such as, Ann Landers, the Church, neighbors, or community organizations, no longer seem sufficient.

On the institutional level, family and marriage also must compete with and challenge other, increasingly organized social institutions, for example, education, the judiciary, big business, and, of course, the local government bureaucracies. Families never were unionized or organized politically. In the past, however, they were, on the whole, far better integrated in neighborhoods, local communities, and, depending on the circumstances, professional or occupational organizations. This, too, is eroding.

IN CONCLUSION

An essay like this presents its argument throughout its pages. Its conclusion, then, essentially answers the question, so what? In answer to that, let me begin by returning to the "ultimate" causality of the presumed disintegration of family and marriage. By now, it should be clear that I do not believe that either of the latter are disintegrating; both merely are changing drastically. The "symptoms" that concern us during this symposium should remind us of that change but, also, of our collective inability and hesitance to come to terms with it. Dealing with institutional change is more than a simple "scientific" endeavor. Of course, it demands an understanding and explanation of its nature and direction before we can begin attempts to control and collectively live with it. But it also requires recognition that there are important aspects of our environment that, like the weather, lie beyond our immediate control. I doubt that anyone seriously would suggest that we reduce our dramatically increased life expectancy. Yet, I do not believe that the human family evolved to deal effectively with the problems of its aging and severely disabled members. Death solved those problems in the past. As suggested earlier, I do not consider marriage capable of effectively fulfilling the social role of "guardian" in the realm of human sexuality. All it can, and should, do is attempt to sanction the legitimacy of its procreative consequences.

Let me, at this point, introduce a metaphor to help me be more specific in the remainder of my final comments. "Traffic," as a current institution, can be seen as "the set containing all vehicles in transit." It has rules. For example, one is obliged to move on the right side of the road. It is supported by values, such as, being a courteous and careful driver. Traffic also knows a variety of "accidents," but it does not really "cause" them. Mishaps are "caused" by people who operate vehicles under all sorts of conditions and contingencies. Slippery roads add to the risk of driving. Attributes of individuals such as being drunk, having poor reflexes, and being poorly trained, contribute, each in its own way, to the risks of being in traffic. Finally, situational variables, like in the rush hour, "interact" with individual ones. Many drivers tend to become rude and abusive on their way home from work. Reducing traffic problems, thus requires, among else, improving the conditions under which it operates and improving the skills and attitudes of those who are on the road at any given time. Excluding certain kinds of drivers from participation altogether also will be of help.

We can look at the sets labeled "family" and "marriage" in an analogous manner. As in the case of traffic, it makes no sense to hold marriage or family responsible for what is happening to them. Even turning the clock back to a "nostalgic" and poorly remembered past will not help. No one would benefit from such a return to a horse-and-buggy stage. What is left, then, is to improve the conditions under which these institutions must function in modern societies and work to improve the level of interpersonal skills, attitudes, and understanding of those who contemplate living in marriages and families. It also might be helpful if those who are unfit to participate could be effectively discouraged from doing so.

The latter point raises, at least implicitly, the need for free and equal choices between culturally acceptable alternatives, for example, that between getting married or remaining single, to have children or to remain voluntarily childless, to limit the number of one's offspring, and the option of being able to leave an unsatisfactory marital relationship. I suggest that in the realm of such choices and the availability of alternatives, our society and its predominant culture still are lagging. Singlehood, for example, remains, in many ways, an unequal option. Intimate bonds outside marriage, especially sexual ones, still are considered "deviant" in many social settings. Single parenthood, even when unavoidable, remains stigmatized and economically hazardous. Adoption, as a rational alternative to biological parenthood remains to many a "last resort" option. And so on, and so forth.

In essence, though, most of the above "inequalities" represent instances where our collective past, so far, has failed to catch up with the realities of the present. They can and are being corrected, often without too much fuss, and do not require a basic rethinking of either marriage or family. If we, however, begin to think more imaginatively about the institutional realities of marriage and family, other, more unlikely and perhaps more socially risky alternatives come to mind. Even if we reject them at the present time, they may foreshadow events to come. Let me give just a few examples.

Our current "marriage-for-life" value goes back to times in which the life expectancy for individuals was less than 40 years and that of the average marriage about ten years. Currently, the average duration of a marriage is around 40 years, which seems too long for many couples. This suggests the option of a "renewable" marriage contract as an alternative to our existing commitment for life. Such temporary commitments would expire after a specified number of years, and, of course, should include an option for renewal. The idea is not new. Decades ago, Margaret Mead discussed the possibility of a so called "two-stage" marriage. Obviously, she was ahead of her time.

A second value in need of basic reconsideration is the unrealistic, and, at times, counterproductive, evaluation of "biological" parenthood over its various adoptive counterparts. Sociologically, parenting is a major responsibility, a lasting commitment and a behavioral process. Who provides the sperm or gives birth seems, at best, only partially related to effective parenthood. The irrational cultural bias in favor of the biological aspects of human reproduction leads to situations in which young, often unmarried, parents legally "own" their offspring and, as such, can interfere destructively with the best interests of a child and a community.

Finally, to remain a viable and sensible sanction of the legitimacy of offspring, marriage needs to be "protected" against competing alternatives. This only can be done, however, by the elimination of its virtual legal monopoly on all forms of intimacy. By legalizing lasting bonds that simply do not fit into the existing form of marriage, such as homosexual unions, and those between cohabiting adults, marriage itself is strengthened. The assumption that voluntary heterosexual marriage as we know it, is able to compete with other meaningful and viable nonprocreative relationships is wishful thinking. Marriage, as it has evolved as a major human institution, derives its immense social importance from the fact that it provides continuity and order in human societies. To argue that only one, aging institution can continue to fulfill this function in increasingly complex and culturally diverse modern societies is not just naive but dangerous.

In closing this essay, one final comment is in order. The study of how individual marriages and families may go wrong is the domain of psychologists and socialpsychologists. Their research and clinical practice into the "micro" world of marriages and families is progressing remarkably well. Gottman's recent impressive book (1994) bears witness to this development. Such work, however, is only marginally relevant to what concerned me in this essay. Its published results, useful as they may be to clinicians, remain afloat in a societal vacuum, because the linkages between such data and the cultural malaise that seems part of "modernity," and reverberates within the boundaries of its social institutions, remain poorly understood. Let us hope, then, that multidisciplinary symposia, such as this one, will help us to get to know more about what, as of yet, we do not know.

REFERENCES

Beck, U. (1992). *Risk Society: Towards a New Modernity.* Newbury Park, CA: Sage Publications.

Bromberger, S. (1992). *On What We Know We Don't Know.* Chicago, IL: University of Chicago Press.

Cowan, P. A. (1993). The Sky is Falling, but Popenoe's Analysis Won't Help us do Anything about it. *Journal of Marriage and the Family, 55,* 548-552.

Gottman, J. M. (1994). *What Predicts Divorce?* Hillsdale, NJ: Lawrence Erlbaum.

Horowitz, I. L. (1967). Consensus, Conflict and Cooperation. In N. J. Demerath & R. A. Peterson (Eds.). *System, Change and Conflict.* (pp. 265-279). New York: Free Press.

Popenoe, D. (1993). American Family Decline, 1960-1990: A Review and Appraisal. *Journal of Marriage and the Family, 55,* 527-555.

Sprey, J. (1969). The Family as a System in Conflict. *Journal of Marriage and the Family, 31,* 699-706.

Sprey, J. (1979). Conflict Theory and the Study of Marriage and the Family. In Wesley R. Burr, et al. (Eds.) *Contemporary Theories about the Family.* Volume II. (pp. 130-160). New York: Macmillan.

Sprey, J. (1996). (forthcoming). Family Dynamics: Conflict and Power. In M. B. Sussman & S. K. Steinmetz (Eds.) *Handbook of Marriage and the Family.* Second Edition. New York: Plenum.

Stacey, J. (1993). Good Riddance to "The Family": A Response to David Popenoe. *Journal of Marriage and the Family, 55,* 545-547.

Zill, N. & Nord, C. W. (1994). *Running in Place.* Washington, D.C.: Child Trends, Inc.

Jetse Sprey, Ph.D. *is Professor Emeritus of Sociology at Case Western Reserve University. He served as editor of the* Journal of Marriage and the Family *(1982-1986) and has written in the areas of family conflict, family disorganization, and the interface between social theorizing and evolutionary biology. In addition to undergraduate and graduate degrees from the University of Amsterdam in the Netherlands, he holds an M.A. in Southeast Asia Area Studies and a Ph.D. in Sociology from Yale University.*

Rainforests, Families, and Communities: Ecological Perspectives on Exile, Return, and Reconstruction

JOSE SZAPOCZNIK, PH.D.
YOLANDA MANCILLA, PH.D.
Center for Family Studies/Center for Minority Families
Department of Psychiatry and Behavioral Sciences
University of Miami School of Medicine

This paper suggests that the ultimate cause of the disintegration of the family can be located in the breakdown of a social ecology that sustains families, an ecology characterized by active participation, a sense of collective identity as one people, and accountability to one another.

Here is a true story. There is a rainforest on the island of Puerto Rico that is called El Yunque. Once, a girl of ten, who had only known the perpetual and desolate grays of a great Northern city, traveled to this rainforest to spend her summer at Campamento Elisa, a Girl Scout camp. There she found a lush and verdant landscape: an air so clean and charged it seemed to carry the ancient voices of the Taíno Indians, and joyful multicolored birds, and an abundance of lizards, chameleons, iguanas, that scurried along trees and the walls of the tiny cabins, and flowers and palm fronds (oh, it seemed like hundreds of different ones!), each one mysterious and beautiful, and El Río Grande, a playful, powerful river that whispered over smooth rocks under the filtered tropical sun, and swelled and wept under the swift, torrential rainforest rains. The girl loved the coming of the rains, when the tropical exuberance gave way to an utter stillness, and then she would listen deep into that stillness, until the silence was shattered by the sudden and omnipresent rush of the rain.

Yet perhaps she loved the night more than the day, for then the sky was pierced with the entire universe, and if she cupped her hands around her eyes she could imagine herself alone and unencumbered, flying among stars and as free as rain, as if forever in a lucid dream. And then all the night creatures of the rainforest came alive, but the most magical of all the night creatures was the coquí. The girl fell in love with the song of this tiny tree frog, and she listened every night as its lullaby gave way to a sleep she had never known.

The girl found a language in the rainforest, and a community, and a culture. She knew herself to be one with the creatures of the day and the creatures of the night, with the palms and the flowers, the river and the rains. She knew herself one with the night sky. She knew she belonged. The rainforest sustained her, and she grew brown and warm and resilient, and filled with laughter and wonder and silence.

This is a true story, and one day it was time for the girl to leave the rainforest and return to the city. But she could not bear to leave behind her one true love, the coquí. The night before she was to begin her journey, the girl found a small box, and into this box she placed a tiny coquí, and a few succulent leaves for his dinner. The next day the girl found herself in San Juan, and all day long she peeked into the box, and the little frog seemed to sleep. But that night the coquí did not sing, and in the morning he was dead.

And so the girl learned that both she and the coquí are sacred and living creatures who are nourished by the exuberant tropical rainforest that is all of us when we are one people. She came to understand that homesickness is a hunger that can kill a coquí just as surely as it can kill a child, or a family, or a people. This is a true story, and the girl was to return to the rainforest again and again, until she became a woman, and each time, she knew herself home.

I. THE EXILE

We are all homesick, and we know we will die of our homesickness. For each of us, there is something: a beloved, a town, a tree, our grandmother's cat, something that means *home*, that is desperately missed, with a nostalgia that envelopes and compels us into action, as if we could reclaim and reconstruct the past, or seduces us into inaction, as if nothing could ever carry us back, as if nothing could ever be the same again. It is easy, and comforting, and yes, perhaps necessary, to rest in these memories, so familiar — in the sense of *family* — they orient our daily lives in countless tiny ways, imbuing value and meaning and substance to our experience of who we are, of where we belong, of how we locate ourselves in time.

So essential are these memories — our own private nostalgia — to our conception of who we are, that we are careful not to disrupt the integrity of the whole, the collage of images and words we have constructed of our experience. We respond quickly to any challenge to our recollections *"that's not how I remember it, so that's not how it happened"* we say to our sister when she retells a shared childhood incident, as if to say, *"if I cannot locate myself in your remembrance, then I do not exist there, at least not as I know myself to be."*

There is an *ecology of memory* that is as fragile as it is tenacious. We will hold fast to these memories of who we were because they weave the fabric of everything — our parents, family, home, friends, school, church, community — that came to form us, our values, our selves. Disrupt one memory, and the ecology of self we have constructed reels, every other memory readjusting to the fit. In a sense, then, psychotherapy is a reconstruction of memories, a journey into the ecology of our thoughts about ourselves, our families, our experience.

● ● ●

In Miami, Florida, there lives a community of Cuban exiles. We have diligently reconstructed, out of our shared memories, out of our *collective nostalgia*, a social and cultural and economic world in which to locate ourselves as a people. Rather than allow the experience of exile to disrupt the ecology of memory that claims us forever *cubanos*, we have oriented ourselves, as a community, as a people, to the past as we collectively remember it, and to a future that seeks to reclaim what is past. And while we have worked to build a new community in Miami, and while the collective memories have undergone much painful challenge and readjustment, and while the generations have struggled to understand each other as they have *"biculturated"* at different rates, even the very bicultural children of Cuban parents, born and raised in the United States, when asked *"what are you"*? readily respond *"Cuban."* We know — one of us was born in Cuba, and one of us was not; we identify deeply, by heritage or by lived experience, with other peoples — Jewish, Andean, Puerto Rican — but we are both inextricably Cuban, we are woven into that collective memory that is our people in exile.

Yet in our work with Cuban families in Miami, we have noticed a gradual but important shift in the sense of collective nostalgia. Families that entered into exile in the early years of the Cuban Revolution insisted on passing on to their children not only a Cuban identity, but a conviction that they would one day return to the island. Many young Cubans state that they will go back to Cuba if the "system" changes, to live, to work in *la reconstrucción*, the reconstruction. Cuba is their *homeland*, and for lack of personal memories, they have taken on the collective memories of the community — of how things were, and how they should be.

In contrast, many recent arrivals — the *balseros* who brave the Florida straits on makeshift rafts — say they will not return to the island, at least, not for a very long time. *"I have bad memories of Cuba"* they say, memories that will take time to heal. They are not a part of the collective nostalgia; they have woven their memories out of other experiences, out of lives we do not know or understand. Theirs is a greater ambivalence, a sense of not being oriented to anything, if not their hope in the future itself.

We are one people, but we are two sets of memories, two ecologies. How these two ecologies will finally achieve a synthesis — as they must if the Cuban people are to move forward as one — is a question to be answered, perhaps, in the forging of new, shared memories; in the reconstruction that is already beginning, the reconstruction that is more than just about buildings and infrastructure and legislation. It is a reconstruction of hope, and of knowledge, and of memories. It is a reconstruction of a rainforest for an exiled "coquí."

• • •

In our Center for Family Studies at the University of Miami, our front line work with Cuban exile families over twenty years has taken us from "first wave" exiles to the Mariel refugee camps to the *balsero* experience. In thinking about the conditions that are conducive to the development and sustenance of strong, functional families, we find we have learned a great deal from our work with this exiled Cuban community in Miami. The large, multigenerational, extended Cuban families were dismembered by the Cuban diaspora, as we found ourselves in Spain, Puerto Rico, Venezuela, New York, New Jersey, Miami...to this day a number of Cuban communities thrive in countries all over Europe and Latin America. But Miami remains by far the largest of these communities.

Our encounters with Cuban families in the 1970s revealed parents and children in pain — and at the core of their pain was the very real fear that children would acculturate to the predominant "Anglo" environment, leaving behind all that parents considered essential to their own concept of *familia* — beliefs, behaviors, that spoke to basic Cuban (Latin American) values — such as respect for elders, the dignity of each individual, the duty of parents to their children, and of children, perhaps especially adult children, to their parents. It seemed to these parents that all they had relied on to ensure the continuation of these values and thus, of a strong and supportive family, had been left behind in a Cuban society that they increasingly held up as the standard against which all other societies must be measured. It seemed to these parents that their children were refusing to participate in the collective memory of Cuba.

Our work with Cuban families at that time often consisted in helping parents to understand, and to learn to locate themselves, within a new, and for many a radically different, social, ecological and cultural context. As the Cuban community was attempting to re-create a *Pequeña Habana*, a "Little Havana" in Miami, these parents were also engaging in an active process of sorting out for themselves what attributes of the old and new cultural environments were to be valued and nourished, as essential to maintaining a strong, functional family, and what attributes were damaging to this end. Perhaps the most painful realization for some parents was that many cherished customs — chaperons for young girls, for example — would have to be let go. At the same time, many Cuban women were discovering, for the first time, a sense of themselves as competent individuals in the outside world, and as a result were more willing to reconsider their goals for their daughters.

At the core of this process is the orientation to a new ecological context in which the family must find ways to nurture itself, the reassessment of what is to be valued in both the old and new ecologies, and at the level of the community, the attempt to re-create attributes of the old ecology which are viewed as sustaining families. How each family ultimately defined what aspects of their ecology were essential to their survival was, in the end, a deeply personal decision to be negotiated among parents, adolescents, grandparents, children. But one consideration emerges clearly for us: the Cuban exile families were greatly nourished and sustained by a sense of community that provided identity, belonging, shared goals, and strong, interdependent social networks, in which adults, as well as youth, found a sense of inclusion, of role, of being needed and wanted.

Cuban exile families left behind a social ecological context that they believed supported families, and learned to re-create in their new environment those aspects of the old social ecology that they considered valuable and worth saving, and to identify aspects of the new social ecology that were equally valuable and worth adopting. The Cuban "success story," as a community, has been well-documented and continues to this day. There is a downside to this story, to be sure — political intolerance, materialism, rejection of other groups, including other Latin Americans, who may be viewed as racially different, have characterized many Cubans — but the Cuban community is not unique in this respect. *What is perhaps the ultimately valuable lesson to be learned from the Cuban exile experience, is the emphasis on a collective sense of identity, of a sense of place even in exile, of belonging to something larger, and of a responsibility to that larger context that demands active participation towards its sustenance.* Cubans do seem to share a sense of oneness, of accountability to each other, that has been lost in many other communities, and out of this sense of oneness, have built a strong and thriving community that in many ways has been able to nourish its families.

We are all homesick because, like the Cuban people, we are all exiles. And like the *coquí*, our families are dying of homesickness, of nostalgia for the social ecology that once sustained us. We have exiled our families from the ecologies they once named *home*.

What happened to the Cubans is a metaphor, a microcosm of what has happened to society at large. We find ourselves, as a society, estranged from what we remember as being sustaining and nourishing to us as children. Even in the absence of "perfect" nuclear families, we remember extended families and neighborhoods that sustained us. Yet today, we find ourselves banished from our childhoods, our hometowns, and from the common everyday elements of society that nourished our families. And so we look around and lament its passing.

We attempt to re-invent these elements for our own families, but find our communities do not support us in our efforts, because as communities we seem to lack a sense of shared values and goals — the warm, carefully woven cloth that once nestled us in our childhood families. As we remain trapped in our *private nostalgia*, we look increasingly to material ways in which to achieve, at least, the appearance of what is past. We trivialize our own longings in many ways. The popularity of fashion and home decorating trends that re-create the look of times past, speaks to this yearning for re-connection with something older than ourselves, with something worth passing on to our children. In our nostalgia, we have come to believe that if we could somehow capture the superficial appearance of our childhood homes, we would once again possess the sense of family and community that imbued those homes. And like the young Cubans in Miami, who never really knew the island, those of us who did not know a strong, loving childhood family and supportive community, have borrowed from the collective memory of our society to construct a sanitized image of a *Father Knows Best* world.

Just as the Cuban people, who long for *the return*, must now face the painful task of reconstructing a social ecology that includes and sustains everyone, so must we as a society, who also long to return from exile, forge for ourselves a social ecology that is not exclusive of any group, that in sustaining families, sustains everyone. Because, *like in the childhood communities we remember, everyone has a family, everyone belongs, everyone cares, everyone has an important and meaningful role to play, a sense of place and a responsibility for the well-being of all.* We must ask, if we are all exiles from what we once knew as *home*, from communities that once supported families, then what is this *homeland* to which we long to return? What does it look like? How did we lose it? Who, or what, did we allow to colonize us, to direct the course of our lives, to divest us of our families and communities? And how is the ecology of this homeland to be reconstructed, and who is responsible, who is to be held accountable, for its reconstruction?

• • •

The global, physical ecological model that has emerged to understand and address the problem of the destruction of the physical, planetary environment, provides a useful model for beginning to think about reconstructing a social ecology that sustains families. Central to the global physical ecological view is the understanding that *multiple symptoms of ecological destruction,* such as the destruction of the rainforests, or the contamination of our groundwater and oceans, *are the result of multiple individual and societal behaviors,* such as inattention to the value of rainforests in sustaining the balance of the global physical ecology, or a lack of understanding of the multiple individual and industrial causes of contamination of our waters. The ultimate cause of the physical ecological destruction of the Earth has been framed as a lack of awareness and understanding of how our behaviors affect the planetary ecosystem, or given that awareness, the unwillingness to change our behavior, whether as individuals or as a society.

The physical ecological movement has attempted to create and foster a *global consciousness,* both at the individual level (such as in the "Give a Hoot, Don't Pollute" campaign, home-based recycling, "buying green," vegetarianism), and the societal level (such as in the establishment of the Environmental Protection Agency, and in community-wide recycling and clean-up efforts). This global consciousness holds us collectively accountable for the impact our day-to-day choices and behaviors have had, and continue to have, on the global physical environment. In the process, the physical ecological movement has been able to frame the problem of the destruction of the physical ecology from a historical perspective that is at times benign, and at times not.

For example, the development of technology has led to products that damage the environment, yet it cannot be argued that as a society, in our early efforts to improve the "quality" of our lives, we intentionally set out to damage the environment. Indeed, in the early days, we did not understand the potential damage to be caused by these products — the automobile, for example — or by the industrialization and modernization of society in general. However, as we grew in our knowledge of the harmful impact of some industries, we began to see cases of companies fighting against environmental regulation, or moving to Third World countries to escape these regulations. Financial gain became more important than accountability in helping to preserve the environment. Similarly, on an individual level, many of us grew up at a time when we did not think twice about throwing away newspapers or empty cans, yet we did not intend to harm the planet with our behavior. Today, many of us have made a habit of a new behavior — recycling — while others of us continue to feel inconvenienced by the requirement that we change our behavior.

The solutions are not always simple or painless. For example, the loggers in the United States northwest, or the poor farmers clearing out areas of the Brazilian rainforest, are simply attempting to make a living for their families, although in the process they are damaging the planetary ecology. The global physical ecological movement continues to struggle with such issues as it seeks to foster a planetary ecology that sustains human communities even as it protects and preserves fragile biological ecosystems.

• • •

Following this global physical/ecological model, we suggest that *the ultimate cause of the disintegration of the family can be located in the breakdown of a social ecology that sustains families, an ecology characterized by active participation, a sense of collective identity as one people, and accountability to one another.* These are among the principles that our "founding fathers" articulated as essential to the creation of a fair and just society (albeit limited in their view to White men). Their vision unleashed a process that, as it evolved, brought greater equality and inclusion to other groups such as women and minorities. But as our society grew larger and became increasingly modernized, active participation, collective identity and mutual accountability gradually waned.

Just as we have, collectively and individually, inadvertently or carelessly, created the conditions that damage our physical ecology, as a society we have engaged in behaviors that have failed to support, and have ultimately damaged, the social ecological conditions that sustain families. These behaviors represent our failure to implement the principles on which our country is based, and include our reluctance to participate in creating a better society, as well as our negligence in creating the conditions that permit all members of society to participate fully. They also include our failure to be held accountable not only for our own behavior, but also for that of our neighbors.

As these primary principles (active participation, common identity, mutual accountability) that sustain our society have waned (please refer to Figure 1, level 1a), the social ecology that sustains families has become tattered (level 1b). This breakdown of the social ecology has in turn led to multiple primary symptoms (level 2), such as unemployment, availability of drugs, individually oriented — rather than family-focused—programs of social assistance, and schools that prepare children for modern technological society without adequately addressing the needs of the entire family. The breakdown of the social ecology, together with these primary symptoms, contribute to the damage experienced by families and communities (level 3).

Finally, we identify two types of secondary symptoms (level 4), that are caused either directly or indirectly, by the factors in the preceding three levels. One type of secondary symptom is usually labeled as *"anti-social"* because it describes behavior that is troublesome and disruptive to society (such as criminal and violent behavior, domestic violence and abuse, child and adolescent problem behavior, school drop-out, reliance on welfare, and substance abuse and addiction). The other type of secondary symptom is more subtle in nature, but we suggest it is equally as destructive to society, and might be labeled as *"insularity."* Insular behaviors that are destructive to the social ecology reflect the natural tendency to isolate or protect one's own family and immediate community from perceived threats in the larger society, while at the same time neglecting to participate in the resolution of those very threats from which we attempt to protect ourselves. Insular thinking results in denial of our common identity and mutual accountability, thereby aggravating the ultimate cause of the breakdown of the social ecology.

Once the behaviors that reflect the secondary symptoms (both anti-social and insular) are in place, an extensive array of settings and social networks continue to validate, encourage and sustain these behaviors. Antisocial behaviors find a home in street hangouts and crack houses, and are supported by social networks, such as the increasingly ubiquitous youth gangs. Similarly, insular behaviors find a home behind walled-in communities and security gates. Insular behaviors are fed by fear, and are maintained by distancing behaviors.

Today, most of us immediately recognize that a global perspective is imperative when thinking about our physical ecology. While we recognize that individual and local community efforts are essential to the preservation of the planet, we understand that it is not enough for only one or two communities to participate in this process. We know that all communities and all nations must be involved, because we all share the same physical ecology. We do not say *"Let us control auto emissions in our own neighborhood, and let the other neighborhoods take care of themselves."* Of course, we all breathe the same air, and the efforts of one neighborhood will not suffice to clear the air that visits all neighborhoods.

Unless we all participate in the effort, we will all suffer the degeneration of our environment. Our common air, our common groundwater, our common soil, must be protected collectively and with an eye to the larger ecological context that renders us inextricably interdependent. We do not claim the right to damage the environment, but rather, we hold it in a sacred trust. *The physical ecology does not belong to us, or to anyone: it cannot be privatized; it cannot, ultimately, be owned. We cannot isolate "our" ecosystem from the multiple ecosystems that, together, give life to our planet.*

In the same way, a global perspective is essential to an understanding of our social ecology. Yet so often we view our own family, and perhaps our own immediate community, as our only responsibility. We fail to recognize our interdependencies, our shared social ecology. We forget that, if a neighboring community is in distress, that distress will eventually, in some manner, visit us as well. We say *"Let us ensure a quality neighborhood school for our children, a school of caring teachers and plentiful resources, and let the other neighborhoods take care of their own schools."* But of course we all breathe the same "social ecological air," and the children who attend that impoverished school are no less present in our lives.

Are we aware of the lives of these children, these families? Do we hold ourselves accountable to them? We organize baseball teams in our neighborhoods — but would we do it for them? In a healthy community, when one family is hurting, or destitute, or ill, neighbors bring food and laughter and kind words. But some communities in distress have lost the ability to respond to overwhelming external conditions, their resources are compromised, their families unable to assist each other fully. And the surrounding communities, the neighbors of that community, *have lost the will* to help them overcome their pain.

As neighbors, we have become fearful, wary, skittish. We have forgotten about our shared ecology, we have come to believe that, if only we can secure and nurture our own family, our own community, we will be safe and healthy. We attempt to privatize *"our"* neighborhood, to isolate it from the neighborhoods that collectively bring life to our world. We construct private communities, protected by private security forces. We send our children to private schools, and we socialize at private clubs. *We have forgotten that our social ecology is also a sacred trust, that it does not belong to us, but to everyone, that it cannot, ultimately, be privatized or owned. We cannot isolate "our" social ecology from the multiple social ecosystems that, together, bring life to our world community.*

Most efforts to remedy the ailments of society have focused narrowly on the "antisocial" symptoms because they appear to be the most painful and disruptive to society. Yet we have failed to address the other kind of secondary symptom that is represented by our collective insularity. It is perhaps this failure that has led to our inability to fully understand, and consequently fully resolve, our social dilemma.

In family systems theory, the strategy we have used here might be described as *spreading of the identified patienthood.* The *identified patient* is the family member who is the repository for the pain of the family, as expressed in symptomatic behavior. In this paper, the identified patient is represented by the antisocial symptoms that are troublesome to society. In family therapy, we assume that the symptomatic behavior of the identified patient draws attention away from the behaviors of others that contribute to the current conditions. Thus, a strategy in family systems therapy is to identify the broader range of behaviors that contribute to the current conditions. In this paper, the more extensive behaviors that contribute to our social dilemma are reflected in the collective insularity through which members of society deny a shared identity, relinquish participation, and abdicate responsibility for the greater good.

III. THE RECONSTRUCTION

As in the global physical ecological movement, the task of reconstructing a social ecology that sustains *all* families, demands the active engagement and involvement of us all — as parents, youth, professionals, citizens, scientists, as members of local, national and global communities — in proactive and watchful behaviors that attend to the social ecological factors that either damage or sustain families. The solution requires basic changes in how we make our lives within communities, in how we hold ourselves accountable to those communities through our choices and behaviors, and in how we define the concept of *family*. In this paper, our definition of *family* attends to what is *"familiar,"* to what is known and remembered as being nourishing, rather than being merely present-oriented. But we also see *family* as an evolving construct that must be ever inclusive of all people, rather than as an insular, "nuclear" unit that is oriented to its own individual survival at the expense of the social ecological community of families that ultimately sustains us all. Perhaps most profoundly, *the reconstruction* involves a fundamental shift in our prevailing world view about the causal factors behind our most troubling social conditions, and about the process that must be undertaken to arrive at ecologically-based, integrated and holistic solutions that reflect and honor our basic interconnectedness and interdependencies as a people.

• • •

One strategy used by the global physical ecological movement is to look at a secondary symptom, such as air pollution, and to explore its antecedents. Of particular interest are antecedent behaviors that occur on a large scale, and that initially might have been well-intentioned, such as the development and use of the automobile. As we have come to recognize the automobile as a significant cause of air pollution, we have had to acknowledge that our behavior, which relies heavily on the automobile, must change accordingly. Thus, to contribute to the reconstruction of the physical ecology, we must explore and use alternative modes of transportation that are "eco-friendly." Each of us must demand and expect vehicles with better emissions standards, we must support national policies that require such standards, and we must be watchful that American-based companies overseas comply with such standards. As a nation, we must urge other countries, through our international treaties, to implement effective national emissions control policies. And through our professional associations, we must encourage our friends in other nations to support such policies.

In the case of the social ecology, one such large-scale effector is the educational system (while we focus on the school system by way of illustration, we acknowledge that multiple, interacting effectors contribute to the disrepair of our social ecology). A major function of schools is to prepare youth to function in a modern world, and this is clearly a necessary and well-intentioned goal. In the case of economically, socially and politically resourceful communities, parents have a voice in the daily life of their schools, and play an instrumental role in setting and directing the agenda for those schools. Rather than become distanced from their children, these parents join school committees, interact with teachers, school administrators, and other parents, vote for school board representatives, and become an integral part of the modernization process of their children. In doing so, they weave traditional values and modern concepts into their children's educational process. The dialectic process, which evolves from the parents' attempts at influencing the schooling of their children, in turn influences the parents and broadens their understanding of and support for the modernization process.

The cycle of mutuality and reciprocity between parental values and interests on the one hand, and the forces of modernization represented by the schools on the other, reflects a *post-modern process* in which iteratively, tradition and modernity interact, dialogue and adapt to one another. Neither ignores nor neglects the other. The moral value here is on creating an *inclusionary process* that builds on the common goals of parents and schools for the education of children who are at once rooted in parental values and fluent in the language of the modern world.

In contrast, families with less economic, social and political resources, often find themselves marginalized from their children's schools. Many face limited access to school personnel because of language barriers, as well as cultural differences in the conception of the role of schools and of parents within schools. Unable to enter into dialogue with the societal forces responsible for preparing children for the modern world, these parents are thus denied a voice in shaping the modernization process of their own children. The schools unwittingly nurture a distancing, a cultural schism, between parents and children in the same family. Unaware of the difficulties faced by parents with less access to resources, schools go about their business of teaching without adequately addressing the developing gaps at home. These families and their schools become the victims of the modernization process, not realizing that their victimization occurs because of their inability to create a dialogue, a dialectic process, between traditional and modern forces and values.

Our system of government is intended to protect the less powerful from the more powerful. In a case such as this, it might be argued that it is the place of government to protect families, the more vulnerable, from the modernization process reflected in the schools — without preventing the modernization of subsequent generations of children that is required for the continued intellectual and economic development of the country. Modern schools were not created to protect families, but to form citizens who could fill the anticipated workforce needs of the nation (just as the development of the automobile was not intended to protect the physical ecology, but to create a more efficient mode of transportation necessary to support the industrialization of our economy). In the family area, if there were a "family protection agency," such as exists for the physical ecology in the form of the Environmental Protection Agency, then such a family agency would certainly regulate school activities that inadvertently undermine parents by excluding them from the modernization process of their children.

• • •

In reconstructing a social ecology that sustains families, we must make difficult choices that compel us to consider both *moral content* and *moral process*. Moral content is concerned with the *content of values*, as exemplified in the debates between creation theory and evolution theory, between sexual permissiveness and sexual conservatism, between "pro-life" and "pro-choice." Moral process is concerned with *social and personal processes* that reflect *how* we make our lives in family and community, as exemplified by inclusionary versus exclusionary behaviors, democratic versus autocratic systems of decision-making, and ecological versus insular world views. This paper promotes a morality that reflects ecological, inclusionary and democratic processes, in contrast to a morality that is insular, exclusionary and autocratic.

Many of us belong to communities, churches, or social and political groups whose members honor deeply held values, are working intensively towards the fulfillment of common goals, and share a profound sense of belonging and accountability to each other. These groups exist at both ends of the political and social spectrum, and carry a multitude of labels such as "fundamentalist" or "liberal" or "feminist" or "conservative." These groups promote divergent moral content, but are similar in moral process. Their passion has led them to a process that seeks to "win over the other," rather than to a process that seeks to find ways to include the other. While all are well intentioned, they unwittingly contribute to the further disruption of the social ecology, and families become the battleground for their differences.

This chapter proposes an *alternative moral process* that is inclusionary. We call upon the major social forces that are struggling to heal our society to find ways to build on their common interest for "saving families." We call upon them to construct a larger *moral ecology* that is inclusive of different moral perspectives. We believe that families are sustained by a healthy social ecology, and that the "whole" social ecology we seek to construct is in turn based on, and sustained by, an inclusionary moral ecology.

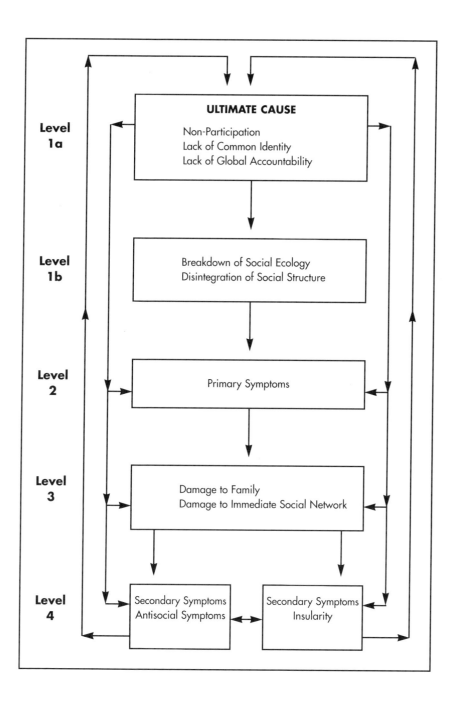

● ● ●

The reconstruction of healthy, functional families depends on the reconstruction of a social ecology that attends to the factors that support families. We maintain that we are all collectively responsible for the quality of the social ecology in which we make our lives, and that this social ecology must be viewed in broad, "global" terms if we are all to be served. We must all actively participate in making this happen, in the spirit of a shared, common identity that links us all as neighbors, *as family*. For not a single family falls, that we do not all fall together. And not a single family rejoices, that we do not all rejoice.

We do not claim easy answers, but we call for a social ecological movement encompassing a comprehensive process of education and awareness that is both intensive in nature and extensive in scope, a change in how we make our daily lives, and a collaborative interplay between public leadership and private participation, equivalent to the movement that has attended to saving the physical, planetary environment. In the same way, this is a process that must be played out at the level of local and federal government, in the arena of social policy development, and in the everyday choices of each one of us.

Jose Szapocznik, Ph.D. *is Professor of Psychiatry and Psychology and Director, Center for Family Studies/Center for Minority Families/Spanish Family Guidance Center, University of Miami, Florida. Dr. Szapocznik has over twenty years professional experience in the area of substance abuse prevention with minority families and has received considerable recognition for this work. He also serves on numerous advisory boards and federal committees in his area of expertise. Dr. Szapocznik has published over 100 scholarly books, chapters and articles in professional journals.*

Yolanda Mancilla, Ph.D. *is Assistant Professor of Psychiatry at the Center for Family Studies/Center for Minority Families/Spanish Family Guidance Center, University of Miami, Florida. Dr. Mancilla is currently Project Director for the Center's community-based youth gang prevention and Hispanic family leadership programs in East Little Havana.*

THE DETERIORATION OF THE MODERN FAMILY

PETER A. WHITE
Founder and President
International Skye Associates, Inc.

RESPONSIBILITY

The principal task of the modern family is to raise children who can take charge of their lives as adults. This is distinct from the historical family, whose principal task was to assure the physical survival of family members. When the modern family succeeds in its task of raising children who can take charge, it gives the world young people capable of the highest and most rewarding state of being: the state in which responsibility is possible.

The responsible individual looks first to herself. She understands that to accomplish anything in this life, she must decide where she wants to go, make plans to get there, and take steps to implement those plans. She is not a loner: she knows that her success will probably depend on getting help from others and that it is up to her to get that help. Her attitude precludes blaming and whining; her eye is on her objective, not on assigning reasons why she cannot reach it. She is neither single-minded nor obsessed, but she never gives up, although her objective may change as she makes discoveries along the way.

The responsible person is one who cares. He cares first for himself, understanding that his mind, body, and spirit are his being and that he must attend to all three as his parents once attended to him as a child. In his self-care, he becomes able to care for others, extending beyond the limitations of his fears and taking the risk of love, without taking over the others' lives. Finally, he accepts and relishes the truth, which he realizes he cannot fully know in this life but to which he dedicates himself, first in small ways and later, as he grows in spirit, in perhaps great ways.

Responsible people commit to eternal relationships of marriage and attack the baffling work of raising children with vigor and dedication. They tell the truth, pick up litter when they find it in their path, join communities, and participate in the welfare of the group as a whole. They are people who fail regularly in all of these things, but their failures are irrelevant. They are aware of their eternal frailty and are courageous enough to take a chance on changing and growing. Fortunately, there are many responsible people in our world. Regrettably, a great many people are irresponsible.

A world in which responsibility is broadly understood and accepted — one in which responsible behavior is the norm — would be one whose institutions, such as organized religions, educational organizations, governments, business and labor organizations, media, philanthropic and nonprofit foundations, social clubs, neighborhoods, and every other community, would reflect and support responsibility.

Successful families would make such a world possible. (Given human imperfection, it would be more realistic to say that the more effective families are, the more the institutions of the world are likely to reflect and support responsible behavior.) Effective families produce individuals who, on their own and in concert with others, act responsibly. In the long run, the institutions of society cannot require irresponsible people to act responsibly. And when irresponsibility prevails, social institutions come to reflect and support irresponsibility. This is what we decry in our world.

Family is the vessel of responsibility. Responsible behavior emanates from family, so family is the fundamental unit of human life. But to be effective — to raise young adults who are responsible — requires an enormous commitment to responsible actions on the part of parents. And raising responsible children can only be accomplished by people who have themselves become responsible. It is most likely to occur when the institutions of the world reflect and support responsible behavior and when people tend to act responsibly on their own. This, in turn, is most likely to be the case when families are successful overall in raising responsible young adults.

DOWNWARD SPIRAL

Human experience can be seen as a continuum of causes and effects, in which causes become effects and effects become causes. We act as individuals, in relationships with others, and in society. We act in relation to our physical and spiritual environments. Our actions affect people, places and things, who in turn influence others based in part on how we influenced them. What they do influences us. All is connected, as a circle.

But a circle is flat, and human experience is not flat. It improves and declines. If it improves, the circle becomes an upward spiral; in decline, a downward spiral. The family is the key influencer in whether the spiral of human experience is upward or downward because of the family's role in raising children to responsible (or irresponsible) adulthood. Adults act in ways that make their own lives and the lives of others better or worse. Adults create social institutions that influence the lives of others. Life is tied to the environment and to the spirit, which are influenced by adults, responsible and irresponsible.

The appropriate question, therefore, is not so much what contribution any part of the spiral, in isolation, makes or fails to make, but why the spiral is downward for so many. Why is it not an upward spiral of strength and empowerment? Why is it a spiral of deterioration?

We are inclined to ascribe the causes of the deterioration of families to a variety of sources, in particular to a decline in values. As sources of that decline, we look for causes. We point to television, movies, and literature, and we regret the anti-family tone presented broadly in the media. We point to a government that seems to corrupt by supporting immoral behavior and to a judicial system that has nationalized and institutionalized childish squabbling. We point to people who divorce, ascribing to them a moral weakness that undermines the family structure. We blame men alternatively for acting autocratically and for wimping out. We blame women for having children without taking responsibility for motherhood.

We are adept at finding causes, and what we have found is correct, insofar as it goes. But while these and other forces have caused the deterioration of the family, they were effects before they were causes. Why does government pass seemingly anti-family legislation? Why does television send anti-family messages? Why are divorce rates soaring? Why have values deteriorated? Do these things happen because evil people in Washington, New York and Hollywood seek to undermine the fiber of American life? Regrettably, such a tempting premise cannot support a quest for the truth, nor can any premise that blames a particular individual or group, or even particular causes such as government's failures or a decline in family values.

The moral weakness we decry in institutions exists because the constituencies of those institutions demand it. Television's support of irresponsible behavior is a response to what people want to see and to behavior that people want supported. The evening news reflects not the world as it is so much as the world interpreted to support the attitudes and behaviors of viewers. The same is true of government and education: institutions can lead but only if their constituents want to be led. Otherwise, institutions reflect.

Divorce cannot be denied as a cause of family deterioration; it is family deterioration. But divorce is not inherently evil or even a weakness. Divorce results from people having poor role models for marriage and from their inability to understand, much less effect, a timeless commitment to another person. Marriage is an act of responsibility; responsibility emanates from family. High rates of divorce are caused ultimately by the inability of the modern family to raise responsible young adults.

Gender-related problems, which are certainly causes of family deterioration, are no less caused by family deterioration. Men are lost without the fathers who traditionally informed them about being men by living and working with them each day. Today, they cling to autocratic models that have no validity in modern life, or else they become demoralized, unable to lead or follow. Women seek to fill the gap left by absent (physically and morally) males, and seem at risk of reinventing themselves in a way that precludes motherhood.

Racial hatred, which prevents a peaceful community and which threatens civil war in America, has historically understandable roots, but is inflamed and nurtured by the childish desire to blame and scapegoat, which in turn is cultivated in politics and popular culture. The instability created by racial hatred is a destabilizing factor in the family because it precludes true community, and it is fueled by the failure of the modern family.

It is a mistake to look outside the institution of the family for the causes of its deterioration, because deterioration of the family is the reason for deterioration of the family. So we must know family better.

THE HISTORICAL FAMILY

For several generations the family has been in a process of change. The modern family is very different from the historical family, and it is important to appreciate this difference to understand the downward spiral.

The task of the animal is to survive and perpetuate its species. Its concerns are primarily food and shelter; its instincts are survival and procreation. This is no less true of the human animal. Each species has its own organizational unit to facilitate survival and perpetuation, and for human beings this unit has been the family. The family, working as a community, has directed most of its energy to the fundamental mission of survival.

Although we know little about our hunting-and-gathering ancestors, what we do know and what we can infer supports the fact that family, with monogamous partners producing and raising children, has been the basic human organizational unit from the time of the emergence of Homo sapiens. The discovery of agriculture and the emergence of crafts and, later, merchants and traders enabled the family to stabilize and to become more efficient in survival and perpetuation. But, by modern standards, life-threatening forces of disease, adverse elements, and marauding outlaws and animals, were constantly present in all phases of advanced civilizations through the nineteenth century. Life expectancy was short compared with today's span. The possibility of dying was for people, as it is today for most wild animals, an ever present millstone.

Family life then may not have been pleasant. Hardship from external forces was omnipresent. Internally, autocracy and what we would now regard as abusive behavior toward women and children were commonplace. Intimacy was less an ideal of sharing than a reality of being cramped together in barely adequate shelter. Children were conceived, born, and reared in part because of the procreative and nurturing instincts, but in equal part to increase the number of family workers. Divorce and other, less civil ways of ending a marriage had usually been the province of the wealthy few. Mid- and low-income partners rarely divorced, in part because of their greater adherence to the sanctity of marriage and their fear of the stigma of divorce, but primarily because necessity precluded disintegration of the family. Separation made survival a greater challenge, so most families didn't separate. If marital love or fear of God weren't enough to keep families intact, the harsh realities of surviving alone were. The family bonded together to defeat the adverse elements, but it was far from an ideal experience. Still, the family, for the hunter-gatherer, agricultural, and for much of the urban industry phases of human society, did bond together. It was a strong, close unit. It had to be to survive.

It seems likely that the practices that caused families to be cohesive in the past differed little from those that have the same effect today. In our work at International Skye, we delineate the "Elements of Care" as the essential practices most conducive to raising children who can take charge of their lives as adults.

The Elements of Care are:

• Necessaries (food, clothing, shelter, medical attention — goods and services to sustain life)

• Affection (appropriate touching and words or sounds of love)

• Affirmation and Support (confirming another's desire to explore and achieve)

• Guidance (teaching skills and values)

• Boundaries (standards of behavior expressed in concrete circumstances)

• Respect (listening to the opinions, beliefs, and feelings of others)

- Trust (giving the opportunity to act responsibly), and

- Letting Go (the culmination of all these and the recognition of the end of childhood).

Although for most of history the emphasis on child rearing has been less on developing the child as an autonomous individual than on producing someone who could help the family as soon as possible, these Elements of Care were critical to an effective family's raising of children. Further, the standards embodied in certain principles — truthfulness, openness, commitment, care, teaching and learning, respect for authority, ethics, personal growth, and others — were pragmatic ingredients for a family that needed to work together to survive. They were ideals in a sense, but they were adopted as operating principles because they were directly relevant to the family's mission of survival.

In historical families, fathers spent their days with sons and mothers with daughters. Children were expected to help and were instructed and shown by example. Boys learned how their fathers dealt with the world, girls learned how their mothers did.

In the home, boys and girls learned by instruction and example about marriage. The commitment of marriage was, ideally and of necessity, reflected in the home. Parents married, stayed married, and acted as partners in the struggle for survival for important reasons. It seems unlikely that the character of the marriage partnership was debated as much then as it is today. Husbands and wives needed each other, and their children needed them to work together. As we teach in our work today, the strength of the adult partnership is the linchpin of and the model for family as community.

THE MODERN FAMILY

The modern family has lost its traditional motivation. Most Americans — most of advanced society — are no longer preoccu-pied with survival. We might get sick and die. We might be killed by lightning or by criminal violence. We might even be eaten by wild animals. But none of these threats seems imminent to most people. Modern citizens of advanced societies are the beneficiaries of enormously important discoveries that represent victory in mankind's war against the elements.

The late twentieth century family in advanced societies, certainly including the United States, is in transition. Its mission to keep every-one alive has been accomplished for the most part by previous fami-lies, which produced scientists and other discoverers and builders who found systematic ways to protect us from evil. Disease is relatively under control, infant mortality is low, and life expectancy for those who survive infancy is great and growing greater. Attaining age 90 is no longer uncommon, and breakthroughs in medical care and preventive health seem to expand the frontiers of life expectancy almost daily. Although crime and violence are increasing, they are, by historical standards, under control in all but pockets, mostly inner-city, of modern society. The wilderness has been tamed, so attacks by wild animals are rare.

When members of advanced societies arise in the morning, we do not usually concern ourselves with how we are going to survive the day, the week, the month, or even the season or year. We do not worry about having enough food to sustain life. We feel that we have a fighting chance to avoid or survive serious illness. We are cautious, particularly in big cities, but we are relatively confident of being able to avoid violence.

Because of our separation from the threat of imminent death and because of discoveries and inventions during the past 200 years, other institutions of society have taken over roles previously filled by the family, and, consequently, the environment of the family has changed. These changes include education in schools rather than in the home, the termination of work as a family responsibility, the location of work in factories and offices away from the home, the democratization of travel, and the fact that entertainment has become largely a passive, individual activity. Even the home itself has changed and spread out, with families no longer sleeping, much less eating and bathing, in a single room.

The implications of these changes are enormous. Family life is no longer a matter of survival, and the enforced intimacy of the family has evaporated. External social institutions, like governments, schools, businesses, and the media, have taken over old familial functions. Boys no longer spend most of their working hours with their fathers, and girls are apart from their mothers. The purpose of the modern family is far less clear today than when working together to survive was its principal function. The family is grasping for its place in a world of seemingly infinite freedom.

What the historical family had to do to survive — raise capable, responsible children — the modern family does not have to do. The structure of society, with all its frailties, has been strong enough to support modern life even though irresponsibility is widespread. Yet, no one can seriously believe that the trend toward irresponsibility can continue. As discussed earlier, social institutions reflect the collective will of their constituencies. A government can extend its benevolence (however one may define true government benevolence) somewhat beyond the time in which the people are themselves benevolent. But that is because of bureaucratic inertia. Government cannot, over the long run, be better than the people it serves.

Therefore, as families fail increasingly to raise responsible adults (and assuming that no institution successfully replaces the family) society moves increasingly toward chaos. It would be a tragic irony if, when human beings succeed in improving life to the point at which the family is no longer necessary for survival and when the family fails to do the work of raising responsible children, nature recreates the family by recreating chaos in which the world becomes again a dangerous place and family becomes once again essential to survival.

The modern family stands, as Adam and Eve stood, at a crossroads. We are safe from the constant threat of death, but there are certain disciplines required of us to keep our place. We must decide whether to follow those disciplines or to neglect them and fall back into chaos.

The disciplines I refer to are those mentioned in the preceding section describing the work of family. They encompass the Elements of Care once applied to raising children who could contribute to the family's mutual effort of survival. They encompass commitment to marriage, in which the stage is set for the growth of all family members in the community of the family and in which parents nourish each other in a love that fuels the enormously taxing effort of providing the Elements of Care and raising children who can take charge of their lives as adults. With minor modifications, the same effort that was required of the historical family is required of the modern family. The principal change is that physical survival is no longer at stake.

Responsibility begets responsibility, and irresponsibility begets irresponsibility. The modern family is in a downward spiral because the work of responsibility, which in our age seems voluntary, is being neglected.

THE FAMILY OF THE FUTURE

We have seen that the modern family deteriorates not as the result of a discrete influence, or set of influences, but as a phenomenon that fuels itself in a downward spiral. We have seen that the family began this spiral roughly as it succeeded in its battle against the elements for survival. The family has been victorious over adversity (though perhaps not permanently) but not over freedom. Does freedom doom the family? Is adversity necessary for the family to be strong and cohesive? Does freedom necessarily send it into a downward spiral from which it cannot recover? What intervention might reverse the spiral and create for the family of the future an upward spiral of empowerment and fulfillment?

This is not a small question because, as we have seen, the causes that are effects, such as anti-family government action or anti-family media messages, are reflections of who we are. They reflect the prevailing levels of responsibility, and to expect them to be the sources of our growth is to expect the mirror on the wall to make us better looking. Of course, we know of circumstances where institutions of broad influence can help — even government and TV. My point is not that changing the things that serve us poorly can never help. It is that we must find a new source of power — one that is greater in magnitude than the power of the declining cycle, one that can confront the cycle and help reverse its direction from deterioration to empowerment, one that can empower families and restore responsibility in them so that responsibility will yield responsibility.

There is such a source of power. It is one we recognize and have begun to tap, but it is one whose potential we have not come close to understanding, much less realizing. The source of power I refer to is community. The purpose of this paper has been to describe the decline of the modern family, not to suggest remedies. That awaits another paper. But, in closing, I think it worthwhile to say a word about the process that I believe can turn the downward spiral upward.

COMMUNITY

We usually use the word community to refer to a political subdivision where people live: a village or town, a suburb, or even a city. Sometimes, community used in this sense refers to neighborhoods. Another common use of community is to describe a group of people with common cultural, social, or political interests. Thus, we refer often to the African-American community, the gay or lesbian communities, or groups that have other common characteristics and common points of view.

I speak of community more broadly. I refer to it as a coming together of people with something in common — a joining of hands to share and move together toward a common, agreed upon objective. Two friends may be a community if their friendship has real meaning and purpose. Families may be communities. Members of religious organizations, such as churches and synagogues, may come together as one in community. Social clubs or other groups may be communities united in a single sense of direction, with common objectives, and with shared standards for behavior. Neighborhoods or areas in cities may constitute community in the sense I use it; so may cities themselves, as well as towns and villages. And, mysteriously, all of these units of personal interaction may not constitute communities. It depends not just on a conjunction of interest; there must be something more in the relationship, something that makes the group one and, in making it one, infuses it with extraordinary power.

To stand as a true community, the members must have made a commitment — to the mission of the community, to the standards by which members agree to conduct themselves, and to each other. This commitment must manifest itself in respect, in which those involved are accepted for who they are and regarded as important members worthy of having both a stake and a say in the business of the community.

When these characteristics are present, something happens that elevates the community and its members and calls them to be more than they were previously. In the embrace of community, people hear and are motivated to respond to a call to responsibility. The spirit of community can be a force to reverse the downward spiral of the deteriorating family.

Family therapy, an important and successful influence in the reversal of deteriorating patterns in families, could be described as the creation of community in families. The concept of "total quality management" is an effort to tap the power of community in business. Movements such as Alcoholics Anonymous have effected enormous social change, bringing about a process for arresting a disease that for centuries was thought to be incurable by using the concept of community to call and empower people to take responsibility for their lives as adults. These examples of community building are leading to other efforts to capture the power of community and to use that power to instill and reinforce responsibility. Community is being used to empower people to take responsibility for housing, the safety of neighborhoods, health, and education. I recently toured an area in Americus, Georgia, where government-built and owned public housing stands on one side of an inner-city street and community-built, family-owned housing stands on the other. The community-built homes, though somewhat smaller and perhaps even plainer, are better cared for, as are the yards around the homes. I am told that the lives of homeowners often improve dramatically as the experience of community empowers them to take responsibility for their ownership and perhaps reverse the downward spiral of their individual and family lives. The houses on two sides of a street in the Georgia town stand for me as a metaphor for the possibilities of capturing new power from nontraditional solutions.

To return to the theme of this paper, the decline of the modern family — the critical issue of our time — is a spiral of declining responsibility. It is doubtful that the elements within the spiral could change and reverse the course of the spiral itself. A superior force might, however, be able to reverse it. I believe that community is a process that can yield such a force.

 **Peter A. White**, *founder and president of International Skye Associates, Inc., is an advisor to families. He developed the International Skye methodology, which stresses taking advantage of opportunities and solving problems according to the needs and goals of each family as the family defines them. The Skye approach integrates modern thinking about business and finance with timeless wisdom from religion, philosophy and the social sciences. Mr. White is a frequent speaker on wealth and is writing a book. Prior to founding International Skye, Mr. White practiced law, serving until 1986 as a partner in the firm of Fulbright and Jaworski. Mr. White received his J.D. degree from Duke University in 1969 and his B.A. from Kenyon College, cum laude in 1966. He lives in Washington, D.C. with his wife, Susan, and two sons.*

THE DECLINE OF MARRIAGE AS
THE SOCIAL BASIS OF CHILDREARING

BARBARA DAFOE WHITEHEAD, PH.D.
Vice President of the Institute for American Values
New York City, New York

With each new report from the Census Bureau, we are reminded that American family life is changing. The continuing rise in the percentage of children born out-of-wedlock; the historically high levels of divorce; the increase in the percentage of unwed teen births; the decline in the age of sexual initiation and the normalization of premarital sex all testify to the fundamental reorganization of family life and intimate relationships in recent decades.

The question of what these changes mean for the nation and the society provokes intense debate in both political and scholarly circles. This paper will not attempt to address, much less resolve, this debate. However, since our views of family change are inevitably influenced by our own disciplinary and personal perspectives, I do think it is useful to identify my own biases at the outset. I have two. My first bias is toward the child. A large body of popular and scholarly literature has chronicled and analyzed recent changes in family life, but for the most part, this literature has looked at these events from an adult perspective and especially from the perspective of the changing experience of American women.

While this approach is valid, it neglects the fact that adult and children's experience of these events are different. Even women's interests in family life are less closely identified with children's interests than in the past, as historian Carl Degler has observed. Thus, I will focus on children's experience, and my judgments will be influenced by impact of family structure changes on children.

My second bias is historical. Much of the recent research into family life comes from the social sciences, particularly sociology and psychology. The historical perspective is not entirely missing in the social scientific literature, but it is used selectively to "debunk" popular conceptions or "myths" of family life, especially the myth that the nuclear family of the 1950s represents the historical or "ideal" American family. In this respect, the social science literature shares much in common with popular literature. Consider, for example, the following titles of books which take up the demythologizing of the post-war family: *The Way We Never Were; Embattled Paradise; Ozzie and Harriet Are Dead.* As a generational protest by baby-boomers against the fifties family, this approach has popular appeal, but as history, it represents something of a straw man argument. There are very few reputable contemporary historians who make any such claims about the historical representativeness of the post-war family. Indeed, the consensus opinion is that the post-war period represented an unusually stable and highly familistic moment in American life. Therefore, it seems more useful to look to the historical evidence for signs of continuity and discontinuity in children's family lives. I intend to point to a major discontinuity: the decline of marriage as the social basis for childrearing.

I

The family lives of American children have been fundamentally restructured during the last decades of the twentieth century. As the result of the escalating levels of unwed childbearing and historically high levels of divorce, a growing proportion of American children are likely to spend part or all of their childhood in single-parent families. Many will also be members of step-parent families. If current trends continue, it is estimated that as many as 60% of all children born in the 1980s are likely to have their families disrupted by divorce or nonmarriage.

Why did this restructuring occur? The reasons are varied and complex, but many scholars cite a major ideational shift in western societies as a primary cause. According to sociologist Alice S. Rossi, "Westerners are shifting from a concern for their children's futures to a self-orientation that gives priority to individuals desires rather than to the needs of spouses and children."[1] This shift has profoundly altered the social and psychological bases for childbearing and childrearing in American society.

I want to call attention to two ways in which the change is manifested. First, marriage is declining as the central institution of family life. This does not mean that marriage itself has fallen into disfavor. Americans are a marrying people, and marriage is highly regarded as a means to achieving intimacy and personal happiness in relationships. Americans remain starry-eyed about the magical transformation wrought by marriage, even when it comes to the revolving door of celebrity marriage. We fervently hope that Elizabeth Taylor will find true happiness with Larry Fortensky, her eighth husband, and that Julia Roberts and Lyle Lovett will make it through their first year of marriage. But marriage is less important as the social basis of childrearing than it has ever been in the nation's history. Increasingly, marriage and parenthood are coming apart.

The second way that this ideational shift manifests itself is in the greater tendency to see marriage and parenthood as individual pursuits rather than socially defined roles. Getting married and having children is no longer a requirement of adulthood nor a response to social norms. Increasingly, these important life events are dictated by individual goals and purposes. Psychologist Elizabeth Douvan observes that we used to judge an individual by the way he or she managed social roles; now we measure roles by the rewards they hold for the individual.[2]

Additionally, both marriage and parenthood are defined in expressive terms. One elects to be married or to become a parent because it is "what I want to do." This understanding is widely accepted: as one pastor told the *Los Angeles Times*, "it is everyone's choice to fulfill a dream. If a woman can't find Prince Charming and wants a baby and is ready, society should not dictate what is acceptable."[3]

The emphasis on the expressive side of parenthood is most dramatically evident in the small but growing "single mothers by choice" movement. One of the leading popular books on the subject, *Single Mothers By Choice*, advises women on how to avoid the social and legal entanglements of involving a father in the rearing of a child. Its author, Jane Mattes, warns: "You need to be aware that putting a father's name on the birth certificate opens up a hornet's nest of potentially serious legal complications."[4] But Mattes is not alone in seeing motherhood as an expression of selfhood. In one recent survey, a majority of Americans, including 70% of younger adult Americans, agree that women should have the right to bear a child out of wedlock without reproach.[5]

Taken together, these two changes suggest a trend toward a 'post-marriage' society, marked by the decline of marriage as a child-rearing institution and the rise of a more voluntary system of family relationships, with easily dissoluble ties and more contingent and limited commitments.

It is worth underscoring how rapidly all of this has taken place. A popular book written in the 1970s offered what seemed at the time to be a utopian vision of future family relationships: "My grand-daughter, at the moment unborn, may live well into her nineties, if not beyond, and be married at least twice, maybe three, perhaps four times. Her divorces will be no-fault divorces. It is also likely that she will be the complacent biologic mother of two or three children by various fathers and the affectionate social mother of another brood via her several husbands and their ex-wives."[6]

To a remarkable degree, this forecast proved accurate. In the early 1980s, the distinguished historian Lawrence Stone noted:

...the characteristics of the post-modern family are as follows:... sexual relations have been almost entirely separated from both the biological function of procreation and the legal institution of marriage...Despite the high psychic and economic costs of divorce, marriage itself is now only a temporary arrangement. It is predicted that today one-half of all marriages will end in divorce, so that we are moving into an era of serial polygamy.[7]

Because a post-marriage society is characterized by more fragile and impermanent relationships, it is also marked by greater churning and instability in family life. In the past, family instability was caused by high mortality and morbidity, but these causes are largely absent today. As social demographer Samuel Preston noted in his 1984 Presidential address to the Population Association of America: "It seems incredible that we have reached this level of instability when collectively we have better health, more teeth, better odor, and more orgasms."[8]

From an adult perspective, greater fragility and instability in familial relationships is not necessarily undesirable. More open-ended and contingent commitments may provide greater freedom and opportunity for adults to seek and perhaps find satisfying relationships. When marriage fails to offer emotional satisfactions, when it proves difficult, disappointing or demeaning, it can be abandoned. Importantly, too, when marriages are easily dissoluble, there is greater opportunity for women to escape abusive and violent marriages than in the past. (Nevertheless, there has been no decline in domestic violence with the rise in divorce. Some scholars suggest that this is because domestic violence grows out of sexual possessiveness and jealousy rather than out of marital institution itself.)[9]

Moreover, the ability to shape and reshape family relationships endows individuals with a greater sense of possibility. When nothing is forever, then anything can happen, if not today, then tomorrow or the next year. This engenders a sense of hope and optimism, even when the reality doesn't always measure up. *The Wall Street Journal* recently reported on a Department of Agriculture study that measured divorced mothers' perceptions of their post-divorce lives. The women's appraisals were remarkably sunny. Over 60% considered their career opportunities better after divorce, and 54% reported that their overall situation for caring for their children had improved. The researcher concluded that despite heavier work and childcare burdens, the women enjoyed greater freedom from spousal conflict and therefore, had an improved outlook on life.[10]

However, though it offers advantages to adults, a more voluntary system of family relationships is problematic for children. Children have an important stake in a marriage. Marriage provides the basis of children's primary attachments and the foundation of children's social security. A large body of evidence suggests that children suffer emotionally and economically when these primary attachments are severely disrupted.[11] Consequently, in a society where adults increasingly engage in marriage and parenthood as individualistic and expressive pursuits, the basis of children's security is threatened. To be sure, parents' interests and children's interests in marriage have never been identical. But for reasons I will explore in this paper, their interests are now increasingly divergent and competing. Thus, the principal challenge of a post-marriage society may be stated as follows: how to reconcile the adult pursuit of individual happiness with children's needs for secure and stable family attachments?

II

WHY DOES MARRIAGE MATTER TO CHILDREN?

To answer that question, it is necessary to offer an overly broad and simplified, but I hope useful, historical observation. Two great structural changes in children's family lives have occurred in modern western societies. The first occurred sometime in the mid-seventeenth century with the advent of what historians call the "modern nuclear family."

Historian Lawrence Stone describes the change as a shift from families organized around the kin group to families organized around the married couple. This shift involved a corresponding shift in the pattern of authority and deference, from one characterized by a hierarchical distribution of power, the arranged marriage and the fostering out of children, to one based in a more egalitarian distribution of power, companionate marriage, and the child-centered family.

The new family structure contributed to higher levels of parental investment in children. With the decline of kin responsibility for children, the responsibility for the economic upkeep of children fell more directly on the father, while mothers began to assume responsibility of child nurture, rather than handing the child over to the care of servants and wetnurses. As a result of declining mortality rates, moreover, there were greater incentives to invest in children. Thus, a more affectionate ideal of childrearing emerged during the eighteenth century.

But the restructuring of the family around the married couple had a second profound impact on children. It made children dependent on the permanence and stability of marital bonds. At the heart of the modern nuclear family was a radically new marital ideal. While marriages in the past had been dictated and regulated by the larger kin group as an "economic deal or a political alliance," the new marriage ideal was defined by individual choice and mutual regard. Thus the foundation of family life was rooted, not in property or status, but in affection.

In these new, more streamlined families, organized around the married couple, children's fortunes were closely tied to the quality and stability of spousal affection. Compared to the marriage arranged by the kin group and dominated by patriarchal power relationships, the companionate marriage offered many advantages for marital partners, especially for wives. However, bonds of mutual affection proved a fragile foundation for marriage. Therefore, at the same time that the new marital ideal fostered greater parental investment in children and a greater childcenteredness, it also contributed to a new source of vulnerability for children.

Because of the patterns of early immigration, the "modern nuclear family," defined by companionate marriage and child-centeredness, became the dominant family structure in the new American republic. The rise in the 19th century of a "separate spheres" domestic ideology linked women's identity and status to that of children, further increasing maternal investment in children.

The second historic restructuring of children's family lives began in the late 1960s with the rise in voluntary family disruptions. In 1974, divorce replaced death as the principal cause of family breakup. The same period saw a rise in unwed childbearing, from 5% in 1960 to close to 30% in 1990. Although the divorce rate leveled off in the mid-1980s, the percentage of births to unwed mothers continues to increase. From the child's perspective, it is hard to exaggerate how significant this restructuring has been. Indeed, the historical demographer Daniel Scott Smith notes that the period of most rapid change in the history of the western household, at least since the Middle Ages, lies in the immediate past.[12]

Because of children's dependence on marital stability as the basis of parental investment and affection, the weakening of marriage has had harmful consequences for children. Yet, given that structural reality, there has been remarkably little attention devoted to the interests of children in marriage. Indeed, over the past two and a half decades, the trend both in the popular advice and scholarly literature has been to focus on the adult interests in marriage. To cite a single example from the advice literature, consider the following: in *Quality Time: Easing Children Through Divorce*, Dr. Melvin Goldzband writes: "All the comments about the needs of children for intact families should not cause any divorcing parent to consider reconciliation for the sake of the children."[13]

III

The decline of marriage often leads to parental, and especially paternal, disinvestment in children. Though the family is no longer economically self-sufficient, it remains the central social institution for transferring resources between generations. Historically, the principal beneficiaries of these transfers have been children, and the most prominent group of donors have been adult men. In a post-marriage society, however, the family structure for male investment in children is weakened as is the incentive structure. Men who live apart from their children are less reliable providers than married fathers who share a residence with their children. Fathers who have never been married to their children's mothers are the least likely to provide regular income support to their children, partly because they have not been identified and paternal identification is the essential first step to securing child support and partly because they tend to be younger and poorer than divorced fathers.

Contributions of nonresidential fathers to the family household are dramatically less than the contributions of married fathers who live with their children. Nonresidential fathers (mainly divorced) who reliably meet child support obligations contribute an average of $3,000 a year to their children, while married fathers contribute a much higher proportion of their earnings to the family's maintenance and care. (According to 1990 figures, the median male wage is $30,000; this figure may be taken as a rough proxy for the median paternal income available for investment in children.)[14]

The loss of paternal support is not offset by higher levels of maternal support. Most children live with their mothers, and despite improving wages, greater work force participation and better economic opportunities for women, single-mother households lack the earning capacity of the two-parent, and especially, dual-earner households. Median family income for married-couple families, with at least one child under age 18, was $41,260 in 1990, compared to a median income of $13,092 for single-mother families with at least one child.

Consider this gap in light of the very conservative estimates from the U.S. Department of Agriculture for a no-frills annual childrearing budget. According to USDA figures, a middle income married couple with one three-to-five year old child would spend a total of about $8,000 in direct annual expenditures.[15] Obviously, a single mother with a $13,000 income and one similarly aged child would have a hard time achieving even this modest level of expenditure, a level that would be expected to increase as the child got older.

Nor is the falling off of family investment in children offset by increasing public investment in children. Although overall public spending on children continues to rise, it has not increased fast enough to lift children out of poverty. European nations do a much better job than the United States in reducing child poverty through tax and transfer policies. In western nations that treat children as generously as they do their older citizens, government benefits lift from half to three-quarters of poor children out of poverty.[16]

Nonetheless, reducing poverty among children is only a first step in securing the bases for economic well-being. Indeed, the decline in family investment in children could not have come at a worst time. A post-industrial society requires a "high investment" childrearing strategy, because economic success depends on longer schooling and the acquisition of more sophisticated technical and conceptual skills than in the past. Thus, in addition to increased public spending on children, lavish expenditures of parental time and money are required to endow each child with the competencies for achieving economic independence. According to a study by Thomas Espenshade, a middle-income family raising a first child born in 1981 can expect to spend $150,000 per child to age 18, assuming a low inflation level (5.2% per annum). Anticipated college costs, which are increasing at a level higher than 5%, obviously boost that projection, perhaps as high as $310,000.[17]

Moreover, in America, the principal responsibility for postsecondary education rests with parents. Public spending on education drops dramatically after high school. Compared to a country like France, where university education is "free" for eligible students, the United States depends on families to bear the principal cost of preparing the next generation of American workers and citizens for life in a global economy.

Consider, too, that most states do not require child support after age 18. At the very moment when parental investment in children's education ideally should increase, legal requirements for child support end. The consequence is that many college-eligible students in disrupted families have a hard time realizing their educational goals.[18]

The economic disinvestment in children might be compared to the earlier family disinvestment in older Americans. In the 1940s, the sociologist Talcott Parsons argued that poverty among elderly Americans was due to a diminished sense of obligation for their support within the conjugal family. Samuel Preston points out that it is not too farfetched to think that the family may be divesting itself of the economic upkeep of children, largely as a result of widespread family disruption.[19]

However, there is an important difference between these two classes of dependents. The elderly have been the beneficiaries of public investment for roughly half a century. As the result of a generous tax and spend program, a large proportion of elderly have been lifted out of poverty. Indeed, the reduction of poverty among the elderly is one of the great social achievements of the twentieth century. During the same period that the elderly have improved their economic status, however, children have lost ground. In the mid-1970s, about 15% of young and old Americans were poor. In 1991, only 12.3% of elder Americans were poor, while 22% of children were poor.[20]

A second key difference between the elderly and children is that the elderly hold the franchise. Because they vote in large numbers and because their numbers continue to grow, the elderly possess great political power. Children, on the other hand, represent a shrinking proportion of the population and are not able to vote, much less organize politically. Thus, it is probably unrealistic to think that children can pursue the same route to improved economic well-being that has worked so well for older Americans.

With high levels of divorce, we see yet another pattern of family disinvestment in children. Not only is there evidence of diminished capacity for intergenerational transfer of resources, but there is also a sectoral shift in investment — from the family sector to the professional service sector. This pattern is especially strong among middle- and upper-income families.

A large divorce industry made up of lawyers, investigative accountants; real estate appraisers and salespeople; pension specialists; therapists and psychologists; expert witnesses; and private collectors of child support has sprung up to harvest the fruits of family discord. However necessary their services, these professionals are the recipients of family income that might, in happier circumstances and earlier times, been invested in children.

IV

This pattern of parental disinvestment has been accompanied by a shift in notions of parental obligation to children. As parents are less able or less willing to invest large amounts of time and money in children, as parent-child relationships are forged across separate, often distant households, there is a growing emphasis on the affective side of parental commitment. Today, more than in the past, notions of parental obligation place greater emphasis on expressive rather than instrumental considerations as the central requirement of family life. Above all else, what parents "owe" children is love, sympathy, and understanding. It is the emotional interior rather than the structural exterior of family life, the strength of affective bonds rather than the stability of marital bonds, the feeling rather than the doing that counts.

A corollary to this is the emphasis on adult marital satisfaction as a key determinant of children's happiness. Today's conventional wisdom is that happy parents make for happy children. Conversely, parents who are unhappy in marriage will damage their children's prospects for a happy and secure family life. Leaving an unhappy marriage or refusing to marry a child's biological father because he is an unsuitable husband is commonly thought better for the child than a commitment to raise the child in an intact family.

This argument has some merit. High conflict marriages are distressful and damaging to children. Indeed, children who live in households dominated by constant parental strife and violence often exhibit emotional disturbances long before the parents divorce. Nonetheless, divorce does not reliably institute a new reign of family peace and harmony. The aftermath of divorce often brings intensified conflict, even violence, over postdivorce issues like custody, visitation and child support. Nor are high-conflict marriages the only marriages that break up. Parents leave marriages for a much broader set of reasons. For children in stepfamilies particularly, the idea that parental happiness determines children's happiness is flawed. A parent who finds a new partner may be ecstatically happy, freed from the loneliness and economic hardship of solo parenting, while the children may be resentful or hostile to the new stepparent.

V

As a result of these trends, we might characterize parent-child relationships in a post-marriage society as moving in the direction of "low investment, high affect." While no one would argue with the idea that strong affective bonds between parent and child are vital to child well-being, there is reason to believe that affections alone may not be enough to foster good outcomes for children. And there is the very real danger that a sentimental rhetoric of caring and sharing will eventually replace the daily donations of parental time, attention, and supervision that are the currency of parental love.

To paint so bleak a picture without offering a shred of hope is probably unAmerican. Therefore, I conclude this discussion with two suggestions that may, at the very least, slow this trend of childrearing outside of marriage.

The first is to turn away from an adult-centered focus on marriage toward a more child-centered focus that takes into account children's interests in parental marriage and recognizes the central importance of marriage as an institution for childrearing.

The second and more radical suggestion, is to reconsider marriage as an essential social institution. Over the past two and a half decades, marriage has been subjected to a withering critique. This critique was prompted by the best of intentions: to improve marriage by creating more egalitarian spousal relationships and by establishing a fairer division of responsibility for housework and childcare between spouses. However, this critique did not so much improve marriage as breed cynicism and despair about marriage as an institution.

As a human institution, marriage may be perfectible, but it will never be perfect. Yet it serves some very essential human purposes: to bind fathers to their biological children; to foster high levels of parental responsibility and investment in children; and to regulate sex and childrearing.

As a society, we have developed a kind of amnesia about the purposes of marriage that extend beyond the self. In recent years, we have tended to view long-lasting marriage as a matter of accident, happenstance and luck, rather than as an achievement based on intention, effort and struggle. Finally, we have — to belabor the point of this paper — rejected the notion that marriage exists not only to serve the needs of adults but also "for the sake of the children."

Quite possibly, it is too late to change the minds or behavior of the generation of adults who have participated in the divorce revolution. But there may be an opportunity — indeed, a responsibility — to try to reach the children of the divorce generation with a different message about marriage.

[1] "Parenthood in Transition: From Lineage to Child to Self-Orientation," in *Parenting Across the Life Span: Biosocial Dimensions*, ed. Jane B. Lancaster et. al. (NY: Aldine de Gruyter, 1987) 38. See also Carl Degler, *At Odds: Women and the Family in America From the Revolution to the Present* (NY: Oxford University Press, 1980), 458.

[2] "The Age of Narcissism: 1963-1982," *American Childhood: A Research Guide and Historical Handbook*, ed. Joseph M. Hawes and N. Ray Hiner (Westport, Connecticut: Greenwood Press, 1985), 591.

[3] "Single Parent Issue Touches Sensitive Nerve," *Los Angeles Times*, Thursday July 22, 1993, E1-2.

[4] *Single Mothers By Choice: A Guidebook for Single Women Who Are Considering or Have Chosen Motherhood* (NY: Times Books), 1994, p. 112.

[5] "Most Believe Dan Quayle Was Right: Kids Do Fare Best in Two-Parent Families," In Focus, Family Research Council. Survey conducted in September 1993 among sample of 1,100 randomly selected adults. Margin of error is plus or minus three percentage points.

[6] Davidyne Mayleas, *Rewedded Bliss: Love, Alimony, Incest, Ex-Spouses, and Other Domestic Blessings* (NY: Basic Books), 1977, 3.

[7] "The Historical Origins of the Modern Family," O. Meredith Wilson Lecture, Department of History, University of Utah, May 11, 1981, 24-25.

[8] "Children and the Elderly: Divergent Paths for America's Dependents," *Demography*, 21:4, November 1984, 444.

[9] See, for example, the interesting discussion by Martin Daly and Margo Wilson in *Homicide,* especially the chapter entitled "Till Death Do Us Part," 187-213, *passim*.

[10] "Divorce Doesn't Damp Mothers' Lives," *Wall Street Journal*, Friday, August 12, 1994, p. B1.

[11] See my summary of the research evidence in "Dan Quayle Was Right," *Atlantic Monthly*, 271:4, April 1993, 47-84.

[12] "The Curious History of Theorizing About the History of the Western Nuclear Family," *Social Science History*, 17:3, 325-353.

[13] (NY: McGraw Hill, 1985), 58.

[14] "Money Income of Households, Families and Persons in the United States: 1990, Bureau of the Census, Current Population Reports, Consumer Income, Series P-60, No. 174 (Washington, D.C.: Government Printing Office, August, 1991).

[15] Family Economics Research Group, "Expenditures on a Child by Husband-Wife Families: 1990," (Hyattsville, MD: U.S. Department of Agriculture, January 1991), 7.

[16] Danziger and Danziger, *op.cit.*, 68.

[17] *Investing In Children: New Estimates of Parental Expenditures* (Washington, D.C.: The Urban Institute Press, 1984), 5-6.

[18] See especially Judith S. Wallerstein and Shauna B. Corbin, "Father-Child Relationships After Divorce: Child Support and Educational Opportunity," *Family Law Quarterly*, vol. XX, no. 2, Summer 1986, 109-125.

[19] *op.cit.*, 443. My discussion is based on Preston's excellent summary of the divergent paths of the elderly and children.

[20] Sandra K. Danziger and Sheldon Danziger, "Child Poverty and Public Policy: Toward A Comprehensive Antipoverty Agenda," Daedalus 122, no. 1 (Winter 1993), 59-60.

Barbara Dafoe Whitehead, Ph.D. *is Vice President of the Institute for American Values, a nonpartisan research organization in New York City devoted to issues of family and civic well-being. She has written extensively for many publications and is currently working on a book on parents and children in a post-marriage society, an expansion of her widely noted cover story in the April, 1993 Atlantic Monthly. Dr. Whitehead earned a B.A. from the University of Wisconsin and a M.A. and Ph.D. in American social history at the University of Chicago.*

Balancing Family, Work, and Leisure

JACK G. WIGGINS, PH.D.
Parma Heights, Ohio

My practice as a clinical psychologist focuses on family. When dealing with family issues, work and leisure activities must also be considered. These three spheres should be addressed simultaneously in order to gain a clear understanding of the behavior of individuals. To understand family dynamics, individual values and behaviors must be compared and contrasted. Galinsky, Bond and Friedman (1993) estimate time spent in family, work and leisure. Family, and its seemingly infinite variety of experiences, requires about 43% of people's time and energy to provide vital satisfactions and perform routine survival chores. Work supplies the essential economic basis for family survival. Therefore, it has a profound impact on family lifestyle. The average worker spends 37% of their time at work, traveling to and from work, or in education and career development. Leisure activities occupy about 20% of people's time. Leisure supplies an added value to family life beyond the requirements of daily chores and child rearing. Thus, no evaluation of an individual is complete without inquiry into these three domains of family, work and leisure activity. Family, work and leisure are not viewed as three separate spheres, but rather overlapping activities which weave together to form the fabric of life.

A diagram of the interplay of family, work and leisure may be useful. Although unequal amounts of time are spent in these three activities, this does not necessarily represent a balanced view of life. A balanced picture of family, work and leisure can be visualized as three overlapping rings of approximately the same size representing the life space values of an individual, as in Figure 1.

FIGURE 1

F = Family

W = Work

L = Leisure

THEORETICAL BALANCE OF LIFE ACTIVITIES

Some individuals tend to emphasize work to the extent that this comprises the largest sector of life experience, with family and leisure relative small overlapping circles in that person's scheme of things. This pattern of behavior is generally thought of as a workaholic who leaves little time and energy for family and leisure. (See Figure 2)

FIGURE 2

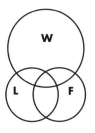

F = Family

W = Work

L = Leisure

THE WORKAHOLIC

Theoretically, there should be a counterpart to the workaholic who places work over family or leisure. However, in practice, this is something that is seen infrequently in as pure a form as the workaholic. There are some people, who are fairly well consumed by family interests, whose energies are devoted primarily to maintenance of the family and have relative little time even for leisure. The epitome of this model would be the queen bee in an insect colony who spends her entire time in procreation, leaving the work to the drones and having no time for leisure. There are autocratic individuals whose need for control of their lives and environment are not limited to their own work and leisure activities. They extend their power to regulating activities of other members of the family. The autocratic male views other members of the family as a part of his own ego and tends to control other members of the family through giving privileges and punishments based on his self-proclaimed devotion to family. We also find overcontrolling matriarchs who have the power to regulate the activities of other members of the family and define the limits of work and leisure.

Perhaps, a more common manifestation of individuals who take their primary satisfaction from family, are women who adopt a highly home-centered model and men who become child-centered parents. A child-centered couple take great pleasure in the activities of the children and spend a great deal of time teaching the children various sports or other expressionistic activities, such as music, dancing, and art. (See Figure 3)

FIGURE 3

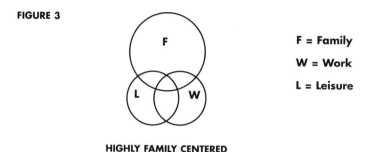

F = Family

W = Work

L = Leisure

HIGHLY FAMILY CENTERED

There is still another pattern which needs to be identified and represented by a figure in which leisure plays a major role of organizing time, energy and relationships. This is represented by leisure comprising the largest sector of life experience with family and work comprising a relatively small part in their value system. In this characterization, the pleasure and sense of achievement through leisure activities takes precedence over work and family. Since leisure is defined in terms of personal satisfactions, this individual may be compared to the myth, Narcissus, who fell in love with his own reflection and eventually drowned trying to discover himself. Clinically, individuals who over-emphasize their personal prerogatives are referred to as Narcissists and are represented by Figure 4.

FIGURE 4

F = Family

W = Work

L = Leisure

THE NARCISSISTIC INDIVIDUAL

Thus far, the descriptions provided have been of the individual, rather than addressing family relationships. The idealized relationship among family, work and leisure has been presented as each being equivalent to one another in time, energy and meaning. In real life, this is almost never the case. No two individuals place exactly the same value on family, work and leisure. Assuming that an individual's value system is not heavily weighted towards family, work or leisure, we can focus on the interactions between individuals which facilitate their ongoing dynamic relationship as a couple. This is referred to as "bonding" which can be defined as a sustained interactive relationship which is rewarding to both individuals.

Bonding occurs more easily and is more successful if the couple comes from similar backgrounds, has similar values and satisfactory coping skills. If the couple comes from dissimilar backgrounds, have dissimilar values or inadequate coping skills, conflict resolution becomes more difficult. Those less able to negotiate their differences are more likely to threaten each other merely by representing their dissimilar goals to one another. To overcome marital dissonance, both marital partners need to be mutually invested in their current situation, with common goals to reduce the risks to their bonding process.

Bonding may take place in one or more areas of family, work or leisure. The strongest occurs when there is a participative relationship in all three areas of life experiences. Bonding takes place when the interaction between the individuals occurs with minimum risk. Risk is experienced when there are potentials for rejection, criticism or loss of esteem, fear of rejection or criticism. Risk is reduced when initiatives to interact are met with responsiveness, acknowledgment, and receptiveness. In order to maintain this dynamic, people must engage one another on a regular basis with a sense of low risk.

Even when individuals have similar family values, work ethics, and compatible leisure interests, it is possible for conflicts in the mutually agreed upon value system to occur. A common place example is when one person may be in a work mode and when the other person is on a family or leisure mode and miscommunications occur. Thus, there can be many opportunities for miscommunication and disappointing interactions. Another case is where a couple meets at work, falls in love and marries. The mutual interest in work dissipates when the woman leaves her job to raise the family. The couple may find their mutual interests are no longer there. Then their marital relationship may require considerable effort to build bonds between them to maintain family stability. Marriage of childhood sweethearts who bond because they are in the same school together and know the same people can be another example of inadequate bonding. When the young couple is out on their own, their mutuality may diminish.

They grow apart, as their personal interests become emphasized and are less influenced by their prior relationships.

To reduce the risks to family bonding, each partner must have adequate skills in conflict resolution. There must be a recognition that conflicts are normal in any ongoing relationship. The partners must not see conflicts as being pathological, but rather normal expectations based on prior agreements worked out between the two of them which may not apply to the current situation. Or, as my Murphy's Law calendar says, "All solutions create more problems." Agreements between people must be kept in order to prevent disappointments which are seen as rejections. However, there are changes that naturally occur in the conduct of daily affairs resulting in misunderstandings about what agreements have been reached. These raise questions whether the matters under discussion are really violations of those agreements. The people involved need to have a way of expressing their views without threatening the other. While skillful articulation in communication is very helpful, it is also essential that there be good listening skills. It is not enough to state your point clearly so it can be understood. There must be a receptive receiver to understand the message given. There also must be sufficient time and opportunities or a "give and take" dialogue between the people to negotiate a resolution. In counseling, troubled couples' problems in communication are principal causes of deterioration in family relationships. While external forces can and do change family, work and leisure priorities, families can usually tolerate the stress resulting from these changes. As long as there is active dialogue and a willingness to try to understand and adjust, families do adapt and weather these crises fairly well.

The above illustrations represent an idealized family structure and four different types of individuals who can contribute to a dysfunctional family. If either family, work or leisure are overemphasized to the exclusion of the other two spheres of influence on the individual, it will effect the kind of person with whom they can bond and form a stable family relationship. Hence, there is a need for individuals to achieve a balance between family values, work ethics, and participation in leisure activities.

If an individual is overcommitted to one area of their life, it leaves little room for the bonding to take place in the other two areas. When only one area of bonding occurs, the family relationship is essentially unstable and vulnerable to external pressures which may create conflicts of interest between the marital partners or among the family members. In order to balance family, work and leisure activities, a marital partner must try to compliment the activities of the person who is dedicated primarily to a single activity area, while at the same time compensating for the limited outlook of the spouse. This frequently creates a certain amount of tension in the mate who feels they are compensating. A person who is compensating by helping their spouse, generally feels victimized, ignored, frustrated or angry in their attempts to normalize the family and balance activity patterns. Such tension is wearing on the marital relationship and over time depletes the reserves of the compensating partner. Under these circumstances, the family may become destabilized by seemingly minor frustrations. Destabilization of family may occur when children are old enough to attend school full time so the woman can work, or the children are old enough that they will not be harmed by the separation of the parents.

In the case of the workaholic husband, the woman may become tired of being the primary trainer, protector of the children and social chairman for the family. She may eventually go on her own seeking a career for herself, rather than contend or try to compete with her husband's work.

The autocratic male who tends to dominate the family, often tries to do a variety of things to preserve and keep the family intact. These include bullying, bribing, or any other tactic which will give them dominance or control of the family. Family members may rebel and become alienated from the family in order to avoid domination. For the matriarch, divorce is also considered catastrophic to their visions of family and their self esteem for the role they have had in the family. These women who have experienced divorce, preserve their bonding with their children and generally do not get remarried.

For the couple who has become child-centered in their activities, the loss of children through maturation and leaving home may be very devastating. When this occurs, we often find adult children in their 30's living with their natural families.

The Narcissist, since family and work mean relatively little to them, may participate in family activities as long as it serves their interests. These individuals are detached and may have behavioral excesses such as gambling, alcoholism or tendencies to spend too much time in bars. Their relationships are transitory and last only as long as others are willing to tolerate their chauvinistic attitudes. With relatively little bonding in all three areas, family relationships are less stable and more vulnerable to external forces leading to disintegration or dissolution of the basic family unit.

There is another consideration which needs to be acknowledged in regard to this three-sphere view of the integration of family. When family members organize to form a business it tends to create an overlapping of family and work spheres similar to the one described as the highly home-centered pattern. (See Figure 5) Spouses tend to have confusing bonding patterns in a family business where the work and family ties comingle. Sibling rivalries of childhood can be carried over into jealous competitions in the work and family relationships. Even when siblings can work things out between them, these family relationships can deteriorate in the stress of business. The business is likely to suffer when future generations are added to the work force, creating very important questions of leadership for a family business.

FIGURE 5

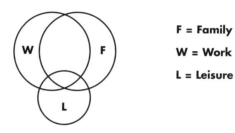

F = Family

W = Work

L = Leisure

FAMILY BUSINESS PATTERN

Just as the pressure of family dynamics can interfere with work efficiency, work can invade the spheres of family and leisure. Interestingly enough, leisure can invade work and family as well. For example, lottery winners who find themselves with unaccustomed discretionary funds, sometimes give up work to focus on leisure and family only to discover that they have destabilized their relationship with their spouse. Retirees and disabled workers report their wives saying, "Our marriage may be for better or for worse, but it's not for lunch." Under these circumstances, the marital contract and working relationships must be renegotiated in order to find the balance between leisure and family activities. Sometimes this even results in role reversal where the spouse who had kept the home gets a job while the retiree or injured worker begins to manage the household activities and homemaking chores.

For the majority of people, work still is an intrinsic portion of their lives, along with family and leisure. The question is often raised about the impact of family on work and work on the family. Galinsky et al. (1994) recently completed a study of the impact on family on work versus work on the family. In studying stress, workers were asked about the spillover in both directions from job to family or from personal and family life to work. Measures of job to home spillover were frequently of experiencing no personal or family time, housework left undone, bad mood or no energy due to work. Home to job spillover was associated with refusal of overtime, refusal to travel far to work, lowered productivity, and problems with the supervisor. The time frames for measuring this were not comparable. The home to job spillover questions referred to situations which occurred in the last year. While job to home spillover referred only to the last three months. Thus, there was four times the opportunity for home to job spillover to be reported. However, the results of this survey indicated the job to home spillover was three times as great as that from home to job.

In this report, as hours worked increased, there was correspondingly less time to spend with family or in leisure. Employees with no spouse or children at home spent 2.84 hours per day for themselves on work days and 6.55 hours on days off. In contrast, employees in dual-earner families without children had less time to themselves — 2.11 hours during work days and 4.94 hours on days off. Employees with children in addition to employed spouses had even less time to themselves, averaging 1.44 hours on work days and 3.44 hours on days off. This was approximately half of the personal time the employee would have if they did not have a spouse or children.

This same study of 814 workers revealed 40% of the workers reported that household work was not done due to the amount of time they were spending on the job. "No personal time due to the time demands on the job" was cited by 35% of the workers. "No time for family due to job pressures" was indicated by 24% of the sample. Workers who were able to spend more time on themselves on work days tended to be more satisfied with their lives, less stressed and felt that they were coping better. The study supported the importance of leisure, finding "that carving out some time for oneself represents an investment in mental health and well being which may well offset occasional modest reductions and attention to work or family."

In this sample, the average worker spent about 40 hours per week on the job. Overtime and commuting time brought the total of job related activities to more than 45 hours per week, representing about 40% of the waking hours of the average person.

Recently, workers have witnessed a tremendous amount of turmoil in the workplace, with 42% experiencing downsizing of their companies, 28% have seen cutbacks in the number of managers in the last year, 80% feel that their jobs require working very hard and 65% reported their jobs require working fast. Job burnout was reported by 42% of the workers stating they come home feeling used up at the end of the day with little time for family or recreational activities. A national study of 28,000 workers (Kohler, 1992) reported similar results, with job stress more than doubling between 1985 and 1991. Galinsky, et al. also studied job changes workers were willing to make for family. Among workers under age 25, 28% were willing to make sacrifices in their education, careers and jobs for family life with a differential of 21% for men and 34% for women. In a gender comparison, up to 26% of the men and 44% of the women indicated that they were willing to make some sacrifices in advancing their jobs and careers for their family life.

In considering family-friendly benefits that employers offer, it is interesting to see how many people would change jobs to obtain these benefits. Of 865 employees without access to flex time, 26% said that they would be willing to change jobs for this benefit. The percentage was higher for employees with children under age 13 at 35%, than for employees with no children under 13 at 20%. Part-time work was appealing to 12% of the workers regardless of whether children were involved. Willing to switch jobs so they could work at home was stated by 23% of workers. Of those with children under 13 years, 29% would switch, as well as 20% of those without children under 13.

In regard to access, use and willingness to trade salary or other benefits for child and eldercare, 28% percent of the workers had employers who offered a dependent care benefit and 53% of the workers used it. Employers (20%) who offered childcare resource and referral had 11% of the employees using this benefit. For workers without access, 17% would trade salary and other benefits for childcare. Eldercare resource and referral was offered by 11% of the companies with 6% of the employees making use of this. Of the workers without access, 15% say that they would trade salary or other benefits for this provision. Approximately 10% of employers offered childcare at or near the work site, with 12% of the workers utilizing this benefit. For workers without access, 23% would trade salary and other benefits for an employer-sponsored childcare service at or near the work site. Only 4% of the employers gave vouchers to purchase childcare services and 8% of the workers made use of them. Nearly a quarter (23%) of surveyed individuals were willing to trade salary and other benefits to obtain vouchers to purchase childcare. Twice as many employees with children under 13 were willing to trade benefits for access to child and eldercare resource and referral, on or near site childcare or given childcare vouchers. In general, workers with more flex time and leave options, and more dependent care benefits, had more positive attitudes towards employers as measured by feelings of loyalty and commitment. When comparing attitudes by gender, women were twice as willing as men to switch employers for more flexible work schedules or part-time work. Women expressed significantly more willingness to sacrifice advancement on the job for more flexible work arrangements or work at home. This represents a higher professed commitment to family by women.

These data are consonant with the commonly held view that men are more likely to emphasize work and women emphasize family in their personal value system. Data on dual-wage earner families indicate that men are willing to assume more responsibilities in bill paying, cleaning and shopping, in addition to their traditional role of performing household repairs. Women tend to maintain their roles of cooking, but still spend substantially more time in child and eldercare and in doing household chores than men. This finding reveals elasticity in marital bonding in order to accommodate family needs, while maintaining traditional differences in gender roletaking. These shifts in family role assignments have occurred in an era of major economic changes in the workplace and other social foment regarding the definition of family and other social values. It is unclear whether this elasticity is a function of:

1. Adjustments due to economic pressures resulting in more women in the workforce and more dual earner families;

2. Changes in social values redefining family;

3. A different kind of bonding within families fostering greater flexibility in interpersonal relations within the context of family; or

4. Some combination of these factors.

The relationship among values, external forces and elasticity of bonding within families is an open question. Balancing family, work and leisure requires further study of elasticity in bonding. During a time of changing social values and stresses of the workplace this *Symposium on Family: The First Imperative* is a noble step to obtaining essential answers to these vital questions.

REFERENCES

Galinsky, E., Bond, J. T. and Friedman, D. E., *The Changing Workforce*, Highlights of the National Study, Families and Work Institute, No. 1., 1993.

Kohler, S., The St. Paul Fire & Marine Insurance Company Study released October 13, 1992. St. Paul Fire & Marine Insurance Company, 385 Washington Street, St. Paul, Minnesota 55102.

Jack G. Wiggins, Ph.D. *is in private practice in Parma Heights, Ohio as a psychologist where he concentrates on developing fully functioning families. One of his goals in family therapy is to make each member a productive partner on the family team. He has received many awards, honors and recognitions, including a Resolution of the Ohio Senate for his leadership in mental health advocacy and election as Centennial President of the American Psychological Association (APA). He received his Ph.D. from Purdue University. Dr. Wiggins and his wife have three grown children and two grandchildren.*

Families in the 1990s —
The Changing Picture of Who We Are

JOAN LEVY ZLOTNIK, ACSW
Bethesda, Maryland

The 1992 presidential campaign was full of talk about family values. Dan Quayle's attack on the single motherhood of TV character Murphy Brown served as a battle cry for a fight about "good family" and "bad family." Articles appeared in newspapers about the loss of family values and the lack of valuing family. Conservatives and liberals seemed to be lined up on different sides. But there was an underlying question. Was one group for families and the other against families? If one were to venture a guess, we would guess that both groups are on the same side. Both groups are pro-family. They both understand that families are the "primary source of social, emotional, educational, spiritual, and economic support in American society." (NASW, 1993b) They both understand that families are at the core of our social structure, and at the nexus of creating our communities. Then what is the debate about, if there is agreement about the role of families? The debate about "family" and the concerns about the disintegration of family occur for several reasons.

• The structure and demographic characteristics of families have changed over the last 30 years.

• The definition of family is evolving.

• The well-being of families are increasingly challenged by changes in societal and economic conditions.

To value families means valuing families in the 1990s. We cannot judge today's families by our ideal or stereotype of a 1950 or 1960s family. We must understand who today's families are and then create policies and supports to sustain and nurture them so that children will flourish and be successful as they become adults.

This paper will focus on the following:

• Provide a definition of families that has meaning for the 1990s.

• Explore the changing demographics of American families.

• Address stresses in today's American society and the implications for family well-being.

DEFINING FAMILY

How we define families should reflect the broad array of structures that describe families in today's world. To define family as the Census

Bureau did near the beginning of World War II — "two or more persons related by birth, marriage, or adoption who reside in the same household" (McNeece, 1995) does not reflect the variety of settings in which children live with adults today. There are an increasing number of children living with grandparents; living in blended families with step-parents and step- and half-siblings; children living in single-parent families; and, children who are living with kin, with members of their tribe, with non-relatives in foster homes or in group settings. Older persons may share housing and act as family to each other. People are also living together in greater numbers without marrying.

A recent article in the *Washington Post*, "Study Alters Image of 'Typical' Family," (August 30, 1994) highlights a new Census Bureau report about the evolving picture of American families. The Census Bureau's definition of the "traditional nuclear family as a married couple and their biological children living with no one else" describes only half of families today. This type of family, exemplified in the 1950s and 1960s by TV shows such as "Ozzie and Harriet," "Donna Reed" and "Leave It To Beaver," is home to only 56% of White children, 26% of African-American children and 38% of Hispanic children. When the definition of two-parent families is broadened beyond the "traditional nuclear family" to include blended families and adoptive families, about 71% of children, 45.3 million, live in two-parent families in 1990 (Center for the Study of Social Policy, 1992). This includes about 42% of African-American children who live in two-parent families (*Washington Post*, 1994). These figures contrast with those from 1960 when about 88 percent of children lived in two-parent families (U.S. Congress, 1989).

"Traditional nuclear" or "two-parent families" are often viewed as the ideal family setting, yet they exclude the families of about one-fourth of children. These are the children who are living in single-parent families, living with grandparents or other relatives or living in an out-of-home care setting such as foster care. About 10.4 million children live in single-mother families and 2 million in single-father families (Center for the Study of Social Policy, 1992). Many of these children of single parents are living with extended family, as well. Children are not only living with single parents due to divorce or death. There is also an increase in the number of unmarried women who are giving birth. In 1950, only four percent of all births were to unmarried women; in 1986 that figure was 23% (U.S. Census Bureau, 1989). The diversity of today's family structures is reflected in several of today's television shows. We can view TV shows which include several single-parent families living together, male- or female-headed families living on their own, or with the older generation, blended families, single parents who have never married, and a combination of family and friends living together to provide social and economic support to each other.

In 1990, in order to be inclusive of the diversity of today's families and to ensure that one type of family structure is not given more value than another, the National Association of Social Workers (NASW) revised its "Family Policy" to incorporate the following definition:

"*Family* is defined in its broadest sense to include two or more people who consider themselves "family" and who assume obligations and responsibilities that are generally considered essential to family life."

This broad definition is an appropriate one to adopt because it is inclusive, rather than exclusive and reflects the diversity of American lifestyle. It recognizes lesbian and gay relationships and can assist in developing policies that ensure that health care and other benefits are provided to "family members" who are not related by birth, marriage or adoption. This definition also encompasses families of two adults who consider themselves family without having children, as an increasing number of couples choose not to have children. An increasing number of people also choose not to marry, although they may be involved in long-term, sustained relationships with other adults. Such a definition does not judge the worth of single-parent families over two-parent families or vice versa.

As government struggles with welfare reform, how "family" is defined, and what set of social and economic supports are created to "support families" are critical issues that must be wrestled with. As school teachers create assignments and special activities, projects such as "Father's Day presents," or "reading to both parents," or "invite your grandmother to lunch," need to be renamed and rethought to reflect the diverse settings in which children live. Children need to see themselves and their own family situation reflected and accepted by school and social activities. Human service programs also must develop definitions of family which are reflective of the families that they are serving. This helps in appropriately determining eligibility and to whom services should be delivered.

FAMILIES IN THE 1990s

In order to understand how we can best help families today, we must continue our exploration of the picture of families in the 1990s. In this section we will look at families and economic well-being, inter-generational issues and caregiving responsibilities.

Single-parent Families

As previously stated, the number of children growing up in single-parent families today is increasing. In 1989 about 28 percent of all households were headed by women. This is up from about 21 percent in 1970. Among African-Americans, the number of female-headed households is over 40 percent. About 23 percent of Hispanic families are headed by women (Chadwick, 1992). According to the 1990 Census, about 50 percent of children who live in female-headed households are poor and about 24 percent of children in families headed by a single father are poor. These rates of poverty are high despite the fact that 70 percent of children living with one parent have that parent working (Center for the Study of Social Policy, 1992). The incidence of poverty among children in single-parent families has caused great alarm. Children in single-parent families also tend to do worse in school (Committee for Economic Development, 1987). The concern for the status of children in single-parent families has brought about the following types of responses.

• The National Commission on Children issued several implementation guides as follow-up to its comprehensive report *Beyond Rhetoric*. The first implementation guide, *Strengthening and Supporting Families*, states that "All children need loving, supportive homes. Families formed by marriage — where two caring adults are committed to one another and to their children — are best suited to provide such a home" (National Commission on Children, 1993). The guide then goes on to recommend a set of strategies to be implemented on the national and local level to encourage stable marriages to enhance family well-being. While not meaning to put single-parent families and other forms of family in a negative light, such a report seems to ignore the realities of today's families.

• McNeece, (1995) in his article, "Family Social Work Practice: From Therapy to Policy," states that the number of births to single mothers and the numbers of divorced mothers left in charge of raising their children without fathers dramatically increased and that this "among most 'experts' is the single largest factor causing poverty in the United States today." (McNeece, 1995).

Blaming single-parent families for their poverty and their problems, or focusing solely on strategies to create more two-parent "traditional nuclear" families, are short-sighted responses. The demographic changes toward single-parenthood have been occurring for a long time and are a combination of rising divorce rates, increases in teen pregnancy, and an increase of births by unmarried women in every income level. The rising rates of poverty among these families may not be due to intrinsic problems of the women, but rather to our changing economic environment. Two-parent families find it hard to make ends meet without two incomes, single-parent families surviving on one income would certainly find it difficult to make ends meet.

In 1985, in order to explore more fully the needs of families headed by women, the National Association of Social Workers (NASW) undertook a study which resulted in the report *Helping the Strong* (1987). The report identifies disparities between the women's own perceptions of their family situation and social workers' perceptions of their family situation. The women heading families perceived their families to be stronger than did those people who represented the formal service providers. Strengths included independence, cohesiveness and connectedness to neighbors, family and friends. The primary stressor these families faced was financial. This was often coupled with concern about health because many families lacked health care. Rather than focusing on the deficits of these families, the report set forth positive recommendations that would assist and support these families. Recommendations included:

• Pay equity.

• Availability of comprehensive, affordable, quality child care.

• Job training.

• Student grants and loans to assist single mothers in obtaining additional education.

• Incentives to employers to assist with flexible work time, sick leave and job sharing.

• Welfare policies that would — provide adequate income; allow recipients to receive transitional benefits, including Medicaid after becoming employed; provide higher education benefits; eliminate the humiliation of the current application and receipt of public assistance; provide improved training to income maintenance workers that stresses respect, compassion and efficiency.

• Comprehensive, affordable, quality health care for families.

• Support and encouragement of natural helping networks.

• Increased resources to develop support and resource groups.

- Grants to national and local organizations to develop service models.

- New models of educating professionals to educate professionals to recognize and appreciate the strengths and resources of single-parent families.

- Support groups and counselling to help with stressful situations.

- Extended service hours on nights and weekends to help accommodate working families.

- Integrated packages of services that meet related needs, such as mental health counseling with child care.

- Services for fathers and young boys to help them develop better relationships with their present and future children, in order to prevent the estrangement which currently occurs from non-custodial fathers.

These recommendations provide a broad framework of how we can help families. Some of the recommendations have begun to be implemented through national legislation and local initiatives. The Family and Medical Leave Act of 1993, the Family Support Act of 1988, the Child Care Legislation of 1988, the Family, Resource, Support and Education program created in 1990, and the Family Preservation and Support Legislation passed in 1993, all take steps toward meeting some of these service goals. In addition, through the development of school-linked services, comprehensive service reform programs, or foundation initiated efforts, many communities are beginning to increase the amount of community-based, family-focused prevention and early intervention services intended to build on family strengths, not focus on deficits. It is hoped that current attention in Congress to both health care and welfare reform will also address the recommendations made above.

Currently there is increased attention to the responsibility of the male. Several strategies focus on enforcement of child support payments and efforts to keep men more involved with their children. One special project is the "male involvement initiative" within Head Start.

Two-parent Families and Economic Well-being

For two-parent families the road to family well-being also encounters many challenges. Over the past 50 years there has been a large increase in the number of women in the work force. While single women were always likely to work, we see an increase in the number of married women in the work force, including married women with young children. In 1960, 36 percent of women entered the labor force. In 1988, 56 percent entered the work force. In 1960, about 31 percent of married women were in the labor force. By 1988, that figure had risen to 57 percent. Among the most dramatic increases regarding women in the work force, is the dramatic increase of women with children under the age of six who are working. In 1950, only 12 percent of mothers of young children worked, today, 57 percent of mothers of young children work (Chadwick, 1992).

While the number of two income families has increased, the standard of living of many families remains the same as it was in the 1950s. Two incomes are needed to just make ends meet in today's world. In fact, recently there are reports of a growing number of three-job families, with mom holding down one job and dad holding down two jobs.

Although there are more women in the work force, women continue to have the primary responsibility for household responsibilities.

The increasing numbers of women in the work force has led to an increased need for a range of quality, affordable, available child care options. Child care options may range from care by relatives, to family day care, to day care centers, to job-site day care programs. There are also a growing number of children who are home alone after school. These children, often called latch-key children, have created attention. Some communities have developed special call-in support and homework help lines. Other communities have attempted to leave schools open longer to allow the children a safe and structured place to play. The numbers of children home alone have raised concern about the appropriate age at which children should be left alone, or at what age children should be caring for other children.

Due to the changing economy there have been shifts in how people earn their living. Families may encounter multiple job changes and a loss of financial and health care security. Stress in families due to unemployment and job problems has been linked to rising rates of homelessness and child abuse.

Families work hard to be strong and healthy. Research has identified several characteristics of "successful families." These include a commitment to "family values," religious and spiritual connectedness, ability to adapt to changing circumstances, clear role assignments and time spent together (Krysan, et al, 1990). Probably "spending time together" is one of the greatest challenges facing today's families.

Many of the recommendations provided above to assist female-headed families are relevant to assist all families, particularly the development of community-based support programs to enhance informal support networks.

Intergenerational Changes and Caregiving Responsibilities

Longevity has increased as medical care and nutrition improves. The fastest growing segment of the population is over 65. Within the population over age 65, the fastest growing segment is over age 85. This group, over age 85, often constitutes the frailest and poorest of the population. Currently, about 13% of the population is over age 65. By the year 2020, when the "baby boomer" generation reaches retirement age, 25% of the population will be over age 65 (NASW, 1993a).

As the number of older persons increases, there is an increasing number of four and five generation families. These multi-generational families are often interdependent on each other for economic, social and health care support. While popular myths often indicate that the younger generation has abandoned older people, actually about 80% of the care provided to older people with chronic health problems is provided by family members rather than by formal service providers (NASW, 1990).

For multi-generational families, whether living in the same household or not, adults may experience several episodes of caregiving responsibilities. These include caring for children, parents and grandparents, as well as for disabled spouses and siblings. The term "Sandwich Generation" gained popularity in the 1980s as researchers and Congressional committees explored the demands of family caregiving. The challenges included caring for children and parents at the same time, trying to maintain a full-time job while fulfilling caregiving responsibilities and the lack of financial and other supportive services for family caregivers.

The burden on family caregivers has also increased due to the changing health care delivery system. As people have shorter hospital stays, family members are often required to provide health care treatments with little or no preparation and training, creating stresses on family relationships.

Women and men need to balance work, family and other responsibilities. With more women in the work force, there is a struggle to assume traditional caregiving roles in the family and to earn money as well. Caregiving duties may lead to loss of wages and excessive time off from work. The Family and Medical Leave Act, passed and signed into law in 1993 is intended to help protect family members from losing jobs due to an illness, pregnancy, or emergency need of another family member. Also directed toward relieving "caregiver burden," some large corporations have begun to provide a number of "dependent care" or "elder care" programs. These programs may include child and adult day care programs at the worksite, counselling, help with accessing resources, special tax-free accounts for dependent care expenses and flexible work-day arrangements.

The economic burden of family caregiving exists as well. Family caregiving is not compensated in this society, except for families with children who receive Aid to Families with Dependent Children (AFDC). There is no caregiver allowance, compensation to parents with disabled children who may need respite care, or allowance provided to new mothers to allow them to stay out of the work force for a period of time. In fact, the welfare reform debate which is currently underway is rethinking the AFDC program. Rather than focusing on strategies that will help to support mothers in their caregiving roles and to help enhance family well-being, several of the proposals that are currently being debated would put further strains on families. They would put time limits on eligibility for AFDC, whether or not a mother was able to find a well-paying job with health care benefits and quality, affordable child care. These proposals often focus more on how to limit government payments than on how to support the caregiving role of mothers.

In some American cultures, grandmothers have the role of raising children and are the family matriarch. There are also an increasing number of grandparents who are assuming care for their grandchildren, because the child's parents are unable to due to substance abuse or other problems. The American Association of Retired Persons (AARP) has created a resource center to provide information to grandparents caring for grandchildren and a number of family service agencies provide support groups and other resources.

As grandparents and other family members care for children who are unable to be cared for by their parents, increasing attention is paid to the issue of "kinship care" and its relationship to formal foster care services. Social service agencies are faced with dilemmas about what level of service to provide these families and what is the appropriate payment for them to receive. In some communities, grandparents caring for grandchildren may be eligible for foster care payments. In other communities, they may receive AFDC payments which are considerably less. Some agencies require that grandparents go through the foster parent training and evaluation process that any care provider would need to undertake. Other agencies provide special considerations for family members. It is thought that one reason for the dramatic increase in the number of children in foster care in some states is the redefinition of some kinship care arrangements as foster care.

For grandparents caring for grandchildren there may be many stresses in addition to economic ones. Grandparents may try to raise grandchildren to correct failures that occurred in bringing up their own children. Or, the grandparent might feel resentful of bringing up a child just as they were beginning to focus on their empty nest and retirement. In some situations, as the child's parent who has experienced a drug problem tries to get his or her life together and regain custody of the child, family relationships can be strained over who is the "fittest" parent — grandparent or parent. Often the child is caught in the midst of a conflict between people who should be nurturers and protectors.

With changes in the economy, there are many entire families that have moved back in with the grandparents in the 1980s and 1990s. This may have reversed the trends that occurred between 1950 and 1980. The number of children living in two-parent families with a grandparent dropped from 9 percent in 1950 to 3 percent in 1980, and the number of children in single-parent families who lived with a grandparent dropped from 26 percent in 1950 to 12 percent in 1980 (*Washington Post*, 1994).

To address the needs of families due to the increasing older population and increased caregiving responsibilities, a number of strategies can be undertaken.

• Informal support networks — family and friends, neighborhood and cultural programs, and church groups, may need assistance from more formal community service agencies in order to provide more support to families.

• Caregiver allowances should be considered to help caregivers who are unable to participate in the work force receive compensation for their caregiving work.

• Hospitals, social service agencies, workplaces and community centers should offer a range of supportive services, such as general parenting seminars, groups for caregivers, meals on wheels, respite care, etc., to help ease caregiver burden.

- Services that are developed must reflect and be sensitive to cultural, racial and ethnic differences and the differences in rural, urban, and suburban communities.

Picturing Strong Families

To help ensure the well-being of families in the 1990s we need to be aware of the challenges that families today face. We also need to recognize the diversity of families by using a broad definition to define "family." We need to understand and respond to the diversity of families due to cultural, racial and ethnic differences, due to geographic differences and due to the structure and needs of that individual family. There is no one solution to family well-being, no magic bullet that will make all families strong. What we need to do is to focus and build on the strengths of all families, and to provide an array of prevention and early intervention services which will provide support to families. We need to promote partnerships among families and create communities that work together with families to promote family well-being and the health of the community. Services should be developed to fit family needs, rather than trying to fit individuals or families into categorical services. Family-focused services should provide formal and informal support, promote the development of informal support networks and recognize the interdependence of the generations. Persons providing services to families should be educated and skilled to understand and respond to the needs of children and their families. The government should take leadership in promoting policies and services that enhance the social, economic and physical health of families and should expand the development of early intervention and prevention programs for children and youth. Churches, synagogues and community centers must work together to partner with families to create an array of social, spiritual and recreational supports to help promote family well-being.

Families are our future. For a strong future we must support, value and invest in all families and not spend our energy valuing one type of family more than another.

REFERENCES

Center for the Study of Social Policy, (1992). "The Challenge of Change: What the 1990 Census Tells Us About Children," Washington, D.C.

Committee for Economic Development, (1987). *Children in Need: Investment Strategies for the Educationally Disadvantaged,* New York.

Krysan, M., Moore, K., and Zill, N., (1990). "Research on Successful Families," Washington, D.C., Child Trends.

McNeece, C. A., (1995). "Family Social Work Practice: From Therapy to Policy," *Journal of Family Social Work,* 1 (1), pp. 3-17.

Miller, Dorothy, (1987). *Helping the Strong,* Washington, D.C., National Association of Social Workers.

National Association of Social Workers, (1990). "Aging Policy," *Social Work Speaks,* Washington, D.C.

National Association of Social Workers, (1990). "Family Policy," *Social Work Speaks,* Washington, D.C.

National Association of Social Workers, (1993). "Social Work With Older People: It Could Be For You," Washington, D.C.

National Association of Social Workers, (1993). "Supporting Children and Families," Transition Policy Paper, Washington, D.C.

U.S. Bureau of Census, (1989). "Studies in Marriage and the Family, Washington D.C., U.S. Government Printing Office.

U.S. Congress, House Select Committee on Children, Youth and Families, (1989). "Children and Their Families: Current Conditions and Recent Trends," Washington, D.C., U.S. Government Printing Office.

Vobjeda, Barbara, "Study Alters Image of 'Typical' Family," *Washington Post,* August 30, 1994, p. A3.

Joan Levy Zlotnik *is a nationally recognized expert on services for children, families and older persons. She is currently working toward a Ph.D. in social welfare at the University of Maryland — Baltimore and providing consultation to associations and human service agencies. For the past seven years, she has led the* National Association of Social Workers (NASW) activities related to children, families and older persons, promoting the development of community-based, comprehensive, family-focused services for vulnerable populations and creating strategies to encourage competent, qualified social workers to work in public human service agencies. Among her publications are Social Work Education and Public Human Services: Developing Partnerships (CSWE, 1993) and AIDS: Helping Families Cope (NASW, 1988). Ms. Zlotnik and her husband live in Bethesda, Maryland and have two children.